A Matter of Life

---

when gender doesn't work

a woman's view on having been transsexual

Eva C Moser

According to psychiatry[1] the general prevalence of transsexuality
*in biological males is **1 : 37,000**.*

*Governmental authorities of the Netherlands have stated that it is **1 : 11,900**[1]*

By the year 2000 there have been at least 27'500 male to female gender-
reassignment surgeries in the US on US citizens in the age group of
20 to 65 years (not including "illegal surgeries" and surgeries abroad).
This puts the probability that an individual of this group has
*had surgical reassignment at an absolute minimum of **1 : 3,000***

In a presentation by JPMorgan-Chase[2]
*the prevalence of transsexuality is given as **1 : 500***

Statistical extrapolation of the steadily increasing reported numbers puts
*the effective prevalence at up to **1 : 200**[3]*

*Health-Insurance premiums would have to be raised by **11 cents per year**[4]*
to have the entire treatment of insured transsexuals covered
A single dose of Prozac, Ritalin or Viagra costs at least 10 times as much

The average life-expectancy of transsexuals without any
*treatment is given anywhere in the range of **23**[5]***-27 years***
*With proper medical treatment it is **77 years**[6]*

---

[1] *The American Psychiatric Association*
[2] *JPMorgan-Chase presentation on: "The Cost of Transgender Healthcare Benefits"*
[3] *Olyslanger Conway: "On The Calculation Of The Prevalence Of Transsexualism"*
[4] *JPMorgan-Chase presentation (see 2); Cost estimates for US-insurers, cost includes mental-health treatment*
[5] *Scottish Equality Network, worldwide average for transgendered people*
[6] *NHS-Tayside Gender Equality Study*

In memory of all the woman who have paid the

ultimate price for being denied life-saving treatment.

1. Transsexuality. 2. Human Rights. 3. Disability.

ISBN-13: 978-0-557-01391-3

Library of Congress Control Number: 2009903077

Yin/Yang-Teardrop graphics-design copyright © 1989 by Eva C. Moser

A Matter of Life

---

when gender doesn't work

This book is available in a low-cost edition entitled A Matter Of Life - a
woman's view on having been transsexual *available at online retailers
and from the publisher at www.lulu.com, id 7914429*

German edition: Eine Entscheidung Fürs Leben - Wenn das Geschlecht nicht stimmt, *ISBN-13: 978-0-557-05192-2*

THE BELOVED FINE-PRINT

This book isn't intended as a work of art, it is life at work. I could have published it as a trilogy in four volumes[1], 250 pages each with lots of empty spaces, an attractive format using 28 lines a page, a large font and 10 words per line with double-spacing. Doing this would certainly have appealed to my creative side, it would also have cost at least three times as much to buy it!

If I wanted to make money writing books I presume fiction would have been a much safer choice - even though you will see that reality is at times not just stranger than fiction but (unlike good fiction) downright unbelievable!

On another note I would like to mention that the contents of this book may give the impression that it could be based on my life. If this indeed were the case I wouldn't have deliberately invented or misrepresented any facts, I would however have avoided any reference to persons and places I presume would rather like to remain anonymous.

For legal correctness *please note that everything in this book is entirely fictional.* I have chosen the narrative form of "reality telling" as an artistic style because of its dramaturgical effect, any and all relations to *"the real life experience"* (persons, places and events) are altogether unintended and entirely coincidental. The contents is for entertainment only, it is not to be construed into either medical advice or guide to treatment nor is it intended as such.

Furthermore I would like to point-out that the contents of this book would have to be classified as *"mature subject matter"*. I personally don't think that the term "sexual contents" as used in "entertainment rating systems" would be applicable, however the topic does relate to reproductive biology. More particularly the interpretations of transsexuality certain third parties have put forward are highly sexualized. It is also in the nature of the subject that male and female reproductive anatomy will have to be part of the contents. Some individuals may therefore feel that this book may not be suitable for minors.

Am I ever grateful that we have lawyers!

---

[1] *We will hear more about people who get their trilogies in four instalments later!*

I would like to thank my partner for accepting me as I am; I would like to thank her for her compassion, her love, her support and her sharing her life with me. I would like to thank our children, they have been and are my inspiration for life! I would also like to thank all of them for giving me the many hours to write this book, I know they missed me just as I missed them. I love you all so very much!

There are more people I would like to thank but at this time it is not possible for me to do so here. I hope that at some time in the future this will change.

I.   INTRODUCTION

This book is - in no small part - based on my own personal experiences and the experiences of a few people who also happen to be labelled 'transsexual'. It is not representative, not scientific, it is not research and it is not all-inclusive.

It is a book about life's experiences when gender doesn't work and while it may give some insight into how transsexuals are treated and/or mistreated it is not intended as a guide to treatment or as a reference for such treatment.

Transsexuality is relatively equally distributed among the human population[1], the experience of life people who were given the label 'transsexual' go through is therefore about as diverse as humanity itself is. This is one view of it, *my* view.

To start I would like to put forward four statements. If you feel you understand transsexuality and transsexuals I invite you to validate your opinion by these statements. If you are looking for an introduction into transsexuality, are just interested, would like to learn more about it or think that this might apply to you personally I invite you to compare these statements to your own thoughts, your own views, your own feelings, your own experiences and your own life:

I.   I am a woman. I have always been a woman. I was born a woman. *I have never changed my sex, never 'transitioned' from male to female,* how could I, I never was male. What I do is change my appearance and to some degree my body to reflect who I am. I have done this so I am able to live my life in a way I experience as meaningful, but also because today this is the only way to make society accept me for who I am.

II.   I am a woman who was born with a birth-defect, a rather severe congenital physical disability: *I was born with the wrong reproductive system.* What I do is deal with this disability and its symptoms and side-effects as good as I can in the best way I can find. I think this is the most ordinary, normal and appropriate thing I could possibly do.

III.   I am labelled 'transsexual' not because of who I am, what I do or how I identify. Other people do all the same things I do without getting this label, more than half of the population identifies as I do and they all do not get the treatment I'm getting. The one and

---

[1] *The long held claim that there are far more male to female transsexuals than there are female to males does not appear to be true as figures from the last years have shown [see B.3]. However there still appear to be far fewer older transsexuals than there ought to be assuming equal distribution. Among other considerations a higher than average suicide-rate will have to be considered as an explanation [see B.34].*

only reason I'm being labelled and treated as I am is *because you perceive what I do differently when I do it.*

IV. There would hardly be any transsexuals and the surgery for that "sex-change" would be about as much of an issue as heart-bypasses if this condition were treated *as a medical condition.* It is not transsexuals who make transsexuality a rather visible "borderline lifestyle", *it is psychiatry and psychiatric dogma which creates transsexuals and forces us into living what they call "the transsexual phenomenon" - and the media exploiting us for living it.*

If, so far, you have disagreed with me at least once then I suppose you're the person I have written this book for. If you agreed to everything then read on! I might just surprise you on the next page. And if you're still looking for explanations why I write what I write, you may just find these in later chapters.

I don't want to show that this "experience life" is different for every one of us, in my opinion and experience this is self-evident. What I would like to show is that it can in fact be so dramatically different, solely depending upon the point of view one takes to interpret it, that the various conclusions drawn from such interpretation can be completely contradictory. I hope to show how this comes about and why this contradiction alone causes misunderstanding, pain, impossible expectations, absurd treatments and death.

While I have tried to keep the reading light wherever possible what I am writing about still is *a matter of life.* And for far too many people it is one of ending life. What I write about is, for hundreds of thousands of people, lived reality. It used to be just that for me too. Life isn't always light and it isn't always fun and joy. So this book isn't either. Nevertheless I have made great efforts to not let everything drown in misery but to add some humour where I thought it appropriate. Because life is light and fun and a great joy also!

This book is presented in four main sections. The first three, *Discovering, Becoming* and *Living,* predictably deal with life before, during and after treatment.

While this seems rather obvious and "the usual thing to do" I have also divided it into a personal part relating to my own experiences (chapter numbers starting with the letter 'A') and a more generalized part dedicated to general considerations and background information (chapter numbers starting with 'B'). But rather than to present the personal and the general sides in separate parts they are intertwined. Because this is how life happens also.

Self-awareness and self-acceptance don't take place in sequence, they happen simultaneously, interwoven with many other internal and external threads in life which, in the end, may or may not find each other. And if, sometimes, they do find each other some understanding may happen. Only in the life of a transsexual physical self-awareness and emotional self-acceptance *never* find each other. When - after treatment - this finally becomes possible all we can understand is that we too can not comprehend! Because it is not possible.

The last part of this book, *Reflections,* tries to show what this does to us and how society copes with something that by it's very nature isn't understandable.

My life started out with a small problem. Almost three decades ago I found out that this could be taken care of in an afternoon in an operating room.

I was not allowed to have my problem solved but was instead given the choice to live a life that was not truly my own or to choose death instead.

It took me 27 years to make up my mind. In the end I chose life. It is not worth dying over a psychiatric dogma.

By now I have been given the solution to my original problem. The price I had to pay for my life, for being physically normal, is that I am now emotionally incapable to be who I am.

Getting my life, having this problem fixed, leaving my disability behind could have been one of the most joyful events and experiences of my life! However social attitudes and in particular an absurd, misguided, unrealistic and downright deranged medical system has seen to it that instead this turned into the most depressing, most miserable and most life-denying experience I have ever had to live through.

II.   WE, TRANSSEXUALS AND ME

Throughout this book you may notice that while I say I identify female (and not transsexual) I often use the pronouns 'we' or 'us' when I refer to transsexuals. There are several reasons for this, one of the more important being sheer readability. But there is also the fact that the statement "I am transsexual" was at some time in my life perfectly correct, only to me this describes a condition, not an identification.

When writing about transsexuality the first major stumbling-block is that there is no universally accepted definition of the term 'transsexual' itself. The use in fact ranges from "transsexuality does not exist" to "a transsexual is whoever self-identifies as such" to "...only people who are deemed to be by some group of self-styled experts" to "...people who cross established or perceived social gender lines in any way whatsoever, either temporary or on a permanent basis". And that's just to get the list started...

Some people use the term to identify a person who is designated one sex and says he/she is, should be or would like to be the other. Given this definition transsexuality is *a description of a temporary condition in need of treatment:* After there is enough evidence to have the designation changed the condition no longer exists because then the person presumably agrees with her designation.

Others however use the term to identify people who have been designated one sex and either say he/she is, should be or would like to be the other *or actually have had that designation changed*[1] (presumably after surgery). Given this definition transsexuality is *a life-long condition* which, once identified, can never be overcome *as a matter of principle.*

Then there are yet others who use an "in between approach": They basically say that they use the second definition but whoever they can no longer identify as being transsexual and can no longer point a finger at isn't. This view has the obvious disadvantage that it is entirely arbitrary, the label 'transsexual', at least for people who identify the same as they are officially classified, *becomes exclusively dependent upon circumstances, looks, and the eye of the beholder.*

Apart from the definition itself being rather unclear there is the issue as to how I should refer to myself? Should I say "I am transsexual" *instead of* saying "I am a woman" *or* should I say "I am transsexual *and* a woman"? Or "I am a woman *who happens to be* transsexual"? Or maybe "happen*ed* to be transsexual"?

I'm glad that, just being a woman, I don't have to ask myself such hairsplitting questions!

---

[1] *This works like that commercial on financial investments: "Not every change qualifies, individual designations may vary and past identification is no guarantee for future designation!"*

III. A WORD OF CAUTION

Before you read on I would like to allow for a word of caution: I have no formal training in psychology nor psychiatry, my educational background is engineering. As an engineer I see emotional issues differently, I see things from a pragmatic and practical perspective whereas psychology and in particular psychiatry sees things from a theoretical and interpretative position.

For an engineer it is more important to get things working than it is to fully explain these, this I gladly leave to science. I have no problem taking things for granted as long as they make sense and I work on the premise to leave things alone that work just fine and don't need fixing - there's plenty out there that really does need fixing, so let's do that instead.

It therefore happens at times that my views on certain issues may deviate *slightly* from the "generally accepted consensus". Actually, now that I think of it, this happens with almost predictable regularity and my views tend to be rather dramatically dissenting time and again...

Therefore if you feel you may find yourself easily offended this book may not be for you. If you have a heart condition or suffer from high blood-pressure you might want to consult your physician prior to reading it [consider talking about Spironolactone[1] to your doctor].

---

[1] *Spironolactone (Aldactone, Novo-Spiroton, Spiractin) is used to treat hypertension, it is also used in the treatment of male to female transsexuals to suppress testosterone.*

CONTENTS

-	*The Beloved Fine Print* .... *VII*	
I.	*Introduction*... *IX*	
II.	*We, Transsexuals And Me*.. *XIII*	
III.	*A Word Of Caution*.. *XIV*	

Part I   Discovering 21

A   **Awareness Dawning**
B   **Exploring Madness**

A.1.	*Once Upon A Time...* 25
B.1.	*And Just Where Should I Start This?* 26
B.2.	*May I Introduce Jane and John*................................. 28
A.2.	*Help! I Don't Want My Sex Changed...* 30
B.3.	*A Note On Female To Male Transsexuality* 34
A.3.	*...And Neither Do I Need Plastic Surgery* 38
B.4.	*To The Root Of The Problem* 40
B.5.	*Worse Than The Worst Criminals!* 43
B.6.	*Dogmatists And Dogmatic Treatment*........................ 47
A.4.	*I'm Definitely Not Crazy!!!*....................................... 55
B.7.	*Transsexual Choice* 57
B.8.	*Gender And More Delusions* 62
A.5.	*Overpaid, Oversexed, And Only One Problem* 65
B.9.	*Closing The X-Files? Case #1: Kinsey*....................... 67
B.10.	*For Laughs: The Eva-Scale Of Scientific Truth*......... 72
A.6.	*All You Need To Be Is A Sexual Pervert* 74
B.11.	*Closing The X-Files? Case #2: Benjamin*................... 79
B.12.	*Closing The X-Files? Case #3: Money*....................... 87
B.13.	*Even More Laughs: Stretching The Eva-Scale*........... 92
A.7.	*Can We Have Children?* 94
B.14.	*Homo, Hetero, Bi, Don't Know And Don't Care*......... 97
B.15.	*And Just How Do I Really Know?* 100
B.16.	*Could This Be A Congenital Physical Disability?* 106
A.8.	*And I Pronounce You... Wife And Wife?*.................... 110
B.17.	*Testing The Limits* 113
A.9.	*Three Strikes And You're Out!* 117

Part II   Becoming 121

A   **469 Days Of Slavery**
B   **Living Madness**

A.10.	*This Makes So Much Sense!*	*125*
B.18.	*Binary Gender, Continuum Or Gendersoup*	*127*
B.19.	*LGB's And T's*	*131*
B.20.	*Cisexuals And Normal People*	*136*
A.11.	*For They Know Not What They Do!*	*140*
B.21.	*Only In 4" Heels And A 14" Skirt*	*142*
A.12.	*Where Irreparable Harm Starts*	*145*
B.22.	*Booby Trapped*	*147*
B.23.	*One Giant Leap!*	*151*
A.13.	*Making Myself Transsexual*	*154*
B.24.	*A Matter Of Convenience*	*156*
A.14.	*You Must Be Mental - In A Good Way I Mean!*	*159*
B.25.	*When Dogma Gets People Killed*	*160*
A.15.	*My Life In Your Hands!*	*162*
B.26.	*Love, Pain And Compliance*	*163*
A.16.	*Can You Be A Woman Now?*	*167*
B.27.	*No Right To Remain Silent!*	*169*
A.17.	*Sorry, I've Never Had A Sex-Change!*	*173*
B.28.	*I Wish I Had Started Sooner*	*175*
A.18.	*Arbeit Macht Frei!*	*178*
A.19.	*A Word On Hormones*	*182*
B.29.	*Mental Choices*	*185*
B.30.	*Money For Nothin' And Your Chicks For Free!*	*187*
B.31.	*One More Word On Hormones*	*191*
B.32.	*Transition??? What Transition?*	*193*
A.20.	*She Needs Surgery, Not Counselling*	*196*
B.33.	*Medical Nightmares*	*199*
A.21.	*Going Nowhere - Really, Really Fast!*	*204*
B.34.	*When Suicide Is Not A Cry For Help*	*206*
A.22.	*Dollars And Nonsense*	*208*
B.35.	*Of Course I Have Always Known...*	*215*
A.23.	*Bending Reality*	*219*
B.36.	*Transsexuals And The Media*	*222*
A.24.	*How Do You Do Today?*	*226*
B.37.	*For All The Wrong Reasons*	*227*
A.25.	*Psychiatry? Thanks, But No Thanks!*	*230*
B.38.	*Your Life Has Just Been Cancelled!*	*232*
A.26.	*Female Minus 59 Days*	*234*
B.39.	*Absence Of Evidence Is Not Evidence Of Absence*	*236*
B.40.	*Ok. Transsexuality. Just What Is This Again?*	*239*
A.27.	*Being Of Perfectly Sound Mind...*	*248*
A.28.	*Epilogue*	*250*

Part III Living...253

A   **Healing**
B   **Madness Never Again**

A.29.   *Back To The Future!* *257*
B.41.   *Legalize It!*.. *259*
B.42.   *No Future!* *262*
A.30.   *Transaction Without A Receipt*...................... *265*
A.31.   *Mirror, Mirror, Who Is The Fairest...* *270*
B.43.   *New: Obsessive Self-Righteousness Disorder*........ *272*
A.32.   *I Am Not Mental, It's Everybody Else...*.............. *276*
B.44.   *New: The Reverse Munchausen Syndrome*........... *279*
B.45.   *It Just Never Gets Real Enough*...................... *282*
B.46.   *Spiritual Self-Expression Or Mental Illness?* *287*
A.33.   *It Is Only A Matter Of Life*........................... *291*

Part IV Reflections 299

C   **Failing To Understand**

C.1.   *And Just Why Isn't This The End* *303*
C.2.   *With Minimal Collateral Damage* *304*
C.3.   *The Ultimate Catch*.................................... *308*
C.4.   *Racism, Sexism And Featurism*....................... *310*
C.5.   *The Most Invisible Minority* *312*
C.6.   *Absolute Power Corrupts Absolutely*................. *314*
C.7.   *Look, It's All A Game!*................................. *319*
C.8.   *Forever Guilty For Who I Am*......................... *321*
C.9.   *In An Ideal World Where We Are Free To Choose* ... *324*
C.10.   *Just Trust Me!* *326*
C.11.   *Hope* *328*
C.12.   *Final Note*.. *330*

Appendix...337

App.I.   *The Yin/Yang Teardrop (Cover)*..................... *337*
App.II.   *Chapters That Didn't Make The Cut*................. *339*
App.III. *Quotes That Didn't Make The Cut* *344*
App.IV.   *Notes And References* *345*

PART I - DISCOVERING

A

AWARENESS DAWNING

B

EXPLORING MADNESS

The United Nations, General Assembly Resolution 217A(III) of 10 December 1948,

Universal Declaration Of Human Rights[1]

Preamble [excerpts]:

Whereas recognition of the inherent dignity and of the equal and inalienable rights of all members of the human family is the foundation of freedom, justice and peace in the world,

Whereas disregard and contempt for human rights have resulted in barbarous acts which have outraged the conscience of mankind, and the advent of a world in which human beings shall enjoy freedom of speech and belief and freedom from fear and want has been proclaimed as the highest aspiration of the common people, [...]

Article 1:

All human beings are born free and equal in dignity and rights. They are endowed with reason and conscience and should act towards one another in a spirit of brotherhood.

---

[1] *Official wording quoted from www.unhchr.ch udhr lang eng.htm*

A.1. ONCE UPON A TIME...

There I was. Experiencing myself a woman while I was told that I was a man instead. The worst part of it was that, looking in any mirror around observing my anatomy, I actually had to grant these people a rather acute sense of observation because, just seeing my reflection, even I could not avoid noticing that they indeed had *a point.* Never mind, I knew who I was and if I was born wrong then I most definitely wanted to have that fixed! Fortunately I'm not exactly short-changed in the self-confidence department, so there I was, looking for options, searching...

That was, well, once upon a time. True, I like to cheat on my age but I suppose I would not get away with telling people that I am 25 or thereabout these days, so I may just as well admit that this was some 30 years ago. All right, a little more... But could we just end the discussion on the issue? I promise, I'll be more forthcoming on other topics... All right, let's just agree, I was searching, something like half a lifetime ago...

Information wasn't all that easily available back then, but there was some. And what I found was, well... different from what I... hoped for? Or just expected? In any case it rather soon became apparent that I would be hitting a few snags on my way. Well, right before I got started on that way to anywhere!

Snags? All right, as you will see that is the understatement of a lifetime. *Guaranteed!*

---

[1] *All quotes appearing on the side of pages have been part of my real-life experience, most are from the past 24 months. I have not altered any of the contents, though I have abbreviated some and made changes so individuals cannot be identified.*

[A female friend] You really want to be a woman? [Me] I don't want to, I just am... [She] Nobody wants to be a middle-aged woman in this society! You must be crazy to want this! [Me] That's what the psychiatrists say too...[1]

B.1.   AND JUST WHERE SHOULD I START THIS?

Most authors choose to explore transsexuality by telling their personal story or by collecting research, by philosophical introspection, either as external observers or from the insider-perspective. I'm going to do this too, at times, but I'd like to start one step back. I'd like to ask the apparently simple question: *Just why do I write a book about this anyway?*

Transsexuality is, on a whole, a rather simple issue: I do not agree with the biological reproductive capacity I was born with, so I want this changed. Well, as good as it gets anyway. As we will see the details are a little different from what it would be if I were to disagree with the shape of my nose and wanted *that* changed, but on a whole it really is rather similar: I see a surgeon and he gets the problem fixed. It could be done efficiently, privately, quietly. Just like that nose adjustment.

If it were my nose then people might notice, or they might not. It would likely come down to how much change there was and of course if that other person had seen me before or not. If I have genital surgery then I don't expect too many people to notice. I mean, *honestly…*

But for some reason there aren't too many books out there titled *"How I got my nose-job"*, because if you want a nose-job, well: You just get one! The one sticky point somebody might encounter on her quest to getting that rhinoplasty, as it's called in medical circles, might end up in a book titled *"Who's paying for my new nose?"* but the local library isn't exactly bursting with these titles either…

So why do transsexuals write books and nose-job-, hair transplant-, tattoo- and piercing-parlour clients do not? Even kidney transplant recipients by far don't write as many, although there are far more kidney transplants done every year than genital reassignments. What is different? Well, the difference is not in what we do, it is in *how we do it.* It is not a matter of who we are, but rather *how we are perceived.* And this in turn isn't an expression of either what we feel or what we need, *it is an expression of how we are seen by others, what we are made into by them and how we get treated along the way!* Because I can't just go and see a surgeon to get that problem solved, instead I have to adhere to strict guidelines and get permissions first, there is no way around this if I'd like to keep this legal.

It is important to understand that this doctrine I have to follow is made-up by mental-health and not by physical medical requirements. Therefore the requirements and conditions imposed are not biological, biochemical or even medical in any sense *but rather behavioural in nature,* they are *subjective* rather than the result of a lab-report (such as testing that somebody is in general good health before going into any elective surgery), and these behavioural requirements are imposed on us for years or decades and not rarely an entire lifetime instead of days or weeks.

Well, I suppose this is putting it nicely because really *what it comes down to is that we are told how to behave, how to look, what to say and what to do* in order to qualify to have a medical problem solved. More cynically I could say that *we are told who we have to be in exchange for a permit to continued existence.* And of course one of the first expectations is *that we are to call this life and be happy about and thankful for it!*

This is where we are today - and where our treatment has been for the past 50 years or so. However it isn't my intention to offer an extensive history-lesson, a few fragments on how we got to where we are now will have to do. What I intend to show is how this works today and how this refined system of behavioural conditioning works through pain and withholding treatment and by implicit and explicit threats and rewards. How this gets us to how we look and behave, but not who we truly are!

In the end I, like so many other transsexuals, write a book about the depth of an exceptional experience, I write a book about a treatment that doesn't work as it should but is amazingly painful because it gets done so wrong, has little to do with what I need and nothing at all with who I am. But more than anything else I write a book about manufacturing the impossible! No, not "making a girl from a guy", this is impossible anyway - *what I really write about is how psychiatry manufactures it's own sanity and how they're getting away with it!*[1]

I would like to do this by showing that who we have to be is entirely artificially created, how and maybe even why this happens and in the end I would like to show how this gets to be a self-fulfilling prophecy, why ultimately the very expectations of who we are and the conclusions drawn from observing our compliance makes us exactly into what's expected of us!

---

[1] *I did consider **"Manufacturing Insanity"** as an alternative title but decided against it because this book isn't primarily about the workings of psychiatry but about the experience of social and medical treatment as a transsexual. Today psychiatry is a mandatory part of this but transsexuality and therefore the experience of it has existed long before the first psychiatrist has ever started practicing and it will be here long after the last one will have closed his "gender practice".*

B.2.   MAY I INTRODUCE JANE AND JOHN

It makes sense to better understand transsexuality to compare it to a few other severe conditions. To do this I would like to invent two "composite-personalities", Jane and John, who will serve throughout this book to illustrate to whom I compare myself, how I react to my environment and why this becomes understandable when compared to the reasonably expected reactions of John and Jane.

As this is not a scientific work I am at liberty to freely invent my "test-subjects" and as I don't pretend to need a "scientific style" I can give them names, not referring to them as "subject 1" and "subject 2".

[I find "subjecting" tentatively appropriate when the object of the research is, say, ants or snails, but completely inappropriate, dehumanizing, and demeaning for human-beings (or any animal who is capable of an emotional response). Some researchers will likely argue that naming people (or anything alive) makes us identify with these people while keeping them anonymous makes us keep a distance, getting less involved. While this may be true I ask myself what this 'detachment' might be good for? Maybe it's just easier to be unethical to "subject 1" if the research calls for it than it would be towards Jane Smith? And while it is true that some psychological and behavioural, indeed biological and medical research is done with individually naming animals, even people, it is still rather common to not do so. Of course given some of the research that's happening I suppose a psychiatrist would often want the same detachment a president gets when signing a piece of paper which will have the effect that 100,000 people get nuked, rather than having to stab each and every one of them personally. I suppose one just gets a better night's rest if the dreams are about signing a piece of paper rather than...].

Nevertheless I will highlight the sections of Jane and John so they'll be clearly visible. After all, these parts are the ones that are, maybe, completely speculative while the rest is at least based on my life's experiences, thoughts and emotions. I would certainly feel it wrong if the reader could not distinguish between the normal speculations of a woman and the mental thoughts of a de-facto certified deranged gender-dysphoric male.

Please meet Jane: Jane is a 32 year old paraplegic. She uses a wheelchair to get around, lives with her partner, they have two children, age 6 and 8, and a dog. Jane works part-time, takes care of her children, brings them to school before she goes to work, picks them up afterwards, walks the dog. Once a week she goes to physiotherapy. Jane lives a life on daily medications. Before her accident she was a phys-ed teacher and an outstanding athlete, volleyball being her preferred sport. Then, at age 26, just after recovering from her second pregnancy she got struck by a drunk driver while riding her bicycle to work. When she woke up she found herself in a hospital bed and was told that she would never be able to walk again.

Please meet John: John is 44, he was born with Prune Belly Syndrome (aka Eagle-Barrett Syndrome), a condition which affects multiple organs of the abdomen, in particular abdominal muscles, the urinary tract and the reproductive organs. Most people who have PBS are identified male, therefore the affected reproductive organs would typically consist of the testicles and the prostate. His life rotated around doctors and multiple hospital stays up until his 25th birthday. At age 3 a partial renal failure was diagnosed, at age 8 regular dialysis was necessary. By age 18 John had suffered complete renal failure, by then he was on dialysis 3 times a week. In spite of all this he managed to get through high-school and was attending university when one day at age 25 he got the call to check into the hospital to receive a kidney-transplant. Ever since he has lead a relatively normal life, he works as an industrial architect for a construction company. The one issue he never came to terms with is that due to his condition he was born infertile and although sexually normal he remains single.

Both John and Jane have what is typically referred to as a "physical disability", for John this has been a life-long issue, for Jane it was a very abrupt impact in her life that changed everything for her. But in spite of all the adversity both of them lead independent lives, both of them are integrated in society. Both also have very specific needs, medical as well as others.

A.2. HELP! I DON'T WANT MY SEX CHANGED...

It took some searching, but at the age of 17 I found that what I needed was what they called *"a sex-change"*. I checked into the largest library I could go to and eventually found out that there was only one way to ever get one: I would have to be diagnosed mental, presumably by a sane person! Or to be more specific I would have to be labelled "a gender-dysphoric male" and I would have to prove that I was a severely incurable dysphoric case. This seemed to me a rather absurd diagnosis because, as a woman, how could I possibly be a gender-dysphoric *male*? I mean at best I could be a gender-dysphoric *female* but this diagnosis did seem rather unappealing to me as gender-dysphoric females apparently, if they're severe, incurable cases, get a phalloplasty[1] and honestly, I thought I already had one penis too many! So, do they expect me to pretend that I am a man so I am allowed to be a woman *without* testicles instead of one *with* these???

Never mind as this seemed to be the only way to get there I continued to read that book I was staring into. The text said that in order to qualify I needed to exhibit a "strong and persistent cross-gender identification" and a "repeatedly stated desire to be *the other sex* ". Well, it took me a few readings an some thinking to get what they actually were after... I don't want to be *the other sex*. I'm a woman and I feel just fine being one! Why would they think I wanted to be a man? This is *what I don't want*!

But then it clicked, I understood! The whole point appeared to be that the people who had written this really worked from the premise that the best way to deal with me would be *by refusing to accept under any circumstance who I am* and by finding a solution to my problem *while never giving up rejecting the idea that I could truly be a woman and instead take me for a man!* I found this extraordinarily strange and irritating and I have - to this date - except for a few hyper-cynical explanations no idea why any reasonably sane person would possibly do this! Wouldn't any decent treatment start with *accepting what the patient says and experiences instead of denying it?* Would it not make sense to work with who the patient is instead of *making her into something the therapist decides she has to be?*

So I need to say that I want to be *"the other sex"*. Which would be *my own sex*. The one I feel and say I am. Because *that* one is *"the other one"*. Right? And this is then called "a cross-gender identification", because I identify the same way I feel, *but it gets labelled "cross-gender" for the simple fact that the therapist doesn't agree with my*

---

[1] *Phalloplasty: Surgery to create a penis (phallus) and usually a scrotum*

identification? And once they all believed what they wanted to believe in I would - maybe - get that 'sex-change' to - in their opinion - have the gender I say I can't change changed and end-up - in their opinion - being even more mental because then I will claim that I was right?

My first conclusion along that long journey was that my self-identification apparently isn't something I have and feel for myself (which naïvely I presumed), *but it is something I get assigned depending on the view of the person who treats me!* If they say I can't identify female then I can't! Because...? ***Because <u>the therapist say so</u>?*** Well thank you very much for so much openness, trust, consideration, acceptance and understanding... Now just how come they're actually interested in treating me anyway if that's their attitude?

There were other conditions I needed to meet, conditions which seemed even more absurd. For example I would need to show "a strong and persistent preferences for cross-sex roles in make-believe play" and "intense desire to participate in the stereotypical games and pastimes of the other sex". By now I had learned that they meant 'female' by either "*other* sex" or "*cross*-sex"... But still, I had to check about five times as to the gender of the author before I knew that I could not believe what they were looking for, but indeed the author of that particular book was *male*! I didn't check but surmised that the person was older than I was, after all the author sported a medical degree and most people don't get these before they're at least 20-somethings?

So what was the guy looking for? Me volunteering to play Cinderella in a high-school-play or knitting during recess??? I mean, honestly! Had I done this I could just as well have signed a request for being slaughtered by my school-mates, if not physically then at least socially. After all even without showing off that passing for a female came rather naturally and without much of an effort and that I really could sew and knit was I deemed the oddball and I was quite intelligent enough not to deliberately add this... So I chose to do the lights when they played Cinderella and played chess and cards in recess instead of knitting. The thing I don't get is why anybody would seriously have expected me - or *required* me for that matter - to go out and commit social suicide to prove, five or then years down the road, that I indeed had identified female and was predictably trashed-up for it? This seems particularly strange given the fact that the person who wrote this had been in male changing rooms and formed male peer-groups *himself!* Doesn't he know better than to expect this from a male teenager if she wants a social life, if she wants to live free from being trashed-up or worse ...

Unfortunately this was by far not all of the bad news... There was more absurdity, a lot more: I should have "asserted that it would be better not to have a penis". Well, really... Just imagine: There I am, a woman in that well-known male change-room setting, surrounded by maybe 25 typical guys my age (choose anything from 4 to 99), doing what they do best: Pretending 'theirs' is bigger and fantasizing they had better success using it? (That second part may not apply to pre-teens?). Would anybody honestly claim that this would have ended any better for me if I would have been the only one in there without a penis? As to my experience just about anybody who would think this has no idea whatsoever of males...

Now what I off and on wished for was that I would have been born with ovaries instead of testicles. Apparently the sex-ed my mother had given me well before kindergarten was quite good enough to get me to understand that not the penis gives a person biologically male reproductive capacity but the testes. One doesn't get testes from having a penis, it's rather the other way 'round, isn't it? But wishing for having been born with ovaries instead or even wishing for a pregnancy and motherhood was apparently much to abstract an expression of one's identification as to count for anything, so it wasn't even mentioned. (While any urge to gratify a male sexually appeared to be just what the doctor ordered!)

If that would have been it, thank God! But it wasn't. The next shock hit when I read the passage that *"this isn't concurrent with a physical intersex condition"*. Now I am a woman with a set of male reproductive organs too many and a female set too few and they say I can only qualify for *physical* treatment *if this is not physical*? I don't know, I mean I might just be very, very stupid here, but if *this* is not to be deemed *physical*, what is? Or if my interpretation of what's physical and what's not is that dramatically different, then either me or that other author must truly suffer from a severe mental condition!

Well, I have said it initially: Fortunately I'm not exactly short-changed in the self-confidence department. So I had no problem assigning the mental illness part to the other author instead of myself. But of course I was equally certain that the people who seemed to believe what this individual wrote would have this the other way round. The snag: Unfortunately it appeared to be *them* who were in control of *my* treatment, not I.

This truly was about as bad a shock as anybody would need for a decent depression, but I wasn't done. So I read on. The last bit hanging there, at the very end of the page of that library-book, the most essential bit: *To qualify for treatment this needed to cause "significant distress or impairment in social, occupational or other important areas of functioning"*. Only I didn't have any of these! Yes, people thought of me as odd, different, but somehow I didn't think that this would be quite it - quite good enough. After all one of my few friends at high-school was gay and he got laughed at, harassed, even beaten-up and nobody from the officials appeared to think this could be in any way 'significant'. I was apparently doing a really, really good job at surviving in spite of having one of the more unusual conditions out there… Really the only severe problem I had was emotional and that wasn't anywhere on the list!

Well, maybe emotional problems aren't significant or of enough importance to a psychiatrist to merit mentioning or indeed any of his attention, never mind treatment; *but they are most definitely vital to me!* Although maybe that's just because I'm a woman? But then again, maybe emotional problems would qualify under *'other functioning'*? Because if not I would have to conclude that I were not deemed worthy of treatment *because I did too good a job of surviving in spite of the problem?*

Before I returned the book to the library I had read this passage a few times. Well, maybe a hundred times. Thinking things over. And the more I thought about it, the more I got reminded of a Milos Forman movie I had seen not long ago starring Jack Nicholson featuring another variation on the theme of psychiatry gone wrong. Oh shoot!, now I've given away my age after all… Anyway, at the end of that movie the character played by Nicholson gets a lobotomy[1] to solve all his problems - a treatment I had previously found in several 'scientific' articles on the issue and treatment of what these 'experts' called "gender queers"…

---

[1] *Prefrontal Lobotomy: Surgery to cut the connections to and from the prefrontal cortex (PFC). The PFC is the part of the brain associated with high-level social behaviour, complex personality expression and abstract temporal reasoning. Simplistically seen the functions of the PFC are what differentiates us from other primates, it is the part of the brain that makes us human.*

B.3. A NOTE ON FEMALE TO MALE TRANSSEXUALITY

[A friend] So you want the second-class treatment in society now? [Me] Yes! Because up from fourth class that's a two class improvement!

Although I am writing this book exclusively from a woman's perspective (psychiatry would probably call it "from the perspective of a severely gender-disturbed male", the media would call it "from the perspective of a male-to-female transsexual"), some parts of it are of a more general nature and touch far reaching issues outside transsexuality or gender-concerns, issues any and all people who are in some way 'different' ought to be concerned about and some issues everybody should be interested in because they define our very humanity, how we see ourselves and how we shape our society.

To keep this book readable I generally use the term 'transsexual' to describe a "male to female transsexual" and I don't insert statements such as "in the female to male case this would be considered…" or "the equivalent procedure for a female to male would be…". I find that if I would do this extensively the contents would not be any clearer but it would become rather cumbersome to read. I would however like to point out that *this is in no way meant to value either one of the conditions over the other.* Both conditions (male-to-female ['m/f', 'mtf'] as well as female-to-male ['f/m', 'ftm']) are just *different* and unlike other people I would like to limit myself to write on what I'm familiar with. I nevertheless have some insight into ftm because medical science assumes that both are one and the same, so we often end-up getting the same wrong treatment and then find this to be equally inappropriate, just for different reasons!

Let me start by addressing something of a myth which seem to persist in medical circles as well as in the media: It is often said that for each f/m case there are maybe four to five m/f cases. So biological males identify female some four to five times more often than biological females identify male. Such assumptions are convenient when the intention is to define transsexuality as a sexual perversion (these are psychiatrically defined to be a predominantly male issue) or as an extreme form of transvestitism (which they define as exclusively male, see later). The "few female cases" may then be deemed "an aberration" or even marginalized into non-existence!

Truth is that there are in all likelihood about as many f/m's as there are m/f's. As we will see the difference in the numbers lays in the perception of the cases, the availability of medical treatment, the interest psychiatrists show in the two conditions, the acceptance of these by psychiatry and a few other factors. But before we get into details I would like to make something very clear I find many people do not understand (or even think about): *M/f transsexuality and f/m transsexuality are two entirely different conditions with only little resemblance!* For this very reason it is completely absurd that we are treated the same, deemed the same, submitted to the same protocols and requirements, even officially categorized identical.

I don't think that the differences in medical treatment would require much explaining, a quick look at the female and the male reproductive system should suffice to appreciate many of these. And we both need what the respective other case needs to get rid of!

Nevertheless we do have common concerns: These range from similar legal problems to concerns in regard of our psychiatric treatment - but then again, both the legal system and psychiatry do treat us as if we were the same, so we may both end up having a problem with this very fact. There are common concerns as to social acceptance and integration, though these are few and the majority do seem to be unrelated to medical treatment, or to say this better, seems to be only related to the *un*availability of medical treatment and not to our condition as per-se.

I did promise earlier that I would come back to highlighting a few facts why it could be that psychiatry finds fare more m/f's than f/m's. As usual I see the issue as a complex result of many influences, you just never seem to get a simplistic interpretation from me. But honestly, there isn't! I would like to list a few of the thoughts that come to mind but eventually you'll have to make-up your own mind if you think that these make sense, these make enough sense to explain a 1:4 or 1:5 gap, or what other reason there might be.

➤➤**Acceptance:** Many psychiatrists define transsexuality as *an exclusively male to female issue* (they would call it "a male pathology"). It appears reasonable to assume that because there are fewer therapists who are willing to accept that the f/m case actually exists fewer f/m's than m/f's may be able to find a therapist and get treatment, thus fewer would make the statistics.

➤➤**Cheating:** Medically all procedures an f/m transsexual would likely want are, with the exception of a phalloplasty, *routine treatments for female identified biological women*, including the complete removal of the female reproductive system (hysterectomy) or of the breasts (mastectomy). It appears reasonable to assume that many transsexuals have received such surgeries without any doctor ever knowing of their identification! On the other hand the equivalent procedures for m/f's are virtually never used in general surgical practice *on male-identified biological males*, on the contrary: While the female reproductive system seems to be up for grabs for the slightest suspicion of a (potentially freely invented) family pre-disposition to, say, cancer, the male one will likely be protected at any cost, including the life-expectancy of the patient. Males routinely opt-out of orchiectomy[1] even if this is in-

---

[1] *Orchiectomy: Surgery to remove the testes, commonly also referred to as 'castration'. However (a) medically (particularly in veterinary medicine) 'castration' describes 'neutering' of both male and female animals while the term 'orchiectomy' only applies to removing the testes; (b) in the realm of urban legend the term 'castration' is often used to describe an amputation of the penis (this may or may not include the testes), the medical term orchiectomy does not include the removal of the penis.*

dicated for medical reasons, say when a testicular cancer has been diagnosed, and will prefer a less effective treatment, they will routinely opt out of surgery for prostate cancer and prefer statistically less effective radiation treatment instead because surgery potentially affects "sexual performance" permanently while radiation therapy does not.[1]

➤➤ **Cost of surgery:** Many transsexuals only ever seek the assistance of a psychiatrist when they know that they want surgery, have the money and only need permission for it. Genital surgery for m/f's costs anywhere from $8,000 to $20,000[2] while the f/m case runs more in the neighbourhood of $75,000 to $150,000[3]. As this is often "pay it yourself" it would seem reasonable to assume that fewer f/m's can afford it. There hardly seems to be a point in getting permission for something one can't afford, so they don't go to psychiatry for it and don't make the statistics.

➤➤ **Quality and invasiveness of surgery:** Today's m/f surgery usually allows full social (and sexual) integration. Depending on the technique used this is usually either a single surgery or two procedures within only a few days. In most cases the procedures give excellent emotional, visual and sexually fully functional results, typically few - if any - skin grafts are needed. Meanwhile the result of f/m surgery often leaves much to be desired, full sexual function is impossible[4] to achieve with today's methods and the process is far more invasive (multiple surgeries, extensive grafting of tissues from multiple locations, months of healing between procedures). Therefore it is to be expected that many f/m's opt-out of surgery (or at least the phalloplasty) at this time. They either prefer to wait until better procedures become available or feel the quality of a potential result would not justify the risks and side-effects. Again, many individuals will opt-out of psychiatry because they don't need it and won't make the statistics

Do these arguments (and the many I have not listed) account for a five to one misconception? I don't know. But there is one last argument to be made, maybe the most important: Even though the first genital f/m[5] surgery was only some 16 years after the first m/f[6] case (as documented by modern medicine), general acceptance by psychiatry took several decades more. As the number of m/f cases has over time steadily increased, from a handful of allowed

---

[1] *If the surgery does not completely remove the cancer one can often get radiation treatment as a secondary measure afterwards, however if one has undergone radiation therapy surgery is typically not possible as a back-up at least for some extended time because of the inherent tissue damage radiation causes (and thus surgical wounds would not heal properly)*

[2] *Total cost of a typical vaginoplasty. Usually this is one surgery, sometimes two in short sequence (a few days apart), rarely it is done in two stages within 6 to 12 months. Of course as so often in life one can spend a lot more if one absolutely insists...*

[3] *Total cost of a typical phalloplasty and, unlike the m/f case, necessary separate procedures (i.e. hysterectomy). Today a phalloplasty typically includes several surgeries for a complete creation of a penis and a scrotum, these are usually at least several months apart. The estimate also includes a hysterectomy which is an obvious precondition but due to the extent is done as a separate procedure. Furthermore it includes a mastectomy and chest reconstruction which is usually necessary and would often be done as yet another separate procedure. Of course more expensive procedures are always available.*

[4] *No spontaneous erections, often limited sensation/sensitivity, some sexual practices (i.e. anal intercourse) may not be possible*

[5] *Michael Dillon received genital reassignment surgeries in 1946-49 in the UK*

[6] *Lili Elbe received genital reassignment surgery in 1930 in Germany*

cases each year worldwide in the sixties to more than 15,000 surgeries in the year 2000, so has the number of f/m cases, ever since the condition became more generally accepted. *Therefore the difference in reported numbers may simply be a catch-up issue[1]!*

---

[1] *Statistically the average annual increase in cases over the past 50 years has been in the neighbourhood of 15%. A factor of 4 to 5 therefore represents a time lag of about 10 to 12 years.*

A.3.   ...AND NEITHER DO I NEED PLASTIC SURGERY

If ever I would make it through this jungle of absurdity, I learned, and finally got that permit for this "sex-change" they then call the procedure anything from *"plastic surgery"* to *"a cosmetic procedure"*. In the dictionary "cosmetic surgery" is defined as: *"An operation that improves the physical appearance of the body"*. Now I whole-heartedly agree: "sex reassignment" surgery would be an improvement to my appearance and I would add 'function' as well. But honestly, from their perspective seeing everything the way I didn't they might just as well call the procedure 'eviration' or 'neutering' (why not *'fixing'*), so indeed I had to admit that calling it "cosmetic surgery" wasn't that bad a choice. Not as bad as it could have been anyway. Of course it makes complete sense that they can't see this as "organic surgery" *because this would be akin to admitting that the problem is of a physical nature!* If they define it as *cosmetic* then they can at least get away with claiming that this is all - *and exclusively* - about ego and looks...

From my own perspective I neither think of it as "cosmetic" or "plastic" nor do I think of it as "sex change" or "gender-reassignment". Because I don't need a sex unassigned and then another assigned, I already have one and I'm quite happy with it, thank you very much! All I need is *to have my physical function brought in-line with my emotional one.* So at best I need **gender-alignment** or in this context maybe better **genital and hormonal alignment** as today it is not possible to give me my own functional hormonal system[1]. If this gets done by bringing my physical appearance in line with my emotional self-perception, all the better!

Yes, John could have gotten that kidney-transplant on a kitchen table, he could have had a cut from the back all the way to the front and the surgeon could have used surgical staples to close the incision afterwards. And yes, this might just have worked and it really makes little to no difference in the functioning of the kidney, does it?

But they don't. Just about every transplant-centre tries to do this with as small a cut as possible, even if this might make the surgeon's work slightly more difficult. They use sutures, even though this is more time-consuming than either staples or clips.

True, this costs a little more, but then again the result is a lot more aesthetically pleasing. And no, that kidney transplant isn't considered "plastic surgery" just because it allows John to use a public change-room without being stared at. And of course

---

[1] *This is why I will refer to "gender reassignment" as "gender-alignment" for the remainder of this book.*

John, just as every other transplant patient, gladly takes looking human afterwards, on top of getting the benefit of the transplant.

But while for him this "little improvement" means that he's not being stared at, for me the difference between a vaginoplasty[1] and an orchiectomy[2] (which solves the problem on a purely biochemical level) isn't just about being stared at in that change-room, it is being thrown out of that change-room and locked-up in prison for having been there! Besides this there are other likely far more important emotional aspects to support this choice, but in my opinion the legal problems alone fully justifies all the added expenditures.

So yes, if this gets to be visually indistinguishable or even appealing, all the better! But I would have settled for anything that would have made me feel emotionally right. Things like achieving sexual functionality was at best a remote concern. Sort of: It's nice to have, but really, if this were not possible I would not have given it any second thoughts.

Again, this doesn't seem to be the officially prescribed view at all. In fact this rather appears as if this were all about my capacity to serve as an object of sexual desire. After all I am not deemed male or female along the line of how I identify nor how I behave nor how I look or appear or socialize or even what reproductive capacity I have. I am deemed male or female *solely along the line of having a hole to stick something in or having something to stick into that hole!* If you find this offensive, well, I do too!

Yes, of course this surgery removes an organ or two (both testicles) and creates a new one, the vaginal canal. But apart from that this works by the principle of RRR - Reduce, Reuse, Recycle - because, with the exception of internal reproductive organs, the female and the male parts are just about the same.

No. I would not call this "cosmetic surgery". Because *it does remove organs and create new ones.* Cosmetic surgery *corrects* or *improves* a function, it doesn't create one *and it most certainly doesn't remove one.* This is "organic surgery" just as John's kidney transplant (or that orchiectomy a testicular cancer patient may require), removing a diseased organ and replacing it with a healthy one, with the one difference that in my case I can be my own donor as all the bits and pieces are anatomically there, just in the wrong places and some need to be cut down to size. For the rest some surplus tissue of whatever is left will do just fine. Ok, that's not entirely true. I'll have to continue to take estrogen as it is as of yet not possible to create ovaries from testicles (or from any of these bits and pieces I could contribute to this). I'll end-up being medically equivalent to a post-hysterectomy female, but apart from that...

---

[1] *Vaginoplasty: Surgery to create the vaginal opening, typically includes the relocation of the urethra and depending on the type of procedure may include creating the labia and/or clitoris; if testicles are present these are removed.*

[2] *Orchiectomy: Surgery to remove the testes.*

B.4. TO THE ROOT OF THE PROBLEM

Apparently I don't seem to have much trouble to self-diagnose and find the appropriate treatment. But why am I not allowed to get it? Well, the problem appears to be that there are two ways to define my condition: *Either* **I could be a mental male**: *I am playing female*. In this case I would have *a mental illness*, likely some form of "delusional disorder". This calls for mental treatment: Helping me to see and accept myself as a male. *Or* **I could be a female with a birth defect**: *I am a woman born with the wrong reproductive system*. In this case I would be *physically handicapped*. This calls for medical treatment: Hormonal and surgical correction of this disability to whatever extent is possible.

It can't possibly be both as *these diagnoses and treatments are mutually exclusive:* If both treatments would be employed at the same time and both would actually work (making me mentally experience myself as being male while at the same time medically changing my body to female) I'd end up being a female believing she's male - which hardly seems to be a desirable result!

Obviously I expect the experts to only send me to a treatment that does at the very least *have the potential* to generate a positive result? *So if both treatments would be known to work applying these simultaneously could easily be called the most mental treatment on earth?*

But if only one of these treatments should be used, one would have to know which of the above descriptions would make for the better diagnosis and treatment! I for one have my preference, but that's only my personal statement. Can I be trusted?

On the other hand I can only have a mental illness if such an illness is defined to exist. So let's have a look at that definition of mental illness:

There are two definitions out there that are in general use. The first one is: "Mental illness is any disease of the mind; the psychological state of someone who has emotional or behavioural problems serious enough to require psychiatric intervention"[1], the second one is: "Mental Illness means a mental or emotional disorder [verified by a diagnosis contained in the DSM-IV or ICD-9-CM] that substantially impairs a person's cognitive, emotional, or behavioural functioning, or any combination of those"[2]. Not surprisingly **psychiatry uses the first definition as it *leaves the decision of what actually looks***

---

[1] *Quoted from wordnet.princeton.edu perl webwn, search term "mental illness", a typical definition often used in medical texts.*

[2] *Quoted from Disabilities Services Act of 2003, Illinois General Assembly Public Act 93-0638 (text slightly simplified). This is a typical definition found in legal codes of most countries.*

pathological enough to require their intervention <u>exclusively to psychiatrists</u>! Meanwhile legal systems (at least in "western nations"), including the Canadian and the US as well as the European Union and all its nations, the United Nations and the WHO use the second definition *which deems (at least) all individuals who are not substantially impaired (i.e. function in society and personally without causing or having significant problems) <u>to be free of mental illness</u>.* While even this second definition is still highly subjective (in particular the condition "contained in the DSM or the ICD" restricts the definition of mental illness to an arbitrary selection of pathologies selected by professional organizations), **it nevertheless makes the same difference as <u>"guilty until proven innocent" or "innocent until proven guilty"</u>!**

I neither had nor ever caused any of the above mentioned impairments, significant or otherwise. So if I don't find myself impaired, why would I want a sex-change? Yes, I am emotionally and behaviourally (particularly intimately) impaired, this could in fact get serious enough to induce a suicide. *But the impairment isn't caused by a mental problem, it is the result of two different aspects of a biological problem*: First: For a female to look, physically experience herself and sexually function male, well, it is just plain wrong. To put this into perspective: Some people get clinical depression because they don't like the shape of their nose… Second: Being physically wrong on the level a transsexual is physically wrong isn't exclusively an emotional problem, it is a biomechanical one also. This isn't "I don't like the length of my penis", it is "I have the wrong set of organs". When a female is kept at male hormone levels *this causes a well known set of emotional problems similar in almost every woman who has ever tried this!* The most often reported side-effect in biological women who take testosterone (other than f/m transsexuals), such as in elite-sports for doping, are *depression* (some reports suggest that at regular male levels this happens to 4 out of 5 women) and *suicidality* (this may be the case in more than half of all women at male levels). Nevertheless for some reason psychiatry claims it absolutely not understandable why transsexuals might react the same way…

Of course there is also the matter that medical treatment has a success-rate of 90%+ for hormonal alignment, 99%+ for surgical genital alignment. If you remove the biochemical and the biomechanical problem you remove the related emotional problems! Meanwhile, just like "curing homosexuals", *psychiatric therapy has yet to produce a single case of a "cured transsexual"*…

I have a functioning life and what I say I need is for all intents and purposes meaningful and helps me, gives me a better life. Why do they need to shatter this if what they offer is years of pain, irreparable damage and a 0% success-rate with their treatment? So what's the "mental-health community" up to anyway? Denying me the decent, socially productive life I happen to have on the grounds of *what? Having the life I like is wrong? Feeling good is wrong? Being different is wrong, particularly if no one notices?*

As you probably suspect by now all this insight doesn't mean that we don't have to do whatever the psychiatrists have in store for us, it indeed doesn't mean that the definitions in the DSM or the ICD get changed or removed or that any medical association anywhere in the world would put an end to the entirely arbitrary, illegal and abusive use of "mental treatment". (True, if they would change this "for us" this might just have implications for other "mental illnesses"). It means that *I have the legal right to get genital surgery at any time, but practically I can't get it because this right is denied to me by a professional organization self-enforcing a completely arbitrary decision as a "professional standard"!*

B.5. WORSE THAN THE WORST CRIMINALS!

There are quite a number of mental-health conditions and thankfully the American Psychiatric Association has figured out what they all are. They publish their findings about every decade in a diagnostic manual called "DSM" (the "Diagnostic and Statistical Manual of Mental Disorders"[DSM]), currently it's the fifth revision which the APA calls DSM-IV.

There are a handful of mental conditions which appear to be stable and remain seen as a "severe affliction" throughout the millennia (things like Alzheimer's, Dissociative Disorders, Paranoia or however these used to be called so many centuries ago), the rest though varies greatly over the years. Homosexuality for example was certainly not seen as "a mental illness" during the Roman Empire but was made into this later, only to be removed again not too long ago. Poverty used to be seen as a mental illness, as was leading a nomadic lifestyle - and I hope I don't have to mention that this is seen differently today, officially anyway.

What's deemed "a *severe* mental affliction" in one edition of the DSM may be *missing entirely* in the very next and what is normal today may just be deemed mental in the sixth major revision (which they will call V, officially due in 2012). Seeing all this instability one might be drawn to the speculation that the basis for the decision what's in the catalogue of today's mental conditions and what's not might rather be based on philosophical, religious or political positions of the DSM's authors than any hard evidence... And even if they would deny such motivations vehemently (which of course they do) and argue that they're after all medical doctors and not politicians, how are they possibly capable of making such a determination in regard of transsexuality? After all, it is exclusively self-identified and therefore "hard evidence" is impossible to come by! Or is it this "guilty until proven innocent" preference? But then again, since when has the preference of "guilty until proven innocent" over "innocent until proven guilty" become a medical imperative instead of a political, philosophical or religious one?

As an example one can find such mental disorders in this book as Nr. 301.7 (Antisocial Personality Disorder)[DSM]. Somebody has it, among other possibilities, when this person doesn't conform to what the government says, takes up arms and starts to fight against the ruling regime. Of course the APA didn't want their own national founding fathers accidentally declared sociopaths, so there's one more condition in the definition of

43

this "severe mental illness": A person is only crazy if his/her actions "substantially impair that person's cognitive, emotional and/or behavioural functioning"[1]…

I can certainly understand that *loosing a revolution* could be a problem for the people involved as there are sure to be some presumably painful consequences which are bound to impair the emotional, behavioural, even cognitive function of such a person; being executed is just one example from the typical range of such consequences… What I fail to see however is *why loosing a revolution is a mental illness while winning one is not,* just because one does not suffer the negative consequences of one's actions if one ends-up being head of state instead of death-row inmate? I also fail to see why political, economical or other external influences which, presumably, have prompted such an event and have contributed to its outcome would be of any consequence *for an individual's medical diagnosis* - and that's after all what a psychiatric label is.

More generally *I for one would say that revolution, particularly if it is against tyranny, oppression, abuse and artificially imposed suffering **cannot be a mental disease.** Wanting to live in an orderly world with just and equal rules and the equal application of such rules to all, a world with freedom of expression, a world without officially sanctioned or even tolerated oppression **is a normal human desire - even if the target of such a revolution might be psychiatry itself - no matter if one wins it or not!***

Now clearly just about every psychiatrist would ejaculate the term "foul" somewhere around here, he would interject that I misinterpret their handbook (although there doesn't seem to be too much room for misinterpretation *in that particular chapter*), that every case would merit individual review, a personalized diagnosis, that no definite diagnosis and certainly no treatment could be defined *unless the patient has been personally examined* (usually this requires an extensive amount of time), and *that such "summary justice" is not medical treatment.* Honestly, I could not agree more!

It seems that not just I agree, society as a whole does too! Society and psychiatry even seem to be doing this to a degree which I find at times beyond belief. Paedophilia for example is defined as a mental illness. However *no paedophile can be sent to mental-health without either freely consenting to go or by order of a court!* This seems to be how things are done in our society: If somebody is convicted of sexually abusing children by a court of law (or even openly admits to it) *this does not automatically mean that the person is also deemed to merit the psychiatric label of paedophilia or any related treatment, it does not even warrant a single mandatory visit to a psychiatrist to find out **unless a judge says so!*** Every case merits its own review, even the one of a *convicted* criminal. Every single one, except transsexuals…

---

[1] *Excerpt from definition of Antisocial Personality Disorder, DSM.*

I neither have nor ever had any kind of mental or emotional problem which I could not resolve myself - with the single exception *that I was denied treatment* for a certain physical condition by mental-health. No judge has ever decided that I should have to see a psychiatrist or that I would lack any capacity which could impair my judgement *to making any and all decisions in regard to my own life.* Nevertheless, **I find myself summarily convicted of having a mental disorder! Without any examination whatsoever, without ever having seen a psychiatrist!** Based on this pseudo-diagnosis I am denied medical treatment to solve my problem. *Because according to it **I am deemed incapable to even understand if I have the capacity to make decisions in regard of my own life or not!*** Hasn't this trap been called "Catch-22" in another context before?

Every rapist, every mass murderer, every paedophile, every other human being *is deemed competent to make decisions,* is deemed mentally healthy *until proven otherwise*, even after conviction of such a crime. *Every single human being is entitled to this - except transsexuals! **We are officially deemed mental just because of how certain people want to see us!*** And we find ourselves not in the position of fighting an accusation of mental illness *but in a position <u>where we are by decree defined to be insane and then have to try and prove that we're not!</u>* And we have to do it all from a position *where we are denied the capacity of understanding if we are mentally competent or not!*

As of how I'm treated by duly authorized officials, am I to conclude that my case, that being transsexual, *is deemed to be something far worse than being a paedophile, a rapist or maybe a serial killer? **After all, none of these get summary convicted by mental-health or forced into mental treatment solely because of who they are or what they did!*** None of them need to have their medical care approved by a psychiatrist. **And they all get their chance to defend themselves** *because they all are deemed innocent until proven guilty, <u>they all are deemed mentally competent until proven otherwise!</u>* **No matter** *that these criminals have proven beyond a reasonable doubt by their very actions that they seriously lack in some fundamental mental capacity!* Us? **We get convicted <u>without any proof whatsoever, on a mere hypothetical suspicion on what we could be!</u>***

Of course after surgery psychiatrists will deem it *entirely normal for me to always have seen me as a female* as - from their perspective - I am one *by proof of looks* (well, with nudity anyway). In fact if I'd see a psychiatrist these days he would in all likelihood not even ask about how I identify and just assume that what my self-identification and my legal documents say would be the same *unless I'd say otherwise.* And why would I? After all thinking of myself as male is now a mental illness for me…

Let me ask a somewhat pointed question here: If we agree that I am mentally the same person after genital surgery as I was before and my psychiatric designation nevertheless changes from "mental male" to "normal female", does this mean that - from the point of view of psychiatry - all normal females are in fact mentally (and probably also physically) handicapped males and the only difference - from a psychiatrist's point of view - between a "normal female" and the former me (a "mental male") is that normal females are born with their genitals on the inside *which entitled them to the nicer label at birth, for the same mental disorder?*

B.6. DOGMATISTS AND DOGMATIC TREATMENT

Whenever a large institution or bureaucracy doesn't have any success in doing their work and they'd like to take cover behind something the thing they do is to form a committee. One of the first tasks of such a committee usually is to designates its own members 'experts'. These 'experts' then in turn work out some 'standards' to adhere to. Then nobody has to take it personal when they fail while doing their work! After all, they all adhere to *"the commonly accepted standard"* as defined by *"a higher authority"* - their own committee! And in doing so they provide *"the best known treatment"* because the foremost experts on the subject (they themselves) have defined it and if that doesn't work, nothing else would have! Right?

In our case that standard is called "The Harry Benjamin International Gender-Dysphoria Association's Standards Of Care For Gender Identity Disorders"[HBIGDA-S], this uses to be published by "The Harry Benjamin International Gender Dysphoria Association, Inc." which has transitioned in 2007 into "WPATH" ("The World Professional Association For Transgender Health, Inc."[WPATH]). One would assume that this would mean that their main publication ought to be renamed "WPATH Standards Of Care For Gender Identity Disorders" but, to date, they didn't seem to have had time to implement this. However that name may be it appears to be somewhat unpractical to use this cumbersome designation repeatedly in a book. I will thus henceforth refer to it as *'dogma'.*

While I certainly don't recommend reading this dogma it is now available free of charge for download at *www.wpath.org*. They used to *sell* it to their victims for $20.-, but that seems to have changed after a few people have put copies on the internet.

I have hardly ever come across a comparably unethical document though the *Malleus Maleficarum[1]* may just come close. In my medical library it is only comparable to promotional texts of the last few "psychiatric glitches", things like phrenology or eugenics. But as the dogma is what's imposed on us even by the most well-meaning doctors (that is the ones who have not had their licenses revoked for "letting us go to easily") we're just about forced to have a look at it. So how does this work, officially:

First and foremost dogma works by denying us access to medical services if we aren't deemed compliant by the psychiatrists in the system. *Medical treatment is given as a reward for "good behaviour".* Nowhere else in medicine is it known that deprivation of medical services is a valid tool to enforce compliance to medical *and in particular non-medical (i.e. social and behavioural) conditions.* But this is only the first time we will

[Medical professional, about mental-health] They shouldn't do this to you, this treatment won't work on you anyway...

---

[1] *Malleus Maleficarum (English "[The] Witch Hammer"), first printed in 1486 as a "handbook for witch-hunters".*

encounter a profound lack of medical or human ethics. Dogma imposes a sort of 'schedule', a *"minimum-timeline"* and a *"predefined, fixed sequence of the type of treatment"* onto us. This is done with no regard whatsoever to the patient's condition, needs, dignity or wishes and as we will see with a flagrant disregard of her physical as well as her mental health, personal safety and at potentially enormous sacrifice to the quality of the result of treatment. So how does this work:

Dogma sets the following schedule called "triadic treatment" as minimum requirements (every institution is at liberty to add further conditions or extend "minimum requirements"):

Part 1 of "triadic treatment"

Psychiatric treatment starts (if there is no indication one needs to be made-up).

➤➤ The type of psychiatric therapy is completely irrelevant, just 'treatment'. Dogma doesn't require "verified treatment success" or even "presumed treatment efficacy" (as this isn't possible anyway), just "proof of attendance" and compliance to the satisfaction of a therapist.

Part 2 of "triadic treatment" (only after successful completion of part 1)

The first medical treatment that can be made available by the treating psychiatrist is Hormone-Replacement-Therapy (HRT). To qualify for it the patient must:

➤➤ be at least 16 years of age

➤➤ have been in continued psychiatric treatment for at least 3 months

➤➤ have been deemed mental by said therapist (i.e. *certified to suffer from "gender-dysphoria"*). This requires the psychiatrist to believe, according to the definition of "gender-dysphoria", *that "the desire to be the other sex"* **must have been present for at least two years.** How this is established is entirely up to the therapist's personal preference. Some accept testimony. Others insist in "more tangible evidence" such as photographs of oneself crossdressing or evidence of having used a "female name", such as a credit-card in this name. Yet others accept third-party testimony such as interviews with friends, parents or guardians (if one has any). But there are also places, among these a majority of the larger psychiatric institutions, who state that *they accept this claim only if it has been made to an accredited professional (i.e. a psychiatrist or medical doctor). Meaning that a patient with no prior history of psychiatric treatment will, at the earliest, be believed to be transsexual exactly 2 years after the first therapy-session! Her life, her appearance, her emotional state and well-being as well as any other evidence whatsoever will simply be ignored!*

➤➤ obtain the permission from this psychiatrist in the form of a "letter of recommenda-tion" to get the prescriptions for HRT from a GP or get the prescriptions directly from the psychiatrist.

➤➤ Dogma suggests that the patient starts living "the desired gender-role" *some time af-ter going on HRT*, first "part-time", later "full-time", however not few psychiatrists and institutions are known not to prescribe hormonal treatment to people *who do not already live in accordance with their behavioural- and dress-code* (i.e. don't look or behave sufficiently 'female' to *the therapist's* expectations).

Part 3 of "triadic treatment" (only after successful completion of part 2)

At this point dogma allows any surgery (subject to 'recommendation' in writing by psychiatrist) except genital reassignment[1]. To qualify one has to:

➤➤ qualify for all of the above, plus

➤➤ have been on HRT for at least 6 months

➤➤ still be in continued psychiatric care as described above

➤➤ provide proof of "significant improvement of her mental health" since commence-ment of psychiatric treatment and show "significant stabilization of her gender-identity" (no details are given as to what this is or how it could be demonstrated)

➤➤ obtain the written permission from psychiatrist to get this surgical procedure

➤➤ if this surgery includes orchiectomy then *permission from a second authoritative per-son is required,* dogma says that this may be a second psychiatrist, a psychotherapist or a PhD psychologist specializing in human behavioural psychology

Part 4 of "triadic treatment" (only after successful completion of part 3)[2]

At this last step dogma finally allows genital gender reassignment[3]. To qualify a pa-tient has to:

➤➤ qualify for all of the above, plus

➤➤ be at least 18 to 21 years of age, depending on the country one lives in (presumably because mental people merit different treatment durations depending on the prevail-ing political system?)

---

[1] *This is the day a transsexual is allowed to apply for surgery at a clinic of her choice, not the day of surgery itself. Depending on the clinic waiting-lists for breast-surgery can range from 3 to 6 months (some doctors may not accept pre-op transsexuals for this procedure), waiting-times for orchiectomy can be similar or longer if done at a clinic specializing in gender-reassignment or at least weeks if done locally. If one can find a doctor willing to perform the 15 minute procedure that is...*

[2] *The term 'triad' comes from Pythagorean philosophy, it stands for the number three, a TRIAD is therefore supposed to have THREE parts, not four...*

[3] *This is the day a transsexual is allowed to apply for surgery at a clinic of her choice, not the day of surgery itself. Depending on the clinic typical waiting-lists for genital surgery can be 9-15 months.*

➤➤ have been on HRT for a minimum of 12 months

➤➤ have been in continued psychiatric care as described above for at least 12 months[1]

➤➤ provide proof of having lived "the desired gender role" with no interruption ("full time") for a minimum of 12 months (no definition is given to what "living a gender role" actually means and how such prove may be obtained)

➤➤ satisfy the employment and socialization criteria dogma sets out

➤➤ provide proof of having assumed "a further stabilization of one's gender-identity" and "significant, lasting improvement in mental health" since commencement of psychiatric treatment (no details are given as to what this means or how this could be demonstrated)

➤➤ obtain a second permission from another authoritative person, dogma says that this may be a second psychiatrist, a psychotherapist or a PhD. psychologist specializing in human behavioural psychology

➤➤ usually this comes with the expectation that one remains in psychiatric care for life (however after surgery this typically can no longer be enforced)

Superficially this sounds, at least in general, straight-forward, even at times reasonable. But there really are a few rather basic issues with it:

➤➤ Forcing a group of people into mental-treatment because their self-identification fails to meet certain expectations is a violation of the UN charter of human rights, in most countries this is also illegal

➤➤ Forcing only *selected* people with the same self-identification into such treatment (i.e. transsexual women vs. biological women) is discrimination

➤➤ There in fact exist people who do just fine without the assistance of a psychiatrist (who would have thought?)

➤➤ Most of the requirements of dogma are largely open to interpretation or are subjective or even entirely arbitrary

➤➤ None of the restrictions of dogma and none of the conditions it sets out have anything to do with our self-identification or are related to diagnostic results of verifiable medical tests

---

[1] **The theoretical minimum time is actually 15 months of continued mental treatment!** *One has to be on hormonal treatment for a minimum of 12 months but <u>before this</u> a minimum of 3 months **prior to being allowed on HRT** is required.*

≫ The way this dogma is set-up, in particular that it implicitly states that *there is no urgency* and that *there is never any need for immediate treatment,* makes our requests for gender-alignment look as if it were not necessary medical treatment. After all, if there are no cases in which treatment is ever urgently needed and several years of delay are always acceptable then all cases can be postponed time and again and eventually indefinitely without causing significant harm

≫ Forcing an individual into mental treatment without any evidence of any behavioural problem whatsoever is illegal

≫ Restricting our rights to make decisions, in particular restricting the rights to freely decide over our own bodies is a human-rights violation

≫ Linking social behavioural expectations such as being unmarried, being employed or identifying heterosexual (after surgery) to providing medical treatment is in sharp contradiction to the medical oath, it is unethical and discriminatory

≫ Dogma specifically limits our access *only to hormonal treatment and a very small number of surgeries* (such as breast augmentation and genital surgery). Other surgeries which are far more invasive or socially visible, such as facial and voice modification, leg- and neck-extensions and many others are freely available to everybody at any time. People who do not require or wish *these specific restricted treatments* but live the other than assigned gender-role anyway aren't even considered. This double-standard can only be explained by *this being a targeted measure to single-out people who need these select treatments (in particular presumably genital alignment).* Such narrow targeting shows that this is indeed not a measure to "help and support", because if it were then everybody with similar concerns would merit help also

≫ The mandatory character of this dogma *amounts to socially endorsed punishment based on the grounds of who we are* or what we need. This punishment is handed out by a private interest-group *bypassing the legal system,* its safeguards as well as any and all avenues of recourse

≫ *The absolute minimum required treatment time* at a facility requiring proof of "gender-dysphoria" by presence (the standard for a majority of large institutions) is (assuming) a 3 months wait for an initial visit, then 24 months for the diagnosis, then 12 months on hormonal treatment and then a minimal 9 months wait to obtain surgery, *a total of 48 months or 4 years,* not including recovery from surgery. This is assuming that everything happens as quickly as possible and the psychiatrists sign their prescriptions and letters on the first possible day - which in itself is just about unheard of. (Realistically the expectation should be about 6 years). This in itself is abusive. It is also painful and harmful, this wait indeed turns deadly for many

Besides all these arguments there are a few practical problems with this dogma. One of the more obvious would be that it is just about impossible to define what "living a gender-role" actually means. If a therapist insists that this is wearing 4" heels and a 14" skirt in his office and fails a woman for wearing jeans and sneakers, well, then that's what he means by "living female". Personally I think that there just might be something fundamentally questionable with that person's view of what a woman is... Nevertheless sadly enough in far too many places *this is exactly what's being asked of us!*

Dogma requires that we are "full-time employed, -students or -volunteers". This, apart from being generally discriminatory, I find sexist as some of the most typically female roles in our society, for example being a mother or a housewife, a farmer's wife or an in-home caregiver for an elderly or handicapped person are, sadly enough, deemed as worthless as not to merit any financial remuneration. So people who clearly occupy some of the more feminine-identified and socially meaningful positions our society has to offer will never qualify for any treatment! Are these people "too much stereotypically female" to deserve being woman?

On the other hand being a registered prostitute employed by a brothel (in a country where prostitution and brothels are legal) is quite ok because, after all, a sex worker in a brothel has a full-time job and regular income - and that's the criteria! Now I don't want to debate here if this prostitute provides a "social meaningful service" (and why there are customers who specifically look for she-male[1] prostitutes), what I dispute is that a person who cares 24/7 for children at home with no pay whatsoever does not. [And if you allow me a more personal remark I find that therapists who accept prostitution as a meaningful occupation but deny the same to mothers, caregivers, housewives or unpaid co-workers in a family business ought to work on their own ethics instead of declaring other people crazy and denying treatment arbitrarily, all in line with optimizing their personal financial benefit. But that's just the opinion of a transsexual who's been declared a lunatic herself and therefore might not count for much].

As so often I also have a problem with "psychiatric logic" here: When somebody works as a prostitute or actress in porn-movies or anywhere in that industry then I suppose gender-alignment surgery would have a rather dramatic impact on the particular appeal this person has for her clients or employer? Gender-alignment might indeed make her unemployable... Or it should at least be expected to have a major impact on her work and likely on her remuneration? I mean - but honestly! Just how could this possibly have escaped the average male psychiatrist???

Just by the way: This doctrine of full-time employment also discriminates against people who have retired or are on disability, part or full-time. Except for direct discrimination it is not understandable why any such person should not be entitled to any particular medical treatment. Indeed I have a great problem to understand why *doctors* who have taken an oath

---

[1] *A she-male is an individual who appears female but has male genitals. She-males typically like to keep their male genitals functional (often for sexual activities) and thus would not want genital surgery and limited or no hormonal alignment.*

to treat people in need would possibly accept such standards of social selection, never mind write these!

Dogma furthermore distinguishes between 'eligibility' and 'readiness'. 'Eligible' means that a patient "has done her time", "shown never-ending compliance", accepted all the degradation without complaint and hopes to get to the next step in her treatment. 'Readiness' means that the psychiatrist deems the patient 'ready' for that particular step. This is comparable to the process of parole for prisoners where a committee decides if an inmate is to be released early, i.e. having been sentenced to 4 years but being released after only 3. Only with transsexuals this is turned upside-down: A single person decides not if the woman in question is to be granted her treatment a little sooner but if punishment should be extended potentially indefinitely! No reasoning needs to be given as to why 'readiness' is denied, so on top of that already completely arbitrary and highly abusive schedule (which is called "a *minimum* standard") any additional criteria a psychiatrist may dream-up can be enforced. In fact most larger psychiatric institutions who provide treatment to transsexuals simply insist by decree that *'readiness' requires 1 to 3 years of additional waiting over and above the required one-year waiting prevision of dogma* to be allowed on surgery. If a psychiatrist (or a psychiatric institution) defines that no patient can be 'ready' if she did not have at least 4 years of psychotherapy at this facility or a minimum of 100 sessions on the bill, well, that's that for the patient. There is no recourse.

I personally do not understand the term 'readiness' at all. I suppose one can see this two ways. One view is that *one is never ready* as the experience to go on hormones as well as the experience of any surgery whatsoever, from a root canal to a kidney transplant to gender-alignment *can only ever truly be appreciated after the fact*. Therefore technically one's ready and understands what to expect *right after it has been done...*

The other view is that *I was born ready.* I'm a woman and for a woman having no testicles and a vagina is just about as normal as it gets! There's no "getting ready for this", "getting used to it" or "having to think about it", this is just simply right, age or waiting doesn't change a thing. This is right at age 88, at age 18 and at age 8. But somehow psychiatry manages to find *something in between being born ready and never being ready at all,* something like *"psychiatric readiness".* It's assigned to each and every patient with no transparency of reasoning whatsoever. As it is completely arbitrary it isn't in any way consistent from institution to institution or psychiatrist to psychiatrist or even case to case.

A few parts of dogma are clearly and directly unethical. For example HRT can be commenced *immediately,* i.e. the patient can skip mental treatment and psychiatric approval, *if the patient has demonstrated that she obtained hormones 'illegally' on the grey market.* Now I find it outrageous that illegal activities are promoted by psychiatry in this way, or if seen the other way 'round, *that people who are stupid enough to adhere to the law or to prescribed procedures and expectations would be punished for this by being sent to mental-health for it* and by having additional requirements and waiting-times imposed on them! This is maybe one of the parts of the protocol where it is most clearly visible that mental treatment is never intended to 'cure' us or 'care' for us but is exclusively designed as a punishment for the stupid ones, the honest ones, the compliant ones.

While I quite understand that it makes sense to get people off grey-market HRT and into an environment where they get advice and have access to laboratory-checkups, I don't understand why everybody else would not merit the same consideration and efficient treatment, *why somebody who has demonstrated that she is willing to bypass rules* may (or may not) be sent to mental-health *but is rewarded by medical care immediately!* And even if she is sent to mental-health, a positive decision, a 'recommendation' and 'readiness' for hormonal treatment as well as potentially years of waiting are suddenly no longer a consideration!

Most interestingly, the patients who are given HRT immediately because they had already started on their own in the end don't do any worse than their control group (the ones who adhere to dogma), they may in fact even do better, but so far it seems that no psychiatrist has had the time to make a study of this!

Of course this gets really absurd, if not mental, when one reads in the introduction of dogma that *"The designation of gender identity disorders as mental disorders is not a license for stigmatization, or for the deprivation of gender patients' civil rights"*[HBIGDA-S] when misdiagnosing us for the purpose of stigmatization and deprivation of our civil rights, including deprivation of medical treatment, is the first, last and only thing this dogma does…

A.4.   I'M DEFINITELY NOT CRAZY!!!

That disorderly gender identity I mentioned in B.6? Well, I don't seem to ever have had that either. But just what do they expect? Somebody who does not know if he/she is male or female? Or somebody who feels male in the morning and female in the afternoon except on rainy days? This could conceivably be call 'disorder', but if somebody agrees with having it this way? I'm certainly not going to start inventing limits to people's identifications... My own? Well, it was just boringly always the same and always female, nothing ever changed and I felt just fine with it. Which is about as far from 'disorder' as it gets, isn't it?

What I did not find normal was that I had testicles and that I had to live on male hormone levels and everything that comes along with that. If they had called me "a testicle-dysphoric female", that would have seemed somewhat appropriate. Somewhat. Although I would have to add that this would be strictly limited to *my own* testicles, this isn't "testicle-phobia". Of course on a more general note I couldn't help asking myself just why it was that they thought not wanting testicles could possibly be a mental illness for a woman? Or for anybody for that matter?

To put this mildly, there seemed to be a few rather fundamental issues that the people who were holding the key to my treatment and I seemed to see *slightly* different. Now this could have different reasons: It could be because they in fact had no clue as to my condition and were completely ignorant of my experiences and people like myself. It could be that every other transsexual really was completely different or that I was the first case of something that had never existed before (or at least they had never seen), though somehow I didn't think these explanations to be very likely. Or it could be that I really was mental and just needed to see the truth: That I was not a woman but a male suffering from gender-dysphoria instead. I mean seeing things that dramatically differently...

Now there I was with a few things to consider about my life. How infinitely easy it had seemed only a few months prior! Back then I actually thought of being a woman as something normal...

I was 17 when I learned all this. The closest I had ever gotten to mental-health was a session of career-counselling provided by our high-school. That session had failed to reveal anything I didn't know before and I had opted to continue trusting my own skills and instincts into making decisions to my own life instead of delegating these to somebody whose mental capacity I didn't trust.

[Me] I'm not doing this for a living, I'm doing this for life! [Friend] I suppose it would be mental just to be difficult to be mental just for a living? [Me] I see you have no idea what some people do for a living these days!

I analyzed what information I had collected very, very thoroughly and weighed the pros and the cons. Should I learn to see myself as a deranged male instead of as a normal female? Should I ask for *this* treatment or take my chances with a possible future suicide? The decision took the better part of a second. I opted to take my chances at trying not to kill myself over a guarantee to get killed by this treatment.

B.7.   TRANSSEXUAL CHOICE

No matter where one suspects the roots of transsexuality, biological, biochemical, other, there is the question as to why this happens in the first place. It is not at all obvious that transsexuality exists - or is it? For decades the medical community did not accept that this is real and that we need appropriate help. Even today there are not few people, medical professionals and others, who doubt that what we say is true or who claim outright that they know us all to be mentally deranged liars. I know better and fortunately I can prove it:

I have two premises I start from:

➤➤ I accept that gender-designation is commonly derived from how our genitals look just after birth (and let's just for the sake of argument exclude biologically indeterminate individuals, forged documents, bureaucratic and medical mistakes and so on and assume that this identification is always 100% accurate).

➤➤ I furthermore assume that self-experience as either male or female is made-up in the brain. (It could also, in a spiritual context, be the soul, but as we will see this would not make any difference to the argument). I derive this conviction mostly from the fact that even people without identifiable genitals and people who have had their genitals or reproductive system destroyed or removed due to illness, accident or whatever (note: people who do not say that they are transsexual) *continue to identify the same gender* after the fact, and that they neither report any change in conviction nor become 'ungendered' just because they have lost reproductive organs or visible genitals or both.

I must therefore conclude that biological gender (the genitals, the reproductive organs) and subjective gender-experience (the brain) are made-up *in two physically separate parts of a person's body.* These parts have developed more or less independently from a very early stage of development. We can assume some kind of mechanism that would safeguard for a matching outcome, that somebody with male reproductive organs would develop male visible genitals and male secondary sexual characteristics (i.e. usually taller, more muscular, heavier, develops a low voice during puberty, potentially body-hair,...) as well as a male identification. (And vice-versa for women). One avenue we know of which does just that are hormonal influences, but there may well be others. Or we can assume some kind of mechanism we start out with that would do the same, genetics would be an obvious candidate for this.

[Friend] I haven't seen you for a while, what have you been up to lately? [Me] Ah, well, the usual... Taking care of the kids, enjoying summer and having a little sex-change...

While I leave it to others to work-out how this works in detail it is to be assumed that both influences would normally act together to contribute to the final result. However, we're not talking about an assembly-line here but rather about biological growth. Biology allows for variation and such variation isn't just normal, biological diversity is in fact built into the very mechanism of how our cells work and reproduce. On top of that there's always the variations that environmental influences contribute, everything from natural (and artificial) radiation to maternal hormone levels during pregnancy to natural and artificial chemical influences and many more are potential or known candidates of interference.

Whatever the reasons are, *the imperative conclusion is that the correlation between biological sexual or genital development and emotional development can never be 1 (or 100%), but something less than 1.* And however good this correlation is, however good the mechanisms are that should 'guarantee' a matching outcome, *there will be individuals where these two attributes will not match.* These individuals, at least, would be transsexuals.

There may be other conditions, other influences that could make an individual identify other than her birth-certificate suggests. I don't know if such an identification could be acquired later in life due to social influences or pressures or due to exposure to biological, biochemical, even physical changes or influences, but it would seem far-fetched to exclude this outright. In any case *this would only ever increase the number of transsexual individuals.* The one thing that can be derived with certainty is that *there is a mathematical certainty for transsexuality to exist.*[1] (The same incidentally is true for homosexuality). Or in other words: *Transsexuality is not a choice. It is a biological necessity!*

I have great difficulties to understand how medicine and seemingly large part of society can define transsexuality (and homosexuality) as 'abnormality', 'illness', "mental condition", 'deviation', 'fetish' or worse if rendering proof that this is a necessary and normal expression of the process "sexual reproduction in sexually different individuals" is that simple. *The very existence of transsexuality (and homosexuality) is founded in who we are, it is not good or bad, right or wrong, **but it is a necessary and predictable expression of the process we call 'life', it is one of the many variations the sum of which we experience as being human.***

And while I could see that society makes the mistake of judging people because of *who* they are instead of *how* they are, particularly ancient and pre-scientific society, I think at least scientific medicine should know better!

There used to be a time when John and Jane would not have survived their conditions. John would either have been killed shortly after birth when it was noticed that he had a physical problem or he would have died early in childhood. Jane would have died after her accident or she would likely have either been killed or left to die when it became clear that she would never again be capable to follow her group of hunter-gatherers. Jane and John would have been deemed "a burden to society" and left behind.

---

[1] *This is even correct within the theory that emotional gender self-perception is an exclusively learned trait (which I find is exceedingly absurd as an idea): After all it wouldn't be the fist time that somebody is found to have learned some fact 'wrong'!*

Over time this changed. Not only does our society these days have the resources to support individuals who can't for any reason contribute more than they need, but we also deem it wrong to leave people to die if help is possible, we deem it wrong to kill people instead of providing support, whether for a certain period or for life. In having, as a society, evolved past mere existence we have found that there are far more ways of contributing than just hunting and gathering, childbirth and child-rearing. We have found art, science, entertainment. We have found abstract and complex ways to contribute to society. We have also found that who will contribute and in what capacity, how much (if it's even measurable) or in what way isn't predictable at all and it isn't all that straight-forward as we initially thought it to be. Sometimes a challenge only ever generates the need, the determination or the means to create something extraordinary, sometimes having a reason to care for others does. *Over time we have learned that every life is important!* **We have learned that every life contributes, just differently!**

Now I am by no means saying that everything is as it should be in how we treat people who are in some way different, however we must also recognize the many efforts society has made and the many improvements there are:

There is research into how to make John's condition easier to bear, how his medical treatment could be improved. There are studies not only in regard to his treatment in particular but also into transplant-medicine in general. Much progress has been made, indeed the very fact that an organ can be routinely transplanted today was breakthrough research 50 years ago and it was impossible only a lifetime before that. John would simply have died, an agonizing death, he would never have been able to enjoy life as he does today.

Jane's condition is different. While a lot of research is going on and some small progress has been made the break-through of making spinal-tissue re-grow and resume it's former function has yet to be achieved. Much of the current medical attention Jane is getting is centred around making her life bearable, making it easier, making it pain-free, practical. And while many more paraplegics walk-away from their accidents these days than ever before thanks to improved care this is still by no means a cure, once the damage is done this becomes, at best, "enabling medical technology". At the current state of research Jane will have to rely on such "technical supports" as a wheelchair for life. Nevertheless, this technology enables her to integrate socially and experience her life as meaningful, she can be self-reliant. Society is even willing to adapt to a certain degree to make this possible, there are laws on equality to facilitate her social integration, we mandate wheelchair-accessibility in such places as public buildings, transit, schools, hotels, workplaces, we have handicapped parking and washrooms. We adapt, a little, to help - and in the end we realize this is to the benefit of everybody.

Sadly unlike Jane's and John's condition transsexuality is treated very, very differently:

➤➤ There is no significant scientific research or trials into our medical treatment, into sequence, type and quantity of drugs, surgery and the results achieved, with the only noticeable exception of the research and progress in genital surgical techniques which largely is the effort of only a handful of individuals.

➤➤ There is no research into how transsexuality should be seen, how it should be approached by medicine, into when and where which form of treatment is appropriate. There is dogma, this is sacrosanct, in this regard nothing has changed in the slightest ever since it's first inception[1].

➤➤ There are no sociological studies on the economic value and benefit of our treatment and subsequent integration into society, as to the relation of treatment-cost vs. our increased social and economic contributions afterwards, into the best time for the onset of treatment vs. social, emotional and economic results.

➤➤ There are no studies on the benefits and side-effects of drugs, except for the ones done on the general population (non transsexuals) on individuals who take the same drugs, but not in the same combinations and for very different reasons. Often these people are considerably older than we are and often they suffer from severe medical conditions (thus warranting the use of the drugs) which undoubtedly has an impact on the results of any study.

➤➤ Virtually all the knowledge on our drug-treatment is derived from either circumstantial or cross-applied evidence, possibly with the exception of side-effects severe enough to require emergency-treatment or leading to death.[2]

➤➤ There is no legal protection of our right to self-expression of our personality in any national jurisdiction anywhere in the world. There is no legal protection for us to have medical treatment continued once it has commenced and there is no international consensus on how to treat our special legal status in regard of gender-corrected identifications, issuance of birth-certificates, parental rights to children or even the acceptance of name-changes.

---

[1] *These days the sixth edition of dogma is being used in North-America and a few other countries. There are places and institutions where different dogmas are favoured, however these are to my best knowledge all either toughened-up versions of the HBIGDA-dogma or are pretty much copies of outdated versions of that same dogma.*

[2] *The FDA has yet to approve a single medication for either the treatment of transsexuality or gender-identity disorder. To the best of my knowledge none of the drugs widely prescribed to treat transsexuality feature either dosage recommendations, notices on use, effects, counter-indications or cross-reactions for use in our treatment either in the package-insert or manufacturer supplied texts for drug-reference manuals nor is it openly admitted that transsexuality is one of the indicated uses of any particular drug. It almost appears as if putting the fact that transsexuals get treated with the same drug as, say, hypertension patients, post-menopausal woman or impotent males were considered not reputable or damaging to sales, so it is avoided.*

Indeed prejudice against us seems to be ok, it is after all approved by medical professionals as shown in our mental-health stigmatization and the routine-denial of our civil rights by some medical professionals as well as the medical establishment.

On the other hand there never seemed to be a lack of funding for "psychiatric research" into either any type of investigating our genitals or our sexual habits...

We, just like Jane and John, love our lives! We would like to have a social life, we would like to be integrated and we would like to contribute. We would like to be treated the same as everybody else and all we need to do this is some medical help. However unlike Jane and John what we need to achieve this isn't given to us as a matter of course but instead is, as a matter of course, *systematically and routinely denied to us.*

B.8.   GENDER AND MORE DELUSIONS

This chapter could be really short. Could... Let's start with the basics. Ok, very, very basic. Let me give you 3 statements to think about:

(a) Identifying female is not a mental illness.

(b) My genitals are unusual for a female (or wrong, depending on point of view).

(c) Mental illness cannot be diagnosed by examining a person's genitals.

If you agree to all these statements then transsexuality cannot possibly be a mental illness! This is an imperative logical conclusion. (If you would like to read-up on logic, may I recommend the works of Aristotle[ARIS-C] on the subject?)

Well, personally I think I'm done with arguments, that one really does it all. But apparently having an educational background in engineering seems to make me far to rational and practical a woman... So, well then, just for the sake of having some fun, let's go on:

Yes, I could be a delusional male who thinks to be a woman and does this so well that I end-up needing female steroid-levels instead of male ones to feel good... True, this would be some kind of a delusion, but let's just disregard my sarcasm here and for the sake of argument assume that I really were a delusional male and that my "feel-good" hormone level" comes from reading-up on it in a book. Obviously if that were the case, gender-alignment would have to be seen as "giving in to my delusions" instead of "having me freed from them". I suppose that this really must be one of the underlying concepts psychiatrists have in respect to transsexuality, because if that were not the case an alternative explanation as to their caring so intently would have to be found. The ones coming to mind are all, well... Unflattering?

So, let's assume that psychiatry sees me as a delusional male and only gives in to gender-alignment as a "last resort" because they find me absolutely incurable of these. If I have delusions I presume I would have to suffer from some sort of an erroneous belief that I hold true in spite of clear evidence to the contrary. This would have to be that I am a woman in spite of having a male reproductive system?

Let's have another look at the definition of "mental illness": A mental illness is *"Any disease of the mind; the psychological state of someone who has emotional or behavioural problems serious enough to require psychiatric intervention"*[1] (please note: This is

---

[1] *Definition of "mental illness" quoted from wordnet.princeton.edu*

the definition that allows for a wider range of pathologies). I suppose the diagnosis of what reproductive system I have would be done by having a look at my crotch? And mental illness is defined as "a disease of the mind"? So apparently psychiatry locates my 'self' between my legs?

Ok, being cynical again I would have to say that there's really nothing new here, except maybe that this insight was never before touted to be *a scientific insight?*

Just about here a short excursion into psychiatric history seems appropriate as my diagnosis of being mental because that mind between my legs looks wrong (or works differently than anticipated) comes from a long line of attempts by psychiatry *to draw conclusions on mental states and abilities of human-beings by examining parts other than the mind (or the brain if we include neurological problems):*

While I can't provide a full list of such psychiatric horrors here I would like to highlight just two of the more recent: Phrenology and eugenics. Phrenology is a method which claims that it is possible to determine mental abilities (such as 'moral' behaviour, 'intelligence' and many more) of a person by examining the bumps on their head (skull). It was widely used (and accepted) in the 19th century but it is still around and everybody can obtain the services of a phrenologist if so desired. What's no longer done - thankfully - is *to measure people's head-shapes and then throwing them either into mental institutions or jails* because the measurement presumably indicate either a current or future condition that warrants such treatment. Back in the 19th century this was done routinely and most interestingly almost exclusively to poor people. It was generally accepted 'science' that one could not escape one's destiny that was written into one's skull-bumps!

The craze in phrenology only really started to wind down when psychiatry came up with another, more scientific explanation of such severe mental illnesses as 'poverty', 'immoral' conduct or lifestyle or 'imbecility' in the early 20th century. The new fad was to explain it all genetically, hence they called it 'eugenics'.

By this new psychiatric insight people were poor *because they were born with the "poverty gene"!* Because genes can be passed on through inheritance from one generation to the next poverty was now seen as "a hereditary disease"! I certainly don't disagree that there is a "hereditary component" to being poor or rich, but of course that would not be a biological but rather a social and financial one. If one's born with more money in the crib than a small country has for an annual budget then it's just less likely that one ends up poor, isn't it? However the conclusion the psychiatrists drew was quite different: They said that the world should get rid of poverty by simply exterminating all the poor people - and in doing so eradicating the "poverty-gene"... (And just as a side-note: In 2007 the median salary of a psychiatrist in the US was reported to be just under $170,000 a year[1] so I suppose neither the average psychiatrist nor his offspring would be in any immediate danger of being exterminated for poverty any time soon).

---

[1] *Source: salary.com, quoted from CNNMoney.com*

However that may be, this line of thinking lead many countries to pass laws based on eugenics. The enforceable measures ranged from fines to involuntary relocation to incarceration to forced medical treatment including (so called) psychiatric surgery such as lobotomies. A few countries went a bit further in pre-empting people to pass on their genetic heritage and had their "eugenically undesirables" sterilized or "medically exterminated" by the hundreds of thousands[1]. All well supported by psychiatric pseudo-science.

I very much hope that these days we are all a little more enlightened. We ought to, after all we're living in the 21st century, the third millennium! And yes, the craze changes, it always does: These days all the evil in the world isn't explained by bumps on skulls or by genes and hereditary, these days it's all explained by looking at the bumps between our legs and what we do with or want done to these!

Well, honestly! Just what should I say? Maybe: If you ask me it might just not be me who is deluding herself but somebody else? Unfortunately the one thing I don't delude myself into is that, as each time before, the people who dream-up such pseudo-science are not the ones who suffer from it but the ones who hand it out...

---

[1] *The largest program of this kind was "Aktion T4" in NAZI-Germany.*

A.5.   OVERPAID, OVERSEXED, AND ONLY ONE PROBLEM

Over the next decade and a bit I managed to get through high-school not too badly; university followed and yes that was actually a lot of fun! Not just because I was reasonably good at what I did but mostly because there were enough people who, frankly, couldn't care less about anything gender-related.

And then this was over. I was just shy of 25, out of academia and on my first full-time job. This certainly was different - and not because I had some surplus-money to spend for the first time in my life. This world was polarized into sexes! Not only were sexual relationships at university comparably rare to the point of non-existence, at least with the crowd I used to hang out, but there was now a clear, invisible line of separation between male and female, people could get here but not there, they could do this but not that. Worst of all in that place, well, the male version of socialization anyway seemed to be completely oversexed. *Oversexed?* If these people ever stopped thinking about how to reproduce they only did so to have time to think about with whom to reproduce and if depression hit them really badly (well, nobody to reproduce with for more than 24 hours I suppose) they seemed to start thinking about nothing else than how to simulate reproducing on themselves. Honestly, the proverbial rabbits could have gotten some education from these people...

Society, male society that is, seemed to be rather pathologically preoccupied with this particular behaviour... True, I could refer to it differently but it is probably better if I don't. It all seemed to me like an overpaid, oversexed circus and the bad thing was that I was expected to be part of it and play along nicely. I solved the problem by keeping away, as much as possible anyway. Thankfully there were always the few women around to talk to about something else... Well, the one other women who worked there anyway.

I suppose for her the next few years were a nice friendship. Only for me it got to be a whole lot more. I had never been in love with another woman before (however I had been attracted to a few) and I had learned to bite my tongue over attraction towards males because, well, they did after all perceive me as being male so I presumed something else than friendship would have ended badly. If a male identified heterosexual he would not have taken nicely to a "gay advance" and if he had identified gay himself, well... Let's just say that this would not have been an aspect I wished to explore. With a woman of course that was similarly impossible because she perceived me as being male and thus everything would turn out wrong also... So this just never worked for me, either way.

[To a friend] There's something I like to tell you: I am trans... [Friend] You too??? [Me] What do you mean, you aren't trans yourself? [Friend] No, no, I am quite happy as I am - it's just, you're the fourth of my friends to tell me this...

In the end I did tell her how I felt, and that was the end of it. Apparently as a transsexual I am woman enough to make a loving and caring friendship work, good enough to share the deepest feelings, tears and life's good and bad sides, but I am not male enough for her to be wanting an intimate relationship with. Well, I'm not male enough, I admit it and if she needs this I am truly not the one to give this to her!

Up until that time I sort-of hoped that if I'd just lived with what I felt and how I felt but ignored life otherwise this would work, maybe past the day I'd pass on. That would then be that, no solution to the problem would ever have to be found... But it doesn't work like this. Unless I also accepted to stay alone for a lifetime and have the same emotional problems over and over again, this solution would not be workable. Never mind, over time depression over not being capable to feel a true experience of who I am became more and more difficult to keep at bay.

So, there I was: Looking for treatment, again. By then I was 27 years old.

B.9.   CLOSING THE X-FILES? CASE #1: KINSEY

The year is 1948. The could war is taking off rapidly, the Russians have occupied half of Europe and are about to detonate their first atom-bomb, the lines get drawn between the good guys and the evil ones. US Senator McCarthy is getting ready to rid the world of all evil. Communists, homosexuals, others. Simple solutions are called for, and quickly!

Enter one Alfred Kinsey, biologist and behavioural scientist supported by the Rockefeller Foundation. His area of expertise is "human sexual behaviour" and as the positions get taken, who better to ask than the expert on how to classify human beings along the lines of *good and evil sexual behaviour?* His report, delivered in 1948, says that every human can be classified by his "Kinsey Scale" of sexual orientation:

Kinsey Scale (extended*)	
Group	*Description*
0	Exclusively heterosexual
1	Predominantly heterosexual, only incidentally homosexual
2	Predominantly heterosexual, but more than incidentally homosexual
3	Equally heterosexual and homosexual
4	Predominantly homosexual, but more than incidentally heterosexual
5	Predominantly homosexual, only incidentally heterosexual
6	Exclusively homosexual
X*	Asexual

*: Please note: "Group X" didn't appear in the original "Kinsey Scale" but was added by Kinsey later. Apparently he originally did not accept the concept of asexual people, ignored or denied their existence or didn't think this possible.

In the given climate it was non too obvious that this scale was immediately seized to split the population into good and evil whereas the line was typically drawn at the convenience of whoever was out for condemning somebody else to be 'evil' or "sexually deviant".

[Clerk at a government office] To have your sex changed in your ID you need a reference from your doctor [Me] Right, here [She] Ok, that looks fine. So what sex would you like your new document to show???

A lot of people appear to get upset by Kinsey's work for various reasons. Some argue that the world used to be split into heterosexuals and homosexuals and *everything was perfectly simple and clear:* The 'heteros' being the good ones, the 'homos' the evil ones... They then argue that introducing *a floating scale* and accepting that maybe an incidental homosexual encounter would be acceptable, that this person could still be deemed *"pretty much heterosexual"* is a blow to morals, particularly religious ones. Others attack Kinsey on the accuracy of his actual research, the cases and 'subjects' he chooses, they deem the work was unscientific because Kinsey uses his prejudice to categorize people, but obviously this is difficult to prove as it is largely subjective. Yet others attack Kinsey personally, they apparently conclude that if they find something they don't like *in a person's behaviour* (particularly a person's *sexual* behaviour) *then that person's scientific work must be flawed.*

Have I previously mentioned that some people tend to confuse cause and effect while others put things together without any causality whatsoever? I am not about to defend Kinsey here, but I find it noteworthy how often we all fall for prejudice, stigmatization and arbitrary conclusions and then actually believe these!

The one thing most of these groups (and many others not the least quite a few gay and lesbian organizations) seem to overlook is that Kinsey's scale (and much of his research) is *inherently useless because the causality it is based on is flawed.* So, if this is all wrong, just how could we draw a picture of that "human sexual experience" that actually works? Well, let's try to enlighten Mr. Kinsey:

Dear Dr. Kinsey,

Have you ever considered to analyze the human sexual experience by looking at it from a point of view of systems-engineering? You should, because you could learn that human sexuality is far too complex to be seen and described by only one single parameter! You would in fact find that the simplest model to describe human sexuality would need at least three parameters! One possible choice for these is "sexual orientation" (the way humans self-identify sexually), "sexual activity" (the way humans actually have sex), and "sexual motivation" (why humans have sex). There are many more parameters such as "perception of sexual behaviour" (how you then interpret any sexual behaviour you observe), but let's just start with the naked minimum for now.

If you, as a scientist, analyse what these parameters describe you will find that they are each distinctly different. This is, obviously, the reason why we can't unify these into two or one: **Sexual orientation** *is a fixed, system-internal and unobservable parameter. Sexual orientation is typically given as one of the four categories* asexual, homosexual, heterosexual *and* bisexual. *Because it's unobservable we*

---

can't directly recognize it in another person in any way. We can ask the person, but we'd have to hope for an honest answer. **Sexual activity** *is an actually observable act, it is strictly empirical and descriptive. It has external influences (such as the need for a sexual partner) and the individual can modify this behaviour, sexual activity is, under normal circumstances, a choice. Sexual activity typically falls into any number of categories (and sub-categories), interesting in our case would be legal, consensual sexual acts between humans, in which case one of the possible sets of descriptive categories would be* no such sexual activity *(asexual behaviour),* sexual activity with same-sex partner *(homosexual sex),* sexual activity with different sex partner *(heterosexual sex) and* sexual activity with any-sex partner *(bisexual sex). And finally there is* **sexual motivation.** *This is another entirely system-internal parameter, it too is unobservable however it isn't fixed but can be influenced. Typical categories of this parameter would be* sex for biological procreation *(i.e. 'producing' an heir or getting pregnant),* sex for personal entertainment, sex for the entertainment of the partner, sex for profit *(prostitution and pornography, but also to gain social status, influence and so on). There are people who engage in or abstain from any and all sexual activity* for religious reasons. *Again, the list doesn't end there, but you're the scientist, you fill-in the blanks!*

Now the problem is that these three parameters are only loosely correlated *and I presume they come in almost any combination somewhere in the world. You can actually find asexual individuals having heterosexual sex for the sake of getting children. You can find heterosexuals having no sex for religious reasons. You can find homosexuals having heterosexual sex for the sake of social compliance. And so on...*

There are two obvious exceptions: (a) Somebody who identifies asexual isn't supposed to be motivated by "sex for personal entertainment". And (b) if the sexual act is motivated by "seeking personal entertainment only" it is reasonable to assume that a person would not engage in sexual activities which contradict that person's sexual orientation.

Because the latter is likely *you can get away with claiming that* any sexual activity is wholly and exclusively dependent upon a person's sexual orientation **given the assumption that any and all observed sexual activity is motivated by personal pleasure only.** *However even under this stringent condition it is still wrong to deduct sexual orientation from sexual activity* **because not being sexually active does not mean that a person _must_ identify asexual.** *All it means is that the person may not have found an appropriate partner!*

By the same token if you observe heterosexual sexual activity which is exclusively motivated by seeking personal entertainment this doesn't mean that the individual identifies heterosexual, the individual may still *identify bisexual, you just have not observed this behaviour* as of yet. *And if you observe no sexual behaviour at all you can conclude is that the person could indeed identify as* anything, *you just haven't observed it! Even observing an individual over a lifetime will not guarantee success* because an individual may wait a lifetime for an opportunity and it may still not present itself. It is as they say: **Absence of evidence of sexual activity isn't evidence of absence of identification!**

Have you noted that systemic flaw in your research yet? Because your conclusion only works (albeit as we have seen your result may still potentially be flawed) when the motivation of the sexual act you observe in your research is for personal enjoyment only you should have asked the people you examined in your research if this assumption is indeed correct! You may argue that this isn't a systemic flaw, just a practical one and that additional research could solve this, indeed would give the same results? And I agree, the systemic flaw isn't not to ask. The systemic flaw is that *if the sexual act takes place in your laboratory or the people involved agree to let you observe them somewhere else then I surmise that <u>other motivating factors</u> must <u>be present</u>*, at least in a great majority of your subjects. Or do you honestly think that "doing it" while you watch, observe and take notes would generally be considered "adding to one's personal enjoyment" by any reasonably representative cross-section of the population?

But honestly, if you ask me: Waiting until you see people having sex, then asking them what motivated them and if they say it was "for having fun" only then can you draw a still potentially flawed conclusion as to their sexual orientation? Well, to me this seems absurdly complicated, uncertain and time-consuming just to avoid the simple question "what is your sexual orientation"?

But back to your mistake: Just how could you possibly have been so fundamentally wrong? Well, either the idea that people may engage in sexual activities for other reasons than personal enjoyment *is so strange to you that it didn't come to mind - in which case I would like to inform you that there actually are such other motivations! You know, things like wanting children or not wanting to be seen homosexual. - Or you never bothered to ask the question because you would have found that all you were doing was substituting the question of sexual orientation with the one of sexual motivation - without noticing it!*

Yours truly,

Eva C. Moser

The imperative conclusion we are left with is that while there presumably is a correlation between sexual behaviour and sexual orientation *the only reliable way to find the sexual orientation of an individual is to ask and hope for an honest answer. Because no observation for however long will ever provide this information!*

Case closed? Well, apparently not. There's still a "Kinsey Institute for Sex Research" out there with the mandate to "further the research" Kinsey has laid the base to.[KINSEY]

There is however one thing Kinsey's work has greatly contributed to: It has advanced a very, very simplistic view of a very complex experience, human sexuality. Because it is presented as being scientific it has given many people the means to render definite judgement on others, to pathologize behaviour and reverse conclude as to who we are by observing and simplistically categorizing human behaviour. It is this part of Kinsey's wok and this kind of application that will find its way into how psychiatry sees transsexuals, into what some people call "the transsexual phenomenon".

We have already seen that the existence of transsexuality is a biological necessity (see B.7). The same is true for the existence of the entire spectrum of sexual orientations. It is not true for sexual behaviour. Or simply put: *What kind of sex we engage in is our choice. How we feel about it is not!*

B.10. FOR LAUGHS: THE EVA-SCALE OF SCIENTIFIC TRUTH

It's true: In engineering things are often either right or wrong. It at times tends to get very simplistic: Something just doesn't work and one can actually prove that it doesn't! Apparently in social science this isn't the case, one can put just about every statement forward and there may just be *a grain of truth* in it, somewhere! Having a logical mind I would very much like to get to the bottom of this "transscientific phenomenon". To do this I have drawn-up the *Eva Scale of Scientific Truth:*

Eva's Scale of Scientific Truth	
Quality	*Description*
0	Never describes the problem accurate
1	Predominantly misses the point, only incidentally describes the problem correct
2	Predominantly misses the point, but more than incidentally describes the problem correct
3	Equally describes the problem correct and misses the point
4	Predominantly describes the problem correct, but more than incidentally misses the point
5	Predominantly describes the problem correct, only incidentally misses the point
6	Describes the problem correct every time

Please note: Eva's Scale is not extendable because every scientific work always falls in one of only seven categories and is guaranteed to be quantifiable using only one single parameter!

My scale now allows me to measure scientific truth very precisely, lets me categorize scientific statements and quantify this previously non quantifiable experience. And please don't tell me that this is rubbish because I would have to point-out that the entire field of social-science is based upon such and similar methods!

However this may be, I haven't put this here for the fun of it (or have I?) but to *accurately* measure the scientific value of the Kinsey Scale! And after careful evaluation a preliminary review would have to give it a 4. After all Kinsey gets the sexual orientation of his 'subjects' right most of the time, which would allow me to give him a 5, only he apparently doesn't understand why, so I make it a 4.

However upon more careful inspection of that science I am inclined to duck Dr. Kinsey 2 points - and he should be glad I'm not making it more! The reason being that I tried to rank *myself* in that chart of his and found that *I was simply incapable to locate an appropriate description for myself!* My problem is that I used to be labelled <u>heterosexual</u>, now I get called <u>homosexual</u>. Only I always had the same sexual partner and I can't possibly have heterosexual *and* homosexual relations *with the same single* partner? Unless she were a transsexual herself, but this is not the case. I don't think bisexual (equally homosexual and heterosexual) *with only one partner* makes any more sense? And as I am clearly not asexual *this makes me unidentifiable by the constraint of Kinsey's scale!* Kinsey himself however reiterates many times *that every human-being can be assigned a position on his scale.* **Honestly, I do take it *very* personally if I can't find a place *for myself* on a scale which some "figure of authority" says** *describes every human-being in existence!!!* I mean what does he suggest? *That maybe I don't qualify for being human because I don't fit into his scale? And no, this most definitely isn't an invalid reverse conclusion on my part, the negative reverse is actually correct (see Aristotle* [ARIS-C]. *Once again)*!

A.6.   ALL YOU NEED TO BE IS A SEXUAL PERVERT

There was more information available this time, not a lot more, but more non the less. Apparently some people had generally noticed that transsexuals existed and treatment had gotten known even in my own country. Only the last many years hadn't changed very much to that treatment. Well, maybe with one significant exception: Transsexuality was by now deemed a mental illness just about everywhere, to be more precise it was now categorized as *"a sexual perversion"* and officially listed under *"sexual* disorders".

Psychiatrists had made an ingenious reverse-conclusion. They had known a group of people they referred to as *transvestites* for a long time. Transvestites are males who dresses-up female, usually privately and secretly. Psychiatry says they're doing this "for a sexual experience", as per their definition females never dress-up male for this purpose so transvestitism is deemed to be an exclusively "male problem" - or 'pathology' as they'd call it. Furthermore they say that transvestitism is a 'fetish' and as they have already stated that this is *always* done for sexual purposes it is a *"sexual fetish"*. In the official manual[DSM] it is put in a line-up with 'paedophilia', 'masochism', 'sadism' and 'voyeurism'.

I find all this is, at best, very strange. I could just say that unlike other people I don't want to put myself into the position of calling myself an 'expert' on something I am not, but as usual in this book I prefer to bite my tongue and be silent... However that's not what I find odd. What's strange to me is the idea that dressing-up female should be deemed *"a mental illness"! What's even stranger is that this should be seen alongside highly abusive behaviours such as the sexual abuse of children or sadism!*

Apparently the prevailing psychiatric attitude at the time was that transvestitism warrants psychiatric treatment, so it officially gets labelled *"a perversion"* (anonymous polling has in more than one study revealed that transvestic behaviour is very, very widespread, some studies suggest that *more than half of the male population has at least tried this.* So if 'normal' is what the majority does...).

So now what I did before surgery was being a transvestite? Of course unless one would count my *compliance-dressing-up male while identifying female* before I socially 'transitioned' I can't say I ever had that particular experience. But then again, my dressing-up can't have been transvestitism anyway as females can't be transvestites, or so that psychiatric manual on mental illnesses says, doesn't it?

Consequently I can't know how this feels or what this does to a person emotionally. I *can't* know *because psychiatry decrees that this is impossible for a woman!* The (male, as for now) transvestites I know however seem to take great emotional benefits from it, only I don't think that this is always or even predominantly sexually motivated. But then again, maybe I just know the wrong transvestites?

From my perspective it is completely absurd to classify such behaviour as "a treatable mental illness". But here we are again at the definition of what mental illness is [see B.4]. If the behaviour in question needs to be "substantially impairing to a person's functioning" then this cannot be a mental illness as the very opposite seems to be true: *The behaviour actually helps the person in question!* If however the standard for mental-illness is lowered to "any disease of the mind... which requires psychiatric intervention" then *transvestic or indeed any behaviour gets to be a mental illness solely and exclusively because it attracts the interest of psychiatrists!*

Not too long ago masturbation attracted the professional interest of the psychiatric community, consequentially this was said to be a pre-cursor to a guaranteed mental illness. Something called "female hysteria" used to be of even more intense professional scrutiny and so was immediately deemed to be "a mental condition severe enough to require psychiatric intervention". And then of course there was homosexuality.

Just imagine: If the wife of a psychiatrist dresses up privately in their bedroom in a way she never would otherwise *just to please him,* that's ok! But if a male does the same, that psychiatrist then wants to treat him for being crazy??? I just wonder what kind of designation would be handed out if that male would be the above woman's psychiatrist husband...

Be that as it may, there are these transvestites out there and, at least according to statistics, they're more than 100 times more numerous than transsexuals. Or *15,000 times* if one believes the numbers on transsexuality of the American Psychiatric Association. And now the psychiatrists see us *and they perceive us as doing the same* - dressing female - *and they reverse-conclude that we are the same! Because, from their perspective, if we engage in the same pathological behaviour then we have the same pathology!*

Well, not really the same, they indeed conclude that we are in fact much, much sicker because while most transvestites at least keep their perversion in the closet we insist in doing this publicly! While most transvestites do this part-time, we just never stop! While the typical transvestite dresses very sexually explicit (which, for a male psychiatrist, must make the whole thing reasonably understandable) we just do as women do! And worst of all: While many transvestites tell their therapists that this indeed includes a sexual component we state that sexuality - male sexuality - not only doesn't interest us but we go one step further, we actually say that it is not understandable, repellent, disgusting. So if we indulge in something they say is a *sexual* perversion, always, *while saying that we do not want a sexual experience,* well then, *this really must be absolute madness,* right?

True, there is that little snag that I don't see or experience dressing female as being sexually arousing, but why ask, never mind listen to what *we* say, when they already have their minds set? Then there is that other snag that I dress very typically for a woman my age, there's certainly nothing exciting about that - but why look at me when they have a ready-made image of who I am to throw at me? And this again seems to be the major problem: If psychiatry would venture into such unheard-of territory as *trying to see my behaviour from my perspective,* they might just gain some insight! Such as: I am a transsexual *because of an inconsistency between my emotional and my physical self,* I dress female *because this expresses who I am and thus feels emotionally normal to me,* not because it feels in any way erotic or arousing. *If this would feel sexual it would in all likelihood be a good reason for me not to do it!*

But I think there is a far simpler and far more enlightening explanation: *I like to dress myself "culturally appropriate" for a woman,* and to some degree I also like to be identifiable to the world. I don't mind if people can see that I am a woman. I don't hide this and I wouldn't understand why I should. Nevertheless this aspect, how I look, *is only a very small part of who I am.* It may come as a real shock to male psychiatry, but I have, in spite of being a woman, a somewhat more complex personality than they apparently think I am capable of and while I like clothes and I like to present myself nicely there just are a few more sides to my life I find important. Besides clothes and looks I mean…

Personally I find it insulting and hurtful that psychiatry reduces my identification as a woman to how I dress and look and possibly to how I can be used sexually. Not that this were in any way new to woman just about everywhere on the planet but I'm not talking of the attitude men in general have towards us but of people who claim that their area of study is human behaviour and their expertise the human psyche! Apparently all they do is spend billions on research in the past 100 years and waste millions of *man-hours just to conclude that their pre-stone-age view of women is now justified scientifically?* What a sorry state this "behavioural science" must be in - and I wonder what the few women who have chosen this their life's work might be doing there...

But in spite of this appearing to be the prevalent and "scientifically approved" view of womanhood I still go out and claim that clothes, looks and sex are not the driving forces in how I experience myself but rather the results of it! They actually are, to me anyway, some of the more unimportant ones. After all at this point in my life I had none of the above, I didn't dress female or use make-up or anything along that line. I was biologically male, I had a male reproductive system, male sexual function if ever I wanted that and still: I experienced myself and identified female! If this isn't clue enough that a few clothes won't make all the difference either, well, I suppose I really can't help them!

But then again I'm completely missing the point here *because they don't want to be helped!* I honestly don't expect anybody yet alone a conglomerate of PhD's and MD's (some of them women) to *all* be *that* ignorant! And the idea to see something form the patient's perspective isn't all that outrageously unique and new either, after all medicine, even mental-health, is based on the very idea of taking the patient seriously, isn't it? As to why this would not be the case in our treatment, well, maybe the inclined reader would like to indulge in some speculations at this point?

A decade ago they wanted me to pretend that I was a mental male with a deranged gender-identification. If I'd manage to do this for a few years to the satisfaction of a pair of psychiatrists I could expect to, sometime down the road, get my treatment. Ok, maybe a decade down the road. That is if I happen to survive psychiatry long enough.

Now they apparently expected me to pretend that I were a mental male with a deranged gender-identification suffering from a sexual perversion! Well, I did get the distinct impression that this was in no way an improvement to our treatment nor was this the direction I had hoped the advancement of medical science would take...

Nevertheless this time the decision-making did take a bit more than a mere half of a second. I realized full well that I needed treatment and as time went by that need became greater and greater. On the other hand I knew that I would never get it where I lived, the conditions were just getting more and more absurd every time I checked. So maybe not to check again would not make it any worse? I mean one just never knew what depressing idea they might ejaculate next?

But apart from cynical jokes the fact was that with the very few cases they got in that country (maybe a handful by then) the most stringent interpretation of dogmatic treatment was bound to be guaranteed, never mind presenting oneself as a specimen of such a rare freak-condition would likely guarantee the most extensive treatment with a top-ranking senior official there!

I was obviously light-years out of what they expected me to be, never mind my sexual orientation still disqualified me right from the start! So I concluded that I would never get any decent treatment or even just acceptance of my case there. I decided to pack-up my belongings, leave and go where treatment should be more accessible. Eventually I settled for a place a few thousand kilometres away and within a couple of weeks I had applied for immigration. At the time the paperwork for that took about a year. More time went by.

The idea was to immigrate and start living female. I had previously lived public for a short while and I found that this went amazingly well, without any treatment whatsoever. Of course I showed-up male for the immigration-interview and just if ever an immigration-officer were to read this book I would like to point-out that I did answer all the questions truthfully. I was never asked *if I deemed myself male or female,* all I was ever asked was *if the previous government classified me male or female.* I was never asked *if psychiatry would deem me mental,* only *if psychiatry had ever declared me such* - and as I had never been there they hadn't. Their own medical doctor certified that I did not have any medical conditions. Nobody ever asked if I were transsexual and as to that question "any other illnesses"? Well, I disagreed with mental-health back then and I still do. I have always stated it: Identifying female is not an illness, even if some people have tried really hard over the past many centuries to have it labelled as being one!

After I had gotten preliminary approval at the immigration-interview I still had four months to wait for the paperwork to be competed. I had flown over a few times, arranged everything from a place to live to all I needed for compliance to the psychiatric protocol. I needed to show employment or full-time student status, I opted for full-time student and enrolled at university for a post-grad program.

And then it happened! I had just turned 31 and there she was! The woman I wanted to share my life with, the one in a hundred billions I could have imagined to have a family with! I was in love, deeply, badly, desperately, absolutely, completely! And the worst part: She was too - with me!

B.11. CLOSING THE X-FILES? CASE #2: BENJAMIN

The year is still 1948. Enter one Harry Benjamin. Benjamin is a medical doctor, Kinsey refers to him a biological male child who says she is a girl. Eventually Benjamin recognizes that this is a medical condition and starts to treat the child with estrogen. It works well, in time Benjamin refers the child to a specialist in Germany where gender-alignment surgery is known. For some reason (speculate yourself) mother and child cease contact presumably after the girl has received competent treatment in Germany.

It would be very interesting to know what this girl had to go through to get her treatment but even more how, at the time, Kinsey's and Benjamin's views and treatments *differed* from the ones in Germany. It may just have been a sad twist of history that at this very time Kinsey's research found widespread approval and use in the United States cold-war witch-hunt on anybody who did not fit the expected profile, political or otherwise. While the Germans simply did what worked (at least they did so up to the 30-es[1]), Benjamin tried to pathologize transsexuality along the lines given by Kinsey's government approved ways and views. There never was any discussion or evaluation as to which way to interpret the issue was better, more promising, had shown better results. The war was over and the German doctors were on their way out while the Americans were on their way in. The apex of *The American Century* was dawning and everything US was in demand. Everywhere and for everything!

I presume it comes as no big surprise that Benjamin over time tried to define "transsexualism" or "the level of gender-misidentification" as he describes it along a Kinsey-ish simplistic one-dimensional scale just as Kinsey himself did with sexual orientation. And just as Kinsey, Benjamin also derived his "Benjamin Scale" and the resulting classification of individuals *exclusively from observable behavioural parameters.*

In Kinsey's case it is who we have sex with which he erroneously says allows a reverse-conclusion to sexual orientation. In Benjamin's case it is how we dress (or look) which he claims allows a reverse-conclusion to "gender-identity". But every decent scale needs some values in between the extremes ("not transsexual" and "transsexual") and as it is totally uninteresting to examine people who dress 'unisex' (or 'androgynous') be-

---

[1] *I'm not saying that people like Magnus Hirschfeld, a German physician and sexologist, did get things completely right almost 100 years ago and certainly I would like to disagree in general with the 'medicalization' of sexual behaviour, however I would like to give them credit for seeing homosexuality and transsexuality as* an expression of personality, not as a manifestation of mental illness. *Hirschfelds institute and much of his work were destroyed by the Nazis in 1933, the archival newsreels of Nazi book-burnings are generally believed by historians to depict the burning of Hirschfelds books and archive in front of his institute in Berlin.*

My partner is not amused...! The Harry Benjamin Gender Dysphoria Association! [Me, across the room] (He had heard this in the school-yard) [Me, across the room] Can you tell me what "an instrument of torture" is? [Our 7 Year Old, to my partner] Can you tell me what "an instrument of torture" is?

cause this is socially completely acceptable he finds himself another group of people who dresses "gender-inappropriate" to act as the missing link: Transvestites!

Transvestites usually dress very, very differently from transsexuals and they do it for very different reasons. Transvestites typically identify male while transsexuals, *as Benjamin uses the term[1], identify either male or female. But Benjamin isn't interested in such details as how people identify, see themselves or what motivates them, all he cares about is *to find a group of people who he thinks are at times female and at times male,* the more obviously the better, the more offensively the better, because this fits the "in between" criteria Kinsey has defined as well.

Benjamin Scale		
Group	*Type*	*Description*
1	I	Transvestite, Pseudo
1	II	Transvestite, Fetishistic
1	III	Transvestite, True
2	IV	Transsexual, Non-Surgical
3	V	Transsexual, Moderate Intensity
3	VI	Transsexual, High Intensity

Please note that Benjamin, unlike Kinsey, failed to complete his scale by adding the rather obvious "Group 0" (not transvestite and not transsexual) as well as the possibly somewhat less obvious "Group X" (does not identify gender). He furthermore failed to allow for groups to accommodate any combination of 1+2 or 1+3 to designate a person who is a transvestite and a transsexual (i.e. a biological female who identifies male, lives and appears male but dresses female for sexual arousal), although it is logical to assume that such a person could exist. (See, once more, Aristotle[ARIS-C])

Benjamin has been criticized for his scale before, although the fact that every transsexual who seeks medical treatment is still subjected to Benjamin's "enlightened treatment" appears to indicate that Benjamin's views are still widely acknowledged as being correct. Only they are not. They are in fact more flawed than Kinsey's!

Truth is that a biologically male person who is assigned a group and type from the Benjamin-Scale *would most likely identify male if he were of type I, II or III, **he/she would identify either male or female if he/she were of type IV, V or VI.** Furthermore type IV is unclear as it

---

[1] *Back then only the m-f case was medically accepted while existence of f-m transsexuals was categorically denied. This may be seen as a parallel to the idea that transvestites also are always males. It was expected that all transsexuals were exclusively sexually attracted to males **which then got the person labelled "a homosexual transsexual"**!*

remains unspecified if this denotes a person who *does not want* surgery or one *who hasn't had the chance to get surgery, meanwhile the differentiation between types V and VI is exclusively derogatory, misogynistic and abusive:* A female identified post-op male to female transsexual is a woman. As to my best knowledge medicine does not distinguish between "moderate intensity women" and "high intensity women"? Or is this yet another invitation for me to drop a highly sarcastic and sexist remark? After all, Benjamin was male...

As it appears Benjamin's scale *is inherently useless not only because the causality it is based on is flawed the same way Kinsey's is but even more so **because it does not explain transsexuality but something else!*** So, maybe we could fix that Benjamin-scale idea? And maybe we could find some insight into how that "human gender-experience" actually works?

Let's try to enlighten Mr. Benjamin:

Dear Dr. Benjamin,

Have you ever considered to analyze the human gender experience by looking at it from a point of view of systems-engineering? You should, because you could learn that human gender is far too complex to be seen and described by one single parameter!

For your convenience (and mine) I have enclosed a copy of a letter I have sent to Dr. Kinsey, kindly replace the words "sexual orientation", "sexual activity" and "sexual motivation" by their gender-equivalents "gender identity", "gender expression" and "gender motivation". You may also want to replace the word 'sex' with 'gender' where appropriate and make other slight linguistic corrections, but on a whole little correction is needed as the mistake you make in drawing-up your scale is the same Dr. Kinsey makes in his.

If we use "gender identity", "gender expression" and "gender motivation" for a first approximation to understand gender, what kind of individuals do we find? For our simplistic first approximation I suppose we can assume that both gender identity and gender expression only comes in male and female, gender expression possibly also in an androgynous version. For you gender motivation is either "sexual" or "not sexual". So we'll get a total of either 8 or 12 possible combinations respectively, depending on if we include androgynous gender expression or not, but as this case is unimportant in our discussion I would like to leave it aside. The following table displays all the remaining combinations:

Completed Benjamin Scale *(with all possible combinations)*

gender-identity	gender-expression	gender-motivation	description
female	female	not sexual	socially accepted female
male	male	not sexual	socially accepted male
female	female	sexual	sexually enticing female
male	male	sexual	sexually enticing male
male	female	not sexual	cross-dressing male or she-male
female	male	not sexual	cross-dressing female or butch female
male	female	sexual	male transvestite, she-male or drag queen
female	male	sexual	borderline? acceptable female or drag king

Harry Benjamin subdivides the categories 'transvestite' further into 'pseudo', 'fetish', 'true' and 'non-surgical', he subdivides cross-dressing into 'moderate-intensity', and 'high-intensity'. All other cases he ignores

---

Dr. Benjamin, have you noticed? **Transsexuals don't appear anywhere in this chart???** *This is of course <u>because the parameters you are using are not suitable to describe or identify transsexuality</u>…*

In fact you could find transsexuals as well as non-transsexuals in every category of this chart! This is because transsexuality has absolutely nothing whatsoever to do with the interaction of these three parameters used above! **It is really important to understand that all the possibilities this table features in the 'descriptions'-column are <u>personal choices</u> people make in regard to their self-expression. If we make a *choice* in regard to our self-expression or to our activities <u>we call this a lifestyle</u>!**

This misinterpretation happens because Kinsey's model of sexual orientation, fatally flawed and over-simplified in itself, <u>cannot be transposed to describe how humans experience gender</u>! The problem and the difference between the two systems observed, sexuality and gender, is that <u>**sexual activity only has one relevant fixed parameter (sexual orientation) whereas gender has two: Both gender-identity (emotional self-perception) as well as biological sex (reproductive capacity) are both fixed parameters but they are nevertheless independent!**</u>

There is no physical self-experience of sexual orientation because there is no biological representation of sexual orientation anywhere on our bodies! But there is a biological representation of our gender and therefore there is also a physical experience of gender! **The need for surgical genital alignment doesn't come from either gender-motivation or gender-expression, <u>it comes from self-experience of</u>**

***biological sex being different from self-experience of emotional gender (or
gender-identity)****! Or very simplistically put: Being transsexual means that I experience my physical self female even though it is male. Well, female in a disfigured
way... This is not a 'preference' like sexual activity. A homosexual can <u>choose</u> to have
heterosexual sex. <u>He can control his experience of having sex</u>, at its simplest by not
having sex at all! This may not feel good, <u>but it is possible</u>! **As a transsexual I cannot 'choose' how I emotionally experience my physical sexuality <u>because how
I experience my body is not a choice! I can't choose if, when and how I experience my physical self, it is simply always there</u>!***

Maybe a more tangible example would help? Imagine you would experience your
left arm right and your right arm left. To solve the problem you could ask a surgeon to
swap your arms? Well, if you were to ask for this I would say that this seemed absurd, crazy, and very unlikely to solve the problem anyway as your experience of
your arms hardly would swap sides this way. However if we lived in a world where
everybody was born with only one arm, half the population with theirs on the left side,
the other half on the right and you would experience yourself "left-armed" but just
happen to be born "physically right-armed"? Imagine as a kid you would be incapable to catch a ball because you always "do it the wrong way", you could not ride a bicycle, play a musical instrument? You'd have great difficulty to write as your hand-
eye co-ordination just works "left sided"? Eventually you'd manage to learn these
things because all humans can adapt, but each time you had to react quickly you
would revert to your inborn reaction, get it wrong, drop that ball, fall off the bike or
write in mirror-image? Now consider there were a surgery to move your right arm to
the left side in a way as to make you function and look indistinguishably from every
other left-armed person, would you now want this? Would this now be crazy?

Now consider right-armed persons would mostly wear pants while left-armed persons would usually wear skirts. Would you find it completely absurd if there would be
a condition on your medical treatment that you wear a skirt while being visibly right-
armed for a few years until you could have your arm fixed? Would you possibly go
as far as to claim that your way of dressing doesn't have anything whatsoever to do
with how you experience your arm? Would you possibly feel that such conditions set
on your obtaining medical treatment were demeaning, degrading and abusive?
Please judge for yourself!

As a final note to my observations I have the sad obligation to inform you that your
research on transsexuality and in particular your Benjamin-Scale scores a 0 in the
Eva-Scale of Scientific Truth because it never describes the problem and always
misses the point. The reason for this is not your use and expanding of the flawed research of Dr. Kinsey but your substituting gender-expression for biological sex in
your approach. In essence what this does is:

➤➤ *You define transsexuality as a behaviour instead of as a bio-emotional mismatch. <u>You thus are the father of making transsexuality into a lifestyle!</u>*

➤➤ *By stating that your definition of 'transsexual' covers any and all persons who potentially require genital surgery <u>you mandate your expectation of this lifestyle as a condition for this medical treatment onto every person who needs this!</u> You thus restrict medical treatment to a limited number of people who either by chance live your required lifestyle, are willing to adopt or capable of simulating it!*

➤➤ *Your definition invites various groups to hijack the term 'transsexual' for any and all similar lifestyles which would better be described differently. You are thus responsible for making the term for all intents and purposes useless for clinical use!*

➤➤ *By assigning a non-functional term which misrepresents us you deny us identification as a group of people with one single issue: Requiring genital surgery. You in fact expand the scope of our treatment to various other completely unrelated conditions and groups. Because some of these are socially at best marginally accepted you style our medical need into a socially borderline acceptable treatment!*

➤➤ *Your definition of our existence is the reason why we, the people who require this very specific medical treatment (and nobody else), do not exist as a group, have no voice and therefore have been and will remain unheard and ignored!*

Dear Dr. Benjamin! Please understand that it is not my intention to diminish the role you have played in the lives of many desperate human-beings by providing medical treatment to them when nobody else was willing to give it to them. I honour you greatly for this! But maybe you should have focussed your practice exclusively on providing direct medical care. Your efforts at etiology and treatment guidelines are by and large failures, their effects are detrimental to people like myself!

Yours truly,

Eva C. Moser

I can understand why people try to explain sexual orientation as a single 'continuum'. After all there are people who have homosexual or heterosexual sex or everything in between. Only I think this explanation is so simplistic that it ends up being dead wrong! Not because this doesn't account for asexual persons but because at least there needs to be a distinction between people who, on one extreme, "grudgingly agree to sexual contact for the benefit of a relationship" and on the other "initiate sexual contact for pure pleasure" (and everything in between). Or to give a graphic example: A lesbian woman doesn't become bisexual when she falls victim to a (male) rapist! There are many other concerns, this is just to demonstrate *how simplistic* the idea of "determining sexual orientation by observation" is.

For gender-identity all this appears to be very different. I have yet to meet an individual who says "I am 60% female and 40% male". People are by and large at any given time either/or and while some may change at times they always know what they are. Consequently there are very, very few individuals who say they do not know their gender while there are quite many who do not know their sexual orientation or need to revise their assumption on it during their lifetime.

Or to say this bluntly: I could easily imagine an individual who asks himself the question if he would like to go to the gay club or to the heterosexual one because he is uncertain as to what kind of sex he would prefer tonight. However I have yet to be asked by anybody for guidance as to which washroom this person should prefer... apparently we all have the capacity to figure that one out unambiguously!

As Benjamin correctly observes there obviously exist "non-surgical transsexuals": That is if we define a transsexual just for this argument as a person who needs gender-alignment surgery because she identifies differently from her biology. It's an easy and straightforward definition. Only *it is apparently different from the one Benjamin uses.* By this definition anyway a "non surgical transsexuals" would have to fall into about four categories:

➤➤ People who are waiting or hoping for surgery (because they're on a surgeon's waiting-list or wait to get psychiatric permission, save money to pay for it, haven't even started the process of getting anywhere but wish for it and so forth)

➤➤ People who can't go for some reason (such as a medical counter-indication to surgery) or are denied surgery (such as for being unable to qualify according to dogma or refusing to submit to it)

➤➤ People who willingly take suffering over surgery, for example because they would like to remain fertile so they can have children or because they don't accept the concept of surgery to alleviate their suffering (as some philosophical or religious groups do) or because they don't accept the concept of genital surgery as a valid intervention on other grounds

➤➤ People who don't know that treatment exists and thus suffer needlessly (though in a well educated country as ours this group is rather hypothetical these days)

As for others? Frankly, I don't know any.

Jane says that in our society there are about four groups of paraplegics who don't use a wheelchair:

➤➤ People whose wheelchair is on order or needs repairing

➤➤ People who can't use a wheelchair because their particular medical condition doesn't allow it

➤➤ People who for some reason refuse to use a wheelchair (yes, this actually exists!)

➤➤ People who do not know that wheelchairs exist (though in a well educated country as ours this group is rather hypothetical these days)

Jane says using a wheelchair and the availability thereof *is considered normal, dignifying and meaningful*, it is also socially and in most cases economically beneficial.

She furthermore says she didn't have to ask for one, given her medical condition it was just assumed that she wanted one: "They showed me what's available and I got my choice of models. And that was that!".

Fortunately our society knows how to treat handicapped people. Sometimes anyway.

Be it as it may, just as with that wheelchair I have yet to find an individual who says about gender-alignment surgery that "*I need this, but only a little*"... Frankly, I find the Benjamin Scale is about the most absurd categorization there is! *If you know you need this surgery then you need it, otherwise you'd know that you don't! NOT EVER AND WITH ABSOLUTE CERTAINTY! In 99.9999% of all people (or better) it is that simple! I would certainly like to challenge anybody to find any other medical diagnosis that comes with that much certainty!*

Case closed? Apparently not. There's still 'WPATH' out there, the successor of "The Harry Benjamin International Gender Dysphoria Association Inc." with the self-appointed mandate to control and limit our access to medical treatment.

There's one significant difference between Kinsey's homosexuals and Benjamin's transsexuals: While homosexuals could not care less about Kinsey's findings and these days happily go their ways (most of the time anyway) *transsexuals do require by the very nature of their identification treatment the medical system limits to exclusively hand out itself. Thus, there is one point in our lives where "their system" can get hold of us: They can deny and limit their services to us and only grant treatment in exchange for years of compliance and behavioural self-modification to their social and moral standards and expectations!*

That same system has done the same to homosexuals as long as they could, but today they don't have the means to doing this anymore: Homosexuality is legal in most countries and a few decades after that legalization it even got removed from the DSM. Today Homosexuality is no longer "a mental illness", not where I live anyway.

To transsexuals they're still doing this. Why? *Because they can!*

B.12. CLOSING THE X-FILES? CASE #3: MONEY

It is the 50-es. Enter one John Money. He is a professor at John Hopkins University where he works as a psychologist on a subject called 'sexology'. He is involved with the Sexual Behaviours Unit, studying, among others, cases of "gender-disturbed individuals". The terms "gender-identity" and "gender-role" are generally credited to him, as well as a doctrine of connection between the two. His idea was basically to split what people used to understand as 'sex' or 'gender' into several different aspects. Biological sex being one, gender-identity another, gender-role yet another.

Money operated on the premise that every attribute except biological sex was "learned behaviour" and can be changed at will (he sets 3 years of age as a completely arbitrary deadline for this 'learning').

During his time at JHU he got to prove his point in the "David Reimer Case": A few months after birth David was brought to him after an accidental penectomy[1] during an attempted circumcision. Money convinced David's parents to allow male to female gender-reassignment on the infant. This, in his opinion, would remedy the damage. His thought was probably something like "if the child can't be *a real man* because one can't be a real man with testicles only but no penis then we make him *a real woman,* because surely to be a real woman it doesn't matter if one has a reproductive system, a clitoris or anything alike[2]! All that's needed here is to add a castration and a labiaplasty[3]. That'll work just fine and nobody will ever have to know of the medical screw-up"!

Doing this was the ultimate human experiment of Moneys career: David had a twin brother, Brian, so Money would be able to observe up-close the development of two identical human beings, one with male genitalia learning to be a man, the other "identical copy" with female genitalia learning to be a woman!

It was a great success for science and a personal triumph for Money *because it proved his theory that gender-identity is exclusively learned behaviour, that it can actually be changed with a scalpel and assigned by a doctor at his sole discretion!*

Only there was a catch: David never accepted his being female. *Even though he was never told about his past he always insisted in his being male!* After David learned of his

---

[1] *Penectomy: Surgery to remove the penis.*

[2] *A vagina cannot be created in an infant. This part of the procedure was therefore delayed until later, presumably in David's teens. However his parents did never follow-up on this surgery.*

[3] *Labiaplasty: Surgery to create the labial folds of the female genitals. In m/f surgery the term is also used to describe a "limited vaginoplasty" where the labia and possibly a clitoris are created, the urethra is relocated, but no vaginal canal is created.*

[Urologist] That looks quite normal [Me] At times it gets a lot bigger... [He] OF COURSE it gets BIGGER, that's NORMAL! [Me] Yes, but it hurts! [He] I have seen quite enough of your kind to stop asking myself any questions...

history he sought and later found a different medical team who offered him a series of surgeries to re-create his male genitals (in essence an adapted version of a female-to-male alignment).

While the surgeries were considered a success David was never able to overcome his trauma of a lifetime of social and medical abuse prompted by perverted human medical experiments. On May 4, 2004, at the age of 38 years, David Reimer ended his suffering by taking his own life.

I deeply hope he has found the peace we, our society, were never willing to grant him.

I believe it is safe to say that the initial medical mistake of the circumcision but more importantly the unbelievable arrogance of a few ethically challenged professionals who decided that his life could be altered in such a dramatic way, never mind in part for their own personal benefit, is to blame for his destiny.

In spite of David's suicide Money remained as a professor at JHU, a position he had then already held for more than half a century, until his own death at age 84.

This very sad case (and a few similar ones) exemplifies nevertheless several aspects of gender:

➤➤ *Gender cannot be assigned at will.* There is far more to this than social interaction and genitals, although there is that too

➤➤ *Gender cannot be learned.* I don't dispute that gender specific behaviour exists, what I dispute is that learning it or even displaying such behaviour has anything to do with how we experience ourselves, our bodies and how we identify

➤➤ *It is not true that gender-reassignment cannot be reversed.* David's result of a reversed m/f-reassignment was in all likelihood not as good as it could have been because some important parts (such as the clitoris as the tip of the new penis) were lost in the original botched circumcision. On the other hand as with every reconstructive surgery there are compromises, even the best techniques do not allow to reconstruct certain functions and there are inevitable scares which will be there for life. (The removal of the primary sexual organs and resulting infertility remains irreversible at this time)

For Money to make his theories true he must base "gender identity" on a person's own perception of one's *actual* mental processes and one's *actual* behaviour. By doing this he completely perverts the term "gender identity". If "gender identity" is defined like this *it is by its very nature no longer a free expression of gender but it is limited to whatever mental process the current hormonal state allows and it is limited to whatever behaviour society actually tolerates* (because a person can only self-perceive what she actually does and unless she starts breaking social rules and possibly laws she can only actually do what society allows her to do!). *Money's "gender identity" is therefore a "substance induced, socially controlled expression" rather than a "free expression" of somebody's personality. It is self-evident that a "gender identity" defined like this can be externally manipulated!*

Of course I experienced my behaviour as being male before social transition and as being female afterwards. Did I "try to be male"? Do I now "try to be female"? Yes, certainly I did and I do! Both! There are always parts of a life's behaviour one does not do because one wants to *but because one finds oneself expected to.* Only now for me this part is a lot smaller and a whole lot easier to accomplish. Was I "convincingly male"? Yes, anybody can bet on it! This is after all what a transsexual lives...

Or if you want to: *Cases like David's (and so many others, including mine)* **prove that *"gender identity" as defined by psychiatrists who believe as Money did truly is exclusively learned behaviour.* They are however also proof that Money's premise (that his version of "gender identity" is what a transsexual feels and needs corrected) is wrong**!

Apparently now we seem to have two options: Either *we could redefine "gender-identity" as an exclusively personal identification which does not come with any expectation of behaviour or mental process* (or *anything* for that matter), *or we could add a new term with exactly these attributes to the line-up of an already overloaded discussion!*

Money started out by "splitting-up" the "gender-experience" into different identifiable sub-components *and then hi-jacked every single one for his own purposes.* Other psychiatrists and psychologists have since added other terms and then done the same! It never helped, none of the explanations explain anything satisfactorily. Because in the end the problem is more a personality issue rather than of a scientific nature: If a scientist were to introduce the "how I perceive myself"-term and *define that this term were absolutely and exclusively self-identified* (male or female, something in between, changing or maybe something completely different, *whatever* the individual feels) then that scientist would put himself out of a job instantly! Because as per definition no research, no experiments, no further description, no follow-up lecture, no book or scientific publication, no interpretation and no justification for research grants would ever be meaningful. Additional research into explaining the subject would *by definition* not be possible! People would just have to be asked *and trusted! Gender would have to become a choice. Not a personal choice, just like David we aren't free to choose our gender, but a social choice: We would be allowed to be who we feel we are! Just because we say so!* What a wonderful world that would be! But would it?

Because as always, there's a catch: If how somebody identifies gender is a completely free expression of that individual (and therefore *invalidates any categorization unless self-identified)* the same would have to be true for Kinsley's Scale of sexual orientation. *If gender is a free expression and not measurable, then intimate gender-interaction (i.e. sex) also has to be one!* While we could still do statistics on homosexuality and heterosexuality just as we could still do statistics on males and females and on how people behave, dress or have sex, *sexual orientation would also become exclusively and freely self-identified!*

Two biological males could, conceivably, have sex and claim *that this, to them, is a heterosexual experience* because one identifies female - *and we would not have any means to question this self-assessment by any external observation!* We also would no longer know if that statement were given to us *as a statement of fact or as one of convenience!*

This, in turn, would undermine any and all social distinction between heterosexuals and homosexuals, it would make such definition as "exclusively heterosexual marriage" completely meaningless and therefore unenforceable. We all would have to learn how to see each others for who we are instead of how we look or behave. *And we would actually have to talk to, listen to and trust each other!*

If you would like or could imagine a society working on communication and trust rather than one working on discrimination and prejudice you are very welcome to make this choice. After all, it is our own choice: This one or Money's. One we don't know how or if it would work or one we know we find littered with the bodies of the victims of social oppression, abuse, medical madness and discrimination every day.

It is YOUR choice! Because making this society a reality is also an absolutely free personal choice! On the other hand needing it to get a meaningful life is not. Not for David. Not for hundreds of millions of human beings. Not for me.

Case closed!

But of course once again I am missing the point entirely, am I not? Because all there really is to this is that a bunch of hypocritical moralists who tell us that we are all deranged and abnormal freaks and that what we need, genital alignment (or some acceptance of our private, intimate behaviour if we extend the scope to sexual orientation) is a completely unacceptable madness. *Because __when we__ request genital alignment - as how they put this is "our choice for a personal fad" - then it must be denied because they say that __this is wrong, immoral, madness and unethical__! However __if they themselves__ force this onto somebody else with no personal consent whatsoever for their own benefit __then they say that doing this becomes right, moral, scientifically sound and ethical__!*

Just in case anybody would ever get the idea that this might be a self-serving double-standard then the perpetrators are quick at validating their view with pseudo-science, burying what evidence they don't like and inventing what they can't find. *In the end they present evidence and pseudo-scientific proof that we are incapable of knowing which gender we ourselves are __while at the same time they find evidence and prove pseudo-scientifically that they themselves are the only ones who are capable to make this decision for us__!*

Because they now have scientific proof of their being superior human beings **they then assign themselves** *the right to enforce their standard onto everybody!*

Transsexual or not, medically mutilated in early childhood for the benefit of mankind made in their image (or imagination) or not: Just why do we accept this? Just why do we not understand that what is happening here is wrong?

B.13. EVEN MORE LAUGHS: STRETCHING THE EVA-SCALE

Ok. Now I need to rate Money's efforts on my Scale of Scientific Truth. And this indeed has turned out to be more of a nightmare than originally assumed possible! As a matter of fact I have found that I need to revise my stands on the absolute completeness of the Scale of Scientific Truth as I indeed have to create room for a new entry at the extreme low end to accommodate Moneys efforts. To remain in line with other well known scales I would like to name this new category "Quality X":

Eva's Scale of Stretched Scientific Truth	
Quality	*Description*
0	Never describes the problem accurate
1	Predominantly misses the point, only incidentally describes the problem correct
2	Predominantly misses the point, but more than incidentally describes the problem correct
3	Equally describes the problem correct and misses the point
4	Predominantly describes the problem correct, but more than incidentally misses the point
5	Predominantly describes the problem correct, only incidentally misses the point
6	Describes the problem accurate every time
X	**This is not science!**

Please note: The author herself has realized that to accommodate some horrors advertised as science Eva's Scale of Scientific Truth needed to be stretched. However kindly note that the author recognized her own mistake within only a few pages and corrected it quickly. Fortunately truth can always be stretched!

But honestly! Making this correction I feel like one of these very important ancient mathematicians and philosophers must have felt when they first discovered the concept of negative numbers...

Dear Dr. Kinsey and Dr. Benjamin,

In regard to my previous communication I would like to inform both of you that the work of one Dr. John Money has come to my attention. It has important relations to your own work however it is, in my opinion, one of the most dramatic illustration of pseudo-science gone wrong!

Yes, I could have written to Dr. Money as I did to you. As you personally know I at times accept to communicate with people I find behave disreputable, ignorant or unethical if it is in the interest of helping other people. But I too have some absolute minimum standards and so there are people I don't write to. However I did update my "Eva's Scale of Scientific Truth" by another entry: Quality 'X'.

I am writing you to inform you that this extension has taken place and that the new quality-category has been populated by Dr. Money's work. However I would like to caution your optimism: This addition of a new quality at the extreme low end of human achievement should in no way be interpreted as an 'elevation' to any of the existing categories! It is simply a reflection of how low applied science can sink given a profound enough lack of ethics.[1]

Yours truly,

Eva C. Moser

---

[1] *True, this could also be a reflection of my inability to imagine a horrible enough scenario to get my scale right the first time. But I don't want to mention this in a letter to people who work in the field of mental-health as putting forward a suspicion of some mental incapacity on my part might just add yet another label from that catalogue to my already impressive line-up of achievements.*

A.7. CAN WE HAVE CHILDREN?

So there we were. Two women in love, one looking female, the other one looking male. Just when I had arranged to leave behind the country, the continent, the language, the culture and the gender I was born in. I would have dropped everything for a life with her, but I knew that this would at best work for a short while because I still needed treatment.

Two months into our relationship she had decided to pack-up her life and follow me, but being independent-minded she applied for immigration separately (and maybe also because she just might have been a little uncertain as to how this would work-out with us). Anyway, I left, she stayed. The next year was, well... Just like my age I also don't want to talk about my phone-bill... Meanwhile all my plans for treatment had been suspended indefinitely because she had asked the one question that could do this at that time: *Can we have children?* Having children and raising them was, from an early age on, the one thing I felt my life should be about. Only I never believed that this could actually become reality!

Yes, transsexuals can have children. Of course they can. Scientists agree that transsexuality is not hereditary. Never mind I don't see that much of a problem in it anyway, just in obtaining the appropriate treatment!

For a transsexual to have children this has to happen before the onset of treatment or at a very early stage into it. Because hormonal treatment eventually destroys fertility and genital surgery removes it outright. Male to females have the option to store sperm, for female to males this is at this time a bit more tricky. There are two more problems, one is of a practical nature: Procreation requires us to find a biologically appropriate partner. This is, for transsexuals, just a bit more difficult than it is for most people. The other one is of a legal nature: As it is at best *unusual* for two lesbians *to have their own biological children* this is completely unexpected by the legal framework of our society. This in turn has the potential to create some serious problems all in itself, for both the parents as well as the children.

As with everybody else the partner a transsexual needs so she can have children with *has to have the opposite set of biological reproductive organs.* Only in the case of a transsexual individual *this partner will be of the same identified gender! The relationship is therefore likely to look and be seen as (and for all intents and purposes actually be) of a homosexual nature,* unless the partner also happens to be transsexual. However in reality many transsexuals don't disclose their condition until long after marriage and having had children. Unfortunately "coming-out transsexual" to a life-partner sometimes creates problems of understanding and acceptance and may even lead to separation and divorce. But often this doesn't happen and a relationship can adapt or improve, even thrive on such changes. From my perspective relationship-problems as portrayed by psychiatry are massively overblown or even artificially created as in such absurd therapeutic suggestions that it would be easier for children to cope with a parent's death than a parent's transsexuality! The transsexual may actually be intimidated by the therapist (by the usual implicit or explicit threats of withholding medical services) into leaving the family while the children are told that she has died!

In reality what we are talking about is a bit of surgery and a person being allowed to live her true identity, not about something like Alzheimer's where a person gradually degenerates and looses essential abilities to function in a relationship!

Ok, there's that bit about *the essential abilities in a relationship...* I would venture the thought that *this* is a place where it is most visible *how different* the male to female and the female to male cases are, particularly socially and emotionally. Assuming a previous visibly heterosexual relationship (one that could lead to biological children with a non-transsexual partner), imagine the two cases, socially, as seen "from the outside": Either the visibly male partner becomes a lesbian female partner to her already female partner or the visibly female partner becomes a gay male partner to his already male partner. For the non transsexual partner this means that a woman would turn from a visibly heterosexual female into a visibly lesbian female whereas a man would turn from a visibly heterosexual male into a visibly gay male. Now I don't have any research on that topic at hand (and I don't know if any serious research has ever been done) but judging by how important the two genders see sexuality as well as sexual orientation and how acceptable it is for the two sexes to identify and openly live homosexual I assume that one of the two cases would be far, far more socially acceptable and frequent than the other. Which one? Well, honestly, why would anybody ask?

It isn't possible to give a "how-to transition when you're transitioning" or "what to expect when you partner is expecting gender-alignment" in a few pages. Obviously relationships are individual, the people who live these are, and so are the needs and the possible solutions for a life together. But even so, in the end this can never be about sex or appearance or sexual orientation or even about gender. *In the end this will have to be about understanding, acceptance and above all else it will have to be about love!*

There is however one thing I do not wish to omit here: For all the change a relationship will go through to work when one of the partners socially or intimately transitions, for all this understanding to happen, *both partners in a relationship first and foremost need time.* In particular the non-transsexual partner needs time to inform herself, time to reflect, time to accept, time to adapt. *But also **time to find herself in the new relationship!*** Most transsexuals have spent decades finding themselves, have probably waited years before "coming-out" to their partners. *Their partners have not!* If this gets done slowly it is easier for both (and everybody else involved) to adapt. And here I have found that there is a point in "doing this the wrong way round", in dressing-up first and talking about identification later: *To introduce a partner first to our looking female, privately and securely.* Not in particular sexually, though this could well be a part of it also. After all, humans are sexual beings, sex is normal and however done if everybody involved feels good about having sex this would, from my perspective, be the right way of doing it. It does seem to be less of a first step to accept looks and behaviour than it is to understand an identification!

At some point in time there will have to be the discussion as to why the transsexual does this, how she feels about herself, how she identifies. But by then her partner will have had the time to realize that this isn't sexually motivated, she will feel that this is emotional, that this is permanent and really had always been a part of their relation. She will have felt that this encompasses a whole lot more than "the occasional cross dressing". Given enough time a partner can understand that this comes naturally, is a basic expression of self, not as a form of desire. *She will start to see her partner female without clothes, accessories or make-up!* She will understand that this liberates the personality of the transsexual and she will understand that this is likely to, in turn, solve a lot of problems that she has come to get used to while living with her partner. And she will understand that treatment is not optional but life-saving, life improving and life-giving.

She may, in the end, find that she will have to accept something she has always lived with, something she has always felt or known. In retrospect it will likely appear as having been obvious all along!

This will not work in every case, not every partner will be able or willing to go along with all these changes. But it is a lot more likely to work than if the transsexual reveals everything in one step and expects her partner to make a huge leap to follow her only because she herself already there.

On the other hand there is one thing male to female transsexuals who have female partners should understand first and foremost: *Their partners are women, just as they are!* In many cases there will be far, far more similarities and understanding, shared feelings and mutual acceptance between them than there are differences!

At this point only two things remain for me to be said. First and foremost: A big, big thank you to my own partner for accepting me, for accepting all this: I love you! Thank you! And second, there's the consideration that our relationship - any such relationship to a transsexual human being - is in all likelihood only ever possible *because of who the two partners are who live this relationship.* But then again, this is true for every human relationship!

My being a little different, my transsexuality is a part of how we relate to each other. This isn't good or bad, but it may just have been necessary. Our relation may never have gotten anywhere, had I not been who I was. And yes, admitting and accepting this is at times difficult and it is being made a lot more difficult than it would have to be!

B.14. *HOMO, HETERO, BI, DON'T KNOW AND DON'T CARE*

The definition of our pathology requires that *a diagnosis of "gender-dysphoria" (transsexuality) needs to include the sexual orientation of the patient.* As of version IV of that manual of psycho-pathologies the term "sexual orientation" was however replaced by the somewhat more enlightened nomenclature "sexually attracted to male, female, both or neither" as psychiatrists realized, after having used the other classification for decades, that it hardly makes any sense to label a transsexual either 'heterosexual' or 'homosexual' *without specifying if this is seen from my point of view as a physically handicapped <u>woman</u> or from the therapist's point of view as a mentally deranged <u>male</u>!*[1]

To complicate matters further some therapists have by now added *"attracted to trans-sexual partner"* to their list of sexual orientations! They first started this when they no-ticed a serious problem in assigning sexual orientation to a partner of a transsexual. If they characterize my (female) partner heterosexual before I had my surgery and lesbian afterwards they would have to throw-out yet another of their beloved doctrines: ***They would have to accept <u>that my partner has changed her sexual orientation</u>!*** *Never mind without doing anything whatsoever except to remain faithful to me!* The way out of this dilemma was *to assign a new sexual orientation **to her**:* They call it '*transsensual*' and claim this means "attracted to transsexuals". I am highly offended by this but as I don't want to imply derogatory intent I assume that therapists who use this term may simply be ignorant to the difference between '*sensual*' and '*sensuous*'. So for once I'm not going to recommend Aristotle, a simple dictionary ought to suffice!

However I may feel about it, people can now be asexual, homosexual, heterosexual, bisexual, *or transsensual.* I fear the next giant leap for *man*-kind's understanding of hu-man sexuality would be terms for a person who's transsensual *or either homosexual, heterosexual or bisexual?* But apart from my typical sarcasm towards pseudo-pathologizations I don't think this term makes any sense whatsoever as its creators missed the somewhat important discrimination **if the transsexual a person feels at-tracted to *identifies male or female.*** The obvious sexist remark here is to presume that some male therapist only ever considered the case which leads to anal intercourse - but who would be sexist here? From my perspective (and I am certain from my partner's as well) *this is the most significant difference there is!* To remedy the situation may I suggest

---

[1] *According to many "standard works of sexology"* **the sexual orientation of a transsexual should be derived from sexual activity (or desire) <u>in relation to birth-sex throughout life</u>!** *This leads to such totally absurd statements as "a male having <u>vaginal intercourse</u> with a post-op m/f transsexual <u>is gay homosexual activity</u>"* (for both). *Transsexuals I refer to as homosexual these experts call 'heterosexual' and vice versa. From my perspective theirs is about as ignorant a statement as it gets and* can only be interpreted as yet another expression of their not accepting who we are.

femaletranssensual and *maletranssensual?* Add *homotranssensual, hetero-, bi- and atranssensual?* Combined this would then give us any pair of heterotranssensual, homotranssensual,... *and* heterosexual, homosexual,... **so there would now be a grand total of 16 sexual orientations?** That still does not include distinct designations for attraction towards pre- and post-ops (a significant difference if it comes to sex, isn't it?) and it doesn't account for a distinction if a person attracted to a transsexual *is aware of that persons transsexuality or not!* On top of all of this just imagine what sexual orientations loom on the horizon when psychiatrists realize that *transsexuals may feel attracted to transsexuals - in all the variations these come in, never mind any and all combinations thereof!* While they are at it, pathologizing and labelling everybody, may I expect that they will eventually progress to *'psychosexual'* for people who happen to fall for psychiatrists? Or would that be *'psychosensual'?*

Personally I have no idea what this is all about except an apparently pathological obsession (see B.43) to find a back-door for some form of sexism/racism-revival movement, but then again it isn't exactly the first time I get the distinct impression that some of these "sexual behavioural scientists" must live *in a galaxy far, far, far, far away...*

Particularly early medical treatment of transsexuals was based on the idea that if a person was seen as gay (biologically male, sexually attracted to males) and if that 'male' then said that he's "a she", *a surgical sex-change would "rid the world of a homosexual"* (and her partner, if any, as well!) **as the resulting female, presumably still attracted to males,** *now would look heterosexual (however according to the doctrines of the time this woman would continue to be officially classified as "a homosexual male" and even post-op any sexual activity with her male partner would be classified as "gay sex").* So a sex-change was granted *on the grounds of being the lesser of two evils,* the choices to provide this surgery or having to look at one more homosexual? (Did I mention that the side-effects of trying to understand psychopathology include being disgusted, insulted, feeling seriously sick and worse?)

Early medical treatment of transsexuality was in fact (almost) *exclusively* reserved to male to female transsexuals *who stated that they were solely sexually attracted to males! Many psychiatrists denied the very existence of m/f's who identified bi- or homosexual* (who were attracted to woman also or exclusively), or at least denied treatment to such individuals by routinely diagnosing them as "something else" (usually 'transvestites') which, given dogmatic rule, indirectly has the same effect. Not few of these very psychiatrists also strictly denied the mere existence of f/m transsexuals!

While I myself have no understanding whatsoever what my sexual-orientation could possibly have to do with my being a man or a woman *psychiatrists consider this* **the single most important criteria to split the population of transsexuals into people who merit treatment and these who do not - to this very day!** Obviously the ones they expect to be perceived homosexuals after treatment would be the non-deserving ones - but honestly, what else would anybody expect?

It seems rather obvious that *the need to assess our sexual orientation and the requirement to state this in an official medical diagnosis and expertise* can only be seen as an officially approved instrument to further prejudice against homosexuals, or in particular transsexuals who identify homosexual. *Why the American Psychiatric Association* <u>mandates</u> *the very means to further prejudice while providing no medically or therapeutic value whatsoever on a population they already needlessly classify as being mentally ill ("gender-dysphoric") by adding homophobia is not something I would like to speculate on. I simply do not understand how it is possible that medical doctors and individual psychiatrists would not see this for what it is, dispense of it in their practice and ask for this to be officially removed!*

Myself? I have never given my sexual orientation much thought until I started to research treatment and in total disbelief *found that it was (and still is) deemed to be the single most decisive factor!* I still do not understand what sexual orientation, after Kinsey, actually means. Before it was sort-of clear. Sort of. Often this is derived from a religious context where homosexuality is typically defined as "a sexual act between two individuals of the same reproductive sex". Sometimes this definition is narrowed down to "penetrative intercourse" (as can be found in certain legal frameworks also), however I don't exactly understand how this should be applied to lesbians? Or maybe women can't be homosexual after all?

However this may be, ever since Kinsey it is no longer actual sex but *attraction* that makes all the difference for the definition. From my perspective this makes things murky at best, but completely incomprehensible would maybe be a more fitting description:

➤➤ I don't see sex as something I seek out. From my perspective sex is something that may or may not grow from and be part of love. *Does this make me asexual?*

➤➤ I fall in love with human beings, not women or men. *Does this make me bisexual?*

➤➤ I have never actually had sex with somebody who identified male, *so I just might be lesbian?* Honestly, I don't know! Can I maybe check *"all of the above"?* Ok, with the exception of gay male?

➤➤ If, pre-op, *being attracted to me* got people rated homosexual or heterosexual, *does this mean that a man who was attracted to me was deemed* **heterosexual** *because he was attracted towards what he perceived for all intents and purposes to be a woman, while I myself am deemed a homosexual for a mutual attraction?*

➤➤ And, post-op, does this mean that *a man who is attracted to me gets a classification of <u>heterosexual</u> until I tell him of my past at which time <u>he has to re-designate himself homosexual?</u>* Honestly, if that ever made sense…

Of course I suspect that the American Psychiatric Association must, as usual, know exactly! Because I am certain that if they too would not know, they would *never* allow this to be put into their official handbook or require this as part of our medical records! They would never have gone after people they designate 'homosexual' as being mental and they would never have thought to waste any research into something that by it's very nature can't be clearly identified or even exactly specified. Or would they?

B.15. AND JUST HOW DO I REALLY KNOW?

Well, there's that famous line *"I have always known..."*. Or *"I can just feel it..."*. And yes, I have said this too, not only for compliance as *I really do feel this!*

Did I mention that institutions just love to form committees when they don't know how to deal with an issue [B.6]? Whenever such a committee encounters a problem they can't handle but can't get rid of either the likelihood that they end-up giving it a signifi-cant name and delude themselves into believing that this is as good as 'understanding' the problem is quite significant. After all, it's what committees do: Find consensus on the lowest common denominator! Well, to be honest committees are sometimes camouflaged dictatorships and there is at times a little more than just a mere hint of personality-cult involved. Which appears true for psychiatry as well, or maybe even in particular... So when psychiatrists were puzzled by homosexuality they formed a committee named "The Kinsey Institute for Research in Sex, Gender and Reproduction". They in turn invented a cause for homosexuality, named it *"sexual orientation"*. Nobody knows where that comes from, how this works or why we should have it, but hi!, we now know where homosexuality comes from, can explain it, understand everything about it and even know why we can't 'cure' it!

As it was to be expected they did the same with transsexuality. Originally transsexual-ity was not accepted as a condition, then some psychiatrists started to portray it as an extreme, incurable form of sexual perversion, a type of fetish, and because this is said to run along gender-lines only male to female transsexuals were examined - after all psy-chiatry says that only males can have sexual fetishes! Later generations of somewhat more enlightened psychiatrists found that this can't be true, so they invented *"gender identity"* along the line of "sexual identification". Nobody knows where *that* comes from either, how this works or why we should have it, but hi!, we now know where transsex-uality comes from, can explain it, understand everything about it and even know why we can't 'cure' it. Right?

Now from my perspective I see all this a little differently... Amazed? Not really? Ok, well then...:

As for "sexual orientation" I suppose you'd have to read-up A.7. The important point here is that I don't think this actually exists as advertised. As to "gender identity", well I suppose I can't feel that either! Of course I used to adhere to dogma and I gladly told everybody who asked that my gender-identity was female and that I knew exactly. But honestly: All I know and have ever known is *that I identify as being myself* and just why I'd want anything else or why this would be wrong or sick I wouldn't know...

Honestly, how can I be expected to identify FEMALE at birth is besides me! As if I could read an imprint on the inside of my head! When I was born I suppose I neither had an idea that gender exists (well, any other than my own) nor that humans generally come in two genders and not, say, four or fourteen. Never mind that back then I probably did not have any concepts in which to express something as abstract as this anyway. But I presume I was transsexual even back then nevertheless, just differently...

Yes, they can take what I say, what I experience apart, they can potentially identify a social component, likely a physical one, they can sub-divide this into a hormonal aspect and an anatomical one, they can call it sexual or not, and in the end they don't understand more than they did before! Because of whatever they find, whichever part they study, *they examine the symptoms, not the cause,* and while doing so they completely misunderstand the condition!

Let me give you an analogy: Your five year old child doesn't want to go to bed because she claims that there are monsters under it. Now you can go and have a look under the bed, find no monster and then *conclude that there are none there* so the child should get a good night's rest now? Or you could read a scientific article to your child *proving that the existence of monsters is biologically impossible* and because she now understands this she should get a good night's rest? Or you could make *mathematical calculations about the likelihood of ever finding a monster under the bed* versus, say, being killed by a bee-sting, which is certain to assure a good night's rest of the child, right? Or you could do the obvious and explain your five year old that her monster-phobia *is really a mental disorder* coming from her being a sexual pervert because she has been wearing her father's tie and that this is all due to her over-protective, neurotic mother and all she needs to get rid of these monsters is a few years of psychotherapy... Ok, just kidding, right?

Or you could do something completely different: You could just sit besides her and accept that her fear of monsters is quite real even though you don't believe that the monster under the bed is, even without checking. *It is the fear that is real, not the monster, right?* To make her "not fear" you make her feel safe, understood and taken seriously. And while you may have to stay there until she sleeps and let her feel that you care I suppose this will work a whole lot better than any theoretical explanation of it you could ever give or any psychiatric therapy you could ever pay for!

Why does this work? Well, because your child understands (or *feels*) *that you are capable of empathy,* that you can feel fear also, *that you can understand her emotions because you have these too.* Maybe not right now, but you know "how they feel" and what this does to you. You remember fear and she knows this. But you don't have fear right now and this she feels also. And then she can accept that fear isn't necessary right now, isn't appropriate and let go of her own! And suddenly it doesn't matter if there's really a monster under the bed at all...

I can speak in a very, very abstract way about fear, love, lust, greed, the whole spectrum of human emotions. Right now I am doing this in letters and you are quite capable to understand these - because you are capable to have all of these emotions too. You can *relate* to these. And when it becomes a bit more tricky, say you're *heterosexual* and I would like to explain to you *how homosexual attraction feels,* you may not be capable to empathize in the same way as I do because you may never feel homosexual attraction, *but you certainly do understand attraction in general!*

Now I am transsexual. What I feel is not fear or love or any other of these well known emotions. What I feel is that it is not possible to perceive and express my emotional self appropriately within the constraints - emotional, physical, sexual, social, whatever - of my biological sex *because it is the wrong set of constraints.* Of course this is not what I feel but the result, what this makes me experience and conclude and I describe it in a very, *very* abstract way. *Because what I feel is something you don't feel and you never have* - unless you are transsexual. ***The reason for this is that the biochemical misalignment in combination with the biological wrongness only ever makes having this emotion possible!*** Let's just call it - for convenience - *"gender-mismatch".* So I feel gender-mismatch. Gender-mismatch is a basic emotion only transsexuals ever experience[1]. *By definition it is therefore impossible for the non-transsexual observer to understand or recognize what we feel and to draw any meaningful conclusions!* It is a bit as if the parent in the above example would be a person who's incapable to experience fear. How would somebody who is incapable of experiencing fear react to his five year old telling him about her fear of monsters under the bed? Well, this does look as if it could generate quite a few misunderstandings, doesn't it?

You could, at this point, interject that psychiatry really says the same, they just call it "gender-dysphoria". Well, I don't agree:

➤ They define their "gender-dysphoria" as *something that is <u>wrong to experience under any circumstance</u>.* Their absolute position of *not allowing for any "non-pathological gender-dysphoria" as a matter of principle* amounts to claiming that there can't ever be any appropriate circumstances to feel this. This is absurd as (a) no psychiatrist is capable to verify such a statement and (b) ***it is obvious that there are <u>at least some cases</u> in which feeling gender-dysphoria <u>must be considered entirely normal by any standard</u>[2], therefore this psychiatric base-assumption <u>is clearly disproven.</u>***

➤ If "gender-dysphoria" is a mental illness then "gender-euphoria" (an irrational feeling of exaggerated elation about one's gender) ought to be one also - *however psychiatry has yet to either produce a single case of "gender euphoria" or even accept or list such a condition.*

---

[1] *It seems that this experience can be induced by drugs like testosterone in many female identified biological women. I am unaware of any research on male identified men who use estrogen. However as there is quite a number of women who use testosterone and only very few men who use estrogen this may just be a result of larger numbers.*

[2] *It does seem completely absurd to label David Reimer (B.12) "mentally ill" <u>for not agreeing with a forced sex-change</u>!*

➤ Their definition and naming of "gender-dysphoria" implies that the normal thing to have would be something in between "gender-dysphoria" and "gender-euphoria" and that the experience of this should be universal - except for transsexuals. *This makes "gender-dysphoria" nothing else than a designation for "disgust of gender".* Anybody should be capable to feel this but nobody really would because nobody ever had a reason to. *But if this were true then "gender dysphoria" would have to be a "composite-emotion" made up of others we already know and if so psychiatry should be able to give us a good description of how either "gender-dysphoria" or "gender euphoria" feels! Only they find themselves incapable to do this!*

Furthermore they introduce *a term which is in and itself judgmental:* If something is called 'dysphoric' *it is clearly meant along the line of anxiety or depression to a degree of it being completely detached from reality,* hence defining this experience as delusional before even examining the patient. It's really sad that psychiatry deems it appropriate to use derogatory, demeaning and judgmental language to describe 'subjects' and pathologies, from my perspective this is as if they'd call AIDS "gay cancer"[1] instead. (And no, calling it "gender identity disorder" instead doesn't make it any better because I don't have a disorderly gender identity!).

Given this definition of "gender-dysphoria" there is one more argument to be made, one which is more important than any I have listed above: For Psychiatry "gender-dysphoria" is an absurd and irrational experience at the extreme outer limits of our emotional capabilities. *As in their view there can never be people who feel a rational or understandable need for gender-alignment, whoever has "gender-dysphoria" (and thus may qualify for genital-alignment surgery) or whoever has had the surgery has by psychiatric definition lost touch with reality. No examination or evaluation of the patient is ever needed to arrive at this conclusion!* If you ask me, something like this is completely absurd and irrational to a degree where I suspect somebody has lost touch with reality... But then again, I am the patient, not the doctor, right?

This definition also completely contradicts my own experience as I never had such an absurdly negative experience of my biological gender. The best commonly understandable description anybody has ever found is that *being male just felt wrong.* This isn't irrational, it isn't detached from reality, it isn't absurd or overblown and it certainly isn't along the line of depression or anxiety! Not necessarily anyway. These components may all be part of it, *but they don't have to!* Because we in fact experience such emotions *independent* of gender-mismatch. *Which in turn is the very reason why gender-mismatch needs to be defined as an independent basic emotion!* By eliminating this entire range of human experiences, *by not acknowledging gender-mismatch as a separate basic emotion with an entire range of potential combinations with other emotions,* psychiatry irrationalizes (and over-pathologizes) what

---

[1] *"Gay cancer" was a derogatory term used to refer to AIDS before the abbreviation was coined and adopted.*

we feel or (if the criteria is said not to be met) ignores the needs of all individuals who do not express these "co-morbid conditions"!

If gender-mismatch is seen as a basic emotion it becomes normal, *in fact expected* **that nobody can get rid of experiencing it by psychiatric therapy!** This would be akin to finding a therapy which would make an individual stop experiencing something like anger, fear or love. I suppose everybody would agree that such a therapy would have to be characterized as severely abusive and damaging, even if in the end this would not work. But frankly, *I find any attempt at trying to change my gender-experience against my explicit wish or even as compulsory therapy unethical, no matter how little damage this may cause!*

Emotions can be connected to physical experiences of self. For example somebody could feel constant disgust about her experiencing herself as overweight and this could, over time, lead to eating disorders as a behavioural manifestation or it could lead to depression as a secondary emotional manifestation. Experiencing gender-mismatch can have similar consequences. As it is a predominantly negative experience it could prompt everything from depression to anger or insecurity on the emotional side, to behavioural compensation or, at worst, self inflicted harm in either a "self-corrective" manifestation (as in self-castration) or suicidality and suicide. *It could manifest itself like this, but it doesn't have to.*

I agree that, *in severe cases,* it might be appropriate to treat such manifestations as depression or suicidality immediately regardless of the cause. What I do not agree with is that the individual is - from a dogmatic psychiatric point of view - *expected to solve any and all her personality and behavioural problems* **before she is allowed to get treatment for what causes the problem in the first place!** Honestly, I find this is completely absurd! Is it not rare enough that we are as lucky *as to know the exact root cause of an emotional or physical problem? Here we do and we don't seem to care?* Isn't this much rather like asking somebody who has, say, an eating-disorder such as anorexia that she controls her fear of gaining weight, changes her image of self and her expectation of beauty, gains a lot of self-esteem *and only if she can prove that she has achieved this and can demonstrate this for a predefined length of time will she be given food to eat?*

Yes, if so called "co-morbid conditions" are diagnosed they should be addressed. But it should reasonably be anticipated that many of these may just disappear by themselves as soon as the physical cause has been addresses. *But more importantly the great majority of such co-morbid problems only ever arise or become significant* **because we do not get treatment for the cause in a timely fashion** *and we get treated in a de-humanizing, abusive and absurd way!*

You may agree that to make the above anorexic patient comply and gain weight by threatening her with withholding food if she doesn't manage to change her self-image does neither sound like a healthy nor an ethical intervention. It might however just kill her...

Gender-mismatch is, even though emotional, connected to the physical experience of our sexuality. After all transsexuals don't agree with their biological sexual function and biology is physical. Yes and no. I think the application of our psychiatric dogma has proven one thing over time: That we are by and large capable of living our emotionally "appropriate social gender-role" with very few problems and that we feel at least some limited emotional improvement without any surgery if we are given hormonal treatment.

However as from my personal experience I would have to emphasize that *not producing testosterone at biological male levels (i.e. life after surgery) feels vastly different from suppressing it,* but I would have to agree that suppressing it in combination with estrogen treatment had improved my self-experience dramatically already. Surgery has made my life a whole lot easier in many ways, it has made my self-experience finally complete to a degree which makes the previous physical/emotional problem irrelevant. Maybe I can sum this up as follows: *Hormonal alignment has made my self-experience <u>meaningful</u> and <u>understandable</u>. Surgical alignment has made my self-experience <u>normal</u>.*

B.16.   COULD THIS BE A CONGENITAL PHYSICAL DISABILITY?

If transsexuality is not a mental illness then the problem must be somewhere else. Or more directly if I don't have the wrong brain then it must be that I have the wrong repro-ductive system. Because woman do not have testicles and a penis... If I have these any-way then I must suffer from what medicine calls *an intersex-condition.*

Transsexuals are not the only woman who have the same problems, others do too. Only some get designated male at birth while others get classified female. If one gets designated female at birth then having a male appendix is called 'clitoromegaly' (or 'cli-tomegaly')[1] *and having this penis removed is considered normal.* In fact the part used to be (and in some areas of the world still is) "surgically cut to length" routinely with no regard whatsoever to the integrity of the individual or her ability to experience herself emotionally or sexually intact later in life! All "for the greater good of society" - or who-ever was in charge to make such a decision (presumably a person who had at one time in his life taken an oath to "first do no harm") - as then *they* wouldn't have to deal with peo-ple who were different [B.12]![2] If one however is designated male at birth then the ap-pendix is left in place and the same procedure is later seen as a treatment for a severe mental disorder, the surgery re-designated "a sex-change"!

Now I agree that having a clitoris the size of a penis is not my only problem. I have testicles instead of ovaries, I do not have a vagina, a uterus and so on. But there are peo-ple who are designated female after birth who do not have a vaginal opening, they too are deemed intersex. There are people who are born without either ovaries or testicles, these people too are usually deemed intersex-*females.*

There are even people who have parts of both reproductive systems, however in these cases only one ever gets functional if the person is lucky, many of these individuals are infertile throughout their lives. However a great number of scenarios are actually possible as biology is in reality very flexible to cope with unusual anatomical combinations.

Sometimes these "opposite sex organs" (i.e. the ones that contradict the birth-certificate) are actually functional which means that after surgery these individuals can have children. For example somebody born with a vagina but (internal) testicles instead

---

[1] *Aka 'macroclitoris'. The medical term describes "an enlarged clitoris" (sometimes defined as "more than twice the aver-age size") but depending on the underlying condition the clitoris may indeed be the size of a small to normal penis. Par-ticularly in cases of Progestin-Induced Virilisation such female children have on numerous times been misidentified as male at birth.*

[2] *The official reason doctors give for the practice of cutting a girl's clitoris "to size" is that "having this too long is bad for her psychological development", presumably this would have to be her* social *development. Of course I ask myself just what kind of sexual-psychiatric designation these doctors merit themselves given the outlandish acrobatics it takes to pub-licly expose the length of a woman's clitoris (as compared to a male's penis) and just what they might be fantasize women do in their washrooms while they compare the length of their genitals in theirs...?*

of ovaries would likely be deemed female at birth. After discovery the internal testicles will need relocating towards the outside of the body, testicles do not produce fertile sperm when they are at normal internal body-temperature. Fertile or not, if testicles are found and no ovaries such a person will get re-designated male, only males have testicles, right? Wrong! In most legal systems it's *the penis* that makes all the difference! And if the individual desires to have such external male sex characteristics this would call for a phalloplasty. The interesting aspect is that, again, *such a change is not seen as transsexuality, neither the social nor the medical process called 'transition', the surgery not designated "sex-reassignment", it is not deemed plastic surgery and the person would not be painted as mentally ill, even though the creation of the phallus would be exactly the same an f/m transsexual would undergo to get his! Only in this case it's seen as a completely normal corrective medical procedure!*

From my perspective *what I do is exactly the same*. It is true that there is no medical diagnosis for my being female other than just asking me [or noticing what a positive effect treatment has]. But then again, this isn't democracy: Whether I am male or female can't be based on "a majority decision by committee" - and neither should the use of the term 'intersex'. I'm just as much intersex as any of the above. I need the same medical treatment to correct the very same biological mistakes any number of people who today are already accepted intersex by the medical community get fixed. I take the same estrogen every woman who had the misfortune to be born without ovaries (or with non-functional ones) takes, I have the same surgery to create a functional vagina as a woman gets who had the misfortune to be born with an incomplete reproductive system[1]. I have the same urethral relocation every woman who's born peeing through her clitoris gets and so on.

The one difference my intersexuality presents, compared to every other currently accepted by medicine is *that I have just the right combination of these to look, even superficially function appropriately for a male and therefore am misidentified male*. This doesn't make me any more or any less intersex than everybody else out there with any of these other conditions, *it just makes it look less so until one accepts that my brain is a vital (or the most vital) part of my self-identification, my gender and my sexuality!*

The problem seems to be that psychiatry functions by the doctrine: If it looks like a duck, walks like a duck and quacks like a duck, then *it always must be a duck*. Ok, I don't "quack like a duck", or better I get recognized as a woman on the phone, and I probably don't walk like a duck either. But hi! You can't have everything, can you? So I'm a useless, odd, ugly duck. That doesn't make me a swan, does it? Particularly if swans have been declared impossible by doctrine!

---

[1] *For example MRKH or Mayer-Rokitansky-Küster-Hauser Syndrome*

Just imagine:

One day you wake up in a hospital and are told that you won't be able to walk again for the rest of your life! Now consider that you would get *psychotherapy* instead of the *physiotherapy* you expect. Because the doctors are convinced that your insisting in wanting to get around and integrate in society *is a mental illness* and the solution to your problem is *to make you accept that you better not expect anything from your life anymore, never mind ever getting out or having a social life!* You however think that this is *a physical problem* and if you may never walk again, you are surely determined to get a meaningful life in spite of your condition!

But your are told that physiotherapy is at best a remote possibility for later and you can only get it *if the psychiatrists think that you deserve it*. You seem to be the only person (along with a few other paraplegics) who clearly realizes that mental-health is in no way capable of making such a decision as your physical health clearly doesn't fall into their range of expertise. But you are told that you need mental treatment for at least several months until it may or may not become clear that you really might be 'ready' to get physiotherapy, and you should call yourself lucky because in most hospitals that decision takes years! You are told that there are many paraplegics who happily rest in their beds all day long and feel no need to actually do something about this so you should really consider at length if this would not be far better for you too. *Some of these "accepting patients" don't see any prospect of ever getting a meaningful life and commit suicide* - in such cases mental-health experts claim that these suicides are *due to a lack of mental-health-support* and/or a lack of compliance by an "unstable individual"...

You're being given a few months to think about this, with regular mental therapy in between. You're not allowed frustration as this is interpreted as non-compliance, treatment-failure, and you're certainly not allowed depression because then this really is a mental issue - which needs to be resolved *first*. People are not allowed on physiotherapy when they are depressive, any activity whatsoever is then considered very dangerous to the point of being life-threatening!

Should you be one of the lucky ones who are finally let go to physio you are told that the next step - getting a wheelchair - requires yet more *psycho*therapy, at least another year (but usually it is *2-3 years*). You will have to pay for the wheelchair yourself and to get one, you are told, you need a permit *from your psychiatrist* while any progress at physiotherapy *is irrelevant!*

Yes, you know that you want one, you even agree to pay for it yourself *because getting out and about, integrate as fully as you can in society,* **is that important to you!** You imagine that with a wheelchair you may not be quite "back to normal", but about as good as medically possible these days and that your life would be so much better with than without. But you are told that in fact just wanting one, paying for it yourself and making a de-

cent progress in physiotherapy isn't good enough to being given that permit fo.
one. You are instead told that *nobody ever has a right to get a wheelchair*, if you ai
given that permit to order one *then it will be at grace, conditionally upon good behav.*
under life-long psychiatric supervision. Instead you are required to take the "let's wa.
again" pills of which everyone knows that they don't work. They can't, they never have,
not in a single case. They make you accept severe side-effects including diabetes, kidney-
and liver-disease, embolism, stroke and cancer. For at least another year. Meanwhile the
mental-health people insist that you stay out of bed all day long. As you're not given a
wheelchair you have to creep on the floor and while doing this you are expected to maintain employment, socialize normally, be independent and do this all under the microscope
of psychiatry. You are, obviously, never expected to get depressed or even accuse mental-
health of forcing a demeaning and abusive lifestyle onto you, in fact you are to show
thankfulness every time you get seen by your psychiatrist! Only if you agree to do this for
an unknown length of time is your request for that wheelchair *even considered.*

If you still insist that this therapy misses the point, you still don't consider crawling on
the ground for the rest of your life a meaningful option, you keep on repeating that your
therapy should be geared towards allowing you to integrate in society then you're told that
you're dearly misguided! Your therapy is designed for you to accept your condition and
stop complaining about it! Only when you manage to provide proof of having accepted
that your condition is mental and not physical at all and you are willing to crawl on the
floor for life will you then, maybe, be given a permit to buy that wheelchair!

Should you ever get that permit the typical waiting time to actually have your chair fabricated is easily another year, it goes without saying that during all this time continued participation at mental treatment is mandatory.

And if ever you get your chair delivered and do just fine with it, suddenly everybody
will accept that you have always had a physical problem and you will be treated as a normal person! Well, as normal as they come, crippled and in wheelchairs, right?

Of course during the whole process nobody ever considers you handicapped, you have
to make enough money to survive on *and pay for all the treatment yourself, if you're*
unlucky this includes all the costs of mental treatment as well! You have to navigate physical, social and legal hurdles yourself even though you're just learning how to get around
creeping on the floor. Nobody tells you what you're entitled to or how to get it.

Fortunately we consider providing physiotherapy and a wheelchair as well as support to
paraplegics *a human right* should the patients *medical* condition allow for it. Society even
pays for it as it is apparently deemed more meaningful (and cheaper) to integrate a human
being into society than having her/him on long-term-care (mental or otherwise) for life.

Thankfully we know how to treat people with disabilities in a decent and meaningful
way. Or so one would hope.

A.8. AND I PRONOUNCE YOU... WIFE AND WIFE?

Well, ok. So we got married. There was a fabulous feast, the two witnesses did the cooking so I didn't have to for a change and since we didn't think inviting a priest to the occasion would be adding to the fun we were a grand total of four people at dinner. Was it fun? Yes it was! True, there was no same-sex-marriage back then, but for some reason I must have forgotten to ask the government to correct that certificate of mine which proved that - in the eyes of the prevailing law - I was an appropriate partner for, well, my partner.

There was however one somewhat tearful thought along with that commitment: The line goes "until death you parted", but I was very hopeful that for us this would not become true! Back then the fact was that registering a legal change of gender automatically annulled an existing marriage (or, depending upon the prevailing legal system, the official change would only be permitted if previously a divorce had been filed). The argument was (and still is) that a change of the legal sex-designation of one partner would make the marriage an illegal same-sex marriage. Because surely it makes sense to void the marriage based on the legal designation of the transsexual and not the looks of her genitals or her identification for that matter?

The idea somebody had come up with was that I could marry *a woman before* that (legal) gender-update and *a man afterwards*, because I was deemed legally male before and legally female afterwards. *Logically, the one thing I would be forbidden was to have the same partner throughout my life!* Honestly, I find it just a bit absurd that **scripture would be quoted as the reason** *why I would not be allowed to keep a life-long commitment I had made before God!*

I fear this is just one of the absurdities of our lives for which psychiatry doesn't seem to be looking for meaningful solutions, but surely it is more important to establish my sexual orientation scientifically with absolute certainty than to give me the right to continue having my family and my children throughout my lifetime just as everybody else? And I agree, it must be so much better for my mental health when I loose my marital partner and all parental rights to my children the moment I wake-up from that surgery but at least I know that I am a psychiatrically certifiable lesbian! After all certainty, consistency and continuity give people emotional support, don't they?

But besides the opportunity for my typical sarcasm I suppose married transsexuals, particularly the ones with children, are the people who are hit hardest by the prevailing laws on marriage most countries have. We certainly exemplify *how wrong and absurd this interpretation of "heterosexual only" marriage is.* How can anybody who applauds "family values" demand that our children do not deserve the same protection, rights and treatment as everybody elses do? That our children do not deserve *both* parents? What justification do they have *to change their minds on our relationship* and why does any court (and the psychiatric establishment) go along with this? Honestly, I don't know.

Any and all contracts I have ever entered into being legally male remain valid after my official change of gender. The one - *and only* - thing that gets thrown out is my family! If they would just do to our marriage *what they do to every other legal document* the problem would be solved easily and acceptably: Just leave it as it was because, after all, *it was perfectly ok when it was proclaimed.* If one of the parties mentioned in the document wants some changes applied to it (i.e. name or gender) they can file for it and, depending on the laws, the change will be granted or not. If they want the contract invalidated, they can file for divorce. *At their own discretion!*

Of course the more obvious solution would be to throw-out gender in the definition of marriage altogether, but this then would allow for what some see as "homosexual marriages" and are opposed to. I have no idea why some people so often think that they need to impose *their* personal views of how things have to be *onto others,* but then again it appears that I'm writing this entire book because there are too many people out there who feel just that! But in spite of all this I must consider myself lucky: The many delays in treatment have made it possible that I now live in a country where so called "same-sex marriage" is legal! And because of this we will be allowed to remain a family after all, even after my surgery and in particular after the legal change! At least in one of the countries I am a citizen of...

On the other hand while we can stay married we will not be given a marriage certificate that is in any way useful. But why should the people who put-up the legislation for same-sex marriage (or their advisors) have given any thoughts to transsexuals or gender-alignment? I mean apart from passing legislation to specifically tear-up our basic rights? Apparently even after allowing "marriage for everybody" the position *we* find ourselves in still isn't favourable at all.

In so many ways I suppose that *this* is the real reason why "homosexual transsexuals" are so unacceptable to a large number of mental-health practitioners: If they knowingly allow me to get medical treatment they'll potentially find themselves in the middle of a storm of religious fanaticism and gay/lesbian-activism! They have lost this battle twice already, first when they had to introduce special status to religions in their official line-up of mental illnesses ['delusions' are commonly defined in behavioural science as *"a fixed false belief (excluding beliefs that are part of a religious movement)*[1] "] and later when they had to concede that homosexuality did not belong on their list of afflictions worthy of their professional attention. If I were cynical I would have to suspect that the many, many people who have thus managed

---

[1] *Quoted from www.behavenet.com/capsules/disorders/dsm4TRclassification.htm [DSM-IV-TR (text revision)]*

to worm themselves out of being declared mental by psychiatry has risen to being quite a significant loss of business...

And now there are these transsexuals, and for heaven's sake they want the same! Some kind of an exemption for their abnormal behaviour! Because they too think that what they're doing is actually *not madness!* If this goes on like this mental-health will go bankrupt pretty soon, and what then???

B.17. TESTING THE LIMITS

Some people ask: Where does transsexuality come from? Just what is the exact cause of this? I suppose such questions are to some degree justified, however I also think it comes from a deep-rooted desire to find *a cause to blame*. Then, if we know the cause, we could conceivably use this to come-up with a test. Subsequently we could 'help' a person with "corrective measures" so she never needs to be transsexual in the first place!

Over the years I've heard of and read about many suspected causes for transsexuality. Among these are hormonal imbalances during pregnancy, developmental issues in the fetus, genetic explanations, chemical influences on the growing fetus due to exposure of the mother. These are but a few examples of *potentially measurable* causes, there are other proposals ranging from early childhood experiences to abuse to divine intervention that have been put forward, all of these explain little and are useless for any preventative diagnosis or screening as they are neither quantifiable nor clearly defined.

But even if we remain, for the sake of argument, within the realm of *quantifiable* causes we would still encounter serious problems with any such test:

➤➤ Whichever test we would specify, *it is to be expected that there will be individuals who would identify "outside the scope or results of the test".* People who say they're transsexual even though the test says they're not - or the other way 'round. Does this make any test useless? I believe so - but others apparently don't!

➤➤ If we define a test, how are we to apply this to treatment? Should there be "mass screenings"? And in what way would we justify treating people differently if they say they are transsexual but show negative on that test? We already differentiate by assigning the term 'transsexual' to individuals who differ from their legal birth-designation and 'intersex' to individuals who are in line with this designation, but "vary from textbook biological, emotional, biochemical or medical expectations" *and we then go out and put vastly different conditions on obtaining potentially the same treatment* simply based on that legal status of the patient (i.e. mandatory psy-chiatry, waiting-times, costs borne by insurance or patient, stigmatization, social status,…). If we find that such different treatment is unethical then why look for and define a test in the first place?

➤➤ If such a test can either be used before conception (i.e. a test of some form on the parents) or very early during pregnancy, what would be the conclusions from such test-results? Could it just be that parents who test positive for "at risk to have a

[On the schoolyard, a group of female 8th graders chatting while I pass by] You know, the women overthere, she's trans? [Somebody else] Yes, I know … But that's not a big deal, just a few hormones and a little surgery …

transsexual child" would be advised not to have children? Maybe punished if they'd try anyway? Could an early-pregnancy test for transsexuality lead to the abortion of such a child because the parents don't want a transsexual child or because political, financial or social considerations or pressure by medical professionals make such a child unacceptable? Surely these possibilities are real and such cases would happen even if it were not legal! My question here is: In what circumstances do we, in general, have the right to terminate a life or to plan for it's non-existence *because we don't like it?* Are we as arrogant as to take this into our own hands, and if so, where do we draw the line? Who will be socially acceptable and who won't? Would I be socially acceptable? Would my life be deemed "worth living"?

≫ If a test were defined and accepted by the medical community, surely "corrective measures" would follow. But what would this mean? As the future reproductive capacity of a human-being is generally determined by genetic make-up or more specifically by the sex-chromosomes 'X' and 'Y', "XX" for female and "XY" for male[1], it is presumably very difficult to alter the genetic sex of an individual after conception or even after birth. Given this difficulty I expect most 'treatments' would focus on *altering my self-perception*, making me experiencing myself male instead of female. Only if this were possible I would no longer have been myself but *would have been made into somebody else.* Obviously there's the question if this is ethical, if we at all have the right to try and do this? I for one like my life and in spite of all the difficulties I like it how it is! Does anybody have the right to decide that this is wrong, needs changing or should not be allowed as it is?

≫ Apparently there is already a treatment for the condition available! One that works quite well, to the satisfaction of a great majority of individuals who receive it anyway, there is even potential for significant improvements to this existing treatment. Many handicapped people would love to have treatments for their conditions and most treatments for disabilities do neither have the success-rate nor quality of the result ours does.

So what is this all about? Well, there are only two possibilities: Either some people find that our suffering is too great and that another forms of treatment might alleviate this. I think they're searching in the wrong direction. Instead of looking for new treatments making the available treatment *available* would do just fine. *Or it could be that the current treatment is in some way unacceptable to some third party, that somebody else wants us "dealt with differently". For their benefit!*

---

[1] *In human-beings this is true in approximately 99½% of all individuals when tested by means of a karyotype (a test in which the chromosomes of white blood-cells are visually sorted and accounted for), there is approximately a 1:400 chance that the genetic make-up of a person does not follow this "XX:female, XY:male" rule. In addition in all mammals, including humans, maternal cells are passed on to the next generation (embryo/fetus or lactating newborn), some settle into structures of the body where they remain fully integrated (function, grow and multiply) throughout life. These cells would normally be female (XX), so in reality there is no person alive who only has XY cell-lines in his/her body.*

Or, in a more general context, should we ask Jane and John these questions? I am certain Jane as well as John would like nothing more than a complete cure for their condition! For Jane this would either mean a medical cure were available to her, or it would have meant that the conditions of her accident should have been altered in a way as to either make it not happen or reduce the severity dramatically. For John this would either mean a medical cure now or early after birth, or diagnosis and treatment before birth.

In the interest of their health, but also of future cases it would appear reasonable to consider any and all means to make this possible. However this addresses questions which today are deemed to be far outside of medicine. For example how much alcohol somebody is allowed to drink before driving (as presumably Jane's accident might not have happened if the driver would not have been drunk) and what methods society would accept to have such measures enforced. Unfortunately western medicine today does not embrace the concept that doctors ought to speak out or *suggest social measures* or simply *point-out shortcomings and consequences of our behaviours* in order *to alleviate or prevent future illnesses or accidents.*

In the case of John this brings-up the question under what conditions early childhood treatment is appropriate. If such treatment should be delayed, if medically possible, *until the person in question is capable of making an informed decision* **if he/she would actually want such treatment?** Or if treatment should be *forced* on some, any or all individuals suffering from the condition? And if we accept forced measures, *which conditions* would be deemed "to be severe enough" to allow such non-consensual treatment? Should we consequentially accept social measures such as the forced removal of children from non-compliant parents or punitive measures against non-compliant individuals?

What forms of treatment would be acceptable and enforceable? Only the ones with a 100% success-rate and no potential of any negative side-effects (which would obviously be *very* few)? And if not, what kind of inherent or potential side-effects of such forced interventions should be deemed 'acceptable' "for the greater good"? Or let's be honest: *To make the individual comply to society's expectations?* Would death or permanent disability be an acceptable potential side-effect of such treatment? Even if only one in a million treatments had such undesired effects? And if no cure for a severe condition is available would killing the individual "for the benefit of society" be an acceptable treatment?

Our society currently agrees that medically killing a human-beings for convenience is under certain conditions acceptable, even expected. For example when prenatal tests indicate certain conditions (such as Down-Syndrome) society will pay for having "the pregnancy terminated", the child killed as a medical intervention. Even though this decision will almost always be based on a test which is known to return false results! Officially the final decision currently lies with the mother (if a physician refuses to provide an abortion, a mother can "shop around" for the procedure), however it is difficult to say just how much influence the attitudes of particular medical professionals and the clearly stated pressure and expectations of society might have. It is after all much more difficult to take the risk of adding one more baby with Down-Syndrome to the world **when there are so few because so many have already been exterminated - and the mother then has to expect to be blamed for "adding this burden to society" instead of receiving appropriate support for herself and her child!**

And just where does this end? If society or medical doctors believe they have the right to declare a life with Down-Syndrome *not worth living,* who's next? Maybe John or Jane? Because a life on dialysis or in a wheelchair may surely be deemed "not worth living" *by these experts?* Maybe all people with disabilities? The elderly? Addicts? People with incurable illnesses? These who are "doomed to have a difficult life"? Like homosexuals? Transsexuals? *Or everybody, to say it aloud, who may cost society more than he/she is expected to contribute, measured in monetary units?* *And everybody who does not measure up to the social or behavioural expectations of the people who have the power to hand-out such measures?*

If you ask me, there's only one person in the world who's capable to decide if my life is worth living: *Myself!* Nobody else, unless I personally designate such a person, in case I should be incapable to make this decision. No a test, not a political system, not a doctor, not a panel of self-appointed 'experts' and most certainly not a social attitude or expectation! Jane and John, I am certain, would agree!

A.9. THREE STRIKES AND YOU'RE OUT!

Well, it took us a while to figure out that "having children" thing. Ok, the "getting children" thing really. But eventually…

Now just for informational purposes and the inclined psychiatrist who might be interested, *purely professionally of course:* Human biology suggests that one needs *sperm* to fertilize an egg, *not sex!* Yes, I suspect this insight will come as a real shock to many males and likely a good majority of psychiatrists, especially sexologists, even though they are all trained medical doctors. But really, it's true!

But in spite of such highly enlightening knowledge some hard-line psychiatrists and institutions disqualify anybody from genital surgery outright just for having children! One can get away, sometimes, being or having been married by claiming "it was all a mistake" or "we didn't have sex". But if one has children then the thinking apparently is: *This person has had male sex (the children are proof!) so she can't be transsexual because transsexuals don't have any sex pre-op! By having sex a person proves that she wants her genitals as they are…* Some surgeons refuse to see patients for genital surgery *if they have had children or are married,* some accept "proof of divorce". No doctor would refuse to help a pregnant woman during a difficult labour and delivery *just because of her marital status (or lack thereof).* Not today. Today we would see this as atrocious, abominable, unethical. Mother and child are given help in this situation *because they need it, because they belong to our human family.* Not because the mother is married or not! Transsexuals however still are routinely denied treatment by some doctors *because of their marital status.* Besides being discriminatory I doubt that such practices are legal. But if anything they are unethical by any standard. How these doctors can bring this in-line with their guidelines on professional behaviour and their medical oath should probably best be answered by one of the physician in question…

The other factor that's being used, our having children, is just for pure argument flawed. The mistake the practitioners who quote this make is the very same we have encountered in B.8 where the sexual act is used to assign a label on sexual orientation: It just doesn't work! The observation is at best inconclusive because there are many more motivations to having sex than having fun, *wanting children would be one of the more if not the most obvious.* There is also the matter that some biologists and sociologists suggest that up to 10% of all birth-records do not show the true biological father as legal father and as this isn't routinely tested for nobody really knows - or maybe nobody (in power) really wants to know…

[A friend, in a restaurant] Why does he give the bill to me [Me] Because he knows that I should get something out of my sex-change…

When I first researched transsexuality the psychiatric view of us actually *required us to say that we never had sex* to ever be accepted as being transsexual! Some psychiatrists would accept the occasional sexual relationship under condition one said that *one really did not have a sex-drive but "just wanted to find out how this feels".* And it helped to add *"and it sucked"* (or whatever expression one finds appropriate in this context). We were forbidden to have any sort of sex-drive or related satisfying activity. Obviously this just lead to people lying to therapists. But honestly, what else would anybody expect?

My experience? I never had a problem to get a decent male sex-drive. Personally I found myself completely oversexed but this is just another rather common experience of women who get testosterone-treatment. The substance is said to increases the sex-drive, from my own perspective I would have to add that this in particular intensified *sexual perception* (of myself as well as my environment) and why should it matter if the stuff is artificial or biologically home-made? But there's one thing I can say to male sexuality that was clearly different for me: I failed to find all the pleasure intercourse is supposed to provide. The best sex I ever had was foreplay. As for the rest? Can we maybe skip this and do the foreplay again instead?

Of course shortly after my partner and I had met we, well... She thought I needed this! I thought she expected this! So there you go, two people having sex, both of them doing it *just because the other might want it...* Well, thankfully women talk a lot so we figured that one out: For us sex was for getting children and that's that.

After we had all this sorted out - which only took a couple of years - we had three wonderful children together. We did talk about a fourth, but by then I just had to admit that this had become impossible.

The time we had together had given my partner and me just about a decade to get to know each other - and to understand each other. It had also given her a decade to get to know the real me, Eva, privately and personally. By then she had not only understood that *this* is me, she had understood that however much I tried and however supportive she was, in the end there is only one way out. She had understood that living my life is not an option, that surgery is not a choice. And she had understood that I had always "lived my own self", that there would not be a different person living with her afterwards.

There was something else we understood: That this was about the last minute for me to start. That if I were to survive potentially years of waiting we may have waited too long already. Privately I felt if this wouldn't progress really quickly now, with minimum delay, that there would be no chance whatsoever for me to ever see the day of surgery. Three weeks later I had booked an initial visit with a GP I knew to be trans-positive.

The next few months are what this book is really all about. Because I should have gotten my life. But instead you're getting this book!

PART II - BECOMING

A

469 DAYS OF SLAVERY

B

LIVING MADNESS

The United Nations General Assembly Resolution 217A(III) of 10 December 1948,

Universal Declaration Of Human Rights[1]

Article 3:

Everyone has the right to live, have liberty, and security of person.

Article 4:

No one shall be held in slavery or servitude; […]

Article 5:

No one shall be subjected to torture or to cruel, inhuman or degrading treatment or punishment.

Article 16 (1):

Men and women of full age, without any limitation due to race, nationality or religion, have the right to marry and to found a family. […]

---

[1] *Official wording quoted from www.unhchr.ch/udhr/lang/eng.htm*

A.10. THIS MAKES SO MUCH SENSE!

So I had booked an appointment. In a few weeks I would see somebody I knew to actually prescribe the treatment. Hormonal treatment anyway. But I didn't want to wait, I wanted to get going. Somewhere. Anywhere. Just away from where I was... So I took the opportunity to tell people about what I had in mind. But first I gave my new self a trial weekend or two. And just as I showed-up male again some neighbours asked me "Is your sister visiting? You look so alike?" and then "I didn't know you had a sister? You never mentioned...".

Ok, it was high time to be pro-active! I composed a "coming-out letter" and my partner and I went out, visiting neighbours, friends, parents of children at school, the people living in our street, knocking on doors and telling them about me, giving everybody a copy of my letter to read. At times we had our kitchen-walls cluttered with printouts of directories, class-lists of the children, excerpts from the phone-book and close-ups of street-maps checking off people's names, houses, phone-numbers, addresses. Friends, family, everybody who didn't already know and these who did were, well, how many fingers does one hand have? I made it a point to talk to everybody personally wherever possible but I had to write to some people because they were too far away for a personal meeting and I didn't think a phone-call or an e-mail would be quite appropriate.

In the beginning I managed to get myself through just a single one of these one-on-one conversations a day being completely worn out after that, but soon I got better at it, dared to tell two people at once and so on. The questions I got back were mostly very interested, sometimes obviously repetitive, males tended to be interested in "how this works", issues as to surgery and treatment, females in "how I felt", emotional issues, which really didn't come as much of a surprise. By the time the end neared I could give my lecture ten times a day and feel good about it in the evening when I was done!

Generally I found males were far more reserved than females, though this may just be because I was m/f and thus experience and live the world female myself. Some of the one-liners I got back were "welcome to the club!" or "so you want the second-class treatment officially now!", at playgroup the comment was "so we're back to all women!". The one I liked best was from a friend from overseas in a letter I received only a few weeks later. She had known me since early childhood, but there was also the part that she just happened to have chosen a career in mental-health - which I suppose was the one reason why I never had told her before... She wrote a few pages, right at the beginning she said: "Thank you for letting me know! You know, this makes so much sense!"...

Negative reactions? No, not really! Yes, there were people who, afterwards, found that they would prefer not to have anything to do with me, but these were few and some even came back after a while. I suppose it happens, it could have been anything. Had I told people I wanted to go into politics I am certain this would have offended many more of my friends. Getting a sex-change may have been a bit unusual and unexpected but it just made sense to them!

True, there are people who avoid me these days but honestly in retrospect my social transition was not "alienating everybody", it was rather *showing the true worth of people TO ME!* It was certainly one of the more difficult things I had to do in my life, it was definitely very intense but there wasn't anything else I could do if I wanted just this - life!

Yes, I do think that I am in some way a bit of a "special case". After all I have publicly lived all the stereotypically female things for years, except lipstick and clothes. But then again I think this may just be something that comes with age: Unlike a 20 year old who might have spent most of her life at home and at school I simply had more time to establish myself and express a little more individually who I am.

And there is something else age tends to 'solve'. Younger transsexuals need to come-out to their parents and this is particularly difficult if one depends on parents not only emotionally but also financially. If one is still in school or maybe university, doesn't have an income or not one that is sufficient to cover life's expenses, never mind the upcoming treatment. It gets even more complicated if one is still under-age and - depending on the jurisdiction - may need parental permission to obtain any kind of medical treatment.

Both my parents had passed on years ago, my father in fact died when I was in my mid 20-es, so this wasn't an issue. My mother (who survived my father by more than a decade) did know, only I never had to tell her. Well, I suppose it is difficult to hide 'borrowing' her clothes, particularly at age six! At that age one just doesn't do a good enough job so this doesn't remain unnoticed… Initially we had a relationship of 'tolerating' this, her motto was something like "well, there isn't any harm done!". Later however she started to understand that this was something that went far deeper than she initially thought and when I was 17 it was her who brought the fact to my attention that surgical alignment existed. On the other hand I am certain that my father would have thrown me out for doing this. Initially anyway. I don't know how long it would have taken him to make the adjustment or if he ever could have accepted me as I am. And yes, I am glad that I did not have to go through this and find out.

B.18. BINARY GENDER, CONTINUUM OR GENDERSOUP

Which brings us in a rather unpredictable way to the question of what 'gender' actually is. The American Psychiatric Association knows: There are men and women, everybody can be classified accurately and they - The American Psychiatric Association - know *exactly* what each and every single one of us is. Only they're not letting us in on their secret of *how* they know this… Apparently *"they just know"* and we're to "just believe them". *As an act of faith!*

Many people in the "gender community" try to somehow 'fix' this approach. They tell us that gender isn't a simple "male/female either/or-thing" but that it rather comes as a *"gender continuum"*, that there is male and female - *and everything in between!*

I understand their concern in some way but *from my perspective I find it is completely absurd to "try and fix" a system that is irrational and wrong from the get go!*

But there are women and men, aren't there? Even I have to admit this? Yes, I do, only for me this is different… Let me give you an analogy

There used to be countries where the population was split into two groups, one called 'black', the other called 'white'. True, nobody who lived there really was black or white, they all were some shade of brown to light pink. Nevertheless, the social order required people to call each other 'black' and 'white', maybe this came from putting the extremes as far apart as possible (I mean, honestly, brown and light pink really aren't all that far apart, are they?) and maybe the ones handing out that label also liked the idea of the religious implications white and black have in regard to good and evil?

However that may have been, they needed a system to identify *who actually was to be deemed 'black' and who was to be deemed 'white'.* Only whatever way one wants to sort this out, in the end one has to admit that this doesn't work! *Because in reality we're all the same!* If measuring skin-pigmentation is taken as an actual physical reference to make this determination then one ends-up having to re-designate many people over their lifetime or even throughout the cycle of a year *because this changes!* If one takes ancestry (or genetics) to make such determinations one inevitably has the problem that the people who are called 'white' are all descendants of the people who they later called 'black', only over time they mutated into being less and less pigmented until, at some time in the past, *some of them* found that they were *"not dark enough"* to be labelled 'black', *so they became "white blacks".* Now I just presume that the people who use the 'white'-designation on themselves would likely be rather displeased if we start to more correctly identify them as *"mutant blacks"?*

[To a friend] Look, there's something about me I'd like to tell you… You see, I am trans… [She] …Well, this explains a lot…

If we find that *such assignment to a binary system (one of two possibilities) is impossible to support scientifically and is therefore **proven** to be arbitrary we have to conclude that it is unethical to impose and enforce it!* And it won't help if we replace the binary "black/white" with a floating-scale where we add "some shade of brown" in between because that way we haven't gotten rid of the idea of sorting people into black and white, *we only have made it more palatable to society, that's all!* **It doesn't make** *the idea* **right at all!** *But it keeps a system in place that remains unethical however many shades of brown get added!*

And no, I don't have the illusion that people don't perceive each other as being 'white' or 'black' anymore just because we stop assigning such labels officially. I don't delude myself into thinking that people don't get "the black treatment" or "the white treatment" and I certainly don't think that some people *themselves* would not continue to uphold that division and think that they are "the better people" because they put themselves onto a specific side of it. *But I do think that it is progress when our society as a whole stops to accept this, stops to officially designate and officially discriminate!* Because discriminating is wrong. It always is! And allowing "half-way-discrimination" in between doesn't make it right and ethical!

So what does this have to do with men and women? After all, there have always been men and woman, haven't there? Well, actually… No! There haven't always been females and males, never mind men and women. One just has to go back in evolutionary biology a bit further than the time when humanity spread out from the trees of Africa…

But that's different? Right? Because we get everything in between "black people" and "white people" from biological reproduction of "mixed parents"? Well… Now this argument might just be the most powerful one I have ever come across to become a racist! Because surely we can never get "pure bread women" and "pure bread men" if we keep interbreeding women and men?

But still, that's different because men and women have *different biological functions?* Well, true, but then again so does highly pigmented skin and virtually non-pigmented skin. Darker skin protects better against harmful rays of the sun (no sunburns in areas with lots of sunshine) while lighter skin allows synthesis of more vitamin D (no deficiency in areas with less sunshine), to name one of the differences. *This is a biological function,* right?

But still, that's different? Because the differentiation of men and woman is *by reproductive capacity,* not by some other form of biological or even cultural identification? Well, true, but then again why is it different if it affects breast-growth and the position in which we urinate compared to skin pigmentation?

But still, I just don't get it! This is about designating reproductive capacity! This is about who needs to get together to produce children?! Well, yes… But that's not what we are doing, is it? We assign gender at birth, *on pure **speculation of a potential future reproductive capacity!*** We don't make this designation by observing actual biological reproduction or even just fertility, in fact when humans are born we are quite incapable to reproduce and we are quite infertile, all of us!

So instead of accepting what we say that we are *we have certain criteria so we can guess if at some time in a distant future somebody will have the capacity to become a father or a mother!* Some of these criteria are directly related to reproduction but some are not (like the ability to grow a beard). Some are biological but some are not (such as cultural differences like wearing high-heels and a skirt or a tie). Some are only male or female (for example the sex-designation in a driver's license), others allow states in between (as in biological intersex) or something completely different (as in genetics when an individual's sex-chromosomes can be "XXY" instead of "XX" for female or "XY" for male). Some can be completely absent (as in persons born without primary reproductive organs). Some typically remain constant throughout life (like the way urine is passed) while others can change relatively predictably (as the onset of fertility *for these individuals who become fertile*) and some change a little less predictably (like menopause). Some are related to others (one can only become fertile if one has primary reproductive organs) while some are only loosely correlated or completely independent (like height, weight or the pitch of the voice).

In the end what we socially define as 'gender' *is made-up of hundreds of attributes we all blend into one single designation.* Only each and every one of these attributes is to some degree ambivalent, not a single one comes "with absolute reliability" and very few individuals (if any) have all these attributes exclusively on one side. So why then should what we see as 'gender' - the weighed average of all these attributes - be any more "universally correct"? *After all we don't get an ethically sound designation (or decision) by taking the weighed average of a large number of potentially unclear, often unreliable and at times downright wrong ones, do we?* **And we don't make this right by allowing "some shade of grey" in between female and male, we only ever get this right if we stop doing this entirely!**

But I'm still not getting it, right? While separating 'black' people and 'white' people isn't right because in reality we are all the same, *women and men are fundamentally biologically different and this makes the labelling ok!* Well, yes, *we are different,* no doubt about that!

A few hundred years ago people thought so if it came to separating 'black' and 'white'. They too thought that this could be quantified, that this criteria could be assigned *with absolute certainty.* They felt as certain to 'knew' this as to derive other qualities from it, qualities such as 'intelligence', 'honesty' or whatever they saw fit! Only later we found scientific proof that this isn't true after all! We learned that making such determinations is wrong! But not (only) because we found proof that we are all the same *but because deriving any assumptions based on an inherently flawed precondition is unethical! Racism isn't (only) wrong because it doesn't work and because it hurts people, racism is wrong because we are incapable to assign such criteria in the first place except by personal prejudice!*

There is no single or combined method to assign gender to an individual *which works correctly in every case.* **Assigning this attribute anyway, somehow, and then deriving other qualities from it is a form of expressing prejudice, nothing else!** *The only way of guaranteeing that no such sexist prejudice exist, at least officially sanctioned or enforced ones, is to* *disallow the assigning of such attributes officially to people entirely!* Making it "a sliding scale" is nothing but *an attempt to save sexism in some form.* It is just as wrong!

And no, I don't think that people will stop to perceive each other as 'female' or 'male' just because we stop assigning these labels *officially*. I don't delude myself into thinking that people won't get "the male treatment" or "the female treatment" and I certainly don't think that some people *themselves* would not continue to uphold that division. *But I do think that our society as a whole should stop accepting this, should stop to officially designate and officially discriminate! Because discriminating is wrong. It always is! And allowing grey in between does not make it right or ethical!*

B.19. LGB's AND T's

Thanks to the psychiatric definition of transsexuality and their effort to put it into the realm of mental illness we find ourselves in the very same places - social support, community-centres as well as outreach projects of mental institutions and so on - where psychiatrists so kindly tried to help gays, lesbians and bisexuals to "make them normal". After all not too long ago these too were deemed mental but having a more effective (and bigger) lobby and presumably thanks to the fact that living gay or lesbian doesn't require the ascent of the medical community, they got out of their straitjackets a few years ago. Still, we find ourselves in the same mental-health publications, in the same wash-up. After all, they're homosexual, we're transsexual. It's almost the same anyway, isn't it? *Just a sexual deviation...*

And many of us fall for this! There is "transsexual activism", "transsexual gender-politics" and so on. Yes, if this were something like the heart and stroke foundation *where people find each other to help further research and treatment, public awareness and the availability of treatment* for heart-disease and stroke patients I suppose I would join in and help out! Only this isn't the heart- or the lung-, the kidney- or even the breast-cancer-society, this is about penises and vaginae - and *this* changes everything! Reasoning and problem-oriented thinking just doesn't seem to be possible in this realm, after all this is about "the things down there"...

Do I have a different opinion? Yes, as a matter of fact, I do... From my perspective what we currently find, once again, can be traced right back to Benjamin's definition of transsexuality *as a lifestyle.* People who live a lifestyle typically tend to congregate together, form groups, clubs and so on. They socialize *because they share common interests and concerns.* And so do transsexuals. Some anyway. The result is "transsexual activism" and "gender politics". Unfortunately most of it falls into about the following categories:

➤➤ People who want to legalize, promote or make "the transsexual lifestyle" socially acceptable. This typically means legalizing of cross-dressing, cross-living and cross-gender activities, as well as making this socially acceptable. I have lived this life a bit over a year and while I sympathize greatly I am very different from most of these people. After all, they do something freely I only accept as an "in between step" *and only because I was pressured into it!* I have similar concerns while I live she-male as somebody who makes this her lifestyle by choice, *my main concern however is about not having to do this at all!* Most notably while I am forced into this by mental-health most people who live full or part-time cross-gender never get

[At my hair-stylist, a friend goes there too] Have you seen her lately [Me] Just before I came here I've seen her professionally! She's ok, but I think her job is getting to her lately... [He] Was that before or after you were there?

into any contact with psychiatry, seldom have these specific concerns I have, never find themselves forced to do anything, *because they rarely seek the medical treatment I need and therefore escape the trap mental-health sets out by simply staying away!*

⇾ People who experience transsexuality as "being different" or even "being special". Statements like "we're not going to assimilate to society, society is going to assimilate to us!"[1] are powerful. But it is dangerous to assume that such statements *even if made by a transsexual* universally reflect transsexuals. *Such proclamations are of a political nature,* however transsexuality is neither a political designation nor a personal choice. It is my opinion that even though many transsexuals have common experiences *no political or social inclination should be derived from it.*

⇾ Not far from these are people who think that because they're transwomen they actually are "the better women". The thinking is something like "because *they have chosen to be women freely* their identification is stronger than the one of biological women". This is detrimental in two ways. First: People in my position *do not choose to be who we are,* we would indeed much rather like to be just about anything else. Second: This attitude cements the view of certain feminist and lesbian activists that we are in fact males who are out to subvert the last female dominated spaces!

⇾ There are some efforts to facilitate our lives legally. This is commendable, only it is almost exclusively focused on *making the lifestyle more liveable,* such as obtaining documents which show a different gender than is on file. I agree that this is important to people who need this and I needed it also, but again only because I was forced into needing it! From my perspective this is a bit of cosmetics. While it helps to keep a rotten system liveable it also helps to not sink it. I don't want a legal change-of-name with the option to not see it publicised (it is still on public record for everybody to see, it just no longer get printed in the "Government Gazette"), I want a system where I don't have to file for a change-of-name because after surgery, after everything is corrected, *this legal change of half of my identity which remains on file forever only ever creates problems!* I agree that this may be appropriate for somebody who doesn't want surgery (and therefore in today's system will never get her legal gender changed), but for me it is not!

The problem is - again - that lifestyle-definition of Benjamin which makes the term 'transsexual' as inclusive as to let anybody who for any reason whatsoever at times crosses established social gender-lines join in. Some want hormonal treatment, others do not. Some have a problem with mental-health, others desperately need psychiatric support for some time or maybe for life. Some want gender-corrected documents, others don't want to bother with this

---

[1] Stacey Montgomery *quoted from www.bostonphoenix.com/archive/features/00/08/10/TRANSGENDER.html*

and just want a surgical sex-change. The goals of individual transsexuals are *vastly* different and so are the objectives of people who become activists. *Consequentially the individual solutions we are looking for are so extremely different that we end-up forming a group without any common interests!* Eventually *everybody makes their individual problem paramount,* everybody seeks *their own solutions just for their specific issues!* As the treatments individual transsexuals seek *are at times mutually exclusive* so are the proposed solutions - and this isn't just true for medical issues but for social and political one as well! Indeed the way we get set-up *the people who are most outspoken against some of my own interests end up being other transsexuals!* Transsexuals with different personal agendas and often enough I feel that these people have absolutely nothing in common with me!

It is, I suppose, an efficient way to undermine any and all of our efforts and to leave our concerns undressed. *Divide and conquer?* Or is it "divide and ignore"?

Often transsexuals have their greatest acceptance-problems with homosexual groups because with us, I mean, who can say? I am a woman. I live with a woman. I am legally same-sex married and when asked I say that I am lesbian. Only many a lesbian does feel more or less strongly misandristic, so it often doesn't go down well that *"I have been one of them",* if only by perception and legal designation. Nevertheless it is true that I have lived in male society, undiscovered and for quite a while and I understand that some women are sceptical. I understand, not because I find it's right, but because at times I have these same emotions also when I meet transsexuals or people who've had m/f gender-alignment. It isn't right but I better admit it, at times I make these very same mistakes too.

And then there's psychiatry. For them genital 'reassignment' is exclusively a treatment for "gender identity disorder". They explicitly describe, in such publications as the DSM, how this disorderly gender identity manifests. One of the descriptions reads: "Adult males who are sexually attracted towards females, both males and females, or neither sex usually report a history of erotic arousal associated with the thought or image of oneself as a woman (termed autogynephilia)"[1]. Unfortunately the psychiatrists do not tell us what they actually mean by this! Consider these two scenarios: (a) A person fantasizes "it would be nice to be a woman" and then gets a male orgasm from it. (b) A person gets a spontaneous erection and then feels "ouch! This is so darn wrong for a woman"! Both of theses statements describe "association of sexual arousal with the thought or image of oneself as a woman"! Now given that the term 'autogynephilia' is a Greek construct and approximately translates as "love of oneself as a woman" the terms *meaning* probably only includes people who qualify for (a), *however the term's definition is inclusive of both* and is therefore, *with the exception of people who do not have erotic arousal at all, guaranteed to be 100%-inclusive!* (Do I really have to remind them to read their Aristotle?[ARIS-C] *Once again*?).

Unfortunately this is so typical of psychiatry: They don't say what they probably mean. Or maybe they don't mean what they actually say? Or maybe they just can't express their

---

[1] *[DSM]: On Associated Features and Disorders, Gender Identity Disorder*

thoughts? (May I suggest some therapy?). Putting this statement as ambivalent as it is then gets large numbers of individuals to misidentify. If therapists subsequently publish such findings in the category 'transsexual' *without ever telling us how many participants of the study seek genital alignment and how many do not* **they make it look as if people who have had genital surgery typically had this one very motivation!** Of course the way they put this may describe *some cases* correctly but I hardly think that this is in any way representative. However stating their theories as ambiguous as they do allows them to draw the least flattering and most suspicious looking half-truth as a conclusion! I understand that the lesbian community becomes highly suspicious after "widely recognized experts" publish *these* findings!

I very much understand that gays and lesbians have a vested interest in coming together, have common places to go. There they find not only acceptance but also social and sexual contacts, *they find freedom and likeminded people.* I however can socialize just about anywhere I can find women, preferably likeminded women. *Women,* not transsexuals! I neither prefer nor seek-out other transgendered people. If they are, fine. If they're not, that's just as well. *This is because I do not identify transsexual but female instead.* My interests I find better represented by female groups than by transsexuals. But gays and lesbians do identify *gay* and *lesbian. They share common concerns and interests among themselves!*

Thanks to mental-health declaring our problem to be of a sexual nature we get thrown in. Because they say that we make "a sexual mistake", just as they claim gays and lesbians do! *LGBT,* the last letter in the quartet. Well, not quite, as some people have extended this further to LGBTTTQQ2S... (I hope I'm not forgetting anybody!). Some of these letters stand for sexual preferences, some for self-identifications, others for emotional or spiritual experiences; some can therefore be combined while others are mutually exclusive - honestly, this starts to get far too complicated for a simple woman like myself! So may I suggest WAYAYA instead? For "<u>W</u>e <u>A</u>ccept <u>Y</u>ou <u>A</u>s <u>Y</u>ou <u>A</u>re"? There would never have to be any new letters - guaranteed!

Yes, I understand that building communities of likeminded people, of people who have the same concerns is important and that it makes sense. However it appears that most of our common problems, well, of the people who do look for genital alignment, revolve around the availability of surgical treatment *which is withhold artificially.* So if I go to one of these meetings much of what I find is *a training-session on how I have to behave to get good marks at mental-health to obtain my permission for treatment!* True, in a mental set-up like the one we have this makes perfect sense: Social support or integration is besides the point in this system - we just help each other to get what we need! We have plenty of problems to deal with, legal ones, emotional ones, family, friends. There's really no need to create artificial ones - and then to give us room and maybe even funds *to establish support so we can solve these!*

But there's something else too, something even more revealing: This creation of a completely artificial community - *a community exclusively in existence to solve artificial prob-*

lems - **creates that very "transsexual community" psychiatry so happily then takes to define us by!** This, from my perspective, is nothing short of mental… I am a woman, not a transsexual! If I live 'transsexual' then I don't do this by choice but because I am pressured into it by mental-health. Because I need their permission *and because I have to know how to behave to obtain this permission!* And if then I build social structures with other people *who have the same* <u>*artificial*</u> *problem,* if we help each other to trick psychiatry into allowing us to get what we need, *they then take this for proof that we don't integrate into larger society but remain among ourselves,* that we "*seek out* transsexuals" just as homosexuals seek out homosexuals, *that* <u>*we*</u> *create this "transsexual subculture"!* Some psychiatrists even make this proof that we are "incapable to assimilate into normal society"! The next step is then to allege that we do this, "socialize exclusively among ourselves", *because we only want relationships among ourselves, personal or even sexual.* It isn't true, but they make it very, very effectively look as if it were…

B.20. CISEXUALS AND NORMAL PEOPLE

These days there are not few books out there who use the term 'cisexual'. Cisexual is an artificial creation that has come to be used first in internet trans-chat-rooms and then in wider circles in the last decade or so, its meaning is 'non-transsexual'.

The idea of defining a word for 'non-transsexual' is a bit in analogy to *heterosexual* for "non-homosexual". If one defines homosexuals as a distinct group, as *a self-identification* then it is easy to define the rest of the people - who are after all the majority - as *"the normal ones"*. This in turn, as there are now 'normals' and 'homosexuals', makes homosexuality look like *something "not normal"*. If something is *"not normal"* it is *abnormal* or *deviant*, isn't it? Of course homosexuality is neither deviant nor abnormal, it is one of many sexual orientations there are, not more and not less. Therefore having a word other than 'normal' or 'non-homosexual' to describe the majority and their identification simply makes sense, *it makes the designations at least less judgmental!*

I understand what the people who coined and use the transgender-equivalent to heterosexual, *'cisexual'*, are after and what they want to express. If I'm transsexual and most people are not, then the 'normals' are the 'non-transsexuals', *the ones without the label.* And me, I'm the abnormal one, the freak. I may even be in need of "corrective measures" to make me normal, 'non-transsexual' that is, *because not being normal is abnormal and sick,* isn't it?

So, they rename the 'non-transsexuals' 'cisexuals' - now we have transsexuals and cisexuals and presto: *There are no more 'normals' and 'abnormals'!* Now we can all be normal, Right? Well... Not quite...

From my perspective what these people do in many respects misses the point, it misses what I live, it ignores what I feel and it misrepresents what I need. It misses how I would like to be seen and it cements something that isn't true: *It implies that this label 'transsexual' is who I am - but this is wrong, because I am not transsexual!*

Because ultimately transsexuality is not an analogy to homosexuality, not for me and people like myself anyway. And in so many ways I believe that I can - again - trace the problem back to mental-health, how psychiatry sees us and how they treat us. *But more sadly I can trace the problem back to many a transsexual actually accepting this psychiatric view as being correct and true!*

The problem really starts with psychiatry seeing, as I have already mentioned, many divergent groups along one and the same Benjamin-doctrine as being "a little more or a little less transsexuals", but not recognizing that these people are in fact *very, very differ-*

ent from each other. We're all sexual perverts and we really all need the same: A psychiatrically prescribed liberated lifestyle! One treatment and one dogma fits all, and if we don't want it then it's forced onto us *for our own benefit!* But we aren't all the same, we don't all need or even want that lifestyle and *we all require different treatments!* **Because what we live (and what we do) is very individual and vastly different!**

To illustrate what I mean I would like to pick-out only two (or maybe three) groups of people who fall, by mental-health definition, under the umbrella-term 'transsexual'. There are many more but this isn't about preference but illustration.

One of these groups is at times referred to as *"no-op transsexuals".* These would be people who live female, may want or have various medical interventions such as hormonal therapy, facial, breast and other surgery and so on, however "no-op transsexuals" are people <u>who do not desire genital alignment.</u> (Please note: These are *individuals who genuinely do not desire genital surgery but wish to keep their male genitals,* usually fully functional). Many people within this group would argue that they like their male genitals just fine. They would likely use their genitals for either sexual activities, self gratification or other active use but at least have a positive relation to these.

The other group consists of *"pre-op transsexuals"* and *"post-op transsexuals".* These would be people *who do not want male genitals and either* <u>are waiting for genital surgery or have had it.</u> (Please note: Not everybody who has had genital reassignment would necessarily have to fall into the category "post-op" as there are in reality many reasons for genital surgery, the request of aligning physical to emotional self-experience is only one among these). A "pre-op" usually finds her genitals anything from disgusting to abnormal to strange to hurtful and typically lives by ignoring their presence and function, a "post-op" is usually very relived to have the female version instead of the male one. After surgery she may or may not engage in sexual activities.

To me it is self-evident that *these two groups of male to female transsexuals* <u>*are very different,*</u> that *they need to be treated differently* because their treatment needs (and identifications) are *so dramatically different. They are in fact so vastly different that the medical treatments I need and the treatment a "no-op transsexual" would likely require* <u>*may well be mutually exclusive!*</u> In the case of hormonal treatment my motivation for it is so I can experience myself emotionally in a way I find meaningful, *to get a female emotional life,* and if I get physical changes (i.e. female puberty and male sexual dysfunction) along with it *then I take this as an added bonus!* A no-op transsexual however would take hormones (if she[1] would want any at all) to induce physical changes, *to get a feminine appearance, but would typically not want any associated sexual changes* (i.e. erectile dysfunction to the point of no erections or orgasms at all) *and most likely only few of the associated emotional changes.* For individuals who desire HRT at all this would be achieved by balancing the hormone levels very carefully by avoiding to have female hormone levels or go anywhere near these.

---

[1] *For the benefit of readability I assume that no-op m-f transsexuals use the feminine pronoun. However this is not always correct, identifications as well as linguistic preferences vary by individual but most will prefer 'she'.*

Please note: These two (or three if you like to separate pre- and post-ops) groups, however divergent they may seem, *are only two examples of an entire spectrum of how people experience and live gender of whom* **mental-health says they are all the same!** In addition to the groups I have mentioned previously *there are* all the fetishistic groups, *there are* people who seek to find a gender-identity because they don't know who they are, *there are* people who play and experiment with sexuality and gender - *and countless others!*

The problem with which we are presented is that - in my case - *transsexuality is the result of an inconsistency between my emotional perception of my gender and the physical reality of it.* (This is why I need my physical gender to be surgically brought in line with my emotional experience of it, *because otherwise I cannot have an emotionally fulfilling or even understandable and functioning life).* However in the case of a "no-op transsexual" this is obviously not the case *because otherwise the person would not want to keep her male genitals* (and the functions and emotional and physical experience of these). The distinguishing element between these groups is apparently *how one experiences these male genitals:*

➤➤In the case of a "non-op transsexual" I have to assume *that the person makes <u>a conscious choice</u> to live visibly female while having male genitals* (the conscious choice being that she does not want surgery but keep her male genitals). This would mean that *"no-op transsexualism" is an <u>identification</u> of this person,* one which is distinctly different from either male or female, i.e. *"a female with male genitalia".* **This validates that a person can <u>identify transsexual</u> for life <u>instead of</u> identifying either male or female!** If 'transsexual' is *an identification* (such as homosexual) then the creation of the term 'cisexual' makes perfect sense, it makes sense in just the same way as the term 'heterosexual' for "non-homosexual" does.

➤➤My own case, formerly "pre-op-" and now "post-op transsexual" is very different. I identify female, not transsexual. **I experience transsexuality, male genitals and all their effects <u>as an illness</u>** which I would like cured by having that mistake corrected. *<u>I don't make a conscious choice,</u> I was simply born with this inconsistency.* **After corrective surgery <u>I am a cisexual woman myself!</u>**

Because we're *all* called 'transsexuals' (instead of being placed into whatever group we belong to) *the observation of individuals identifying transsexual instead of female is simply "deemed validated" for everybody!* And while I certainly don't want to sound repetitive I would nevertheless like to point-out that this problem, once again, arises from an invalid reverse conclusion: This time it is that one attribute observed in a few individuals of a group *cannot* be extrapolated to the entire group unless this entire group is based on (at least) this very attribute or a subcategory thereof (see Aristotle[ARIS-C]).

Only after the creation of the term 'cisexual' the problem *I* now face is that *in one single stroke <u>my own identification as a woman is now being denied!</u>* Because according to prevailing dogma *I will be designated "a post-op transsexual" <u>instead</u> for life!* **Because, just as**

during segregation under the doctrine "equal but separate", <u>*we now differentiate be-*</u><u>*tween "post-op transsexual women" and "cisexual woman", forever!*</u>

From my perspective **identifying female and being also designated anatomically female is at the very core of the definition what a woman is!** *Identifying (cisexual) female while being designated male because of anatomy is the definition of who I was* - and if somebody calls this 'transsexuality' then I'm fine with it, *but I would have preferred (and still do) a more exact term <u>to describe exclusively just this one condition</u>!*

I find it rather sad that of all people *transsexuals* come up *themselves* with the term *cisexual* and its definition. So ultimately we have brought this about onto ourselves! Because some of us feel that *"separate but equal" is the only way for them to get any life at all during their lifetime!*

In the end the one reasonable thing to do would be to simply accept that I'm a woman. This would leave all the other terms for other people to describe themselves as or identify by. However this would have to be done *as a differentiation in designation <u>by medicine</u> because as of now they officially assign the labels 'female' and 'male'.* But then, they could have accepted *this* right from the start - that is if they had ever listened to what so many of us say…

I understand that many readers may be critical of or even outraged by this passage. If so, the one thing I hope for is the understanding that these two completely contradictory views don't come from one being right and the other being wrong but that it comes from squeezing many mutually exclusive paths of life, many vastly different self-experiences, self-expressions and self-identifications into one single group.

Doing this isn't just over-simplistic, *in this case it is very, very destructive!* There isn't a 'right' and a 'wrong' way to live gender, all of them are *right*. However all these different people have vastly different needs. If they - and all the other people who end-up in this psychiatric wash-up - get treated the same *this very likely ends-up hurting most or even everybody who is involved in some way!* Well, maybe it doesn't hurt *the psychiatrists* who find themselves in this set-up equally badly as it does us, or maybe not *all* of them...

And just in case anybody would ever be tempted of accusing me to corner the term 'transsexual' and thus exclude everybody else? Well, I don't call myself a transsexual and I only ever have for the benefit of mental-health or at times to make people understand that I get thrown-in with this definition! As I have mentioned I would be more than happy to entertain the thought that *everybody else* is free to identify transsexual - *and get another designation myself.* If you read B.16. you'll find that I have no problem with being identified as a physically handicapped woman pre-op and simply as a woman post-op. I am most definitely not trying to tell anybody anywhere that they're not transsexuals, *what I am trying to say is that it is me who is not!*

A.11.   FOR THEY KNOW NOT WHAT THEY DO!

Finding a doctor who's actually willing to treat one of us isn't easy. But then again, I did choose the place where I live for this and I had a pretty good idea where to go - or better: Where *not* to go! Well, ok: I knew who to ask to tell me where to ask to get somewhere I could ask to see somebody…

So I eventually got directed to the health-centre where I would be looking for my treatment. Medical treatment that is. I was there to get an appointment, eventually first in the line-up, a rather full waiting-room behind me. Two secretaries organized the line-up and kept track of files, in the background were several more people handling files, a few nurses looking at notes. "Any preferences as to your doctor?". "Well… No, except that the physician should be open to providing hormonal treatment to transsexuals…". "You… WHAT???". I repeated a little louder: "I am transsexual and I would like *hormonal treatment*…!". The secretary turned around and shouted to the people who handled files in the background *"DOES ANYBODY KNOW WHO'S TAKING ON TRANSSEXUALS!!…?"*. An almost infinite number of eyes seemed to be turning towards her - and then towards me!... Do I have to mention that I was out of there just about as fast as I could after having gotten that appointment…

A few weeks later, there I was again, time for that "initial appointment" with my new GP. Sitting in that waiting-room, hoping. Being rather nervous. Nervous? Ok, they have yet to invent the word that would encompass all the emotions I had right there. I assumed he would know why I was there, after all I had asked for a trans-friendly GP and trans-treatment when I booked and I expected this request to be passed on. It's a "community care" group-practice, subdivision of a major hospital, right in the "gay district". They're there because otherwise many people would not get decent healthcare. Or any, I suppose. But one also gets the typical mix of people who see doctors: Families with small children, older people and everybody in between. And yes, transsexuals. They see more every year, which is why just about every major healthcare centre has seen us by now and a fair number doesn't mind to take us on anymore for general health-care even if they don't specialize in psychiatry themselves.

Finally it was my turn: "Come in! You don't mind if we have a med-student present, do you?". The doc was friendly, a good and positive first impression. While his med-student sat in his usual place he started with the customary questions about general health. She first wrote my particulars on a form, then started taking the procedural notes.

Well, it was a good idea to have a check-up, I hadn't had one in maybe 10 years. After 15 minutes or something he pronounced me generally alive and came to the point: "So why are you here today?". Well, either he genuinely didn't know (though I suspect he did) or he wasn't making this as easy as he could. Ok, I suppose this wasn't his job. So I said "well, I have a bit of a concern which should have been addressed 35 years ago or something ... I perceive myself female instead of male... This really does cause some issues at times so I would like to get this fixed with gender reassignment surgery". From my side that was it.

He? Well, he started to explain that they're *strictly* following dogma (he called it differently) for "sex-reassignment" and how important this is (though he skipped the part where he was supposed to explain why...). After some time I cut in saying that I know dogma well but that I may have some problems with these 'standards'. He asked for clarification and I said: "For one dogma requires me to either be full-time employed or -student or a full-time volunteer but I do childcare and as they are my own I am not exactly getting paid for it. So, I suppose by WTO-standards this would be called 'unemployed' which will never get me anywhere with *this* dogma - never mind that childcare is in all likelihood what about 90% of the woman on the planet do at some time in their lives, so if that's not female enough...". Well, this time I got interrupted. The physician asked his med-student: "What did you put in that field just there?". She: "Unemployed...". He: "Please change that, put something else there". "But what? HE *is* unemployed...". "Ok. First, let's put 'Eva' here, she'll have that changed anyway, no need to start off wrong. Check 'female' here. And change that one, she's right, she'll never get anywhere otherwise. And let's change that one too...". He now leaned over his student and started to change about everything she had written. After a few lines he turned to her and said: "Why don't you have a seat overthere for now and let me...". She looked at him, by now rather confused. His reply: "Ok, let me take it from here...". She just looked more puzzled. He, more insisting this time: "LATER!...".

Five minutes after that I was out, a couple of requisitions in my hands. We'll check you out medically to see if there are any potential problems for hormone replacement therapy and I'll need that psychiatric approval before you can start. We have in-house trans-support, contact them, they'll have some ideas as to where you could go. Come back in three weeks, by then we'll have all the lab-work in!

B.21. ONLY IN 4" HEELS AND A 14" SKIRT

There are women - 'biological' women - who refuse to dress feminine, women who don't wear a bra, women who cut their hair a half-inch or less, women who enlist in the military or work in heavy industry, women who distract themselves with extreme sports, women who lead countries and corporations, women who do virtually everything men do, and with very, very few exceptions they can do it just as well or better! And if you pressure me for an exception, well, I have yet to hear a female basso profondo (low bass) sing in *The Magic Flute*, but who knows, given the ever increasing number of women who get testosterone treatment I may yet have this pleasure...

It is obvious that today gender-roles aren't what they used to be. There are hardly limits to what we can achieve these days, given the right circumstances. Yes, it is no doubt in many areas more difficult for women, but then there are also areas where men have it more difficult, say in midwifery or as kindergarten teachers. But males do all this too - and so they should!

For some people this is a bit of a problem of a particular kind: What if somebody dresses like a race-car driver, goes with a bald head, teaches skydiving as a profession and spends her free time at the shooting-range? What if that person hates boobs and gets her exercise in the kickboxing-rink? Well, fine. Now what if that person is biologically male and says she is a woman and asks for genital-alignment? But really, she doesn't want to change *her lifestyle*, because she is just that kind of a girl?

From my perspective that's perfectly ok. She is the only person who feels who she is and for me that's that! Of course for psychiatry it's not...

According to dogma we need to demonstrate that we're "living female". But just how do we do this? Well, I suppose this all depends upon the views of a therapist or the general ideas a particular institution stands for?

The problem is that *if femaleness or femininity needs to be proven then the more 'proof' that's requested the more stereotypical one will have to be to qualify!* Well, presumably stereotypically female *from a male psychiatrist's point of view?*

There are two main problems with this approach: The first is that in our culture so many expressions that used to be gender-stereotypes *have been watered-down into use by everybody.* Things such as piercing (particularly ear), long hair, make-up and fragrances, wearing jewellery, dressing in pants and so forth. Personally I find it is a good thing if freedom of expression is taken more seriously, when people dare to show who they are, when showing one's identity becomes more acceptable and the means to self-expression become more accessible. However *this makes it more and more difficult for me to show how stereotypical a woman I am because by now there are so few exclusively female expressions left.* The second problem I have with this is that, *because of the lack of identifiable general cultural stereotypes, more physical ones are likely to be expected and these are often more sexually overt.* Eventually this, at some places, gets as far as people having to dress-up and present themselves *in a way nobody would in normal life...* Well, unless one wanted to advertise oneself for the sex-trade...

Now I don't know if these (almost exclusively male) psychiatrists just want to find out how desperate we are or if we should possibly consider ulterior motives on their parts but I really would like to keep my book friendly and not claim that any particular psychiatrist might be in the trans-business *because he's a lecher and his profession opens him an avenue to get what he seeks for free without any potential legal ramification whatsoever.* Because psychiatric and medical associations surely would never tolerate something like this?

Nevertheless truth is that dogma speaks at length about obtaining soft skin and a more feminine butt through hormonal treatment, it goes on about the effect on growing breasts and alike. Dogmatists make it a point that "no changes in the male voice can be expected from it", because a soft, high and sexy voice seems to be important. If everything fails they point-out a number of surgeries girl might want so girl can *look* the part. **Meanwhile they completely fail to mention any emotional impact of HRT whatsoever** *(except for a side-note on the loss of male sexual function)!* To me *this really exemplifies how superficial Dr. Benjamin and his successors see and interpret femininity as well as transsexuality!*

But if we talk about femininity it might be a good idea if we tried to find out *what a woman actually is* so we would know just what might be expected of us? Looking around we could, among many other contributions, find the following about what women truly are:

> *[...] That particularly in this time of transition and change we ought to keep in our minds what being a woman means and what duties women have.[...] We have not excluded women [from public life] because we despise them but because their value is of a different kind. Women have at all times been more than just sex-partners for men, they have been his work-partner too. Nobody would dream to remove women from professional life, work and generating family-income; however it must be said that there are things which belong to men [...] The general feminization of men has brought on a masculinization of women and this has lead to removing women from their traditional duties and has as such created a mere caricature of femininity [...] This needs to change and in spite of the danger of being called reactionary the first place for a woman is at home serving her family, giving birth [...], because women's duty is to raise our youth [...] But luckily women have started to understand that they can't win by gaining rights and giving-up duties. [...]*[1]

---

[1] *Excerpts from a speech Dr. O. Hamel and Dr. J. Goebbels gave on March 18, 1933 in Berlin on the occasion of the opening of the exhibit "The Woman", translated by the author*

Now there at least we know what's expected of us and where we belong! And if we don't like this (the above excerpt is, should you not have recognized it instantly, from a speech one Dr. Joseph Goebbels gave on March 18, 1933 in Berlin on the occasion of the opening of an exhibition titled *"The Woman"*) or just might have a medical problem and can't get pregnant, well, then there's always the sex-trade, isn't there? It's still a clearly female-dominated profession and if even Goebbels suggests that woman should not be removed "from their professional activities" that then must be ok! True, many a she-male appears to be getting her share of that business these days also but who's to look *that* close? Never mind I suppose showing-up at the therapist's in 4" heels, fishnets, a 14" skirt and a very low cut décolleté might just naturally add to the DDD-implants, the narrow waist thanks to liposuction and extracted ribs, extensive facial alterations and the surgically extended legs...

There you go, that's a decent picture of woman and femininity to adhere to, isn't it? True, it's misogynistic and abusive, but who cares, if that's what's being asked because it is approved by Dr. Goebbels? And more importantly by dogma and male psychiatrists or the institution one just happens to go to? Which now makes me realize how dismal a failure I myself must be at being a woman...

And yes, if this would have been the condition set *on my life* I would have complied and done this also. I would have taken this sexist abuse and exploitative degradation just as I did every other. I would have complied. I would have done as told, whatever would have been expected. I would have ruined my body by getting all these surgeries. I would have suffered months and years, maybe paid with a lifetime of pain for it. Because, honestly, this is the most female stereotype of them all: *"Do as told and be quiet"!* And *this one* most of us do to absolute perfection!

A.12. *Where Irreparable Harm Starts*

It was time to have the paperwork updated to reality. Id's, driver's license, passport, social insurance, health-card, everything. Of course it would have been helpful if there were *one place* to get this done all at once, co-ordinated and all at the same moment. It is, after all, somewhat inconvenient to have to file taxes with documents issued in various different names and genders… When the name stored in the province's database (that's where tax-returns have to be filed) and the data stored in the federal governments social-insurance records (that's what data they expect on that filing) is not the same this just tends to raise many red flags and requires numerous and cumbersome explaining…

As everybody who ever has had this problem knows: There is a particular order in which this needs to be done. Usually this comes with weeks to months of waiting between filing an application and actually holding each new document in hands. One office wants two supporting documents for a change to be accepted, another one wants three, and not everybody accepts the same…[1]

It all starts with a legal change-of-name which can - thankfully - be obtained with the old set of documents. This takes a few months during which I - unfortunately - have no idea what my name is, my *legal* name I mean, because of course one doesn't get notified as to *when* the change legally takes place until weeks afterwards when the paperwork and proof of change finally finds its way into the mailbox. True, I could have red the government gazette where all such changes are advertised to the population at large and in doing so I would have known this within 36 to 72 hours. But honestly, I was not in the mood of having to spend any more money to get proof of yet another human-rights abuse in writing. Yes, I do find it abusive if the government insists to publicize my change-of-name - along with a 'reason' for it, reading something like *"reason for change: Gender-identity disorder"!* I could just as well take out an ad in a daily to inform everybody of the fact that I am labelled crazy! I am absolutely certain that if the government would feel the need to publish some other medical condition (just to name an example: A list of all the people who suffer from erectile dysfunction) changes would be implemented very quickly! Treating transsexuals like this is, apparently, quite ok.

The next step would be to have everything else changed, right? After all what I get back from that legal change-of-name is an official government document indicating that my name has legally changed? So the naïve observer would expect that with this every

---

[1] *Even though I have changed everything expediently and usually within days of holding the necessary paperwork for the next step in my hands I have, as of 3 years after I have started this legal change, not every governmental document changed. I'm in fact still waiting…*

government office would gladly replace my existing documents with new ones? Of course this isn't actually true as *the government itself doesn't accept it's own document as proof of their own change* to, say, issue an updated driver's license! Neither would anybody else change anything: They all wanted at least an updated driver's license (or a passport) as "additional proof"!

This now wasn't exactly a case of absence of evidence, after all I had quite appropriate proof of that change, but in spite of this there was plenty of evidence of absence of any changed documents! In the end I suppose looking at it from a mental-health angle - given all the training I had in this field - helped to solve the problem... Or let's just say the problem got solved because I no longer expected things go make any sense whatsoever? Or maybe as some other people have, I too have after a while simply given up asking myself questions about how stupid and mental the world really is. [See quote on page 87]

My eventual progress? It all started with the insight that in today's world every girl needs a credit-card to get anywhere! Of course nobody was willing to issue me a card in my new (and current) name, after all I neither had a credit-record nor a bank-account (nor any legal way of proof of address for that matter) nor a driver's license showing this name. To get around that particular issue, just temporarily, I called VISA and ask them if they could issue me a "partner-card" to myself in my new name (keeping the main account, credit-score and all the references in my old name). The following telephone-conversation ensued after I had explained my problem: "Sorry, we can't issue you a second card in your name, we don't do this anymore, you know, new security guidelines after 9/11". "Well, it would be *on a different name*"... "Yes, then that's no problem! What name would you like on your new card?".

Honestly! If ever a terrorist hears of this he now knows that he should better use a name *different from his own* to obtain a cover-up credit-card! Of course the idea of not using his own name as a cover was likely obvious even before reading this, even to the more severely mentally challenged terrorist? Well, maybe not... Because if he still insists to have his own name on his cover-up card he can now, for reasons of national security, no longer obtain one! Ok, haven't I said just a few lines above that I should stop asking myself certain questions about making sense of reality and the sanity of certain people?

Anyway, with that new evidence in hands it was no longer a problem to have my bank-records changed. After all, I now was in possession of *"supporting evidence"*, so the bank could do as I asked. True, it was *the very same bank* and *their own credit-card department* who issued that new card (the original as well as the new partner-card), but then again, does life really have to make sense? And do I really have to point-out all of life's surprises just as I have promised to make an effort not to question reality anymore? After all, treating reality this real might just end-up being really bad for my real mental health? Right?

Whatever my mental health (or anybody elses who has ever had to deal in any way with such regulations for that matter), having my first corrected bank-statement in hands along with the official change-of-name certificate and the new credit-card it was now time to convince *the government itself* to take their turn at issuing new documents *of their own* to me...

B.22. BOOBY TRAPPED

Many transsexuals feel that they are being abused in the psychiatric system, either by their therapist directly or anonymously by the system, for the fact of being pressured into it for no good reason, the stigmatization, the extent or the duration of treatment or the influence this has on one's life. Concerns range from exploitation to harassment to blackmail, extortion, denial or delay of medical treatment or worse. But why don't we just do the obvious: Leave and see another psychiatrist? Yes, this would be the reasonable thing to do, only the trap is laid-out for us in a perfect way to prevent this!

As the issues which play into this are many I'd rather like to put these in a list and let you decide which one might be most significant. From my own perspective it is obvious that this would be different for every individual but it works or worked on virtually every one of us in some way. Including myself.

➤➤ People form a relationship to a therapist. This is normal, but because of what we do our connection is different, it goes a lot deeper than such connections usually go. After all, what we do isn't just a little self-finding or solving of a given problem, it is *living self-acceptance on the deepest level possible* - and the therapist gets accepted right along with it.

➤➤ Many are exploited in these offices, sometimes personally, sometimes even sexually, but every time emotionally and financially. Because we should not be there and we know it! True, some of us need support, but that should be very, very different. The way this works today is severely abusive. Abuse often makes victims helpless.

➤➤ The therapist holds the key to our medical treatment. Especially when therapy has already been going on for a long time we may even be told that surgery could be just around the corner. In this situation few people will consider change because the very next session of abuse could, conceivably, be the last one! Only some therapists seem to be promising this year after year after year...

➤➤ Changing a therapist is inherently painful because people will have to start at zero. To roll out a life which for all intents and purposes never was ours, *again*. This is painful, but the next therapist will inevitably insist on it.

➤➤ And who knows if the next psychiatrist will insist on re-starting the clock for all the waiting times *right at zero?* And if not, he most certainly will insist on having known the patient for at least that one year dogma prescribes or, if a miracle hap-

[At Medical Imaging, a female nurse] Sorry, I thought you were a woman... [Me] So did I but I was told otherwise! [We both laugh, but she gets a male nurse anyway...]

pens, the 3-6 months national professional standards require before any "expert opinion" can be given.

➤➤ For many of us the psychiatrist is also the person prescribing hormonal therapy. I strongly advise everybody to seek the help of a general practitioner for this and see a therapist only in addition. After all, psychiatrists are ill qualified to take care of medical issues such as general healthcare or even potential surgical complications (but - and I really don't want to look as if I'd repeated myself - often psychiatrists don't appear to have too much of a problem to declare themselves competent in something that's not their specialty). However more importantly this separation gives the therapist less power as *dumping him no longer will result in an almost certain interruption in prescriptions.* A new psychiatrist is after all not likely to prescribe hormones on a first visit.[1] He may also insist on changes in dosage, the type of estrogen prescribed or the method of administration, often this is simply the case because "his product of choice" is different from the one the patient has been using. This sometimes causes serious problems and even if not, adjusting often comes with a number of potentially very unpleasant side-effects.

➤➤ Often the slowest and most questionable therapy is provided by large, well established mental-health institutions. In many places these institutions are the only ones who are in a position to grant cost-coverage for their own services as well as possibly for surgery by either governmental, insurance or social agencies. Theoretically a patient has the option to see another (independent) psychiatrist, but this would typically mean *that she would have to pay for such psychiatric treatment herself* (and potentially her surgery). Given the amounts this costs many women just can't afford this.

➤➤ The options to find a therapist are greatly limited as few psychiatrists accept transsexuals. They may just claim to be fully booked or if one gets an appointment without mentioning the reason this often ends in a claim of 'incompetence' as this is the most professional excuse to dismiss a patient. Since treatment is straightforward and not difficult to understand at all I suspect that the real reasons might rather be found in a psychiatrist not accepting transsexuality as "a real condition" or genital surgery as a treatment, or that he doesn't accept dogmatic treatment (to which he would have to adhere to) and doesn't want anything to do with it. He may also just be transphobic. It happens...

➤➤ We at times suspect that there might be ulterior motifs why a therapist would accept transsexuals in the first place. True, it could be as simple as a profound wish to help other people - but that's highly unlikely as if this were truly the case then shouldn't

---

[1] *It is highly cynical that dogma allows doctors to prescribe HRT on a first (or early) visit with no psychiatric approval or mandated wait-times if the patient has taken these illegally, while at the same time this same dogma does not contain any previsions whatsoever to mandate, suggest or even allow for a simple continuation of an existing legal long-term treatment!*

it be expected that therapists give us access to treatment instead of denying it? A relatively benign ulterior motif could be their need to find patients to fill their schedule and honestly it doesn't get any better than writing bills for treatment everybody agrees doesn't work and therefore no positive results will ever be expected... And yes, this exists, I don't deny it. Unfortunately the reality is that our condition also *attracts* a very specific group of predominantly male therapists. *After all each therapist has to subscribe to an unethical dogma, has to impose and supervise sexist behaviour and sadistic timelines or he ends-up providing treatment in sharp contradiction to "commonly accepted professional standard".* Because we know this many will not change as they feel that the situation they're in is bad, but it might just be a lot worse somewhere else. The motto is: *"Better keep the devil you know..."*

▸▸ Women who start at large facilities, particularly institutions who treat people who are severely mentally ill or institutions who provide therapy to criminals, will likely be overwhelmed and intimidated by the sheer administrative and medical power such organizations wield. The very institutional weight they feel behind their treatment suggests that *this really is the only way of doing things* and that everything is set in stone anyway (many of these organizations use public or charitable funds to advertise just how unique and good they are). The women might be thinking that they get the best quality and most efficient treatment because, after all, they are being treated by the biggest, most powerful and best known institution in town!

▸▸ People generally fear the unpredictable. They know what they have, it might just be bad, but at least *it is predictably bad.* Change might well be worse and of course there's no going back.

▸▸ Continuation is valued highly by the system. So any change *first and foremost reflects badly on the patient.* If a patient then claims that *the change is due to a problem the therapist (or institution) caused* most feel that *they wouldn't be believed anyway.* Many of us are of the opinion that *doctors trust doctors far more than they trust patients (or even facts), never mind patients they deem mentally not quite competent*! We feel that if this were not the case we would most certainly not be treated the way we are!!!

▸▸ A new therapist may think that a patient who has changed once may just do so again! So any change is likely to lead to difficult questioning and potentially mistrust at a new place: It certainly might be interpreted as *"shopping around for the easiest alternative"* and this in turn is likely not interpreted very positively at all.

▸▸ If a subsequent therapist were to ask for a treatment-history or some kind of description of "treatment achievements" we would find ourselves in a position where we had to ask the previous therapist to write something about us and hope, in spite of having just dumped him, this to be objective! We don't exactly expect impartiality as the only things we ever get from this system is prejudice, dogma, misinterpretation, denial and ignorance. So *we instead expect to be punished for looking somewhere else by the worst possible interpretation of our efforts (and then some)!* Honestly, nobody believes it possible that our therapists hand out all the abuse and rake-in all the profits without understanding what they're doing…

So if changing a therapist still looks attractive after reading this, well, the situation must be horrendous! Therapists know this *and they are counting on it!* We're truly booby trapped: Every move will just hurt some more!

B.23. ONE GIANT LEAP!

There is one thing I find in dogma I agree with. Sort of. My change in public life (or as they like to refer to it: My 'transition') takes time. I don't know if it's a year or two or five or forever. But it does take time. The question is *for whom it may take this time?* For the transsexual? Or maybe for the therapist? Or for other medical professionals? For a partner, for children, family and friends, co-workers, others? This is of course if one actually intends to live publicly female, only today this isn't a matter of choice - well, not *our* choice anyway...

As from my perspective: Yes, going public, telling people, starting public life, being miserable at it at first... Yes, it does takes time. And if you ask me for a figure, my personal experience was a few weeks, maybe 3 months. True, this depends largely on how prepared an individual starts out and to some degree on one's physical looks, though society is a lot more forgiving about this than most of us would probably give credit.

I would certainly acknowledge that this was a very, very intense time of my life, but I would like to point out that the intensity was only partially because of the "public coming-out", to a much larger degree it was because I knew that I would be getting nowhere on my own *and that I had to do this while feeling physically completely wrong.*

I full well understand that changing one's social role and appearance in this way is a major adjustment. The question, as I pointed out, is: *For whom?* I certainly do not need to accept myself for who I am. I do this 'transition' **because I know who I am** and *because I have acknowledged this at least to a degree which makes me accept public humiliation, starting a life with a very uncertain future and accepting that I will have to submit to any and all decisions some stranger I have not even met would make!* I do this *because for me, this is a matter of life!* I know I can do it, I don't even think this is much of an issue. Be myself! Honestly, what's the big deal? Everybody does it. Or don't they? How sad it were if they wouldn't! But will I be allowed to make this a matter of life? Or will it be made into a matter of death instead?

So by the time I get there, when I knock on the doors of mental-health, there's *nothing* left to do except getting permission for medical treatment. I live 'myself' to their expectations, I suppose they refer to this as "the real life test". I apparently have very few practical problems and even fewer personal ones doing so and these "few problems" all had good and obvious reasons, such as not having a valid id, not one I could use anyway.

What now has to happen for any further progress? A psychiatrist will have to accept that I am who I say I am! *But how can I make anybody accept something like this?* Well,

[Chain-store, they don't take my credit-card. Manager] Do you have a driver's license? [I show him my temp. DL-without picture; He] Do you have another ID [Me] Certainly [I show my temp. health-card - there's no picture on that either]

I can't. Of course I can't! Accepting a person and taking her personal beliefs and her identification seriously *is* <u>*subjective*</u>. In fact this is about as subjective as things ever get! Either somebody is willing to see, to accept, to believe or to just take me by my word or he's not. In which case there's really nothing I can do!

I understand that people who have seen my before and after could interpret this as being rather dramatic. *From their perspective.* I mean *it's from living male to living female - overnight!* Only *from my perspective* <u>*this is expressing what a lifetime of accepting myself has shown me, not a single day!*</u> What I don't understand is that psychiatrists could not possibly give me some credit and accept that for me this isn't dramatic at all! **I just become a little more myself!**

For the therapist there's one more problem: *My self-finding doesn't happen in his office!* <u>*In fact it happens everywhere else except in his office!*</u> **Because that therapist's office** *is the one place where I am not allowed to be myself,* <u>**where I need to be somebody else!**</u> <u>**Because that therapist insists in providing therapy**</u> **to "my old self",** *the one I really never was!*

This change is a very small step for me, a minute increment in my life's journey. *Only for everybody else it looks like one giant leap!* <u>*Because it is that last infinitesimal increment that's needed so everybody else no longer has the luxury to ignore who I am!*</u> <u>*Because THIS forces THEM to start to question THEIR own views of me*</u> **- and maybe their views of just a little more than myself!**

Or to paraphrase history: ***That's one small step for a woman, one giant leap for everybody else...*** [Well, I was tempted, but in the end I thought that I had already offended plenty of people and therefore opted not to use *man*kind there...]

I indeed suspect that this is at the very core why so many well meaning people, including psychiatrists, have such a problem with what they call "our transition": **The experience is just so dramatically different for me than it is for people who observe!** There's no possibility of understanding there, there can only be acceptance and the insight that *for people like me this is possible, this is right, this is the only way and this is going to work just fine!*

It is, I suppose, the "emotional background" on which we live our lives which is so dramatically different. Mine comes from decades of having lived a life I accepted only because I was told to, not because I would have chosen it as an expression of myself. Decades of thinking about why this is, trying to make sense of it, feeling what would be right, meaningful, what would work - and being denied what I found time and time again. People who have never been transsexual, never lived life like this never understand this. *Because they never have to!*

So, in the end, what really takes a year or two or ten or whatever a psychiatrist dreams-up is not the time it takes *us* to be 'ready'. *We are born ready, just like every other woman anywhere in the world!* It is the time it takes *everybody else* - and "everybody else" has psychiatry stand in for their decision-making, to uphold society's expectations and their moral standards. Or maybe to stem the tide on something that is, well, not really acceptable?

It is not we who need to accept ourselves, it is society who needs to accept us! **Consequentially there is no meaning in this waiting and this treatment** *for us,* **there's only meaning in this** *for society around us!*

Our stigmatization at mental-health, being called crazy lunatics, our dogma, how we get treated, medically, legally, socially? **Whoever wants to find meaning in this** *from our perspective* **will never find any!** *Because this is solely designed to satisfy their needs!* This isn't staged to provide treatment to us at all. **It is there to limit our numbers, to select the ones most palatable to society, to condition us, to re-make us** *according to their expectations* **and to keep us quiet!** *To give as little treatment to as few of us as possible while still have as many of us as possible submit to this system and their control freely.*

In the end this is why we are stigmatized, ostracized, why our treatment-conditions are not of a medical but of a behavioural nature! *This is why the system so heavily favours hyperstereotypical individuals who are this to a level where they almost become socially unacceptable for it.* Because these are the ones most likely to disappear afterwards, never to be seen by society again, never to create any waves. Because these are the women who will integrate invisibly and disappear if they can, live in the shadows if they can't. *This is why the system so heavily favours people with co-morbid mental conditions* because these are the ones who most likely are either incapable to voice an opinion or if they do are most likely to be ignored. *And this is the reason why everybody needs to be declared mental for needing genital alignment: Because it is the perfect set-up to discredit myself (or anybody else who has had or needs this surgery) should I, after years of such mental treatment, accidentally still be capable to utter a coherent sentence never mind write an entire book about it!*

Because ultimately when the real decisions need to be made they're not ready to accept us for who we are. Not *really!* Because accepting us would mean *that they would have to re-evaluate who they are! What their society is. What they do to each other and to themselves. They would have to change their own beliefs to accommodate our lives. But even worse: They would find that they would need to change their own beliefs to accommodate their own true lives! And this they do not accept!* So they let us rot instead. If we die waiting, well, all the better: One less transsexual to deal with! And if we kill ourselves, maybe because of how we get treated by that very system, well, even better! Not only one less transsexual to deal with *but one more proof that we truly are the crazy lunatics we are said to be!*

If anything brings out *just how far apart dogma and our reality are,* **this would be it!** There can never be mutual understanding. *The one thing there could conceivably be is **acceptance.*** But this would be one small step *they* would have to take!

A.13. MAKING MYSELF TRANSSEXUAL

Why show up as a male at mental-health if that's not what they want to see? First impressions count - even (or in particular) at mental-health! So it was time to show some obvious, visible, pro-active compliance... *Before* I went there. Before I even knew where to go...

Making myself a textbook transsexual wasn't actually difficult, just add modest cross-dressing behaviour to who I was. Well, *they* call this 'transvestitism' only I was not a transvestite... But then again, nobody cares about who I am anyway. After all, we're talking mental-health here: They insisted to see me as a male in drag, see me as a sexual pervert and as a fetishist. All that counts is preconception, appearance and sex. Sorry, I'll rephrase this: All that counts is a letter with two signatures!

As to that other part? Being mental? Dogma states that I would have to show "significant improvement to my mental health *thanks to mental treatment*" to be allowed genital surgery. Well, I suppose by now I was just a little too mature to play along with that one. Either they'd notice that I was not mental and could not improve my mental health by means of their efforts. Or... But could we just skip that part here and keep this book positive? Somehow?

I still did think that to challenge the system by even that much would be quite daring, after all even this much was nothing less than not just questioning but completely ridiculing one of the core-principles of dogma. So I thought it best to at least be compliant and play along with the rest. Ok, *pretend* compliance and *look* compliant that is. Actually believing the crap, well, that's another matter...

I had done "female living" before and as mentioned I had spent some time to have "my environment" prepared for this. However it is vastly different to do this "for my own benefit" just because I like doing it and because I find it reflects myself and allows people to correctly identify myself than it is doing this for the purpose of having a life-and-death decision made. I also don't do too many of the stereotypes that go along with "looking female as to mental-health standards": I use lipstick only on rare occasions, usually abstain from make-up, rarely show any leg, don't do high-heels or nylons. I neither think DD-breast-implants are in any way called for nor colour my nails or use artificial ones for that matter. I'm just a woman. And while I am definitely not butch my job is to do a household and raise children, I dress and look appropriately - for that job. If that's good enough, fine. If not, well...

The one thing I admit to is a liberal use of cover-up for that male facial hair that was just not becoming to a woman. Over the next couple of months with the advancement of hair-removal all I did was to steadily drop the make-up until I remained "reasonably passing", without any.

I am willing to dress as I find expresses my personal self, as I would do every day, *but I am not willing to dress-up for mental treatment,* for a therapist! I also wasn't in any way going to accept treatment to be sexual or sexualized, but this I expected to be nicely taken care of by asking for a female counsellor - if they would have one. Some problems just seem to be - statistically - far less likely with women than they are with men. True, this too is a sexist stereotype... But then again, the prisons aren't exactly full of female rapists, female child- and spousal-abusers, female voyeurs and female sociopaths. Yes, these do exist, but there's one stereotype that seems to be very nicely supported by the numbers...

I must admit, I was quite a bit concerned at this point. The time where I could have signifi-cantly lived-up to the expectations of dogma had long since passed and I found myself in a position where I complied at best marginally.

Personally I take it as a sign of a good state of my mental health that I do not comply to absurd expectations of an abusive system. That I am and that I remain who I am, that I am not willing to change my personality, to compromise myself for profit. From my perspective this reflects emotional maturity, is an expression of achieved self-finding and stability in personal-ity. Of course from the system's point of view it might just as well be interpreted as rebel-liousness or non-compliance. Well, as so many things in life this too can be interpreted in a very negative way if certain people absolutely insist...

At this point I felt it more clearly than I ever had before: All the waiting hadn't changed the fact that in the end I would force the person I would be seeing into a choice between dogma and my life. Because ultimately the two had always been and remained mutually exclusive!

Somehow this reminded me of the old-style westerns: In the end the stage would inevita-bly be set for the great showdown between good and evil. Except that I would be going un-armed...

B.24. A MATTER OF CONVENIENCE

There are, or were, many obscure mental diseases, homosexuality being a prime example. Even today there are psychiatrists who proclaim that homosexuality was only removed from the catalogue *"for political correctness"*, implying that homosexuality really is a mental disorder in the medical sense but that this isn't openly admitted anymore because of the bad P/R this causes. However this may be, homosexuality is clearly an expression of the personality of some people, as is transsexuality. Now it is apparently difficult bordering the impossible to get homosexuals to come in for demeaning treatment merely by inviting them, after all most of them most shockingly don't seem to think they're in need of mental treatment because of it at all... Which reminds me of many transsexuals who seem to be thinking along the same line! As another example some ultra-hard-line psychiatrists also consider any and all religious beliefs and practices to be aberrations of the mind. Obviously the followers of religious faiths would neither consider their spirituality nor their practices to be psycho-pathologies...

Homosexuals who did ended up in court because of their sexual orientation tended to be individuals who were either denounced, found to frequent "homosexual establishments" or were deemed homosexual by circumstantial evidence. The people who were subsequently forced into mental-health for being homosexual were by and large not very compliant, many continued to insist that they were not crazy at all in spite of what the psychiatrists claimed...

With us, that's different. Not only does mental-health not have to look for us, *we seem to be knocking on their doors almost in hordes these days,* we are by and large also amazingly compliant and seem to accept just about every therapist's expectation of who we are to be! Every research project fills up quickly with 'volunteers' and the patients appear to be only too eager to behave exactly in the way a researcher would want us to! We're compliant to a degree which is unheard of, make even the sickest psychiatric experiment, the most absurd theory an instant success, we make whatever they want easily provable! Just what else could any researcher in behavioural science ever wish for?

Transsexuals are for example asked to give their support to theories such as: *"Transsexuals are actually male super-transvestites who want to get a female body because just dressing-up kinky isn't good enough!"* or *"the best life has to offer is to experience oneself in a female body and then get a male sexual kick out of masturbating to it!"*. Sexologists have no problem to find volunteers who comply, say this is true, this is exactly who they are! *In return the participants get their permission to go to genital surgery, a treat-*

ment which will make precisely such sexual self-expressions and -experiences impossible!

In my opinion these patients are either supported by such psychiatrists to make the mistake of a lifetime - or they lie to get their permission to have what they full well know to be the real problem solved, in spite of this diametrically contradicting the statement they support for getting this permission signed!

By ignoring such blatant coercion in their 'subjects' researchers who do the above either create useless pseudo-research or they send their patients to a treatment which they should know with only minimal insight to be detrimental to their 'subjects' if what their patients state in their research were actually true! *Either way, what these 'scientists' do isn't research, but whatever this is, it is unethical!*

Dogma guarantees social scientists loads of willing volunteers to conduct their research, just as soon as these scientists are willing to write our letters in return. There's just one catch, if it is one: In any case, even if the research is sound, we won't be objective as our goal isn't to provide a psychiatrist with unbiased research but to get him to sign our permission-form, *which for some reason appears to be far more likely when we don't upset the person who is supposed to sign it...* Interestingly in many areas of psychiatry this does not seem to be of any concern whatsoever, *otherwise 'subjects' who are under the personal discretionary (or arbitrary) control of a researcher or depend on his decisions for their medical treatment in such a way would, as a matter of principle, not be allowed in the pool of test-subjects. Researchers in this field should be asked to submit proof, as a routine requirement of each research project or paper, that the 'subjects' were indeed free of such or similar coercion.*[1]

Yes, it is true, **recruiting us for this kind of research would be impossible if we would not depend upon the psychiatrist's signature for our treatment!** *After all it is to be suspected that they invite us to take part in their research precisely because nobody else 'volunteers' for it (or because they know that no other volunteers were to secure the desired result of their research?).* **This in turn sabotages any and all meaningful science as well as any mental-treatment. Not only in the areas where we're only 'subjects' but also and in particular in research into transsexuality itself!**

This isn't about treatment *for us.* For these psychiatrists *this is all about their own benefit! It is about recruiting obedient subjects from a virtually unlimited pool whenever they need any!* **Because they know exactly that we, as everybody else, will act in our self-interest when it comes down to self-preservation.** *And dogma guarantees that while in treatment with these people their self-interests become ours!*

---

[1] *You might think that this isn't possible because surely reputable scientific journals would check before allowing a scientific paper to be published? Well, yes, they do check or have the clinician in question file some proof that no data has been fabricated. But this proof only extends to financial compensation or other forms of coercion, it does in no way include our letters to allow us to go to surgery. This is because (a) this process is absolutely exceptional and not known anywhere else in medicine, (b) the editors of scientific publications may not be aware of our situation, (c) the 'letter' isn't officially seen as "a permit" but either as "an expertise" or "a referral", both of which occur regularly during normal medical treatment. Indeed I'm not aware of any requirement by any scientific journal even for simple disclosure of the mere fact that 'subjects' are (or are not) awaiting permission for some form of gender-alignment (or other not freely available procedure, should this exist).*

Apparently such social scientists either chooses to ignore these facts or they are for some reason unaware of this. Be this as it may, we're outstanding research-subjects! Thanks to our help even the most absurd, demeaning, de-humanizing, sick and ignorant experiment finds volunteers and even the most perverted research can instantly be proven to be correct! We are convenient, we are compliant, we are available *and we are completely reliable!* We are even willing to call the privilege to participate 'therapy' and pay for it! Honestly, this is hard to beat, isn't it?

A.14. *You Must Be Mental - In A Good Way I Mean!*

So I called trans-support. The nurse who picked-up the phone was friendly, had a very positive attitude. She told me that they had a few ideas where I could go. I had a few ideas where I most definitely did not want to go... The positive surprise: She seemed to have about the same ideas I had as to where I should *not* go! And the rest? To be honest in spite of much research I had not found a mental-health facility I found attractive or even acceptable. So I eventually thought of this rather like a political election: *Pick the candidate I dislike the least...*

In spite of all my reservations I called. Community LGB-counselling, they didn't sport a 'T' as of yet in their name. Eventually I got to speak to somebody who did co-ordination. "Why are you looking for a counsellor?". "I have been advised by my GP to call you ...". "Ok, but what sort of problem is your physician sending you to us for?". "Well, I don't think there is one, except that my GP feels he can't provide medical treatment if nobody from mental-health signs off on it...". "Could you possibly be a bit more specific?". "Of course: They have that psychiatric dogma (ok, I did call it differently) they're following which requires them to have the nod from psychiatry before I can get medical treatment...". "But why would they refuse medical treatment to you - that's what they're there for!". "I agree, but the psychiatrists who have written that thing see this differently..."...

Now please imagine the next 10 minutes of the conversation to continue along the same line of arguments for yourself. Eventually he agreed to give me an appointment with one of their counsellors. Probably he either thought that I was a really disturbed woman or that my doctor must be. Disturbed. Not a woman. I still had some hope that there actually was a difference. Well, between being disturbed and being a woman that is...

Back to that phone-call: "I still don't really know what you want...". "Well, to get medical treatment...". "Yes, I understand this now, but why don't they just give it to you?". "I'm really sorry, but it is not me making that decision, I only do as told...". "By now I quite understand that you don't need counselling and I suppose you find this is nothing but a painful waste of your time...". "I would probably have put that a little differently, but yes, I agree". "Try not to be *that* direct with your counsellor at your first meeting, will you?"

B.25. WHEN DOGMA GETS PEOPLE KILLED

Unfortunately it is one of the realities psychiatry forces onto us: Sexual, physical, emotional exploitation *because of who we are.* This is a very sad result of what is dogmatically done to us, nevertheless it is real and it has turned deadly many times. Some of the cases have been highly publicized, there are even movies that have been made after such horrific stories of abuse and exploitation[1].

The simple fact is that being forced to publicly live a woman's life with male sex-parts (or the other way round for that matter) is not just exploitative, *for some people it is downright dangerous!* People become targets and are attacked by sex-offenders *precisely because of the combination of being a possibly very attractive female with male genitals.* Some people (well, males) just seem to be attracted to this combination, sexually or otherwise. While most of the people who find themselves attracted to a transsexual who is forced to live pre-op she-male will behave, just as everywhere there are some who do not, or who do not in every situation. Transsexuals get exploited, sexually or otherwise *because of this,* some of us get threatened, some get attacked, hurt, raped, killed.

If then such a case ever comes to trial the perpetrators often argue *that they're really the victims,* that they have killed a transsexual *because they were so upset over what they found after they had ripped the clothes off their victims!* Sadly this often works, perpetrators get lower sentences or get off completely. Courts have accepted such absurd propositions as *a pre-op transsexual cannot be raped because she is not a woman - legally!* **But far more often criminals aren't charged at all because of fear by the victim for how she would be treated by officials or the legal system** *or for fear of being publicly exposed as a transsexual during the trial!*

I could argue that this too is the fault of psychiatry and psychiatric dogma *because I believe that many of these cases would not have happened as they did if the women would have been allowed to have their surgery in a timely manner.* After surgery we don't appear to be nearly as interesting a target to most perpetrators! Well, we don't seem to have that "special she-male appeal" anymore... After surgery we are *legally female* and therefore it is *more likely* (but by no means certain) that a rape is also officially treated as such, *that a perpetrator has to expect at least <u>some</u> consequences as a result of his actions,* he can no longer expect to get away by claiming he was "startled by what he found and thus had no other option but to kill". But he is still likely to argue that we're

---

[1] *For example:* Boys Don't Cry *as a feature or* The Brandon Teena Story *as a documentary focussing on the same tragic story*

not really women, just fakes, and therefore forced sexual intercourse isn't rape *according to the terms of the law.* And still, even this at times gets accepted by courts!

I could argue all this and maybe I should. *But there are also people who want a life living visibly female while being sexually male.* These people deserve protection too, protection from perpetrators and legal protection if anything should happen. This isn't a predominantly psychiatric issue, although psychiatric dogma extends the problem significantly, in many cases only ever creates it. This is in fact much more a social issue. But there too psychiatry plays an important role, just a different one: As long as they paint us mentally ill it is very easy for a perpetrator to get away with claiming *that we behaved inappropriately and thus brought everything onto ourselves!* After all, *raping or murdering somebody is normal*, at least as seen by psychiatry! If it were not I suppose murdering or raping would be seen as "a substantial impairment of a person's cognitive, emotional or behavioural functioning" and thus could be found as a pathology in the DSM, but neither one is listed there! On the other hand being a transsexual is mental. *Always!* This does put us into a considerable disadvantage: Inappropriate behaviour, misinterpretation and uncontrolled actions are, after all, *expected from mental people but not from normal ones!*

But then again I could just as well scratch the term 'transsexual' and speak of women in general: How many times has a rapist, stalker or murderer argued that "she enticed him because of how she behaved or dressed"? Personally I find the very argument, if it is made, proof of a mental condition! If "loosing behavioural control" in such a destructive way *because of simply seeing somebody* isn't "a substantial impairment of behavioural functioning", then whatever is? It is sad that neither society nor psychiatry seems to recognize this - and even worse that some psychiatrists lend their hands *to defend* such perpetrators by giving expert-evidence that rapists really may be innocent because "they can't help it"!

If a smart businessman is murdered in his $500,000 sports-car, wearing an Italian designer-suit, shoes and a briefcase that set normal people back 3 months of salary society takes very unkindly to such an act. If subsequently the reasoning the perpetrator offers is *that "the display of riches by the victim enticed him to kill"* then the crime *is seen as much worse, it will likely be labelled 'terrorism'.* If on the other hand the very same argument is used in the rape of a woman, the perpetrator claims that *"the way she looked enticed him to rape her",* then this doesn't make the crime worse, this doesn't merit a designation of terrorism, *this makes such crimes excusable!*

Now some things our society does, accepts, even promotes; some things psychiatry accepts or chooses to ignore *or even defends* (for whatever reason) feel downright sick. And honestly, I don't think that this reaction is either mental or has anything to do with me having been transsexual or a victim of psychiatric abuse...

A.15. MY LIFE IN YOUR HANDS!

[Medical professional] I send you to counselling to get to know you better. [Me] But this way my counsellor gets to know me, not you. If you want to get to know me I'd spend some time with you! [He] That's not how this is done! JUST GO!

Hallo, I've got an appointment for counselling… Ok, they let me wait a while, fill out some forms. Name (sorry, don't know… have applied for a legal change, have not heard anything so far and therefore don't know if the old one or the new one is currently valid to sign a contract, so which one would you like?); Gender (I draw a new box besides 'male' and 'female', label it "transsexual female" and check it); Mental-health history (sorry, don't have any); Income (can I deduct my uncovered medical expenses here and if so do they want negative numbers or should I just put 'zero' in?). There was more, some 6 pages, but these didn't make more sense than the first…

Then my counsellor showed up. I quickly found out that not only did she find it "rather unclear" as to why I was there but she also did not have more than a superficial understanding of transsexuality. But she was ready and willing to learn. I half expected something like this, after all what I had signed up for was LGB-counselling and it appeared that I was the one to add some 'T' to that line-up.

As it so happened I just had a copy of our dogma at hand, I gave it to her as an introduction to what was expected of me. My idea behind it was rather that if she already knew it then I couldn't break anything by giving it to her and if she didn't then, well, she'd have to know why I was there anyway.

Apart from that there was a first mutual introduction, the obvious range of questions. I suppose she found out in no time at all that I had not much of a problem to go deep quickly, to emotionally participate and that I didn't need the "keep talking"-reminder…

She was a volunteer-counsellor, highly intellectual, didn't need things explained twice, connected the dots herself and was really interested. She generally asked the right questions but remained in some ways predictable, though I was never quite certain if this was on purpose. And yes, she did note the problems dogma caused rather instantly…

This lasted about the usual 45 minutes, then "see you next week". I had a very positive first impression, but…

B.26. LOVE, PAIN AND COMPLIANCE

So we are in this therapist's office. We pretty much know what he expects and we depend on him to sign us off so we can get our lives. Well, *any* life worth speaking of really. Dogma doesn't leave any room for interpretation, it is a psychiatrist who makes the decision! For the people in the system right now there is no way to either have that changed or go somewhere else - not in the real world anyway.

We either are "living female" as to the definition of psychiatry already (whatever that means, nobody really knows) or this will come our way at some time during 'therapy' - whatever therapy, *it doesn't matter! Just therapy! Any kind will do! As long as it is with a psychiatrist!* Just as long as we end-up paying the bill! True, saying that it all comes down to who writes the bill and who pays it is very cynical but hi!, given these kinds of requirements how could one not be?

What we do in these offices is seeking the completion to a process that has, in all likelihood, started years ago. That has lead us to finding and accepting ourselves deeply enough that we accept to put the decision of our lives into the hands of some total stranger, submit to an arbitrary process of humiliation and degradation and potentially other forms of abuse, *because we understand: Today nobody is willing to offer us a meaningful alternative to either death or accepting abuse as a condition to obtaining treatment so we can live.*

The above is particularly true for people who only ever seek the assistance of a therapist while already "living full time" to psychiatric expectations, *having dealt with all the emotional and social problems of these changes <u>themselves successfully</u>.* People who maybe have done all this a long time ago. It may well be different for patients who seek assistance *because they have difficulties accepting their identity, their lives,* or maybe are looking for support in emotionally difficult issues such as coming-out. But this is different and I suspect that a person who is asking a therapist "I really don't understand who I am, please help me!" would not at the same time be asking "and by the way I think surgical genital reassignment tomorrow would be a good idea" (and in any case she would do so in a therapist's office, *she would not need to be forced into it!*). People who knock on the door of the psychiatrist "fully transitioned" exist, there are in fact quite a few and many more would choose to do just that if they had the option. *I indeed expect it would be the large majority* if artificial oppression, pain and abuse were to end. But no, if this would end we would not go into these offices at all, would not be counted by psychiatry and would never appear in any of their official statistics!

[Pharmacist] Your insurance card doesn't work, it comes back 'invalid relationship to cardholder' [Me] Try sex male' [She] Why? [Me] Just try it, please [She, tries it, the claim goes through] It worked!!! But you should get that changed...

One of the difficult things to understand is that by accepting this, by entering that office, I, as hundreds of thousands of other human-beings before me, accept that I am officially seen as being "of lesser value" *because I officially acknowledge my incompetence to decide about my entire self. To get treatment we are forced to accept that there are parts of our bodies, parts of ourselves which do no longer belong to us, because as of that moment we submit to somebody elses completely arbitrary absolute power of decision as to who we are, <u>how our bodies look and function</u>, how our lives will unfold in either one of two ways* which could not possibly be more dramatically different.

Now I don't know what your opinion of this is, from my point of view *I am being made a slave if my body doesn't belong to me anymore, if I can no longer decide over it freely!* If somebody else gets to tell me what I can and what I can't do with it, how I can and can't live, *how I'm allowed to think of myself and how not!* Of course it doesn't matter how much of my body that other person gets to have such absurd absolute control over because no matter which part and how small, *it is still a part of me.* Wherever that part is, the rest of me will be also. I mean that's the problem? If I could just drop it I would have done so decades ago…

True, I may have been a slave before because even then I wasn't allowed to make that decision as to how my body should function. But at this moment the system does more: *It makes me choose my owner! Because only when I have a master that master can, at his entirely independent and completely arbitrary discretion, set me free, keep me, let me suffer or die.* He can put any and all conditions onto me, he can ask me to do whatever he chooses to (including pressuring me into self-mutilation by undergoing other surgical alterations of my body I might not have wanted myself or by forcing me to take medications I might not have chosen to take myself) he can further abuse me in any way he pleases, emotionally, socially, physically, sexually; for his personal benefit or that of others, for profit or perversion. <u>*Because as I am a slave there will never be any consequences to this person whatsoever,*</u> *legal, professional or other.* No matter what this person chooses to do with me or to me.

By entering this office and accepting the conditions they have set-out I waive any and all recourse I might have if anything which is not in my best interest would happen. Because there is one thing dogma is (deliberately?) quiet about: If I get abused by that psychiatrist, if he extorts me, exploits me, hurts me in any way, demeans me, treats me disrespectfully, insists in meaningless compliance, makes me the object of some sick sexual or pornographic exploitation, uses me as a tool to extort the healthcare-system or an insurance company or simply hurts me by delaying or denying my medical treatment *I cannot remedy this through the legal system. Because dogma clearly states that, <u>under any circumstance</u> (even if a court of law would accept that I have been mistreated and abused during my psychiatric care[1]) <u>I would not obtain the right to go to surgery</u> on the grounds that further forced psy-*

---

[1] *Never mind that this would be very, very difficult to prove in any case because it would likely require me to find yet another psychiatrist to 'prove' this in court (and one who would actually be willing to contradict a colleague publicly at that), I would likely have to pay for that "expert therapist" service out of pocket and I would undoubtedly be subjected to even more pseudo-therapy to enable this therapist to professionally arrive at a conclusion of abuse!*

chiatric care would now not just be unethical but surely could no longer in any way be seen as legally or morally justified. Dogma states clearly that the abuser needs to sign me off on it, *dogma states <u>that there are no exceptions at all, ever!</u>* So if I would sue I could win my case. But I would also loose my life doing this. Not because this would take too much time but *because in the end what I could win would be that I had to start all over again!* Starting all over again at ground zero with a new psychiatrist, this time in the full knowledge that a court of law has agreed that I should not be there? Who could possibly tolerate this? And who could live long enough to endure this? Have the resources to pay for it all? And even if - who would be sane afterwards?

We have officially abolished slavery some time ago. In the meantime we have granted, at least legally, equal rights to women, handicapped people, social and ethnic minorities, homosexuals and so on. *We have extended these rights to all these groups <u>because it is the right thing to do</u>.* There should be no exceptions allowing any discrimination, but there still are. One is discriminating against transsexuals during and after treatment. I was abused by being enslaved and I don't think that withholding any and all of my rights is ok on the grounds that I am not just handicapped, just homosexual, just a woman and just a member of a social minority but a handicapped homosexual woman who belongs to a social minority!

It doesn't matter if the persons who decide to do this do it in good or bad faith, *they still do it!* Even if they do it thinking that this is the only way to give us our lives they still serve that system, they still accept enslaving me for the purpose of exploitation. Even if they don't play out their absurd absolute power to the full extent of what they could. Even if they take little or no personal advantage from it. *Because what other purpose than making abuse acceptable could there ever be to organized slavery?*

As to my own treatment: I could say that I had the great luck to find the right people? Or maybe I helped a little with that 'luck'? Anyway, I never tested how they would react if I'd cut anything material of dogma short. I suppose I am far too compliant for trying such things anyway, although I shaved the corners as close as I could. If dogma says "a minimum of one year" then this means 365 days to me (I could say that I went through great pains to make it a non-leap-year because surely if the calendar calls for a leap-day then an extra 24 hours of suffering is warranted, even needed in the interest of the mental health of the patient, isn't it?). True, in the end it was 367 days, but then again I suppose I can't complain if a surgeon doesn't work on week-ends, can I? So I ended-up self-imposing dogma to the bone and in return nobody ever cared!

But even if I am not physically or sexually abused I am still emotionally abused *because my medical treatment is given on the condition of behavioural modification!* It doesn't matter if these changes are explicitly requested or if I self-impose these because I have to assume that they are implicitly expected anyway. In this context of absolute power the simple reference to these changes makes them expected! Required in fact! Because if they weren't, then nobody would care, nobody would feel the need to document, to ask or to control! *The very* *fact that a certain dress code ("dressing female") and social behaviour <u>are preconditions to</u> <u>obtaining healthcare</u> and the fact that I would be left to rot as punishment if I were not compliant is abusive! It doesn't matter if what is being asked happens to agree with me - because this too should not be expected never mind set as a condition!*

The fact that this system works without any possible recourse on my part, without any safeguard to protect my emotional, physical and social, even financial integrity, without any kind of external supervision or legal protection is abusive in that it is unprofessional, arbitrary, unethical and, for all intents and purposes, illegal.

Apart from a single person involved nobody ever let me know how this felt *to them* and what *they themselves* thought while doing all this. This is sad because such acknowledgement would - unlike all the useless and painful psychotherapy - actually have helped me!

A.16. *Can You Be A Woman Now?*

This evening, after that first counselling session, our then six-year old asked me "can you be a woman now?". But of course I had to tell him that this would take a little longer, quietly thinking *maybe a couple of years...* His reply, rather unbelieving: "But doesn't she see that you're a woman?"...

Over time the one problem that most clearly manifested itself was that, given the conditions in dogma, neither I nor anybody from my immediate family (nor anybody else for that matter) did know anything as to the progress of that pseudo-treatment. There were no clear expectations, no goals to be achieved, nobody ever set any expectations at all and no noticeable progress could ever be made! I understood well enough that nobody had a problem with me, well, except that I may have been a major inconvenience by just being there: Everybody I had ever seen unofficially agreed to what I needed, nobody could give it to me! The question was: *Would this ever change?* What would I have to do? Did they even know? And how long would it take until they would know? Or make the decision that I merit continued existence anyway?

Certainly I wanted to go on with my treatment. Honestly, I wanted to go on *with my life* and I didn't exactly hide this, but nobody wanted to be found in a position to give me a perspectives on this, my life, or rather on my treatment. Maybe because that would have meant to make some sort of a commitment?

Having no idea if this waiting for treatment would take months, years, decades, *if I would ever get anywhere* was one of the most difficult aspects to deal with. It was even more difficult on my partner and maybe the children, after all I had a few decades of training in digesting that "getting nowhere experience". Things got tense at times, which I find rather normal given such uncertainty. If you steal any and all perspectives of somebody's future, replace certainty with chaos, unpredictability at every level, if you replace the prospect of healing with the one of eternal suffering and continued demise, well, this doesn't exactly add to emotional strength and stability. Or the joy of life for that matter.

The one thing I never did was bring this up in counselling because, after all, *I was expected to be the nice, wonderfully successful and perfectly happy transsexual with no problems!* So I was! No problem! Is this getting absurd? Yes, it was as much before, *but when it comes to be in forced therapy and the one thing you're not allowed to is mentioning any sort of problem?* I don't know if I have missed some of the finer points of psychotherapy here, but wasn't the whole idea when they invented the thing that this should be about people caring, people finding solutions to problems and not about people learning to hide any and all issues? Does this really have to be about people learning to stop caring for others and about others, people learning how it feels not to be cared for, to be let-down, left out or better left to rot? In fact *being punished and abused for caring, showing emotions, for being human?* And then come back in two week or three and do it over again - and feel lucky it isn't every week!

A few weeks into this I started to inquire more directly about where this was going. Some of the dialogues I got during this time to my repeated insisting (honestly, I was quite a nuisance to everybody around me) were: "You're doing everything right, don't worry, we'll get you there", "well, ok, but I am not doing *anything* to get *anywhere* right now", "I told you, *you're doing everything right!*". Or: "You must have noticed that you are quite exceptional - for a transsexual I mean". And one of the more revealing: *"Just play along nicely and you will get what you need...".*

Needless to say that to me this all didn't appear to be too transparent and it all didn't look like top-notch medical science. Well, this is putting it mildly, other far more colourful terms came to mind at times...

Over time some of the people around me succumbed to their frustration of me (and don't ask me for an analysis of just why this could have been...). It was then when the odd "Freudian truth" was thrown after me: To my question "So why do you have this dogma anyway?" I once got the highly enlightening but medically very unprofessional answer: *"So we can say we know what we are doing...".*

B.27. *No Right To Remain Silent!*

There is one effect such requirements have: Many of us feel pressured to lie in a psychiatrist's office. This may start with inventing a sexual orientation or not disclosing sexual activities in order to appear as one should. After all in most cases it is not possible to validate such claims and activities anyway. Recollection of the past can at best be verified occasionally and inventing is usually not necessary, overstating, misrepresenting, forgetting or bending reality generally helps enough to get things in line with how they're expected to be. And what we then do outside of this office? It is our own business, isn't it?

We are not looking for any treatment or even treatment-success in these offices, we're looking for a letter to be allowed medical treatment. That's what we need, and we know it. So what do we do? Well, what everybody in such a situation would: Play along nicely! ***Tell the therapist whatever the therapist wants to hear!*** It is normal, it is to be expected and if we would not accept this we better should not enter that office in the first place!

Such expectations and our behavioural adaptation obviously ruins the very purpose of therapy if there ever was one, because openness and honesty is what makes psychotherapy work. On the other hand we still need to *look* open and honest because if we don't it will be assumed that we are 'hiding' something which - obviously - would warrant even more psychiatric treatment!

Everybody else, in court, in therapy, wherever, *has the right to remain silent.* To not incriminate oneself. Or not having to lie to prevent this. Only we don't! *Because to remain silent is inevitably interpreted as "holding back" and used against us!* But not to have the right to remain silent is highly abusive. Because sometimes I truly don't know, I truly do not remember or truly can not express or explain. Sometimes I feel that I should not say anything *because it affects the life of somebody else.* Something another person has told me something *in absolute confidentiality.* Sometimes *it might be illegal* for me to divulge information. *And sometimes I really, honestly do not have anything to say!* It happens, even to me... But I'm not allowed! If I then remain silent anyway it is interpreted *as if I were concealing something,* because I don't have this right. That I find myself forced to cross all these ethical barriers is abusive, *being forced to lie so I can maintain any trust I have been given by another person is abusive also.*

Putting somebody in a situation where her only three remaining choices are "*inventing a lie*", "*breaking an absolute trust*" or "*incriminating oneself by silence and potentially paying with her life by forfeiting medical treatment*" is highly, highly unethical. However

[At the civic centre, I want some documents changed, clerk] We don't do sex-changes here...

given the form of psychiatric therapy and the set-up we are subjected to it is obvious that this would arise, at least in some cases.

The way this works today *transsexuals in treatment simply are not entitled to privacy, to something that emotionally belongs to ourselves alone, something that remains protected, intimate, something that stays out of bounds for the therapist. But nothing is to remain untouchable, absolutely nothing!*

Many solve the problem by going into these offices and lie right from the start, they have a life's story ready for the therapist! Psychiatrists wonder how it comes that we're all so similar, some truly enlightened therapists even openly ask themselves how it is possible that we are all similar to the point of being virtually identical! *Truth is their own expectations of who we are get reinforced every time they see one of us pretend to be what they expect! Because for our own benefit we don't deviate from what they expect, we all present the very same lie to them!!!* **This is clearly a self-fulfilling prophecy: The expectations of the therapist** *creates the 'illness' he* **wants to see!** *Because we're interested in him finding just what he expects we "play along nicely".* **If he then finds that we are the same, that we live that standardized, expected lifestyle, mirror any and all of his expectations** *we get our treatment and our lives!* **While he gets an even stronger reinforcement of who we are!**

Right about here, or maybe 10 lines above, *every therapist would have insisted that this isn't possible!* He would have pointed out that *his therapy is designed to "bring out lies",* that it is impossible to spend potentially hundreds of hours in a therapist's office believably being somebody one is not. And I understand, I even see many of the traps laid out for me, but others I do not - and still, I, just as every other transsexual, navigate around these in spite of the therapist believing that this is impossible! Because there's one thing therapists can't see for sheer professional blindness: *The people they treat for this condition are all transsexuals!*

Because transsexuality is the one condition in the books *that makes a human being be somebody else* *to a level of believability unparalleled in any other circumstance. Because transsexuality makes a human being into another human being who is in every respect capable to integrate and function, to express and behave appropriately. In other words:* **Transsexuality is the only ('mental') condition which 'creates' a personality that is in every respect entirely normal to a level where she may in the end easily be more normal than the average "normal person" of the target-group!** *Only it isn't truly her!*

Psychiatrists will still claim that this is impossible. Only they're wrong! The very fact that transsexuality can't be tested for, that we need to self-identify because "they can't find out" is the best possible proof that we manage to evade every trap they lay out for us! After all, if this were not the case a test could be devised easily!

Of course this doesn't work equally well for every transsexual, but the people for whom this doesn't work are typically very obvious anyway (never mind psychiatry almost always misdiagnoses these people, at least initially). *But for most this does truly work well enough to do just this: Absolute invisibility!* Because we don't play, *we live.* We are compliant to a level that makes us not *act* but *be* who we are expected to be. I was told by society to be male *and I accepted this to a level where I was male,* believed that I had to be male and lived male. True, this felt wrong, forced onto me and was not fulfilling, *but it was not copying, playing or acting!*

And now they expect me to be a textbook-transsexual instead, and of course I can do this! I can do this to an absoluteness psychiatrists never deem possible, *because I become that transsexual they want me to be!* Not as a role as in acting, but *as my life!* I accept this because this is what they require me to do in order to have any chance of treatment and maybe, finally, *a chance to truly become myself!*

And just in case: If somebody rather favours the acting-theory (method-acting I presume?), *well: When I went into my first hour of counselling I had more than a quarter million hours of training to draw from in believably be somebody I am not and of all the people I had ever met in my entire previous life only 3 had ever "called me" on it!*

The absurd part of this is that **whoever is better at being the perfect textbook-transsexual typically gets her treatment faster! Or at all!** *So if somebody fails at being male because she has problems doing this, because she fails at being somebody she is not, then she likely also fails at being that textbook-transsexual for the very same reason <u>and then is not eligible for medical treatment!</u>* Because of... Well: **If she is incapable to play textbook-transsexual for a therapist** *then <u>she is automatically deemed incapable to be herself!</u>* This truly must be the most prejudice and absurd medical fact-finding and decision-making there ever was!

When, after years of 'treatment', we finally get our surgery and are free from oppression we find that these many years of this treatment have left us with deep scares. **Our lives as males felt wrong, unsatisfying, emotionally crippled.** *But at least there was one thing: Living male was socially accepted!* **Forcing us to live she-male, often for years,** *guarantees that we add new scars to the ones we already have! It doesn't allow for healing because it is not who we are just as male is not. It is another forced life but this time it is not one we grow into, it is not one that is at least anatomically correct to social expectations, it is one we have to pressure ourselves into emotionally as well as physically and we all have to do this publicly!* Doing this is neither legally nor socially sanctioned, it makes us pariahs of society, it puts us into harms way while it only acts in slowing down our becoming ourselves!

Sometimes I get really angry! That whole system has damaged me so much that I'm now incapable to perceive my world as 'normal'. What I have gotten from it is my medical treatment and my life. At the cost of my savings and my intact and understandable world? It's so absurd: **I can live wrong in the right world or they allow me to live right, but only in an absurd, abusive, perverted world?**

Now I'm done, I have had my surgery and they don't care anymore. I'm no longer "an interesting subject". I interpret this as being allowed to leave this stage. Discarded. Because with it I have for all intents and purposes rendered myself useless for their purposes. Trash of an inhumane society.

So now I can heal. If I can. Because now they have stopped to keep the wounds open they have inflicted themselves. Heal myself. *All by myself.* Not from surgery, this takes a few months, but that's physical, that's easy. Not from transsexuality. Nobody can heal from transsexuality. One cannot heal from not being oneself, from not having been allowed to be oneself. *What I can now heal from is all their enlightened treatment - if I still can.*

And just now they're actually giving me one of my human-rights back: *The right to remain silent!* The right to privacy, to a personal space *just to myself.* They're giving me this back because they expect me to remain silent forever as to what happened and is still happening. But I am not! *Because sometimes one has to speak out even if one has the right to remain silent!* Because there is something else they never understand: **Sometimes to remain silent is convenient, <u>but sometimes to remain silent is wrong</u>!**

A.17. SORRY, I'VE NEVER HAD A SEX-CHANGE!

As convenience would have it my driver's license just came up for renewal so I had one more incentive to actually go there and ask to have it changed. I had also heard that as of January of that year one could have a gender-correction in a driver's license *without proof of surgery* if a doctor would sign it off. Any doctor. So off I went to see my GP, it was February and I must have been the first, because he had never heard of such a thing. He signed it anyway, never mind that strictly speaking I was not in treatment for gender-alignment as of yet, I had just mentioned that I wanted it and he had replied that he could not give it to me unless I got that permission signed by mental-health. But then again I suppose I looked female enough to make all my intentions just about as clear as they ever come, at least to him…

Equipped with all the documents I could find I went to the local office of the Ministry of Transportation. The usual line-up, then it was my turn. I state what I wanted: "Please change everything except my date of birth - yes, I'll keep the category of the license also". "Yes, we had a similar request just recently but I'm really sorry, we can't do sex-changes here, you'll have to go to one of the full-service offices for that…"

Well, I honestly never expected to get a sex-change at the Ministry of Transportation, but I still replied politely "all right, then I suppose I'll have to get my sex-change somewhere else, don't I?". It was about then when it dawned on her what she had actually said…

Next office, same story. I stated what I wanted. A rather young employee gathered all the supporting documents, went through my application, then she said: "I'll have to look-up these regulations on our computer and ask my supervisor, it's going to take a moment. I'm sorry, I've never had a sex-change…". Apparently they had the same problem everywhere, only at this office they seemed to be getting the sex-changes *themselves?* When she came back five minutes later she looked embarrassed, obviously having noticed her linguistic slip, and tried to correct "I didn't mean… I'm sorry… it's just… I meant, it's the first time I had to do a sex-change…". Ok, back to sex-changes as a service! By now she had turned a glowing shade of red, then continued to give me a temporary license with all the changes I had requested. She even took about 10 pictures of me so as to get a reasonably good one, which I found very nice of her. But honestly it is somewhat more difficult to take "a serious looking picture with no smile" when one has difficulties to contain bursting out laughing…

[Mental-Health professional] Are you looking for group-therapy or individual? [Me] I haven't given this any thought. I really didn't expect that you had so many similar cases so you could do this in groups…

Having the rest of the documents replaced was more of the same, generally people were friendly but uninformed. For every document the laws and regulations were different which meant a lot of reading up on government rules and -regulations before asking for it. It didn't help that some of these rules seemed to change every other Monday and the guidelines on how to enforce these couldn't be printed before they were obsolete. Some government employees told me outright that such a correction isn't possible (looking as sincere as if they'd actually knew...) until I presented them *with their own regulations* on the subject!

B.28. *I WISH I HAD STARTED SOONER*

Psychiatrists put great emphasis on the 'timing' of "social transition". Whatever they choose as a cut-off, age 20, 25, 30, they somehow find "true transsexuals" and "not so true ones". Their logic: *If people 'transition' young they're 'true' because that 'gender-dysphoria' was bad enough for them to do so early in life.* Presumably this comes with the silent assumption that, as we'll see in B.37, *there are no old transsexuals because if we don't get treatment early we all commit suicide anyway? **The very fact of my being alive, that I haven't killed myself (or at least tried several times) is then held against me by implying that this is proof of me not feeling a strong enough motivation, therefore I cannot be "a true transsexual"!***

If I would have known that gender-alignment were possible and somebody would have offered the treatment to me I would certainly have wanted this surgery before age ten. But this wasn't possible back then, wasn't known, and it likely isn't possible today in most cases (unless it is a forced, non-consensual treatment for people who most likely don't want it, see B.12). To get treatment I had to leave my country and this just doesn't work as an independent immigrant at age 12, not these days anyway. Did I have periods of 'denial'? Yes, I did, to me it seems rather normal that one would have these if this stretches on one decade after another. But mostly I did not. Instead I chose a stereotypical female lifestyle to cope with the condition. I found an "emotional outlet" for a physical problem!

In the end I think I can say that for all intents and purposes I sought medical treatment *within a fortnight of this becoming practically possible* after having waited and by and large planned for this for the best part of 40 years. Ok, did I ever mention that the definition of 'gender-dysphoria' includes: *"The disturbance causes clinically significant distress or impairment in social, occupational, or other important areas of functioning"[1]?* So in my case this would, once again, be *"other* important areas" because *emotional pressure to a level which brutally influences and restricts my life* isn't even mentioned? Well, maybe emotions aren't worthy of consideration? After all, we're talking *psychiatry* here, right? Or is it because the distress I live *is created by psychiatry and not a function of my mental health at all?*

True, one could say that I should have done this at least 15 years sooner, have some sperm frozen and have children this way. All I can say to this is that while this option is certainly available and may be suitable for many individuals I have to ask you to accept

---

[1] *[DSM], diagnostic criteria 'D' of "gender identity disorder"*

[My partner, seeing me emerge from the bathroom - after 30 minutes] I hope this is just a sign of puberty and nothing permanent...

that this is ethically not acceptable to me, therefore I never even remotely considered this option.

Nobody would make a smoker's treatment for, say, lung-cancer dependent on or deny it based on his choosing to continue to smoke even though a great majority of doctors will tell such a patient that it is ill advised to do so and is very likely to impact very negatively on his treatment, recovery and future life-expectancy. The same is true for testicular or prostate cancer: Many men who suffered from these conditions have rejected the most effective treatment *for fear of a potential impact on "sexual performance"* in favour of less effective alternatives and this too is likely to impact on the individuals future life-expectancy. *Of course this is respected without questioning!*

I believe it is prejudice and discriminatory if my fulfilling my normal biological function in the procreation of life is being held against me in the way it is currently done by declaring me "not a true transsexual" and applying a different designation to me ('transvestite') which then leads to a denial of medical treatment (no gender-alignment surgery for transvestites)! I am of the opinion that <u>I should have the irrevocable right to reproduce in a biologically normal way</u> in spite of being transsexual before I start treatment <u>*without this having a negative impact on the consideration of or conditions put on my subsequent treatment*</u>, *either by psychiatry or medicine.*[1]

If psychiatry draws an arbitrary line as to the 'quality' of a transsexual and the implied driving forces for treatment then *I feel discriminated on the base of geography* which influences the availability of treatment, *I feel discriminated because so-called "late treatment" is deemed as "not being in need as much"* (or not really being in need at all) <u>while it could just as well be interpreted as *"having successfully found ways to temporarily cope"*.</u>

The most absurd part psychiatry puts forward is that they interpret my saying "I would have wished I had started sooner" (which I do, 45 years sooner or something would feel just fine) as "it is true, starting early really does distinguish the 'real' transsexual from the 'fake' *because they all say they should have!"* In reality this expression states nothing else but *my feeling a loss as to the many years of a potentially much better life I could have had and the many experiences I may have missed out on.*

John had to wait several years before a donor kidney was assigned to him. But even before he was officially on the waiting-list he knew that life with a transplant would be a vast improvement to life on regular dialysis. He says: "Emotionally I have always seen dialysis as *delaying death,* the transplant as *receiving life!"*. Of course we could ask him, now that he has had his surgery and feels healthy, leads an active life and no longer has to go to di-

---

[1] *It should be noted that unlike the lung-cancer patient who continues to smoke or the prostate-cancer patient who chooses a less effective treatment for the sake of maintaining his "sexual performance" <u>my having biological children in no way whatsoever affects my own medical condition</u>.*

alysis for hours, 3 times a week, if he would have liked to get that transplant sooner. But why should we? After all, the answer is obvious, isn't it?

If somebody seeks treatment for cancer only in an advanced stage of the illness the cancer isn't suddenly deemed 'unreal'. The person isn't punished for not showing-up earlier nor is treatment deliberately delayed or denied solely based on the timing of the first presentation to a doctor! Or if you like a psychiatric example: If somebody only seeks treatment for depression after an attempted suicide the depression isn't suddenly deemed 'unreal'. Luckily at times even psychiatry isn't that ignorant!

A.18. ARBEIT MACHT FREI!

Apart from me not being nuts enough to ever have merited any psychiatric treatment (or an evaluation) I still had a few other problems left to overcome on the quest for my surgery and now there were a couple more. Mostly procedural problems, but in the end it would hardly matter which hurdle I could not take…

Yes, at that point in treatment I got pretty much preoccupied with getting my surgery. Nothing else in life mattered because what could I possibly plan for in my future if I didn't know how it would unfold even in two weeks? Never mind three months or a year? They expect us to lead a steady, stable life in order to merit treatment and surgery while at the same time they deny us any outlook into what's just around the corner!

Honestly, there were precious few things in my life that would be the same in a female life compared to that forced she-male state. Simply put: As a woman I had a future, as a male playing female I had none. Except looking for treatment to get out of this and hoping to get it while my strength lasted. Obviously after surgery I would no longer have to look for gender-alignment, I could spend my time and energy on something meaningful instead of wasting it on something unnecessary. Truly these two paths could not have been more divergent!

The particulars that went through my mind time and time again were always the same. They remained as irresolvable as ever, not without external help anyway, meaning somebody would just have to tell me what would or should or could be allowed to happen. But that's not "how this is done", nobody ever made any commitment until two minutes *after* the fact! And yes, this insecurity alone eventually tears people apart very, very efficiently!

Some of the questions I kept repeating over and over were as predictable as it gets:

➤➤I didn't know if my counsellor would be willing to write that letter after the required minimum of three months, though I suspected as much given her initial reaction, but there was never a commitment or any security of what could be expected.

➤➤I was told, even before I booked that first appointment, "but we can't write any letters or give references". The one thing I knew was that I was sent there by somebody from trans-support and I just hoped that they knew what they were doing…

➤➤ However I did know after our first visit that my counsellor did not have the dogmatically required academic certification, she had an M.S.W.[1], and this therefore just might not get me anywhere.

➤➤ And even if I would get a letter and my GP would accept this, all he could give me was hormonal treatment. I had no idea as to how this would be interpreted down the road for surgery. But maybe I could use her letter, if she could somehow give one to me, as that "second opinion" for genital surgery. It would help...

So much for procedural problems, but there were others. In particular there was still the issue that I did in no way qualify for that "is employed" criteria. I found that one very abusive, misogynistic to be more precise, because being a homemaker and mother I thought that what I did was not only more than a full-time job (it certainly doesn't get done in 40 something hours a week, it doesn't come with either free week-ends, holidays, bonuses or retirement benefits), I actually thought of it as socially meaningful, it kept me in contact with many other women, it was a fulfilling and yes, at times exhausting life. What I understood least of all was the rather obvious fact that having one of the most predominantly female occupations society has to offer would not be good enough for a transsexuals daily activity? Is this a sadistic form of misogyny or is it just more of that control-obsession the dogmatists seem to have? Whatever it is, apparently while I was not woman enough to merit treatment to also physically be one I was most definitely woman enough to end-up on the receiving end of society's prejudices which appear to be nicely mirrored by mental-health or at least by that dogma on the treatment of what they call "gender-dysphoric males" (transsexual women).

Of course if my job were to sit in a catacomb, say somewhere in rural Nebraska or South-Dakota, with only one or at best two co-workers, day in and out, doing my transition completely underground with no other social contacts whatsoever, diligently waiting and training to put a key into a lock and turn it when told to do so by an electronic message and in doing so spelling doom onto a couple of millions of my fellow human beings by sending these minuteman missiles carrying nukes in the next room their way, well *that* would certainly count as *a meaningful transitional occupation* because hi! *I would be paid for doing that!*

If society decides that my life's task isn't worth as much as the above, in fact *it's worth nothing whatsoever*, then this automatically means that I also do not merit medical treatment? Now since when do we base our compassion on the income a person makes, in the form "the more she makes, the more compassion she merits"? Since when do we hand-out medical treatment only to people who are deemed 100% employed to WTO-standards? Particularly people who are painted mentally ill? [Remember: Genital alignment is seen as "a cure for a mental illness"].

Which one of the two jobs is the crazy one? Being a mother or being a waiter to an arsenal of nuclear missiles? Caring for children or caring for weapons of mass-destruction? Well, the

---

[1] *M.S.W. = Masters in Social Works*

dogmatists have made *their* choice as to which one they find acceptable: Raising the next generation is worthless while eradicating it as a mass-murderer is worthy!

I suppose at this time it might be a good idea to remind ourselves that the people who make such choices, the people who have drawn-up and enforce this dogma, the people who tell me that caring is worthless while killing is worthy call themselves *"medical doctors"*…

Whatever else dogma does and says, I personally have some serious reservations to the ethics and morals of the people who put something like this into a requirement to obtain medical treatment. *Any* medical treatment. From my perspective the question really should not be if I should receive treatment on the basis of such conditions, ***the question should be if people who put forward or enforce such conditions on their patients should be allowed to continue to practice medicine!***

It doesn't matter if my GP understands how wrong this is, doesn't take this seriously and decides "to make something up to be in a position so he can give me treatment". *This is his personal choice! Acting in direct contradiction of protocol,* putting my life before "professional standards" *because his conscience tells him that this is so wrong he cannot accept it!* In a decent world he should never be asked to make such a decision! Obviously other medical practitioners may not look on a given case so kindly, won't break rules, may not dare to. Many will simply insist in full compliance to the letter, will refuse treatment to people they consider un- or underemployed, even to people who are self-employed as this too doesn't appear in the list of "acceptable occupations". Other medical practitioners may pretend and plead 'incompetence' so they have an excuse not to take us in the first place and thus are never given the choice between professional requirements and personal ethics. Of course this very effectively limits our access to medical treatment (in particular to doctors who actually do consider ethics to be of any importance) but, just to be cynical here one more time, it appears that when the hard choices need to be made doctors apparently deem it more appropriate to dismiss patients rather than a deranged medical protocol…

Please note that such discrimination further extends to (a) persons who are retired, as they too can not show an employment-income (in some particularly demanding lines of work the retirement age is routinely set at 55 and can be lower if a person decides to take early-retirement), and (b) to persons who cannot, due to a physical or mental disability or the necessity of time consuming medical treatment for some other condition, maintain full-time employment. It furthermore extends (c) to people who choose to live on a part-time job and income and (d) to people who are under- or unemployed due to other (i.e. economic or political) reasons.

I do not think that doctors should ever draw-up an arbitrary selection process which is based on political, social, pseudo-racial, religious or economic views (or stereotypes) rather than *medical evidence. I think medical doctors should never install themselves as judges of such criteria or act as enforcers of punishment if people do not live-up to their view of the world. **Whoever gets medical treatment and who does not should never be decided by a*** *medical doctor on a social selection-ramp!* I had hoped that even in mental-health the motto "Arbeit macht frei"[1] would be something of the past. But apparently it isn't.

I don't think that society but in particular any person who practices medicine and any of their related professional associations should tolerate this anywhere, *not ever!*

---

[1] *Literal translation from German: "Work makes [one] free", meaning "work will free you", inscription at the entrances of numerous NAZI concentration-camps, including Dachau and Auschwitz*

A.19.   A WORD ON HORMONES

The theory: Well, hormones are... But let's leave the details to your encyclopaedia or the internet, shall we? Practically: There's "Hormone Replacement Therapy" or in short HRT, the idea is to approximate normal female hormone levels. According to dogma this is done to promote everything from breast-growth to fat-redistribution to changes in skin-tone and, in individuals who are still growing, also in obtaining a more general "skeletal feminization". And yes, I can vouch for this to work just as advertised: My skin most definitely requires a whole lot more care than it ever did!

But back to my personal experience: My counsellor had managed to find a way how she could give me a note that I was seeing her without actually making any kind of statement or commitment. Ok, this may be misleading as (a) her statement didn't say anything whatsoever except to repeat my request ("Eva states that...") *while clearly and unambiguously establishing that this was an empirical observation of hers, not a conclusion nor even a fact;* and (b) the only things she established as factual (apart from names and addresses) were the date it was written, that I was there and that to her I looked female (which I thought was very kind of her as at this very time I started facial hair removal, several sessions a week, and therefore needed to constantly let my facial hair grow to an unattractive 3-day-beard...).

Equipped with this document I got an appointment at my GP's, it was scheduled for the day before my birthday. Chance would have it that this lined-up everything, well, perfectly! Clinic rules required me to have a "case history" of at least 6 months, the day I asked for HRT they had seen me for 6 months and 3 days. Dogma required me to have been in psychiatric care for a minimum of 3 months, I could point to an excessive 3 months and 11 days (8 sessions), though not exactly "psychiatric care", and I had done "continuous full time" as per dogma for two days less than that although I had for all intents and purposes lived "full-time" a few months longer.

Never mind, for hormonal treatment "living female" doesn't count for anything at all, dogmatically speaking, it isn't a criteria for HRT! The prevailing thinking in mental-health circles must be that growing breasts for somebody living male is normal, mentally healthy, while having these if one's living a woman's life is lunacy! Ok, did I ever mention this all at times appeared to be nuts? To me anyway?

However crazy the whole thing may have seemed, I thought that was cutting it close enough. There is that part in dogma which allows a physician to prescribe HRT *in exceptional cases* without the written permission of a psychiatrist. Dogma states that, as an example, a person who has obtained hormones on the Rx-free grey-market can be given pre-scriptions immediately, presumably "to give her medical support" (or maybe "to get her un-der the control of that system"?) but of course I had never done this.

My doc just smiled when I entered and said "and *what* do *you* want today?". "I like to go on HRT, here's that letter". He took my letter, put it away and wrote the prescriptions. "There you go". While I packed my things he took that page back out, unfolded it and actually read it. I know that nobody really cared about any contents but I appreciated this non the less. Af-ter all it was painful enough to get it. Leaving his office I felt that I had just received my best birthday-present ever! I also thought I had some idea of what I was in for - but was I ever wrong...

So I started taking the drugs within the hour (of course) and sure enough my lab-results on testosterone soon flirted with the zero-mark. Now I'm not saying I didn't feel good on HRT, yes I did! It was like seeing the world in 3D-IMAX with surround-sound instead of the previ-ous 1910 sepia experience with a mistuned mechanical piano for sound, add a world of odours and flavours to the previous simplistic experience of "sweet, sour, salty and bitter", just to give *some* impression of the magnitude of this change. The most dramatic part how-ever was not cognitive but mental and emotional!

Mental, well, this may have taken four or maybe six weeks. I could virtually feel how the "thinking process" changed. True, there is no "male or female brain" if one makes such dis-tinctions these are always *statistical* differences. But even so my experience of it was one of having a world turned upside down! Not every transsexual experiences this and I very much suspect that this depends upon "how female a brain" one has to start with or how well a "pre-dominantly male brain" accepts this change. Some people get virtually no experience of change, some "think female" from the start while others "remain mentally male" but still *feel* female. It's normal, after all females come with "statistically female brains" as well as with "statistically male brains". Just not equally as often!

The impact on me was, well... significant? After a week or so I needed to bring a list to school so I knew how many kids I had to collect there because three was just a bit too much to remember all at once... And that was on these days when I got to school at all - it is after all a ten minute walk from home with about four turns on the way... Parallel parking? Just forget about that one, will you? So yes, things changed. Rather dramatically actually! One surprise after another, pretty much a new one every day! But much of it I found was tempo-rary. A month later I had no problems anymore to pick up all our kids, find the way to school or park my car, this was just like before. The effect hit hardest a few weeks after starting HRT and by two months into it this was pretty much back to where it was before. There are a few effects that remained: People say that women can't read maps. Well, I can still read maps without any problems just as I always could before. What I now have great difficulties with is to correlate what I see in the real world with what's on that map, pinpointing my location on it or figuring out what direction in reality corresponds to up and down on the paper... Well, maybe women aren't all that bad at reading maps after all, we just have no clue where we are? I usually sum it up by telling people that *I am not geographically challenged* because I have no problem to find the best route from Chicago to L.A. on a map, *I am rather directionally challenged* because I then can't find the highway when I'm actually driving... And yes, just to mention it if you hadn't already suspected: This was never even remotely an issue before because I just always knew where to go...

The true benefits of this treatment however are *emotional*: I now think that what I feel is what I should be feeling, I now have ways to express what I feel. Before I always felt "emotionally locked-up", I was "incapable to express" or "incapable to emotionally experience as I knew I should", I was "emotionally remote and withdrawn, suppressed". This is now gone, I have in fact found that there is even more to be experienced than I ever suspected (or missed)!

I now have means to deal with emotions such as anger and sadness or conditions such as stress a lot better, because I now have many more avenues to express and communicate these. Before it was all "bottling it up" or "suppressing it". With the entire range of well known consequences. It is very difficult to describe the emotional freedom that comes with the hormonal change. That I can now have tears on the outside when I cry on the inside may be a hint as to what this is all about. At age five I dried-up emotionally, it is when this ordeal began. It took me four decades of waiting until I was allowed to have tears again.

There are other areas affected, for example that touching, particularly other human beings, is now a joyful extension of my sensations whereas before I always avoided this. I suspect that I am more visual now, I do "look at" and "physically examine" more and "logically conjecture" less. I am much more social and sociable than before, getting a social life now is a lot easier. I always wanted to share emotionally but most males don't exactly excel in this. On male hormone levels this doesn't come all that easily, now it does - and in communicating with other women I get the same back! These days I experience myself as a part of a social network and emotionally integrated, before I used to live lonely in an emotional desert.

B.29. MENTAL CHOICES

Reality is that when I read most professional psychiatric or psychological publications on transsexuality I find that the psychiatrist/psychologist so often *makes the group of people he/she examines fit their theory instead of adjusting his theory to the people.* This goes as far as psychiatrists seeking out very particular groups of transsexuals to verify their theories, *then they claim that these findings are valid for all transsexuals!* This is to some degree human, but it is also unprofessional and harm- as well as hurtful when such conclusions get applied to other groups of people who do not fall within the same scope.

But the fact of the matter is far more complex than just psychiatrists seeking out matching subjects to obtain the expected results of their research. Most transsexuals who look for treatment are well informed, some authors actually say that transsexuals are "some of the best informed individuals" in any medical or mental-health setting. We certainly know what specific institutions or psychiatrists think about us and what they expect, information - real information - on how people get treated by institutions and individual doctors can be found easily enough on the internet. In my opinion the very fact that there is an entire community out there to maintain such information speaks volumes. When it then comes to treatment we too have our preferences, these of us who have a choice tend to go to the institutions which seem to be most accommodating to who any particular person is. This way we "self sort" by the very nature of where we look for treatment!

In addition there is the fact that some institutions may end-up getting all the cases which, for whatever reason, seek treatment paid for by insurance, charity or government healthcare-plans *because this institution just happens to have the power to grant such expenditures* while others do not. It is obvious to me that the very fact that a person can pay $50,000 or more out of pocket for her treatment says something about this person. I am not saying that having or not having that kind of money (or having a position and an employer where a suitable healthcare plan is part of the package) should be a factor in any treatment or should be of any consideration at all when it comes to healthcare, what I am saying is that the reality of psychiatry is that this is by far the most segmented and segregated branch of medicine there is and having the ability to pay for it simply gives a patient the option to choose where others can't.

There are obviously many reasons why somebody could or could not have this financial background but in general the places who can approve treatment paid for by social-insurance, government or charity (or which provide it free of charge) will end-up with a great majority of the cases who have, in addition to transsexuality, other issues *which prevents the individual from having an income to cover life's expenses <u>and on top of these</u>*

some very costly medical treatment. **Such institutions therefore will never get a representative cross-section of transsexuals** to base any kind of research on. But neither are private psychiatrists or pay-for institutions *because these will just as much get, on average, a very specific segment of patients!*

Some scientists try to solve the problem by seeking transsexuals elsewhere. But this too is problematic particularly if the proposed 'research' in some way degrades, de-humanizes or even abuses people. Because who would participate in something like this? *Unless of course the participants get some kind of a reward for it which they find outweighs any such considerations.* In the case of a transsexual this could either be a monetary reward or that letter of approval for HRT or surgery. So in the end this too hardly looks like a means to get an honest, representative cross-section of the transsexual population! Looking for people at the local trans-bar may get them transsexuals, but not everybody goes to such places, in fact in my opinion it is rather a distinctive minority who does. The same is true for self-support groups, placing ads in 'scene'-newspapers or -radio-stations or post a message on the message-board of a psychiatric institution or whatever approach one would put forward.

I suppose it is in some way a similar problem opinion-research companies have: How to find *a representative* group of people? But then again, it's not! *Because opinion researchers verify their predictions against actual outcome or occurrences!* For example they can verify election-predictions by actual election-results, sales-predictions by actual sales. This way they can, over time, *build mathematical models to predict the number of people who as a matter of principle refuse to answer or lie - and more significantly they can, over time, predict their "typical influence on the result"!* Thus "statistically significant" predictions can be made *even if only a small part of the population is polled and even if many people who are polled refuse to answer and some lie!*

But unlike pollsters psychiatrists who treat transsexuals are typically not interested in the outcome at all! None of the mental-health institutions involved in my care ever bothered to ask me (or anybody I know), ever cared about my well-being after surgery or anything at all for that matter! Maybe the idea just was "if I felt like it I would call"? Well, *given how I have been treated there I don't feel like it whatever my condition!*

I suppose if they really wanted to know they could easily have asked. *But when they finally, after surgery, could have expected an honest and direct answer from me they weren't interested at all to verify their expectations,* **suddenly the therapists didn't care to listen anymore! Apparently they don't need to hear what we really have to say anyway!**

They don't seem to care at all that the great majority of us end-up having normal lives after they let us go! And most importantly: *Apparently they don't want to see that the groups who get the least abuse in mental-treatment are typically the ones who have the greatest success-rate afterwards because mental treatment is, both in numbers of sessions as well as length of treatment, in all likelihood negatively correlated to treatment-success! Or in other words: Institutions who impose longer waiting-times and require more therapy-sessions are the ones who end-up having a lower success-rate!*

B.30. MONEY FOR NOTHIN' AND YOUR CHICKS FOR FREE![1]

In an amazingly short time I had settled into hormonal treatment, adjusted dosage - and my new life. All these new freedoms certainly did take some getting used to! There are a few new traps also, things like PMS[2] and emotional overreaction, psychiatrists call it 'hysteria', and yes, you may have guessed it, both these conditions used to be mental illnesses! 'Hysteria' finally got removed from the list however PMS may still be found in the DSM[3], *consequentially falls into the scope of psychiatric care and is, to this date, deemed to be caused by a mental disorder, not a physical problem!* So I was just a little too late to get the first one officially pathologized and added to my "list of psychiatric accomplishments" but I presume that at least I'd still be good for the second? However by now I was pretty much used to finding every typically female behaviour ending-up recreated into a pathology in some male behavioural scientist's brain!

And yes, being on a first-name basis with the entire list of female psychiatric pathologies, their definitions, symptoms and often freely invented causes (if any are given at all) I found myself horror-struck one day when I woke up and experienced something I had never had like this before: *A strong sex-drive!* Now what? I was at near zero testosterone and something like pregnancy-level on the female chart and I am getting *what*? *The one thing psychiatry knows to be absolutely impossible at these levels???*

I know that some of the psychiatrists who accept transsexuals treat us, along with transvestites, as a sideshow to their main attraction: Sex-offenders such as paedophiles, rapists, stalkers and exhibitionists. And yes I also know that in their opinion all the above groups as "pretty much the same"! Do I feel offended and insulted by such statements? Indeed, very much so! But I wasn't really amazed because, after all, these very psychiatrists typically see transsexuality as "a super-fetish" and "a sexual perversion" and that now really fits in nicely *with all their preferred clients*, doesn't it?

[*After having informed the neighbours of my intention to transition a high-school student, passing by] Hi there! I've heard... Cool!...*]

---

[1] *Lyrics from the song "Money for Nothing" by* Dire Straits

[2] *PMS: P<u>re</u>menstrual <u>S</u>yndrome: In transsexual woman it is typically caused by estrogen withdrawal (i.e. scheduled or accidental reduction in dosage), in my case it manifests mostly in high irritability, tearfulness, sometimes headaches and occasionally problems concentrating*

[3] *The psychiatric designation of PMS could be found under the heading "<u>L</u>ate <u>l</u>uteal <u>p</u>hase <u>d</u>ysphoric <u>d</u>isorder" (LLPDD) but was renamed "<u>P</u>remenstrual <u>d</u>ysphoric <u>d</u>isorder" (PMDD) in 1993 for the DSM-III-R and remained in the DMS-IV as such. Since the treatment of PMS was (and often still is) not recognized or not accepted for insurance or health-plan coverage many women may still end-up being labelled mental (PMDD) <u>simply for the purpose of making treatment available to them</u>! As with "Gender-dysphoria" the psychiatric term "Premenstrual <u>dysphoric disorder</u>" is highly derogatory and demeaning. I believe if this were a <u>male</u> condition psychiatry would never label it like this! After all there is no "Drooping penile dysphoric disorder" (DPDD) in that book, it's called "Erectile dysfunction" (ED) instead, derogatory terms such as 'dysphoria' or 'disorder' are not used!*

There was (and still is) much publicly funded research on sex-offenders as it appears that helping the world at large to understand and accept paedophiles and rapists is apparently a worthwhile cause (while the victims of these same criminals are largely marginalized and ignored, put aside and left without any help or support, never mind public funding for their issues). Then, after having spent millions of tax-dollars, they come to such highly enlightening conclusions as that all the people mentioned above have an *"erotic targeting location problem"*[1]*!*

I certainly could have told them the rather obvious, for less than a few million dollars: A sex-offender's problem is that he uses the wrong methods, goes after the wrong people and this likely comes from having a disturbed motivation??? And should I repeat it? *I feel highly, highly offended and insulted by these pseudo-expert-psychiatrists publicly declaring that I belong to the same category!* M/f transsexuals that is because there aren't enough female sex-criminals to claim the same for f/m's! True, these days they also declare me a homosexual. And maybe they would have thrown homosexuals in too if it still were the politically opportunistic thing to do? But it was not, so they let this group go for once. For political correctness, even though they clearly have "an erotic target locating problem"? Male homosexuals that is, not female ones because! After all, this absurd theory only covers a select 49% of the population while the other 51% prove this to be nonsense right from the start (haven't these doctors noticed or are they "woman-blind", except when it come to sex?)…

I have more than a bit of a problem when they declare me and my partner sexual perverts *because I locate my erotic attraction on a partner who is about the same age as I am, with whom I have a long-lasting relationship of mutual love and understanding and with whom I have biological children?* I mean, honestly, just what's suddenly so darn psychiatrically pathological about that? Or do they want to scientifically test how close they can shave it before they get sued for libel?

But never mind that for now, what is important here is that psychiatrists have developed a highly enlightened treatment for their criminal customers, it's called "chemical castration". They say it miraculously cures serial rapists and repeat paedophiles! This they base on the premise that chemical castration eliminates desire, sex-drive and aggression. Some even claim that it changes sexual orientation and/or preferences (I suppose they think that this 're-adjusts' that "erotic target locator" to adults instead of children?).

Now chemical castration is pretty much the same cocktail I am also taking with the exception that I also take estrogen. *Only I experience either nothing of what they prescribe I should <u>or pretty much the opposite</u>!* I have *more* of a sex-drive, my behaviour in regard to aggressiveness hasn't changed a bit, I have no change in determination and most certainly I do not feel any change whatsoever in my sexual preferences or orientation! The one sexual effect I can confirm is a reduction of my mechanical sexual ability. I suppose they call it "erectile dysfunction" and I get it big time. From my perspective that's rather welcome but I seriously

---

[1] *"Erotic target location errors in male gender dysphorics, paedophiles, and fetishists" by Freund, K., Blanchard, R.*

doubt that a sex-offender would be docile simply from having ED - never mind there is always that best-selling little blue pill (available without prescription by mail-order worldwide, sex-criminals welcome!) which is marketed as an "instant cure" for ED...

Yes, I could now start to argue that freeing serial-offenders from prison because some psychiatrists claim that they "get cured" by these drugs may just be negligent, that these 'experts' should be held liable by all the additional victims this causes (or I could write another book about it), or I might just be quiet about it *because I am in a position where I need that very psychiatrist to sign my permit for surgery or just my next prescription and he's made it abundantly clear that "feeling something different" will be interpreted as "failure of treatment" and this in turn would potentially lead to the discontinuation of this treatment!*

But it could be even worse: Many of these psychiatrists enlist their paedophiles *and transsexuals* to 'verify' their findings in 'scientific' studies and yes, you guessed it, *the great majority of these 'subjects' all report themselves de-sexed and de-aggressed!* But could this all be nothing but a big lie? I mean paedophiles appear to have a rather good motif to lie: They get out of prison for it! Transsexuals have an even better reason: *They may just get freed from these psychiatrists and get life-saving medical treatment, all in one!*

After thinking extensively about this for maybe half a second, could there be an ulterior motif for some doctors to care as intensely for transsexuals: To get a nicely compliant population of "research subjects" who are prone to blackmail and have no means to complain?[1]

Maybe there is one thing left to say. Or maybe two. First: It feels absolutely lousy to potentially be pressured into a position where I would find myself blackmailed into lying in support of wannabe-science drawn-up by pseudo-experts. Especially because I full well understand that this may well be used to liberate criminals from prison who may just have nothing else in mind than to re-offend - all in exchange for getting my life! And second: I am not at all amazed that *some of these very psychiatrists* are some of the ones who put in most of the effort to keep us seen as mental, support to keep the mandatory mental-treatment of us in effect and to keep the definition of transsexuality it in the DSM, typically surpass dogmatic requirements at their own institutions and on top of everything publicly paint us as instable social parasites leading a fringe life of collecting social-support thus only exploiting society - *while they position themselves as the saviours who are the only ones willing to dig deep enough in the mud to get us out of it.* Well, the dirt they themselves have created to throw us in! Because, after all, they have the most to loose: Their constant supply of compliant guinea pigs, their believability and "scientific reputation" along with their posts at small and large psychiatric institutions, public and private funding for these institutions and their own projects and not to forget a typically sizeable personal income. Add a potential nightmare of legal actions against them by victims of re-offending sex-criminals who were released *on the grounds of such psychiatric research or on direct arguments psychiatrists presented in court or at parole-hearings.* **Because these victims might just be tempted to argue that these**

---

[1] *See B.24 and footnote 1 on page 157*

social scientists should have known that applying coercion in 'research', whether by threat, the prospect of pain or a promise of a reward (or a combination thereof) won't lead to sound scientific knowledge <u>and that the subsequent use of such tainted 'research' to release violent offenders might just be grossly negligent</u>! *Because applying such methods is behavioural conditioning, not empiric science!*

You might just agree: To find oneself in such a position is... problematic?

B.31. ONE MORE WORD ON HORMONES

There's one other issue that comes with hormonal therapy, particularly when one uses rather high doses as is often indicated before surgery. As the levels approach normal puberty never mind pregnancy levels (which are quite a bit higher than normal adult levels) or even surpass these (as is typical for some treatment regimes) what happens to us is what's to be expected for every biological woman: We go into puberty! It is hormonally right and after all that's what the treatment is designed to do…

However there's a bit of a problem… Most biological women do puberty at some time between the age of 9[1] to 16, by the time they approach the 20's they're supposed to behave like adults. Of course many transsexuals are only ever allowed to start this process much later, in our mid 20-es, 30-es or even later. The problem? Well, if I go into puberty at an adult age I'll *feel* like every woman has during puberty. So I feel something like 13-15 years old, but of course *should I start behaving it at my age this would not just be deemed inappropriate but likely rather disturbed!* On the other hand there are a few things women learn during this phase of their lives transsexuals mostly miss out on because we were left out of social female structures during this time. Just to give a few examples this would include the finer sides of dressing, jewellery, everything around make-up, even to some degree behaviour, socializing and social relationships, particularly when it comes to personal or intimate relations. Yes, of course *we see* all this happen around us and we learn much by observing or try it in secret. But that's different to actually doing it - and it's different *from actually having the freedom to doing it wrong and learning to getting it right by "trial and error", it is different if one actually gets some feedback, hopefully some positive or helpful feed-back as well!*

It is maybe a bit like looking at a masterpiece versus painting it? Even the most accomplished art-critic isn't necessarily a good painter just because of his knowledge! Observing may help in getting better at something to a certain degree, but this is only one aspect of learning! If a teenager dresses ridiculously or applies far too much make-up, well, that's ok. She's a teen… If I do the same at age 40+ it is, at best, seen as immature…

I suppose that's just about where an accepting mother or a girlfriend or partner comes in helpful. Of course if one doesn't have any of these a female counsellor would probably

---

[1] *Puberty actually starts just after conception. By the time we are born we are already well on our way of becoming sexually distinct, mature and fertile. This is after all the reason why some babies look male while others look female at birth… The dogmatic view generally states that female puberty starts at age 9-10. Personally I find it typically easy to distinguish biological sex from seeing children's faces even at age 7 to 8 so I must therefore assume that by then gender-specific facial changes are significant enough to do so - which means puberty is well on it's way.*

make a helpful substitute, that is if she would be willing to venture into such unheard of therapeutic territories as talking clothes or make-up! But then again, this isn't exactly what most therapists are trained to do, is it? Even though quite a few psychologists are actually women... Certainly this would help us, but making us fail and look badly in public, then miserable at home is by far a better way to improve our mental health, after all a decent depression creates room for therapy!

It is my firm conviction that most of what society notices about us (apart from the exploitative before and after images and the sex-trade) most likely comes from seeing adults more or less behaving as teenagers do. Because we try to find our ways. Because we try to "fit in". *And because we, just as everybody else, need time, have to learn this by trial and error. Only we don't do it at the appropriate age so we stand out, are seen, noticed.* Some become a laughing stock, society looks at us and says: "Freaks, men trying to be women?", "can't even do decent make-up at her age?" or "can't fool me, I'll always know"!

If somebody were to say of a teenager "she can't even do make-up properly" it would be meant completely different as if applied to a 30 or 40 year old woman. Of course the one "can't fool me" would hardly ever be used in the teenager-context at all!

On the other hand there are all the transsexuals who blend-in just nicely and therefore *never get seen, never get pointed at, don't self-exhibit and never get shown anywhere!* My personal estimate is that in North-America alone up to a million people visibly and openly live the other gender than they were assigned at birth, either full or part-time. Only some 10% of these are actually people who have had genital alignment.

How many of these people have you ever noticed?

B.32. TRANSITION??? WHAT TRANSITION?

The process that takes place when an individual "publicly changes from male to female" is generally referred to as 'transition'. This, to start with, gives the wrongful impression that the person has been male, then somehow recognized that he is actually a she and subsequently decided to start living accordingly. Depending on the openness of an involved mental-health professional we're either supposed to say that "transition will take forever", that we're "never really completely women" and thus "need support (presumably from this mental-health professional) forever" [that is until we have had surgical alignment, then we can pull the plug on it because we can no longer so easily be blackmailed into going there] or we're actually allowed to say that we at some time feel completely female, nothing else.

Of course this isn't true, not in my experience anyway. First I never started out feeling male and then figured out that I'm not, *I started out feeling myself and then figured out that this happened to be female.* Second I have always experienced myself as I do today, I haven't changed who I am. *All that ever happened was that I am now being perceived differently because I look a little different.* **I have never transitioned from male to female, how could I, I never was male!** *What I have done is* <u>*to change how I am perceived so I get accept for who I am.*</u> Important here is to realize that *it is* <u>*everybody elses perception*</u> *that has changed,* <u>*not my identity!*</u> **I remain the same, but the world around me does not:** <u>**Because everybody elses perspective (of me) has changed!**</u>

It is true that unlike woman who were identified female at birth and have been allowed to grow up and lead a life being females I've had a few disadvantages. I had to overcome physical, social, emotional, sexual problems, though I never cared much for sex and I still don't, so that wasn't an issue for me. (For others this may well be very different).

I'm not the only person in the world who has had to overcome a few problems in her life and I'm not the only one who has managed to do so. I'm not writing this to get your sympathy but rather *because I'd like people to understand that in spite of being legally designated male, in spite of being raised as such, in spite of being sexually male, in spite of having a male-ish emotional life biochemically forced onto me, in spite of having been anatomically male, in spite of being treated male by and in society I still do and did experience myself female! I did not put that label onto it in very early life because it takes a while to understand but how I experience myself has never changed.* **Therefore I have to conclude that I have identified female all through my life!**

[Foreign consulate] We can't change your name [to a female one] and sex while you are married. But we can put a "special observation" in your new [male] passport saying that you use the name Eva and are a woman!

Apparently we can inject testosterone into just about any woman, treat her for a male, do all the above, suspend or destroy her reproductive-capacity while doing it, induce a male puberty and thus give her male physical characteristics including a low voice, beard growth, broad shoulders and so on, *and she will still think of and experience herself as a woman* (unless she's a female to male transsexual). *My biological make-up did the same for me, free of charge, no choice.* **But I too, in spite of all this, still experienced myself female. Always!**

So if there is ever a 'transition' it is one of social perception only! From my own perspective it is at best getting used to being seen differently. Yes, my personal experience of it was that I started to have liberties I never had before. Liberties of personal expression and recognition. But these hardly require much of an adaption, after all this is if anything a very joyful, liberating experience!

True, there may be people who don't take kindly to such changes, particularly people who have known "the before" as well as "the after", but there are others also. But honestly, **if *they* can't find it in themselves to accept my self-identification, why would *I* be subjected to therapy *and not* *they*?**

That sounds drastic but really, it is not. I might just agree that *I* could be the one in need of support *if I were the only one to see myself as a woman*. Not because my identification would warrant this. But because if I would be living my identification and this would cause *serious* problems all the time *because nobody could identify me correctly* I may well understand that this might just be an issue. Then, maybe, I should be asked to talk to a counsellor, that's what we have social services for. But if I ever had such serious problems, particularly if this were often the case, then this would be known and/or openly visible. Only, I don't. I get accepted for who I am very nicely. *The few exceptions all are either people who can't accept the fact that they are forced to suddenly perceive me differently or who have knowledge of my former life and, as a matter of principle, **do not accept that this can be right for anybody!***

If people see Jane in her wheelchair there will be some who won't accept her with it. There will be some who want her in an asylum because they don't want to be "exposed to this". Others think that even this is "too generous". They see physically (and mentally) handicapped people as "a burden to society" no matter what and conclude that the best solution to dealing with disability is to have people like Jane euthanized.

Both ideas aren't exactly new and both of them have been practiced widely in the past. At times by recommendation of psychiatrists and with full acknowledgement and premeditated participation of medical doctors.

Today the great majority of people recognize this as unethical. I also sincerely hope that these days nobody in mental-health has ideas such as *to declare Jane mental if she fails to respect and welcome such ideas or individuals or to force her into therapy until she accepts and welcomes such thinking (or simply confiscate her wheelchair and force her to crawl on the ground so she may learn a lesson of how worthless she truly is)!*

I agree that it doesn't help when propaganda is being spread that I do not deserve a little bit of leeway just as every woman in puberty does because I will be making some of the very same mistakes, only 30 years late. Views like I am indeed living out a mental illness and the mistakes I make aren't because of me adapting and learning but because of presumed mental limitations or that I will never overcome this but it is rather a result of my deranged mental abilities *and therefore I deserve no consideration whatsoever* aren't actually helpful. Neither Medically nor otherwise. But even so, *it is not my consideration that is at issue, it is that of other people*, isn't it?

No, this scenario isn't dreamt-up. Humanity is really doing this in thousands of experiments: Forcing an inappropriate puberty onto somebody: It's called 'doping' and it's apparently used rather generously in elite sports. And no, if a woman takes testosterone to change her body for physical peak performance in sports this isn't mental, it isn't a disorder and it isn't medication abuse, neither for her nor for the doctor giving it! There is no mental-health pathology for "sacrificing one's health or life for a shot at personal and national glory". While it may be banned by sports-organization (but of course can't be tested for if the hormone is discontinued in time before a competition as it occurs naturally in every human-being anyway), it is completely ok by the terms of our legal system. One doesn't need a permission from mental-health to do this. It isn't considered child-abuse if done to a minor (as it presumably regularly happens considering the age when people show up at the Olympics). There are no waiting times, no dosage limits, no protocols for meaningful monitoring of emotional or physical parameters, no informed consent on short or long-term health-risks. In fact it may even be considered beneficial in this setting if a woman's regular cycle fails! All the better because all that counts is "peak-performance anytime". And best of all: While the athlete may risk sanctions by sports-organizations if discovered, be banned from competitions and so on, the doctor who writes the prescriptions or provides such treatment apparently hardly ever faces any professional consequences!

If a woman[1] then is acting-out because she was on a testosterone-trip or if she looses control or even gets into depression or tries suicide, well then she deserves every sympathy, doesn't she? After all, she isn't taking this onto herself because she's a mental transsexual but because she is a fighter in the war for the nation's honour and personal over-achievement!

I find that psychiatry's pseudo-science and pseudo-ethics are very nicely revealed when they designate me mental because I would like to live *without* a substance I feel - at my biological (pre-op) level - as interfering with my normal emotional functioning, a bit like a street-drug I really don't want, while these same 'experts' consider it apparently entirely normal to treat human-beings *with the same substance and the same emotional consequences* with the sole objective is that they may achieve super-human physical abilities for a very short period of time in their lives, at any expense. This, in my opinion, is medical madness!

---

[1] *Male athletes have also been known to use testosterone for performance enhancement. The idea must be "to make super-males from males" - with, sadly enough, very predictable consequences.*

A.20. SHE NEEDS SURGERY, NOT COUNSELLING

[A friend, male] You know, ever since you have transitioned there's something that has been bothering me... [Me] About me? [He] No... What bothers me is more that I no longer have any idea who I am ...

Meanwhile I was going to counselling every now and then. It was after the third meeting when my therapist suddenly started to ask some seriously difficult questions. Up to then we had talked about transsexuality in general and in regard to myself, about my emotional, social, sexual life. About who I was, what I thought and felt. About what kind of problems living a pre-op transsexual's life presents, legally, emotionally, socially and so on. Things I could easily answer, with or without tears, depending on the subject at hand as I am quite assuming enough to consider myself the foremost expert when it comes to answering questions about my own life! But now she was asking something completely different: *She suddenly wanted to know why the heck I wanted counselling anyway?*

By then she had not only learned that I thought I needed gender-alignment, she also felt that I was quite capable to make such a decision - and by the way asking for this seemed to make perfect sense! She also understood the one big problem in my life: *That under these conditions I might not live long enough to ever see the day this would finally happen...*

I couldn't help myself but to point out that this wasn't my idea but a result of that protocol of which I had previously given her a copy. "Yes... that... I've read it... It's quite disgusting... They don't actually take this seriously, do they"? Well, unfortunately, they do exactly that! I didn't even have an idea if they were going to accept a letter from her if she would ever find a way to write one, in that scenario nobody was willing to even tell me that much...

Dogma said that this letter had to include, among other positions: "The initial and evolving gender, sexual, and other psychiatric diagnoses; the eligibility criteria that have been met and *the mental-health professional's rationale [but not my own!] for hormone therapy or surgery*; the degree to which the patient has followed the Standards of Care to date *and the likelihood of future compliance* "[HBIGDA-S]. As this was now unlikely to occur in this way (never mind that she didn't have the qualification to make a *psychiatric* diagnosis anyway) I asked her to contact my GP's clinic, the people at trans-support, just to see *what kind of contents they actually expected.* I suppose she was eager to find out *but more so she was looking for some guidance as to what to do with me!* I had left the necessary paperwork to allow everybody involved to talk to each other as I certainly understood that insisting on my right to any privacy would only delay treatment...

So she called the clinic, got one of the nurses there on the phone and asked her questions. I am not prone to the exact contents of that call, however over time I got a few hints as to what it might have been about. Apparently they all agreed that what I needed was surgery, not mental treatment. They also felt that they weren't in a position to sign me off for it... As to mental treatment? Apparently the idea was: *Do something. Anything. Whatever! Just keep me there, we need that for the records!* And that letter? *Just write something. Anything. Whatever!* As long as it is on official paper with a brilliant letterhead that would do just fine!

There was something else they apparently agreed upon: *I was not to be told that they all agreed!* This was now all about them keeping their façade intact rather than my health or my life. I would be given what I needed at minimal compliance - *but I was not to be told this!* I was instead set-up to test the limits of the system *myself,* with my own strength and my own life at stake. *Because ultimately protocol would be given priority over my life!* They all hoped that I may live long enough to see it happen, and cross your fingers for her!

Doctors don't always tell patients how bad their condition is because they fear that if the patient knows then she will give-in and let herself go, thus adding to the inevitable outcome. I don't think that this is ethical but I'm not the one to make such decisions. I only get to hear the result of such thinking and then may second-guess it at my leisure...

Would it have helped to know? Yes, it would have, very much so! Because if I had had a timeline, if I had not had to live in complete darkness as to if I'd *ever* get treatment and what further conditions might possibly be imposed onto it I could have directed my life towards a meaningful future instead of swinging back and forth between planning my own funeral in a few weeks and how to worm any information or a commitment out of people.

Would I have accepted the reasoning for my artificially created suffering? I don't think so. I appreciate that if ever a doctor decides that this is wrong, wrong enough for him that some changes are warranted, if he gives his patient what she needs *immediately, if he would extend the human right of freedom of personal expression without questioning* he would run certain risks. I understand that one of these risks would be that he just might not be there *for all his other patients* tomorrow because he conceivably might be banned from practicing medicine for doing this. This has happened before! He could loose his job. Had I been told *this* I think I would have understood. Maybe I would not have agreed, *but I would have understood his dilemma! This* I would have accepted. Because this is weighing risks, benefits and potential personal consequences which go far beyond practicing medicine.

However what I also understand is that if nobody ever dares to make such changes then there will never be any. And I also understand quite well that if ever a case exemplified all the wrongs in how transsexuals get treated mine may just have been it.

There is something else this set-up fails to take into consideration: Had I been given a perspective on my life, even far out, just as long as it would have been certain and predictable, *I would have felt better, would have done a lot better, achieved more.* It is normal, it is human. To have a perspective in life gives focus, strength and helps to overcome problems and the inevitable low-points. To have none, to be left in complete unpredictability, in a chaos where none of my actions make any positive difference whatsoever will do the exact opposite. This too is normal. This too is to be expected. This too is very predictable. Well, to me anyway.

Whatever the set-up throws at me, whatever the professionals choose to ask of me, whatever they disclose or don't, I will comply. It is who I am and what I do. But compliance needs predictability. *I am incapable (as so many hundreds of thousands of transsexuals in treatment before me) to comply to unpredictability and absurdity - except by suicide.*

B.33. MEDICAL NIGHTMARES

Typically treatment works on the premise that we have to "look female", maybe "behave female" and if we do so for a long time we're then - maybe - allowed *to be female*.

In contrast I myself work on the premise that I am female, female looks come from how I express myself and that my behaviour is perceived as predominantly feminine would, well, be nothing but natural and normal. While psychiatry prescribes that "whoever looks female enough is maybe eventually allowed to be female" I think that "whoever is female will express this in a way suitable for herself without the need for any external pressure". Apparently these views seem to collide on several levels...

One, but certainly not the least important, is *the sequence of our treatment.* Psychiatry accepts only one way, one sequence of how this is supposed to happen. There is only one small tweak they allow us to do by our own preference - and that I suppose is because they don't have control over it as no license to practice is needed for it: We can live female before starting to take hormones (or even see a therapist)! However they still expect us to see a psychiatrist before we can do anything medical at all. Dogma states, in a tone as disbelieving as it gets, *that there actually are people who "just do it", live their lives, know who they are and have the audacity to do all this without ever seeing a psychiatrist!* (The expectation is that one takes hormones until "passing for a male" is no longer possible, then one starts 'living'). However psychiatrists don't accept that just living oneself can be "a real transition" so they enforce any and all rules and waiting-times anyway. *They just never accept any contribution by a patient at all, as a matter of principle! Psychiatrists seem to work on the premise that **only a therapeutically directed self-expression can be an expression of true self!***

On the other hand I work on the premise that I am at liberty to express myself as who I am at any time in my life and in any way I wish, *even if this happens to be female.* By the time I got to mental-health I had simply started because I knew that this would be a condition later anyway - *and because this didn't contradict how I see and experience myself.* Of course I nevertheless had to wait for treatment and of course any and all time I had been living female *before* I started mental treatment counted for nothing whatsoever!

Unfortunately I knew only too well that I could do with some "medical feminization", all I had to do was look in a mirror to see that I was as hopeless for a beauty-contest as it ever got. I most definitely wanted to get hormonal treatment, however my motivation was rather the emotional changes I was expecting rather than the physical ones but honestly, with my looks one takes every help one can get! Only from my perspective it was

[Pharmacist, looking at my insurance-card] You should have your sex changed... [Me] I'm working on it... [She] Here's the 800-number of your insurance company's customer service, they can do this for you...

199

clear from the start: I would like genital surgery to actually feel physically right just as fast as possible! Because although I lived female I at times felt very strongly "dressed-up male living female", or 'she-male'. This felt emotionally and physically very unnatural to me. I also wanted to get rid of my excessive testosterone, not because of looks (although this presumably helps too) but rather because this made me feel "pressured into experiencing myself male" and "narrowed the emotional experience". The way to get there would reasonably have been genital surgery (which includes castration and as such would, to a good measure, correct the testosterone-imbalance), *then* some hormonal-treatment (possibly estrogen only) to a level which I felt comfortable at. Of course this makes sense, so psychiatry required me to do this differently!

Dogma forces us to start with hormonal treatment *as the first medical intervention. It in fact states **that every patient <u>must accept such medical intervention as an absolute condition in order to ever being allowed any kind of surgery!</u>**[1]* Besides the point that this is yet another violation of our human rights and personal integrity, the high doses required "pre-op" are of major concern as several of the drugs, including all hormones used in transgender-care, are known carcinogens. Estrogen in particular also contributes to the formation of blood-clots and not few transsexuals have experienced *(deep) venous thromboembolism* (VTE), a condition in which one of the larger veins of the body, usually in a leg, gets partially or completely blocked by a blood-clot. Clots can potentially come free and end-up stuck somewhere else, most often in a lung. This is then called *pulmonary embolism* and if not any of the above, this one will most definitely prompt a visit to the emergency room, often requires hospitalization and is potentially fatal or can cause prolonged and significant long-term impairments.

So just as a basic rule I'd suggest one takes the smallest dosage possible... Well, that's hardly a sophisticated medical statement but it is simply a fact that the doses required pre-op are far higher than after orchiectomy (or any other surgery that removes the testicles).

Additionally testosterone-blocking is necessary pre-op as the natural level of testosterone would inhibit most of the benefits of estrogen. But due to a devious tweak in biochemistry estrogens (estradiol) and testosterone can be converted into each other[2]. Even if no testosterone is added by means of breaking down estradiol the body still tries to maintain a biologically pre-set balance[3] so if high doses of estradiol are added more testosterone would typically be synthesized as a response (particularly in very high-dose estrogen regimes), so by adding insane amounts of estrogen one also inadvertently adds crazy amounts of testosterone - which then means even more testosterone-blocking or suppression is needed. So even more potentially dangerous (and costly) chemicals are required and even more undesired side-effects are produced!

---

[1] *Except when medically counter-indicated (i.e. history of embolisms, severe obesity,...)*
[2] *The body in fact uses such synthesis to produce all sex-steroids from cholesterol, in particular the synthesis of estradiol from testosterone and from androstenedione (via estrone) is well known*
[3] *In a normal female there is a lot less testosterone present (if measured by number of molecules per blood-volume), so a very small change in testosterone is bound to have a big impact*

After surgery the amounts of all these medications can be significantly reduced, often by half or more, almost always by at least a third. But there's now a catch: If I had never started to suppress my testosterone I may very well be quite happy on my natural post surgical level. But *because* I suppressed the natural testosterone I had for a long time to an extremely low level (compared to my biologically normal level) *I am now an addict to testosterone-suppression, likely for life.* **Had I never started artificial suppression I might just have been ok on my natural post-op levels.** *As a worst case scenario I would have needed the same amount of suppression as I do now, but very likely it would have been less, potentially a lot less.* We'll never know, all we know is that I now am where I am: *Thanks to a mental protocol: A drug addict for life!*

Overall I can safely say that the absurd order of treatment and the waiting imposed before meaningful treatment was allowed *has resulted in increasing my lifetime intake of medications by a decent multiple of what it otherwise in all likelihood would have been.* **This isn't healthy for me, it is medically easily avoidable, it isn't economical, it has at times very noticeable negative side-effects and it may yet get me killed.**

There is another aspect: I kept a chart of measurements of my physical changes, I measured these about once a month (i.e. hip & but-circumference, waistline, breast-growth and so on). This nicely showed how my body adapted to HRT, in that year some parameters changed well in the 15-20%-range. Certainly such changes are also noticeable without taking accurate measurements but I was interested in my progress and wanted this documented.

When we go to surgery (I presume any surgery, but I have no other experience than genital surgery) we're asked to suspend HRT, depending upon surgeon and hospital the requirement is usually around 2 to 3 weeks prior and 1 week post. During this time we reach normal male hormone levels unless the testicles have been damaged beyond functioning.

The reasoning for having to discontinue is rather difficult to understand to me. Officially it is stated that being off HRT, particularly estrogen, lowers the risk of embolism as it is assumed that we get back to the somewhat lower "male statistical risk levels" compared to "female statistical risk levels". I was however unable to find any research to substantiate such a claim (comparing occurrences of embolism in the same elective procedure in transsexuals, woman and men; or comparing similar scheduled to emergency surgeries in transsexuals whereas the group receiving treatment as an emergency measure would not be off HRT), however there are a few significant counter-indications to going off HRT:

First: It feels odd that *something that seems to be of paramount concern when it comes to transsexual women is given no concern whatsoever in biological women!* With biological woman it would be all too easy to have them go into *any* elective procedure *when hormone levels are most favourable. After all every pre-menopausal adult woman has a hormonal cycle so scheduling surgery to take place at the most favourable moment within a women's cycle would surely be called for if there really were measurable benefits!* This isn't done and I therefore conclude that the benefits are either nonexistent or doctors aren't willing to inconvenience themselves to have women enjoy such benefits? Assuming that there really are no benefits might just be the nicer interpretation but given the many question-marks I have already put behind modern medicine I would like to give them the benefit of the doubt on this one. Of course if they actually wanted to know studying this would be really simple, just asking women where they are in their cycle before surgery and then crunching the numbers should give us an appropriate picture. Now there's an idea for a doctoral thesis!

Of course there is the issue of embolism-prevention in general. True, I am an engineer, not a doctor. So from my perspective I would have to ask the question if it has ever come to the attention of a medically educated mind *that all patients who go into major surgery and toler-ate this could benefit from being giving a preventative dose of a blood-thinning or anticoagu-lative agent immediately or shortly after the procedure is successfully completed?* This would simply make sense, far more than any hormonal considerations! If the blood is 'thinner' (flows easier) or has less of a tendency to clot I would expect embolisms to be less frequent or at least less severe if they happen ... But hi!, I'm an engineer who thinks along the line of pipes, pressure and flow-conditions when it comes to the circulatory system, so please take my medical advice with a decent pinch of salt. But still... I would be interested...

Second: I have had a little over 11 months of HRT before I needed to go off for surgery. The impact of this on these "favourable physical changes"? *Within 60 days of going off pretty much all the measurable physical changes had been reversed to pre-treatment figures*, includ-ing breast-growth and abdominal fat re-distribution. It took me 6-8 months to get back to anywhere near the numbers I had measured immediately before going off HRT!

Now I presume getting physical changes is one of the more important reasons why people want to go on HRT, it certainly seems to be the only reason dogma offers. *Only it appears like a bad joke if I have to do this for a year when everything goes down the drain afterwards just to comply to another made-up protocol?* Never mind that I am uncertain if my "final result" in appearance will be equally good as if I had not been asked to go off because I am somewhat doubtful that my body really can tolerate male/female/male/female an unlimited number of times *without any significant influence on that final result*. I am also doubtful as to any potential impact on my overall health and life-expectancy as these are *massive* changes which are imposed on my body *repeatedly and within a very short timeframe*.

Third: Going off HRT cold-turkey virtually guarantees an insane resurge in testosterone. This is in part due to the half-life of testosterone-suppressants (Cyproterone, Spironolac-tone,...) being a lot shorter than that of estrogen (estradiol) but also because estrogen is stored in body-fat while testosterone-blockers are not. The body normally metabolizes some testos-terone into dihydrotestosterone (DHT) and estrogen (estradiol) but because there already is way too much estradiol present this is much reduced. Everything is further compounded if the patient also suppresses DHT[1]. In the end the resurge in testosterone will happen long before metabolizing of it increases to normal levels, *the combined effect will likely result in a peak of insane proportions!*

---

[1] *Testosterone is reduced to DHT by 5 alpha reductase. DHT suppressants like finasteride or dutasteride (Proscar, Avodart) work indirectly by suppressing (most of the) 5 alpha reductase so the conversion can't take place - which means that a lot less testosterone will be removed by this process.*

Giving testosterone to biological females at male levels generally causes depression, even suicidality. We know this from extensive research in elite-sports medicine. Giving it in even higher doses does just more of the same. Well, it did that to me too (how amazing…), I had gotten used to female levels during that year of suppression, my body, but more particularly my brain had adapted. Now I was incapable to tolerate my own biological level, never mind that additional peak I was about to be subjected to…

On this too I haven't found any studies but it would certainly be interesting to compare *the suspected* additional risk to have a severe complication during or after surgery caused by somebody not discontinuing HRT *to the very real one of suicide before surgery due to going off*. How many suicides does it take to allow us **to make an informed choice** *and stay on HRT for the entire time, stay on testosterone suppression alone or go off for an individualized and potentially very short time?*

Of course all this would have been of no consideration whatsoever had I been allowed to go to genital alignment first *and start hormonal treatment afterwards.* But then again, this would be all to obvious a solution, wouldn't it?

A.21. GOING NOWHERE - REALLY, REALLY FAST!

It's pointless to say that this time was rather frustrating. There was nothing to be done at counselling. There was nothing to be done medically. My social life was crumbling under the weight of the needless waiting and senseless uncertainty. My emotional life was strictly downhill, from functional socially integrated active and dynamic woman full of life to disconnected, pain stricken, unproductive and, in the end, suicidal transsexual. What an achievement and credit to psychiatric insight and treatment I was…

True, it wasn't as if ever anybody expected anything to come out of this except a suicide. Sorry, I'll rephrase: Except proof of how compliant a human-being can be. I full well realized that I could not sustain such a life indefinitely, that this would end in some way and probably rather sooner than later. Tensions grew in my private life too, I became increasingly incapable of social exchange, of dealing with problems, any kind of problems, even the smallest. Mine as well as others.

I didn't think of this as being in any way unexpected, irrational or even as being proof of an "over-reaction" or "emotional instability" of sorts. Apart from de-humanizing treatment, exploitation and abuse this was in fact the part of treatment I feared the most - because I knew that this would happen, I pretty much anticipated that I would eventually react like this - and I actually felt that this seemed rather normal…

I had lived physically wrong, socially wrong, emotionally wrong and sexually wrong for my entire life. This I could cope with, sort of. And apparently, at least compared to other people with the same affliction, I even did a rather good job at it. *Now they had added to all this complete social alienation, a total legal limbo, a nightmare of medical concerns, a mental fixation on the impossible, meaningless but nevertheless (or precisely because of this) very painful mental treatment, a life without any prospects whatsoever while deliberately withholding a timeline for the one way out!* This, according to dogma, would be the rest of my life! *Unless somebody finally found that doing this to me, treating any human being like this just might be wrong!*

Because this is - as per dogma - *said to be good for me*? Because surviving this - as per psychiatric insight - *is the condition set onto me to remain alive*? Because this is - as to the brilliance of our dogmatists - *going to show them if I merit to be a woman or not*? Because this experience is - as per understanding in mental-health circles - *going to make me a more whole, emotionally more rounded and mentally healthy individual*? Because THIS is - in their opinion - *<u>the best and most sophisticated treatment possible</u>*!

At the same time this is done to us just about every transsexual in treatment is also expected to master life under the microscope of mental-health, maintain a normal level of productivity and most certainly should not fall into any severe emotional distress or, for heaven's sake, depression! Honestly, I would like to question if this is actually possible! It most certainly wasn't for me. This was all but a pre-programmed downward-spiral into a dark seemingly bottomless pit and the one thing I hoped for was that they would allow me to get treatment before I would shatter on the all but inevitable invisible bottom. I didn't really pretend anymore at this time, but by then they didn't even bother to see me at mental-health anymore. Presumably they had figured out that I was self-compliant to the extreme anyway, to a degree which would guarantee self-destruction.

They had done what they set out to do, had destroyed my old life. They hadn't given me a new one for it of course, this they can't do. At the same time they still put all their efforts into preventing me from helping myself! They can take life, it isn't difficult. They do it every day, sometimes they even plan for it, do this deliberately, are willing to put a huge effort into this. Only when it comes to giving life they aren't actually as good, for some reason it does appear to be somewhat more difficult to give life than it is to take it. That too seems to be a lesson they have diligently learned but not yet understood ...

As to my medical progress? At this point I started to be really glad that I had this daily cocktail of steroids and steroid-suppressants at something between liberal and insane doses. Because by now I needed this desperately so I would not go out and kill myself right then and there...

Now I don't want to sound overly cynical here but if you have ever put a question-mark behind how your tax-dollars get spent or might have gotten the idea that somebody, for example a politician, helped his own interest or got a lavish lifestyle paid for out of your pocket you might want to consider that all mental treatment I have ever received, along with hundreds of thousands or millions of transsexuals, was very kindly paid for (or at least heavily subsidized) by your most generous donation to either the government or your healthcare-plan. Honestly, I do see some room for improvement here... But just in case you might not want to save your money? May I suggest spending it on the advancement of that lavish lifestyle of the politician of your choice rather than on the destruction of my life?

B.34. *WHEN SUICIDE IS NOT A CRY FOR HELP*

[He] I think they're taking us for a couple... [Me] I hope you don't mind!

An attempt at suicide, as seen by the mental-health community, is often interpreted as "a cry for help". But sometimes it's not. For us it's often not. We have asked for help, we have told the people who assign themselves the task to help us what our problem is, we know what can be done about it, we know that there is one - and only one - solution and we know that this solution works in excess of 99.5% of all cases.

We have asked. Most of us nicely though some have screamed a real "cry for help". But we're not getting any help! Or at least the help we're getting is *that we can't get the help we need, can't get what would actually work.* This might be given to us in a few years, maybe. Until then we get pain instead of help. We have cried out *"help us!"* and the reply was: "We'll help you! We'll help you *to become who we say you must be* and if you can be *who we say you are* for a few years then, maybe, maybe…". We have asked because to stay alive we need to live who *we* are and we hoped the reply would be "we see your problem, *there's your life!*". But instead the reply was "we can't see any problems, *but there's who you are!*". **We are given whatever we want, *except our lives!***

At first we couldn't get our lives because there was a biological problem. Now we can't get our lives because there's a mental problem! Only while the biological problem at least is our own, that mental one most definitely is somebody elses! That very system with all these "helpful people" denies us the only treatment known to give us a decent life *because so many of us are incapable of living a decent live to the system's satisfaction (and ours) without that treatment.*

We're incapable to be males. Because we're not! But instead of allowing us to be women the system requires us to live a completely made-up and artificial life: 'Transwoman'. Living she-male while having to say that we're happily transsexual! **But as much as we aren't men we are also not transwomen, we're forced into this under the direction of a therapist!** *And unfortunately so many of us will never be capable to satisfy such sick requirements because to live a normal live they would need treatment first.* **Only mental-health gets in the way by denying us a normal life!**

For transsexuals mental-health is not the solution, mental-health is the problem!

If they find that we're incapable to live she-male, a completely absurd, artificial, made-up social role, *they then deem us incapable to live a woman's life, to live our own social role!* This must be the pinnacle of absurdity in dogma: *If we fail at being who we are not* then we're deemed incapable to be *who we are* - **and get death for it!**

It is easy enough to understand how and why this works, isn't it?

A gay person can't stop experiencing himself as being gay. It isn't possible. So if mental-health tells him that being gay is a disease, a sexual perversion and makes his "not being gay" *as measured by "not having any gay sex"* a condition for his life, what he will probably do is stop having sex. *He can do this because having sex is a choice. He can do this because having sex is behavioural!* **This may not feel good,** *but it is possible!*

I can't stop experiencing myself female. It isn't possible. So if mental-health tells me that being female is a disease, a sexual perversion and makes my "not being female" *as measured by "living as a chick with a dick"* a condition for my life, what they will get is a suicide. *Because I cannot stop experiencing my physical self. Experiencing gender, experiencing one's own body is not a choice! I am because of who I am incapable to do what they ask for because experiencing gender is biological, not behavioural!*

In the end this is what we get: We're not crying out for help anymore, we've done that. The result was people who hear us and say: "No, *there'll be no help* as long as you don't stop crying *and become who we tell you to be!* **We withhold your treatment until we feel compliance is achieved** *and you have become who we want you to be!* And then, after you've been broken into unconditional compliance we'll let you go. Maybe". With this treatment they end our crying for help, I don't deny this. Such treatment is very suitable if the goal is to get us quiet quickly. Dead quiet in fact.

We feel, we see, we're horrified! But we all learn the lesson: Crying out for help only gets us more pain - eh, sorry, help. *More mental 'treatment'.* **Ultimately far too many** *seek a way out from the help we're getting.* **Because the help we're getting is the problem!** If we succeed we're dead. Problem solved, hopefully satisfactorily. If we fail this will be interpreted as 'instability', as *a reason to inflict even more 'help' onto us and getting us farther away from what we need! This we understand also. In the end the very help offered to us becomes the most important motivation to succeed. At suicide.*

And if we actually kill ourselves then this isn't deemed a treatment-induced suicide, a failure of mental-health requiring examination of and change to our treatment. By the mental-health community *this is seen as them not giving us enough treatment!* Because clearly what we want is abnormal and preventing us from getting it is "good medical practice"? *Having killed herself over not getting something psychiatry deems insane is a failure of the person who has taken her own life, not a failure of the system! Providing mental people with something crazy isn't the purpose of medicine and because it isn't, nothing could have been done anyway...* Should we however survive treatment then this is deemed "yet another success of mental-health"! Whatever the outcome, *psychiatry just never looses*!

Transsexuals have one of the highest "in treatment suicide-rates". This, undoubtedly, a sign of our madness! To improve this all we need is ever more control and ever more restrictions on living-out our craziness by further restricting access to that surgery! Because all we really need to improve is ever more mental treatment! Until, in the end, we have only mental treatment, no surgery - and no more transsexuals!

207

A.22. DOLLARS AND NONSENSE

This chapter could just as well have had the title *"And Just Why The Heck Do I Think Society Should Pay For This Anyway?"*. So why do I think society should pay for this? Well, apart from that idea that general mutual support and the medical support of handicapped people are commonly believed to be basic values of our society? Apart from fairness and equal treatment for everybody, as I too have paid all the premiums and taxes to run that system?

Apart from all that? Well, as we will see unlike most disabilities out there, be it Jane's or John's or something completely different like multiple sclerosis, loss of sight or Gulf War Syndrome, our disability, transsexuality, is treatable to a degree which allows full (re-) integration and a normal life. Never mind that compared to all the above treating transsexuality would be very cheap if this were done right.

As with many other disabilities financial analysts have found that transsexuals, after treatment, through their improved general health and better ability to get education, work better paying jobs and have much fewer "co-morbid problems" *will pay for their treatment in a relatively short time <u>themselves</u>, typically only a few years![1]* No, such profitability should not be the measure on which we grant help to handicapped people, it is the very idea of insurance or universal government healthcare that even catastrophic costs, which are bound to incur *to a small number of the insured,* are covered. However if costs pay for themselves over only a short time and these aren't in the "catastrophic range" at all it really - in addition to all of the above - strikes me as a dumb business-decision to not pay for it.

But then again, we're talking politics here and that may just be even less understandable than mental-health! And because it is politics on top of mental-health this in the end isn't a question of paying for my healthcare or not, it instead is remodelled into a quest of how much the system (medical and political) *can profit off my disability!* But this isn't possible? We don't punish people for having medical problems and we certainly don't hand out fines for being handicapped? Well, let's have a look at these numbers. How much does this really cost, in general and to the individual. And where exactly does the money go to?

---

[1] *JPMorgan-Chase presentation: "The Cost of Transgender Healthcare Benefits"*

Unlike economists for whom it seems these days that everything comes down to just one number, the GNP, for us there is more than one financial aspect to this: There are at least a personal side, a socio-economic side and one involving strictly medical expenses. As you might expect I also find plenty of unethical expenses, payments we are forced to make, payments that amount to extortion - and I'm for once not talking of that psychiatrist's bill here!

Direct Medical Expenses:

The minimal treatment of a transsexual (if everything runs smooth and there are no other conditions requiring additional treatment) involves hormonal alignment, this is a lifetime expense, facial hair-removal and surgical genital alignment, these are one time expenses. Technically an outpatient-orchiectomy for $800 should do, but I think given all the social, emotional and legal ramifications it is justified to put vaginoplasty as the absolute minimum here. I mean if this is about talking cheap: There's the $29.95 mail-order kit for the do-it-yourself procedure on eBay… But I think even transsexuals are entitled to *some* dignity…

A vaginoplasty costs anywhere from $8,000 to $25,000 plus expenses such as travelling (ok, as so often in life one *can* spend more if one absolutely insists). Hormonal treatment and the necessary lab-supervision costs in the range of $2,000 to $10,000[1] a year pre-op, about half as much post op and potentially a lot less long-term. As the costs decrease significantly after surgery it is sensible to get the surgery done as early as possible, *for a typical case an average genital surgery would pay for itself (and the insurance company) in savings on the cost for drugs, lab-work and prescription-visits alone over less than 10 years, possibly as little as half as much! (An orchiectomy typically pays for itself in less than a year!).* And that's without including all the added cost in rare *but potentially very expensive* cases when severe side-effects and complications do occur due to the higher-dose pre-op regimes.

Other medical procedures involve surgical feminization of face, body modifications (including breast augmentation as one of the more usual examples), hair-transplants (or more invasive procedures to correct scalp-hair), leg-extension, liposuction in various places, neck-extension, rib-extraction and many more. Many of these procedures easily cost $10,000 *each*, extensive facial feminization combined with hair-line adjustment could cost $50,000. All these procedures are normally paid for by the individual herself.

It is obvious that if treatment is started early in life there will be a lot less pre-existing masculinization of the body and thus fewer drugs and less potentially costly, time-consuming and painful feminization will be needed during treatment to achieve an acceptable result. If treatment is started before the onset of male puberty (or at the latest very shortly thereafter) virtually all of these costs (and the involved pain, risks and loss of time) could be eliminated.

---

[1] *Depending on the type of drugs used, but also on age of patient, how well treatment and particular drugs are tolerated and how often lab supervision is deemed necessary*

Hair removal is a good example: Not only is the procedure excruciatingly painful, it also isn't exactly cheap to get rid of male facial and body hair that only ever started growing during puberty. Removal of the male facial hair alone costs $8,000 to $15,000, this is somehow the absolute minimum to be socially accepted as a woman all day long. [If a biological woman grows facial hair in this magnitude it is deemed disfiguring and the costs of removal are covered, no questions asked. Of course! It's basic human dignity. Transsexual women? Apparently we're not really women after all, are we?]. Unfortunately some people seem to be closer related to apes, this may be why my own electrolysis bill runs in excess of $60,000.

Certain physical features are difficult to reverse medically at this time, some are not changeable at all. Among the first are the lower male voice. Voice surgery is possible but the results are by far not as good and predictable as one would hope for. One of the most obvious examples of the second category is overall body height: Biological males simply grow taller on average and I have yet to hear of the "shrinking treatment". Broader chest and shoulders in biological males vs. females is another example of an as of yet irreversible feature.

Personal Financial Expenses:

In addition to these medical expenses there are other expenses in related fields. In particular I could mention hair re-growth. Minoxidil[1], one of the few products that actually works, costs around $500 a year and needs to be used for life; surgical hair transplants or scalp readjustments are available as a one-time solution but can cost over $25,000.

Often extensive travel is required to obtain surgery. This could cost several thousand dollars for one person and if one has a friend or spouse to be there this more than doubles as this person in addition to travel also requires accommodation. In addition a pre-op visit is useful for most procedures, so an additional round-trip needs to be scheduled. If these are "round the world trips" (as is often the case for genital surgery) this can easily be $5,000 in itself (three trips plus maybe 2 weeks of hotel accommodation for a companion), if it is 'only' a question of flying across the continent (for facial, breast, hair or other surgery) this may still easily be $1,000 for all three roundtrip-tickets. Such costs obviously repeat for each procedure.

There is one expense that's often forgotten: Time off work. Genital surgery requires a minimum of 6 weeks, facial surgery may vary from 2 to 6 weeks. The influence additional restrictions have (no heavy physical activities for half a year, one often cannot wear glasses for many months after a rhinoplasty and so forth) obviously depend on what kind of job one has. The figures are according to several surgeons recommendations but assume that there are no complications. But honestly, taking 3 months off for genital alignment would be my own recommendation, starting the day one has to go off hormonal treatment... There are also

---

[1] *Currently the only FDA-approved freely available treatment for hair re-growth, available in several products. There are other treatments (Finasteride, Dutasteride, Tretinoin) but these are prescription and may not be approved for this purpose.*

simple doctor's visits, electrolysis, psychiatric therapy (my favourite), many visits to government offices and so forth and not everything can be scheduled around work. So if one would peg the total loss of earnings for the entire process at between 6-12 months of salary that would still seem very conservative. How much money this amounts to obviously depends on one's income but it would seem reasonable to assume that people with a lower income would be hit hardest as they are the ones who could least afford to be without a regular income - never mind the medical bills that come in at the same time!

Again, transsexuals would not have these expenses if they were given treatment early in life, for hair-loss this would likely mean surgery typically before the age of 20 but certainly not later than 25 (testosterone-suppression alone does slow male hair-loss but it does not stop it). To avoid all male facial- and body-hair as well as many irreversible skeletal masculinizations the surgery would have to be scheduled some time before puberty, certainly not later than about age 10-12. During this time every year counts. Every month would help.

Socio-Economic Expenses:

Medical treatments have side-effects. Surgeries can have complications or may need revisions due to unsatisfactory results, many of our drugs are known carcinogenic or have other potential serious side-effects. Few cases are needed in order to make the treatment of such side-effects *by far* more expensive than the original treatment was. People may be absent from work for long periods of their lives, they may even die of such complications. This all costs the economy money, the need for longer and higher-dosed treatment and more feminization due to late onset of treatment obviously causes a lot more of these cases and costs.

Every transsexual who is not treated is at risk of depression and other emotional issues, even suicide. Even if only a small fraction do, over time, require related treatments this means still more medical expenses, more lost opportunities for education, more time off work and more costs to society. Besides all these negative impacts, if one assumes psychiatric therapy to cost $200 an hour and genital alignment to cone in at $10,000, it takes a mere 50 visits to a psychiatrist, one year of weekly therapy, to make surgery cheaper than mental therapy (any added cost of psychiatric medication prescribed during these visits isn't even included), *never mind that this psychiatrist and the prescribed psychotropics may only be necessary because of denial of surgery.*

But the most significant socio-economic loss is that *transsexuals statistically will not achieve their full personal, social, educational and economic potential in life if they do not receive timely treatment!* This begins very early in life, mostly due to social problems. Possibly as early as age 6 the person starts to divert considerable effort and time to coping with the condition, effort and time which would be needed in socialization, school and education. Transsexual children are often socially isolated, a problem which typically increases dramatically during puberty. This leads to loneliness, depression and the lack of a peer-group for support and emotional/intellectual exchange. Therefore transsexuals are likely to end up being, on average, less educated and productive than they could be, thus contributing less to society than they otherwise would. If treatment is given early in life I believe the great majority of these sad and far-reaching effects could be alleviated, with greater acceptance these could be eliminated entirely. *It is even conceivable that transsexual individuals could be particularly beneficial to society in certain functions,* if only they and their particular situations in life would be accepted!

Forced and Unethical Expenses:

No, I don't want to point-out here that I - like the majority of transsexuals - had to pay for all the medical treatment with the exception of general care and a portion of the cost of medication myself. This is absurd considering the social benefits of treatment alone, never mind any human-rights issues that come with this refusal of treatment and payment.

I also do not want to focus on the fact that many transsexuals, including myself, have to pay *their mental-treatment* or at least part thereof themselves (according to their respective fee-schedules *a single session* of individual therapy goes for up to $135 of cost-sharing to the patient at subsidized social institutions and for $165 to $240+ at a typical large psychiatric institution, some private therapists charge even more). This too can cost tens of thousands of dollars and the only reason many of us go there is to receive a signed piece of paper finally allowing them to get yet more pay-for-yourself medical services...

No, the real issue I have is that all the expenses I incurred *on medical referrals, with full agreement from a doctor that this is necessary treatment* aren't even fully tax deductible! It is one thing that insurance-plans don't pay for it (which would obviously make it *tax-free* for myself), it is something else that because I have to pay the bill out of my own pocket *the government actually expects me to pay taxes on this money first,* although at a slightly reduced rate. And then, when I spend it, *some of these medical services comes with sales-tax added to the expense!* To me this is simply obscene! ***Instead of paying for my treatment the government actually deems it appropriate to rake-in a substantial financial profit from my disability!***

Another example of such absurd expenses would be me paying in excess of $3,000 in parking-fees so I could actually obtain such *prescribed* medical treatments! Of course if transsexuality would officially be a disability I could have been given a disability-permit enabling me to park for free while undergoing medically necessary treatment. ***But once again the government chooses profiteering off my disability instead of helping me!***

Where it really starts to stink is when the government cancels our childcare-benefits because they say *I'm not the person who can file a claim for these!* The argument goes as follows: I file my taxes with the provincial government. For their purposes I am Eva, *female*. The filing (and processing of all the credits and benefits) is under the federal social insurance system. For the people at social insurance I am Eva, <u>*male, because the rules for assigning a gender-designation are different on both levels of government!*</u> Never mind even after surgery it takes the bureaucrats almost another year to officially correct my status, *meaning another tax-year goes by.* During this time (several years in total) I get a note instead of a payment saying something like *the data provided on the tax-return and the one on file at social insurance aren't the same: Get your record fixed within 30 days or forget the benefits!*

Now sometimes I just marvel at how simplistic some people see the world and I'm simply horrified about how unscrupulous these individuals become when they can get away squeezing another buck out of the misery of somebody else...

In total I estimate that all levels of government combined have raked in a whopping $35,000 in profits on my medical care in everything from sales-taxes on treatment, prescription and non-prescription medications to having to pay partial income-tax on these funds before I could ever spend these to pocketing social benefits to cancelling tax-deductions to handing out fees for everything from parking to systematic extortion for correcting my legal state and government documents. (Note that this amount does not include the bills themselves).

An example of the latter would be obtaining a passport. This costs some $100-$150 in total each time I needed to get one (passport-fee, photograph and getting there. As an unpaid mother I'm generously not including any lost income for the time off work to show-up at that office, never mind the highly entertaining 2 hour wait before I get my 5 minute interview). Now I don't want to argue over the amount of this charge or how this gets done *however I find it outrageous that everybody else gets their passport issued <u>for five years</u> but <u>transsexuals only get it for one</u>* until our administrative gender is finally corrected - which took one of the countries I am a citizen of 3 full years after my surgery (for individuals who for whatever reason don't go to surgery this is *a lifetime expense*)! Because of this *we end-up having to pay five times as much over five years to keep our travel-documents current,* never mind having the hassle to get this done an extra four times! *To me this is yet another $500+ punishment for having been born how I was!*

Even if we would not consider our personal financial expenses, deem our well-being irrelevant and only see this from the point of view of national economy it is still true that the services *we* end-up paying for are more often than not either government or insurance assisted or subsidized in some way (such as prescription visits at the doctor's, general health-care issues, drugs that are dispensed on drug-pans or social assistance, emergency admissions due to complications or even a partial coverage of mental health). So *the more money we need to spend, on average the more gets drawn from all these other sources* - no matter if we want this or not. Whatever the reason, this then ends-up costing *everybody* far more than it would have to!

All in all it is safe to conclude that in just about every respect it is better and cheaper to start treatment sooner in life and have it paid for so the individual can actually obtain it. I certainly don't believe that this is contradictory to what virtually every transsexual wants anyway because in the end it is mostly us who have to bear the brunt of the costs, financial but otherwise as well. *The economically reasonable and sensible thing to do would have to be acceptance, early detection and immediate start of treatment!*

Now somehow I feel I have heard that line before, but it wasn't at mental-health! Because they say the best way to get at this is by refusing to accept that an individual has the condition for years, slowing down and delaying treatment as much as possible and *to guarantee that treatment cannot be obtained before all the damage is done, all the time is lost and far too many individuals have lost-out on a meaningful social, educational and economic integration and a fulfilling personal life, if not worse!*

Psychiatry sets a completely arbitrary minimum age, 21 years is the official requirement for surgical alignment in North-America, 18 years in Western Europe. It must apparently make psychiatric sense to have a three year age-difference between the two continents, but maybe they can prove that European teens are just more mature than their North-American counterparts?

Of course everywhere else in medicine an individual is assumed to be competent to make informed life and death-decisions by the age of 16. But hi! This is psychiatry so a little deviation from the accepted normal must be expected. Never mind we're not talking about life and death here but about genitals and surely it takes a half-decade longer to understand sex than it does to understand suicide?

B.35. OF COURSE I HAVE ALWAYS KNOWN...

And yes, of course I have always known that I am a woman... Well, there's that famous line just about every psychiatrist used to expect although luckily these days that's seen a bit more relaxed and realistic - in most places anyway.

Me? Well... If I look back on my life, kindergarten and before, I can certainly see all these "stereotype-bending" behaviours there. However being a parent I also see all these behaviours in just about every child, male or female. They tend to dress-up, pretend to be somebody else. They do this *in every social role there is*, including cross-gender, *because it just doesn't matter! Children don't analyze and decide, they just play!*

If my 4 year old daughter says "I am Clifford today" (a big red dog from a series of children's books and cartoons) then she's Clifford for a day. Of course if there were a surgery to make her into Clifford... Well, I'd say that this would be a bit, hmmm, *mental?* But then again, I don't expect her to say that she's Clifford every day for the rest of her life! She'll go on to something else in an hour or at least by next morning - after all, it's child's play!

And yes, I too played these games, all of them, only the cartoon characters may have been different a few decades ago... What remains is that we selectively remember our past and this I certainly do also. Just as I suppose many people in transsexual mental treatment do. We very, very distinctly remember all those times we did something that's judged "predominantly female". Of course to be honest I'd have to say that I did try most of these "male behaviours" also - well, it's early childhood, it's all play! Our daughter certainly does but I'm not expecting her to be a guy any time soon because of this! Children play, try to find their place, but they mostly do as their environment allows. *Behaving male was deemed normal for me, so it would not have raised an eyebrow, be followed by discouragement or punishment, it would not even have been pointed out: It would have matched expectations! This wasn't anything special so why should I remember much of it?*

What I find important here is that a good majority of transsexuals doesn't have the experience of having raised children and so they, just as many other adolescents or even adults, assume that *what they remember is what actually happened!* That it is *all* that has ever happened! I find it is easy to fall for this trap, it is a bit like "everything was so much better in the good old days", but was it? Or is it just that *we tend to remember selectively?*

Right from the start remembering ordinary and socially expected behaviour is a lot less likely than the one that failed to meet expectations, was highlighted by being told off

[Consulate] Ma'am you've made a mistake, this is your husband's passport! [Me] No, this is my passport! [Me] No, really, this is mine... And I don't have a husband, I think I'd know...

or even punished! If psychotherapy then puts pressure onto us actually having *selective recall of the "gender-dysphoric kind",* well: We do!

I'm not saying that memories are being made-up (well, I hope not), all I'm saying is that *the recall of events that didn't match expectations back then, the ones that lead to negative experiences and therefore are remembered is further positively re-enforced by psychotherapy* **while the recall of others, likely more positive memories,** *in spite of them being there* **is negatively re-enforced** *because these contradict the therapist's expectations!*

Having to do this repeatedly, therapy-session after therapy-session, if bad luck would have it for hundreds of sessions, these memories might just start to completely dominate everything else! It is predictable. It's a good way to make a past which may have been bad *sometimes* into one that was bad *nearly all the time!*

To me this seems very problematic. It is one thing to use psychotherapy focussed on a specific event in life which occurred once or maybe in a series of incidents over some time, such as abuse, but everybody agrees that there were better times in between, that there would have been a normal alternative, that there will be a better future if the person understands and contributes towards change. *It is something very different if psychotherapy is abused to show to a person that her entire life was in essence worthless and wrong, only consisted of pain up to and including the present - while at the same time telling her that she can't work towards a better future because whatever she contributes remains worthless and irrelevant!*

Jane says: Yes, I could have lamented over why I had my accident for years and years and years. I could have done therapy on this and spent my time sulking in tears over it and be depressed. In the end I would have been in the very same wheelchair I am now, it would have changed *nothing* - except for the additional experience of more pain!

Instead I focussed on my future! On treatment, on getting better! On rebuilding my social life, work, finding friends and solving practical problems. Getting my life on track!

I can't change what happened. All I can change is the future! I do just that and I am glad that I have met so many people on the way who have helped me to achieve this!

Frankly, I would like to venture the thought that most of the psychiatrists who work with transsexuals and who are in a position (or put themselves in a position) to write or influence our dogma aren't too much aware of how small children live, how they behave, feel, what they do. If they had ever raised children from birth to, say, age 6 or 7, they would know better than to say that dressing in a social role which includes changing one's gender *is anything but normal.* They would know better than to claim that this is sexually motivated or even go as far as to state that this is an expression of a perversion, a (presumably dirty) sexual fetish *in a pre-schooler.* Of course it all makes perfect psychiatric sense? I mean if your five year old daughter plays Bob (from "Bob The Builder") *that's normal*, if however your son plays Dora (from "Dora The Explorer"), *that's a sexual perversion???* Honestly, how much ignorance and arrogance must some people have to go out and proclaim just that?

If you ask me: When did I know? I can see female role-behaviours at age 5, even before. I can also see male role behaviour at the same age. The most honest self-assessment I can give is *that back then I didn't care about my gender!* I simply never identified.

The first time I remember that I did ask myself the question what I ought to be was around age 9, by then I answered the question with *"most definitely not male"*. What this would then make me, well, that I really didn't think too much about as it was hypothetical anyway. Of course that was an admission just to myself. I had no idea of the existence of transsexuality or genital surgery so I just kept my mouth shut and did as told...

But there is another side to this. If we ask John the question how he experienced his early childhood, he would likely say something like this:

Although I did not understand anything about my disability, its cause and medical treatment, its name and the effects it was bound to have on my life *I did feel from a very early age that I was somehow different.* I was certainly treated differently, there were things I could not do and things I was expected to do I did not understand.

Understanding my disability came over time. My parents started to explain the medical issues very early, maybe at age 4 or 5, but I really only understood it all perhaps by age 30. Some time after I had gotten my transplant and for the first time in my life had felt really and completely healed. I started to accept that my life may, after all, not be limited by my disability forever, that I would not have to die because of it and that I finally was capable to experiences myself as physically complete, whole and normal.

I did feel the effects of my disability as far back as I can remember, there are some very painful memories back to age 3. I am certain there was more pain even before then but this I do not remember. I did not understand. But it hurt anyway, just differently.

On the other hand I remember joyful, good and positive moments in my early life also. There may not have been as many as other kids have, but it is worthwhile to focus on these rather than on the bad ones. The bad ones are obvious. Why waste any time on these?

The very same is true for transsexuality. It doesn't matter that this disability isn't visible, that it can't be tested for in the lab. The pain is real, *it has always been.* My inability to understand my own pain as a child, my inability to describe it in medical (or psychiatric) terms at age two *is irrelevant in respect to the experience!* There may be a different form of pain once understanding dawns, a different form of pain once one realizes that one is mistreated and abused *because of this* and yet another different form of pain *once one learns that treatment is possible, but deliberately denied.* Nevertheless there is always that first basic pain, this indescribable feeling of "something not being quite as it should be", and this is there right from the start. Every other pain only ever gets piled on top of what's already there!

Transsexuality doesn't start with understanding or even recognizing. Like every other disability this starts with pain. *And while understanding - as far as possible - may be of help, alleviating the pain should be paramount!* **No human being should be left in unnecessary pain and agony. If this happens due to neglect it is social abuse. If it happens deliberately it is criminal. If pain is used to impose change it is downright devious. There is a word to describe the act of wilfully creating pain or of deliberately withholding relief of pain for the purpose of enforcing compliance or behavioural modification. This word is <u>torture</u>.**

A.23. BENDING REALITY

By now I had been on HRT for 12 weeks, half a year of mental treatment had passed, I was going to counselling maybe once every three weeks. Everybody agreed that this was strictly a painful waste of time for everybody involved and was solely orchestrated so I could show compliance to dogma. Everybody also strictly insisted that I continued to go.

But there were a few problems. Dogmatic problems of course. I still wasn't seeing anybody who could sign me off on surgery, but even more problematic: The place I was going to was strictly a "short term service". It was easy enough to get in quickly, but they had a cap of 20 sessions of which, after half a year, I already had 14. This would be over at some time, certainly before I would ever see a surgeon. Not only would I after these 20 sessions no longer be in a position to show compliance, more relevantly staying there I would not be getting anywhere as I still needed to collect the same signatures to being allowed on surgery I needed from the start. I had known this and really I had just hoped that going there would get me on HRT quickly, which it did. But I had a plan B ready: I had applied to go to another place as well. Long-term psychiatric care. There they were ready to take clients for life! I also knew they had trans-experience, their in-house psychiatrists actually were known to have written these dogmatically approved letters. The bad news: Just to get in typically took more than half a year - that's of course why I went to the other place first. So when they called after 'only' five months and offered me to see somebody I accepted immediately!

This also meant that I was done at the first place because the healthcare-system doesn't allow people to do what they call *duplicating services.* Did I mention that dogma requires *two independent mental-health professionals to sign off on surgery?* Ok, getting this done while remaining in treatment *and not duplicating anything* is maybe kid's play for somebody with multiple personality disorder... But by now I was confident that psychiatry would have a ready-made completely absurd solution for this should I fail to demonstrate that particular pathology as well...

So, there I was, first session, new counsellor. "This may be a bit repetitive... As I don't know you we will have to start from zero". Well, I had sort-of anticipated this so I suggested: "You might want to call my former counsellor and get some ideas about me and what we have done (or more precisely what we hadn't done), I certainly wouldn't mind...", I also handed her the printed version of my life, some 6 pages I had compiled for my previous counsellor.

[Me, at mental-health, second counsellor] I need these signatures to get my surgery, can you help me? [She] I think we're way past that stage now...

I am only an engineer and a woman at that, but if I take over a job from somebody else or leave work to somebody else I like to talk to these people, I find communicating to each other helps... But then again this is mental-health and do I really have to say it? *Things are done a little differently there, this is not about "being efficient", "getting results" or even "making sense"*... Just for good measure I added: "And besides, please do send me where I need to go to get the paperwork so I can sign-up for that surgery! You know just as well as I do that if I were allowed to sign-up today you'd still get me for some 12 months until I could actually go because of the waiting-list there...". She thought for a moment, then said *no* and *no!* "And come back in two weeks...".

Session two, two weeks later. I ask again about surgery. By now she had time to read-up on my life: "Ok, here's what I think... This isn't what I am supposed to do but I'd like to talk to your former counsellor, could you get the necessary paperwork signed? And come back in two weeks...".

Session three, another two weeks later. I was back *and I asked again.* Same question, for the third time. "Yes, I talked to your former counsellor and I think you should just try to get an appointment for surgery with that letter you already have. I know it's not what they want but you already have it so you may just give it a try! All they can say is 'no'...". *"I'll have to give the name and address of a current counsellor and a psychiatrist who will sign these dogmatic recommendations,* I assume I can put *you* in?". "Just do as they ask...". "... a psychiatrist?". "For now put in 'to be determined'"...

So I sent in my application: Short medical history? Well, it was really short all right. Previous procedures? That one was even shorter as I never had any. History of mental treatment (do not include treatment exclusively related to "gender-dysphoria")? Same thing. Details as to where I was in treatment: Psychiatrist? I draw a blank. Counselling or second reference? Ok, there I had something. Since? Well, 4 weeks... Additional information (only if HRT is not provided by psychiatrist)? Well, there was *one* question I knew what to put in! At the end it said *"a date for surgery can only be set if all "dogmatic requirements" have been met and at least one detailed letter of recommendation has been provided".* I mailed the package out that very evening.

A week later the phone rang. It was a secretary of the clinic. "You have mailed in your application for vaginoplasty?". "Yes, that'd be me...". "This is a bit... unusual... you are not seeing a psychiatrist, have not been on HRT for a year and you have neither a therapist to verify that you have lived 'full-time' for a year nor a recommendation in due form...". "Well, my counsellor told me to send it as it is, I presume she knows what she's asking me to do...". "Can you come in for a pre-op visit"? I replied "Yes, I can arrange this if you'd like me to" and silently thought about accumulating loads of frequent flyer miles. "Given the circumstances we'd certainly like to see you... As for the surgery, we are currently booking the following weeks...", she gave me the dates. The first possible week for booking started two days after I would have done that one year on HRT! I took Monday (of course). I also got booked on a pre-op two months prior.

That phone-call was 282 days before the date set for surgery. To me this felt like the conception of life! 40 weeks to birth! One pregnancy to go!

Next I was on the phone with trans-support (congratulations!), then my counsellor's answering machine. I left a message: "Hi! I have an appointment! Now all I need is these letters... I have 40 weeks to get these, I suppose you'd better start sending me somewhere! *Now!*".

The minimum in-treatment time before a psychiatrist is in a position to write any evaluation or statement is 3 months - 13 weeks. It's professional doctrine and it's also mentioned in dogma, but of course that's strictly theory. The big governmental organization in town *requires their psychiatrists to have people in treatment for a minimum of two years* until they're allowed to write such a recommendation. But whatever waiting-time is imposed the clock only ever starts to tick after the first visit - often it takes many months to get just that far!

As to the reply to my request? Well, the nurse at trans-support said: "You're going to be just fine! *And if there's still something missing in your file I am sure we can make something up...*". Honestly! I don't know if I had ever questioned the sanity of that treatment more than just then!

B.36. TRANSSEXUALS AND THE MEDIA

Some transsexuals are terribly upset about how we are portrayed by the media. I am too, at times, to some degree. But I also think that many authors an activists go far beyond anything reasonable. True, I don't like the demeaning aspects and I don't like to be seen as a glamour-girl who has nothing but her breast-size, nail-polish and the newest surgical procedure to have her lips enlarged in mind because I'm not like this at all. But there are women who are just like this, transsexual or not. This isn't good or bad, but only seeing this part by far doesn't reflect the entire spectrum of transsexual people just as portraying glamour and sexism would not portray woman in general accurately.

Certainly I don't like derogatory depictions of transsexuality (such as in the movie *"Pet Detective"*) but then again I suspect that our friend Jane does not like derogatory depictions of paraplegics just as John does not like similar depictions of people with birth-defects. I understand if they both are upset about movies like *"Freaks"* where disability is exploited in every possible way it could be for a box-office hit. But in general I think we should "loosen-up" a bit. A movie like *"Transamerica"* is a good comedy, I got a laugh or two out of it even though it is medically largely incorrect.

From my perspective the first and foremost problem with our media-depiction is that usually the media isn't interested in showing what transsexuality is or who transsexuals are. What media-makers seek is a good spectacle that draws viewers, listeners, readers! Parents and schools by and large fail to teach our children that the media doesn't depict "the truth", *but rather offers an ingeniously crafted product either to be sold to them or given away for free to sell them, as viewers to advertisers (or both).* The goal isn't education, *it is to make money!*

There are two ways to get people to consume the media: Either through entertainment or through information. If the goal is entertainment then facts are usually of little concern, after all, it's just that: Entertainment, *fiction.* And it ought to be taken as such! However creating fiction should not be used as an excuse to exploit any and all stereotypes out there and I very much understand if some people hate movies like *"Crash"* for doing nothing else. Predictably this movie then goes on to get a "best picture" award from the *Academy of Motion Picture Arts and Sciences* for exploiting more stereotypes a minute than any other before! Which shows that one person's art is often another person's disgust; but that too isn't new. So if the industry depicts "Sexual and Gender Identity Disorders" in just the same derogatory and exploitative way in *"The Silence of the Lambs"* (where one of the villains is depicted as a male who wants to dress-up female using human body-parts) the result just as predictably ends-up getting another shower of awards from the very same source!

However I hope that just about everybody realizes that as much as *Crash* isn't a scholarly introduction to racism, *The Silence of the Lambs* isn't psycho-pathology 101! Certainly nobody I'd know would take these for anything like this. Thankfully the public is by and large quite capable to make the distinction between the misuse of stereotypes, the fictional and exploitative depiction of the absurd for the purpose of entertainment (well, making money) and reality. Spectators are smart enough to understand that this kind of entertainment lives on fabricating fears of all kinds which are smartly interwoven with fact to make things appear realistically possible *even though they are that at best very, very remotely.* If at all.

From my perspective this gets a lot more complex and at times murky when it comes to informational pieces such as documentaries. Two examples at the extreme ends of this are *"Let Me Die a Woman"*, an exploitative feature-like pseudo-documentary about transsexuality where acting and reporting are indistinguishably interwoven, the facts are few but sex well past the line of pornography appears to be omnipresent. At the other end are informative and very well done pieces like Barbara Walters' on transsexual children in ABC's *20/20.*

The problem many people from the media face is similar to what psychiatrists also find: It is impossible to find *a typical transsexual!* Psychiatrists find people who conform to their expectations. The media-people find individuals who seek media-exposure (usually these people either need money or want to be seen). Unfortunately quite a few of these aren't transsexual at all, but how should the media-makers know? *Sometimes media-makers even insist in depicting an individual as transsexual if she herself maintains that she is in fact a she-male.* They want to depict *transsexuality* but what they often end-up showing is the stereotype about *how real a woman a man can look* or *how fascinating and normal a conversation one can have with somebody who's clearly lost her (his?) marbles?*

This presentation of us, along with the line "males who pretend to be female" or similar ("don't they look believable", "one could hardly tell", "they're almost real"...) is more damaging to us than every derogatory joke there is. The difference lies, again, in perception: Most people understand the difference between an offensive joke and decent behaviour in real life, that such expressions are specifically used "for entertainment". Some sick kind anyway. But when we're being portrayed as "disturbed males" who "play female" more or less believably (whereas the comparison is almost always about beauty or looks, not about what we do or what we feel) and this is offered in a documentary-, real life or news-context, *then the spectators believe that this is an appropriate depiction of transsexuality, that* this *is who we really are - after all, we ourselves would not participate in it otherwise, would we?*

Another often voyeuristic depiction focuses on our 'transition'. The portrayal of living socially male to living socially female. Typically shown in documentaries through more or less kind "before and after" shots. The effect being to gloat at *how the perception of a human-being can change.* And while I do understand that some transsexuals feel compelled to show this process to the world at large - after all, it is a very liberating experience - *I also think that this usually only happens in this way **because psychiatry mandates our lives just this way!***

Generally such docs start either by showing a transsexual in transition and then present some pictures of male-life before or they start with male-life and then continue along that *artificial* journey. Often these end shortly before or after surgical alignment. But of course an individual can only ever be followed *if that individual has already openly identified transsexual! So the whole process of self-finding, coming to a point where one accepts this and seeks a way to express it <u>has already happened</u>!* The filmmakers are in fact *too late* to 'capture' a personal transition - if there ever is one. *What they then depict as "our life's experience" is our <u>social</u> transition.* And while it is true that this can be difficult, that this can be worthy of a documentary **what they depict is our adapting to the psychiatrically enforced transsexual lifestyle while they miss the issue and our becoming ourselves!**

Depicting Jane in how well she can handle a wheelchair and what tricks she can do in it may well impress the spectators. However this isn't a complete image of Jane and it most certainly isn't an accurate depiction of life as a paraplegic. Jane certainly could show many tricks on wheels but in any 45-minute documentary covering her life doing stunts with her chair might take up a minute or so, possibly with a voice-over of her accomplishments in sports. It would never be the centre of the doc and it would most definitely not be styled as her entire life! Or I would hope so anyway…

It is the depiction of an absurd process which only takes place this way *because we're not allowed to do this in a more suitable, natural and normal progression.* I have noted that very few of these documentaries make a point in mentioning this, that "the order things are done in" is not a choice, it is not the result of a treatment-discussion nor an expression of the person's wishes, feelings or needs. *I have yet to see a single documentary spelling out clearly that the transitional process they depict is at least in part but potentially entirely externally dictated and may or may not be a personal expression and choice of ourselves!* But because this isn't mentioned most spectators will predictably assume *that the treatment they see us getting is the best medical science can do for us, that this it is what we want and choose. Many then find themselves confirmed: If anybody wants what they see us live, well then a visit to the next psychiatrist should be in order! And I agree!!! <u>Only this wasn't our choice but that of these psychiatrists we should be sent to for doing it</u>…*

Few documentaries note the pressure we are under and if so they speak of waiting-times due to overbooked surgeons, show desperate people counting down days. **That this waiting is artificially created is rarely ever mentioned and honestly, nobody would take that seriously because this would neither be understandable nor believable to somebody who hasn't lived this!**

But whatever this distortion does to us, one thing is certain: *Transition, living transsexual and in particular being in medical (mental) treatment costs a lot of money.* So if people try to raise funds by appearing in the media, making documentaries or - for heaven's sake - writing books, *even if these may not depict what they feel,* I find this very understandable! Don't psychiatrists and psychologists do the same at times? True, they rarely sell themselves to the porn-industry. Unless one counted seeking public funding for that "systematic study of human sexuality", particularly when it comes to *'empirical'* or *'experimental'* study?

But then again we can also take the *"who is being pressured into selling oneself for sexual or other spectacle"* and *"who is 'observing' and 'studying' it"* as one more sign of who is cleaning out and who is being cleaned out and abused, often for sheer desperation!

A.24. HOW DO YOU DO TODAY?

It was summer in mid-town, the heat outside was unbearable but they had air-conditioning at mental-health. I was 10 minutes early, traffic was at times unpredictable in the big city but that day it was light and I didn't want to stay outside in the sweltering heat. So I got in, passed the armed police-guard (a friendly "good afternoon ma'am!"), the receptionist ("I have an appointment with…", "yes, dear, go right up"), the elevator, then a hallway where I collapsed into the nearest chair. Waiting.

I suppose I was listening to my preferred radio-station when, right on time, my counsellor showed up. "How are you, you look really happy?". "I am, very much so! And how are you?". "I'm fine, thank you!" she said, but made an impression rather like I expected somebody to look after she had just learned that her surgery would be cancelled for no good reason. "…Come in and have a seat…".

"So, is there anything you'd like to talk to me today?". "Well… Honestly… Not really…". "All right, come back in 4 weeks!".

On my way out I passed the receptionist again ("bye dear…"), then the officer, he was holding the door for me ("bye ma'am…").

I had an hour left on the parking-meter - what a waste of time!

B.37. FOR ALL THE WRONG REASONS

Yes, I wanted that surgery. Actually by that time in my life I wanted nothing else anymore with an intensity that came even close. Well, to be truthful *I simply stopped caring about everything else!* My life had been suspended: *Getting surgery was the one, the only thing that mattered.* Suspending life actually helps, it virtually guarantees that there will be no new problems to raise in mental treatment. That is if one's savings-account is capable of sustaining this lifestyle long enough… Well, I did nicely burn through all my retirement savings complying to psychiatrically enforced requirements. On the other hand my life is finite too and at times I most definitely felt that other things than absurd compliance to mental-health and being horrified by their incompetence and behaviour used to be important in my life…

If one hadn't been obsessed by getting that surgery before one certainly - and very efficiently - gets pressured into being obsessed about it after one has started *this* treatment! There are a couple of reasons for this but the really sad part about the whole thing is *that the original reason, becoming emotionally and physically one and whole, is at best a marginal ingredient in the cocktail driving this obsession!*

There was something wrong with me. I had tried to live with this, had found, like millions of transsexuals before me, that this isn't possible. But I had a choice because today treatment is possible: Eventually getting killed by this or getting it fixed. Somehow getting this treatment. Submitting to whatever they concocted to get there or die from it…

The one reason why I chose life, why I accepted whatever they asked of me, was that there were people in my life who needed me to be here for them: My children! So in essence I had created my own obstacle for "the easy way out". As absurd as this seems for a transsexual my own "reproductive success" was standing in my way! Under no other circumstance would I have submitted to this, I would have preferred to continue to take my chances with suicide. *Because in the end there are only two options society is willing to offer to us today: Suicide or abuse! Apparently that's how they want us: Dead or damaged!*

I don't think that I am the only transsexual who has ever faced this decision. *In fact I think many who do understand that system before they are in it ask themselves that very question.* Maybe some might choose "illegal surgery", but for that I was and am far too compliant.

[Voters office] We can't change the sex of a voter, only the name, residence and date of birth. But you can register as new voter. [Me] So I'll have two votes? [She] No… But there seems to be no way to have your other entry removed…

I don't know how many suicides this dogma has caused over the years but if you ask me it is probably one more thing we better don't know. It would just be something else to be really depressed about...

Obviously this dilemma doesn't affect all transsexuals equally. Many I have talked to either tell me that they only ever understood what this did to them *after* they started to recover, either from surgery or later in life. After the threat and much of the pain had already passed. Because this is the time when people start to reflect on how they have been treated. Because it is the time when we need to find ourselves one more time, *when it is finally possible for us to become ourselves.* If we still can that is. Because then, finally, there is no more need to become somebody we are not, not for society and not for psychiatry!

I have asked a few transsexuals what they did during their "self-finding". *Very few made the connection to psychiatry* or even understood that question. Psychiatrists are, as some authors put it, "gatekeepers to treatment". Not guides to self-finding and fulfillment. Why? Isn't that what this should be about? Well, apparently not... And when it comes to professionals asking the most obvious question: "Why do you want this surgery?", well, there's silence. Because the one thing that's absolutely clear in our lives is that we need this. *None of the dogmatists doubt this - and that's why they don't even ask, leave this out of dogma!*

So what then is this process of allowing some and disallowing others, driving yet others into madness or suicide all about? *Well, it selects some people over others according to an arbitrary set of criteria made-up by mental-health professionals or, if we see their framework as a reflection of what society as a whole asks them to do, as a made-up social selection!*

If we look at the entire process from this perspective what they do isn't mental treatment at all, **it is Social Darwinism:** It is in fact the most efficient eradication program ever conceived! Because unlike an open extermination of unwanted people like 'Indians', homosexuals, communists, people belonging to particular religious faiths (whichever it just happens to be), 'gypsies', 'witches' or whoever, *we don't need to be "searched and processed",* **we conveniently self-identify!** *We knock on the doors of the medical people because, unlike all of the above, we need that afternoon in an operating room[1]. **And if then the conditions are set right we don't even need to be eradicated - we quietly self-exterminate!***

In the end they don't even have to put a lethal dose of something into our veins, open the valve labelled 'carbon-monoxide', drop a Zyklon-B canister through a hole or whatever the current method of mass-murdering people may be *because they have found a way to turn our own bio-emotional misalignment into a weapon:* **They re-enforce the problem until we self-eradicate because of our own biochemically screwed-up emotional self-perception!**

---

[1] *Many religious groups perform "bleeding rites" such as male and female circumcision, body perforations or bleeding pain rituals and sacrifices as part of their religious and spiritual practices. In many countries some of these are illegal while in others medical doctors substitute for priests (such as in religiously motivated circumcisions). This is of great concern to me as **the medical profession should not be in the business of regulating, mandating, providing, altering or prohibiting religious or spiritual practices.** I am deeply troubled by medicine actually going one step further and taking advantage of certain religious practices by offering surgeries to revert these so they can be performed again and again (as in hymen-reconstruction).*

Because this selection is not so much about a social criteria as it selects for emotional strength and resilience, lets the ones survive who can tolerate more abuse, I think calling it *EMOTIONAL DARWINISM* would be more appropriate or at least more precise than calling it "Social Darwinism". *But to the people on the receiving end of the extermination the naming of what's happening makes precious little difference.*

And then there are these psychiatrists who ask themselves just why there are so few "older transsexuals"? They pull completely absurd explanations out of their hats as to how this could be *our* fault! Well, if they have read my book so far, now they know!

Myself? In the end I take my chances with 'treatment' because the only difference it makes when I wind-up dead is that it would have been more painful to get there. And there's always a small chance to get through it unseen, isn't there?

A.25. PSYCHIATRY? THANKS, BUT NO THANKS!

The last day when I theoretically could have seen a psychiatrist in time to get a proper mental-health label and be officially designated nuts - sorry, let me rephrase this: And be officially approved for surgery - came... and passed. I had not heard anything from the clinic as to their requirements except for the constant mantra of dogma: *"You need a detailed letter recommending surgery signed by a psychiatrist and a second opinion from either another independent psychiatrist or a psychotherapist as stated in dogma".* The comment at trans-support remained: *"You'll do just fine, don't worry".* No reason was given for their optimism and yes, I was very, very worried by then.

"Psychological support" was in every respect over after that phone-call between the two therapists. By now my second counsellor also agreed that this was all about pretending, we met every 6-8 weeks. Our last session was 116 days before surgery. She gave me a short note saying that I was there off and on and that she would make herself available to me after surgery should I wish to see her. As if! (But I appreciated her being polite nevertheless). At the end she wrote "I am in support of her surgery and wish her well" - which to me seemed sort of self-evident given the fact that she addressed the letter to my surgeon. "Don't send it in, just keep it at hand for your pre-op if they should ask for anything"... In the end nobody would ever ask.

"Take the remaining time for yourself - I understand that you need this a lot more than any counselling. If anybody calls here I'll tell them that you're seeing me regularly and that we missed-out on a few appointments due to circumstances beyond our control...". I thanked her and asked "but I still don't know if I can actually go or not... Having some certainty would really make a big difference just about now...". "This is no longer my decision to make... But good luck!".

I had always thought the decision should be *mine*. Instead this seemed to be turning into a perfect example of the "passing the buck"-principle!

What by now dawned on all of them was that if this would not work out they were guaranteed a suicide; if they'd put me in psychiatric care they could expect the same, only faster. But now it was too late for any additional compliance, for psychiatric evaluations or letters.

There is that saying about the rats who leave the sinking ship? Well, I felt sinking all right. But aren't rats supposed to be smarter than sink the ship they're living on? Or off?

If everybody were to close every eye they had my surgery was 116 days away. By now it dawned on them that, having treated me the way they apparently felt they had to during the previous year, it was doubtful that I had 100 days of life left to live.

B.38. *YOUR LIFE HAS JUST BEEN CANCELLED!*

Psychiatric dogma speaks of 'readiness', it's when they think a woman is 'ready' to be, well, a woman. Psychiatrists tell us to get an appointment with a surgeon, let us pay the bills, make arrangements for flights, time off work, somebody to look after us when we get home, possibly to come along for the procedure and so on. Most surgeons have long waiting-lists so at this time surgery may well be up to a year down the road. But many psychiatrists don't sign our permission until the very last minute so we don't really know…

These days it is unlikely that the combined costs for surgery to the individual ever comes in at less than about $10,000, though it could be significantly more, particularly if the surgery is to take place in North America or Europe. Many woman have saved years to have the money this costs, years during which they may have been forced to pay thousands or tens of thousands of dollars to psychiatrists and other mental-health services, *the "permit for surgery" easily costs a lot more than the surgery itself!*

And then everything is arranged, paid for, and all we need is "final clearance" from psychiatry. Only many don't get this until shortly before the event! Officially I must presume that we aren't deemed 'ready' until five minutes before we board that plane, so we're left waiting, more desperately every day as this event draws closer. I know of several cases where women have been given that "psychiatric letter of approval" *less than seven days before their surgery!*

It must be difficult for somebody who has never lived through such a situation to appreciate what this does to us. There we are, waiting to have our lives changed forever. To get our lives back. Back from a life as wrong as it just about gets! For many this also means freedom from a life of forced mental-treatment, a life of years of oppression, compliance, being controlled, a pretend life filled with abuse. We exchange this for a life of fulfillment, certainly emotional and physical but for many this also makes a meaningful social life possible, for the first time in a lifetime! We exchange a life of artificial limbo for one of stability and predictability. A life with no perspective, no future and no meaning for one we longed for so long, decades, often the best part of a lifetime. *And when it finally happens <u>psychiatry gives us five days of advanced notice to get ready for it!</u>* If ever there was something called 'readiness' and *one needed proof that we're as ready as it ever gets <u>whenever they want us to</u>* then this would be it: **If many of us can prepare themselves within a week and most within a month** *then how come psychiatrists need several years, minimum?*

There is one other side to being treated like this, a very sad one: If a woman gets her surgery cancelled *(her psychiatrist tells her that he is not going to sign that permission or just fails to hand it in)* less than a week in advance this means that she in all likelihood looses most of the money she had invested because no surgeon can make alternative arrangements on so short a notice, neither airline tickets nor hotel-payments will be refunded. This, for many, means that a lifetime of hopes and savings gets crushed in that very instant! At the same time hormonal withdrawal (because hormonal treatment needs to be discontinued several weeks prior to surgery) would be at maximum, this is in essence "a quick version of menopause compressed into a fortnight". This gets combined with an absurd testosterone-peak as testosterone-suppression also needs to be discontinued at the same time.

Psychiatry does not release any statistics on *suicide induced by late-term abortion of gender re-birth*. They don't want us to know how many people get killed by them failing to sign a piece of paper. I have some ideas of who to ask if I ever wanted to find out. I don't ask. I don't want to know because sometimes it is better not to know.

I do not understand how a human-being can treat another human-being like this. Send her to get an appointment, make her pay for it, make her wait many months, have her focus all her life's energy and meaning into this one single event, send her on a horror-trip of drug withdrawal *and then literally in the last minute before her life would finally change for the better pull the plug on her life, tell her she can't go and instead will loose everything!*[1]

Frankly, I can not understand how a professional association of doctors, men and women who have dedicated their lives to a career of healing, could possibly accept, never mind *support* such behaviour! There are some things I can't understand. *There are some evils I refuse to understand!*

I also cannot understand why so many of us are deprived of what we need most for this step in our lives: *Time to get emotionally ready for it!* I doubt that it is a secret to doctors that the result of surgery is, on average, better when the patient comes in well rested, not in emotional turmoil and it seems obvious that this is particularly true for a surgery with such wide-ranging emotional implications. But then, here we go again: I just seem to understand much of the psyche differently from these professionals. This time it's the apparently simple word 'ready'…

---

[1] *Thanks to professional psychiatric detachment such an announcement may well come with a request like "in regard of recent events we would appreciate your contacting us to schedule psychotherapy at your earliest convenience".*

A.26. FEMALE MINUS 59 DAYS

My parents taught me: *Be on time for appointments, maybe five minutes early, certainly not too late.* So after having spent a few hours in airports, line-ups and in the air I was five minutes early for my pre-op. It's a doctor's office all right, so they let me wait. Some 4 hours! Well, they knew I wasn't about to walk-out on them... Fortunately I had anticipated something like this and brought my IPod so I could see a movie. Or two. I certainly was in no condition to read a book... I had also booked my flight back home with half a day to spare so I was not concerned. About the flight. Never mind that interview I was waiting for...

I had asked my GP to send-in a report on my treatment. It was 6 lines, hand-written on a pre-printed company referral form. He had left the entry "Please see this patient for:" blank. (Or should I rather interpret this? maybe as "don't ask, don't tell"?). Under "Referred for the following problems:" He had put *"I am the family physician of this pleasant 44 yo. m/f transgendered lady"*, it continued by stating that he had known me for a little less than a year, that I had seen a counsellor (he forgot about my current one) and continued *"We initiated hormone therapy six months ago, she has done well on hormones"*. All followed by a list of my current prescriptions. A note posted on the margin of the page, bottom to top, read: *"I understand that she has a surgery date booked with you"*. This was what I had for a detailed psychiatric description and recommendation with two signatures. Honestly, to me this appeared awfully thin...

When my surgeon finally called me in I first got a rather sincere apology for the delay, I was told that most people show up may hours before their appointment, that I indeed was booked first that afternoon and now was last just because I was the only one who had bothered to show up on time. I said that I was taught being on time is common courtesy to which he replied in a very helpless voice "so was I".

We sat down in his office, a minute of small talk. He uses the time to have a look at my file, first page. It's the page I had sent in some months ago, the one with next to nothing on it. He turned his gaze away from the paper somewhere far out... "You know", he said, "we get a handful of cases like yours every year...". Then, looking straight at me, "...and don't worry, as for me you can get here whatever you want... So, what do you want?"

Well, I must admit it was some sort of a relief but I also quietly thought *you'd be seeing a lot more of 'us' if you stopped insisting in a detailed and preferably lengthy mental-*

health record... We then went over the procedure (nothing new or unexpected), a short examination followed. After that I was given some details for preparation, going off medication date, a reminder to file the lab reports. Then, just before he got up and walked me to the door: "You're booked in two months?". "Yes, 59 days". "... Yes, of course... Can you do 59 more days?". "Yesterday I wasn't sure if I could do *one* day but now I think I can...". "I want to see you back here in two months... Ask for help if you feel you could use some - there are limits to what you can do by yourself..."

B.39.   *ABSENCE OF EVIDENCE IS NOT EVIDENCE OF ABSENCE*

Basically I had spent 15 month of my life on nothing else but being approved for my medical treatment. It could have been 15 minutes instead! On just about every step I was told "well, you know, *the rules are made for the 'usual' cases but you're just different*". Of course being recognized as different in no way warrants different treatment, I mean just where would this end? But then again I didn't ask directly for it either, just indirectly by being there. And at times by subtly and not so subtly pointing out to people what they were actually doing and what I thought of it... Given the "average treatment experience" I probably got enough "special allowance" as it was.

I have met quite a few transsexuals on my way. Apparently there are many, many "special cases" out there and I have yet to see that "average transsexual", but this is of course not a representative observation. True, there are people who need support, who better think their lives over before getting "gender-reassignment" - or maybe not getting it after all. There are people who misinterpret this as a way out of some other problem, there are people who don't know which gender they ought to be when they ask for help. Clearly some self-finding seems appropriate for quite a number of people. However I hardly find this to be limited to transsexuals, indeed I have found that most transsexuals I have met had a rather more specific and detailed view of who they were and what they needed than most other people ever will. Including if they were in need of counselling or some other form of support. Not all, but many.

If you prefer this bluntly: Are there crazy transsexuals? Yes these certainly exist! But there are crazy politicians, crazy car-salespeople, crazy pilots, crazy doctors, even crazy psychiatrists. I certainly hope that they will all get the help they need but I most definitely don't want to force it onto them nor should anybody else do so unless they imminently or actually endanger or harm somebody. Neither do I think that by the simple virtue of being put into any of these groups (or any other for that matter) is a person guaranteed to be either crazy and in need of treatment or guaranteed to be sane. The same of course is true for transsexuals!

So, am I a special case? Well, maybe. I really don't know. I'm unique, certainly. But then again, we all are!

Do I know transsexuals who I deem not to be and never to have been in need of professional mental treatment? Yes, I do. Is this opinion professional? Well, if you ask me I daresay *that it is a lot more professional than to proclaim that all transsexuals are mental; that all transsexuals are in need of a minimum of more than one year of psychiatric therapy, any therapy, whatever therapy, it doesn't matter at all, just therapy; that all transsexuals are incapable of deciding the order, method and timing of their medical treat-ment; that all transsexuals need professional support to get through their lives; that all trans-sexuals need therapy forced onto them even if they feel it unnecessary because they're all incapable to know when they need it, always! Each and every one, hundreds of thousands at least but more likely millions of people, without a single exception!* **Just because of who transsexuals are?** *Labelling all transsexuals without ever having seen the great majority of them? Making a diagnosis without any need for examination or verification?*

Yes, I actually do think that my opinion on these individuals is more professional and more competent than the one of these mental-health practitioners who declare us all mental, the dogmatists and their therapists who shower us with their labels from high above!

I could argue that this is *for the simple reason that my opinion, however unqualified, is based on actually talking to people, getting to know them* **instead of subjecting them to an ad-hoc process of instant summary justice during which no evidence whatsoever except for the fact of our self-identification is ever considered and the verdict is proclaimed in writing even before a case is heard or the accused has even been seen!** Today we are at the absurd point where many transsexuals were pronounced crazy *long before they were even born!*

But even though this argument appears compelling enough there is an even more impor-tant one: Sanity is generally defined as *"the absence of insanity".* **Because the absence of evidence of insanity is no evidence of absence of it** *no transsexual (nobody at all for that matter) is capable to prove sanity!* Our entire society, our legal system, our morals and ethics are all based *on the assumption that people are deemed competent to make decisions and are capable to understand their actions* **unless** *proven* **otherwise!** I have mentioned Aristotle[ARIS-C] before, several times in fact. Apparently *some* people have cared to read it...

Yes, I actually do think that my opinion is better founded and more competent than the one of the dogmatists and dogmatic therapists. I think this to be the case *for the simple reason that my process of diagnosis is based on a meaningful set of conditions while theirs is based on a set of prejudice, discrimination and arbitrary decisions!* **But most of all because their diag-nostic process is based on an impossible precondition:** *Our need to prove our sanity in-stead of them having to provide proof of any and all alleged insanity!*

When, after years of looking for it, years of behavioural conditioning, years of tor-ture, pain, abuse the dogmatists finally accept that they can't find insanity and finally capitulate *they let us go to surgery* *because they say that we have "gender identity disor-der", a mental illness, and that genital surgery will cure this mental illness!* **After we have spent all this time** *demonstrating under their microscope that we have no significant prob-lems except our physical gender, that our request for alignment is not insane but indeed the most meaningful we could make* **they still don't find it in themselves to certify us** *normal!* **Or at least not mental? For heaven's sake** **they could just declare us outside their scope of practice!** *But we just have to be something. Anything. Whatever!* **And when even what-soever can't be found** *they resort to making something up!* **Define it undiagnosable, uni-**

dentifiable and untreatable! *Because this way it can't be contradicted, disproven or gotten rid of. After all we can't just be allowed to exist, can we? Mentally normal transsexuals?* <u>*Because if we actually existed there would be living, physical evidence of that system being wrong!*</u> And this can't be! Never! Ever! Not even if this hurts us, maybe kills many. *Because keeping a protocol in place, justifying its existence, maintaining the status-quo and securing absolute control is more important than our lives!*

Such schemes typically prompt a well known range of philosophical questions. Each has a very obvious answer - *and each one gets ignored by this system:*

➤➤ *How many "special cases" does it take to make the "everybody is the same" approach wrong?* 99%? 90%? Ten thousand? Ten? *Or is one wrong enough to make something wrong?*

➤➤ *If there indeed are "special cases" then* **who gets to decide who is "a special case"?** *Circumstances and sheer luck?*

➤➤ *What kind of degradation and abuse does a human being have to accept so psychiatrists can make up their minds?*

➤➤ *Why is not* **each and every human being entitled to be treated according to his and her individual needs and abilities?**

➤➤ *How come society allows medical doctors to behave like this and to treat human-beings like this?*

The above is the philosophically deeper approach to questioning this system. There is another aspect. One that may be philosophically more shallow but which personally goes a lot deeper:

If we are not given treatment until we meet the criteria for mental illness (i.e. our emotional or behavioural functioning is impaired severely enough) **we will either choose to simulate such behaviour in order to qualify for treatment or we will become impaired, eventually. Over time even severely. Because the continued withholding of life-giving treatment is a form of torture!**

Constant abuse over an extended period of time on this level <u>**guarantees**</u> *that a person will eventually end-up being severely impaired! The lack of treatment alone would do this over time. Dogmatic mental treatment and forced therapy of an imaginary, invisible, undiagnosable and untreatable condition guarantees that we get there a lot faster!*

B.40. OK. TRANSSEXUALITY. JUST WHAT IS THIS AGAIN?

I suppose by now you, the reader, are either completely confused or brilliantly enlightened? No? More confused than enlightened, really? Well then. Let's see where all the problems come from, because there is a simple explanation! Yes! Really! For once there truly is!

But because I don't want to discriminate let me give you *that other explanation* first, the one of the American Psychiatric Association: "That I am really a very, very sick and mentally deeply disturbed male, indeed one of these most severe cases where no help is possible, nothing works and every effort to instil some sanity is futile. In short: I am a hopeless, lost cause!". Therefore it is actually quite understandable that what I write cannot be understood. Given the severity of my mental disorder nothing else should be expected...

Ok, that was *one* explanation. Not the one I find particularly brilliant and sound, certainly not the one I personally fancy. But what else would you expect I'd say? Fortunately I just happen to have an alternative explanation which describes the issue at hand far, far better:

The problem is that the term *'transsexuality'* (as used in dogma) as well as the designation "gender-dysphoria" (as used in mental-health) *actually **describes two very, very different conditions*** (or 'pathologies', as psychiatrists prefer to call it). The confusion comes about by both populations sharing one *potential* common need: Genital gender-alignment; ***And by mental-health insisting that there is only one condition (or pathology),*** therefore only one avenue to ever obtain this treatment exists **whereas this single recognized pathology isn't consistent with either one of these two actual conditions!**

These two conditions[1] are[2]:

Transsexual (Cross-Gender) Identification (social transsexuality): This is **a predominantly social** condition in which *the individual desires to live the social role opposite from birth-sex*. For these individuals *living the opposite gender-role part- or full-time is normal*. In some, but not all cases genital surgery may be indicated *if the individual so desires*.

Transsexual Intersex (biological transsexuality): This is **a predominantly biological** condition in which *the individual desires to align biological sex with physical self-experience*. For these individuals *a request for genital surgery is normal*. In some, but not all cases living the opposite gender-role may be indicated *if the individual so desires*.

As mentioned, the problem of today's use of 'transsexuality' and the treatment thereof is *that both groups of people are thrown into one conglomerate*. **Or rather that the medical approach is limited to *identifying, diagnosing and treating cases of only one highly specific sub-category of transsexual (cross-gender) identification*** (*sexually* motivated cross-gender identification). **This is then deemed a social or emotional categorization and painted as a psychological problem.** *Because the treatment (usually) requires the authority to write prescriptions (for hormonal therapy) patients are consequentially referred to psychiatrists!*

Now I'm not saying that psychiatry gets this right for the people who really do fall into the scope of their pathology "disorderly gender identity", in fact I think they're getting this badly wrong for most *because psychiatry bases their conclusions and their treatments on a small sub-population within this category and more often than not on people who don't even belong there*. **However I am saying that *this approach leaves several groups of people with no appropriate treatment whatsoever* or, as in my own case, I have to basically sneak through the system, simulate whatever is expected from people *who have a very different condition and then end-up getting a treatment which is, at best, a patchwork-solution along the line of "the best wrong solution I can get for the wrong problem"*.** *In the current system this is the only way for me to ever get any treatment at all because my true condition is neither recognized nor is it accepted - by and large it isn't even deemed to be possible!*

This view of transsexuality doesn't just explain why today's methodology does not work for a great majority of people (there are many other reasons why the current treatment of transsexual identification often doesn't work of which I have previously mentioned several), it also explains nicely why we have such problems in creating interest-groups, why the "group referred to as transsexuals" never fits in anywhere, why there are so many opposing

---

[1] *This separation should be seen* in addition *to the one into an m f and an f m case, in total* there would have to be four different basic types of transsexuality, *each with it's own specific challenges, needs, medical requirements and so on.*

[2] *I separate these two conditions because by doing so it becomes obvious that neither of the two aspects can possibly be a mental illness* and that therefore the current approach of treatment must be wrong for all individuals concerned

interests in "transsexual gender politics" and why we're not welcome anywhere from lesbians to gays to heterosexuals to every group out there: *Because this conglomerate 'transsexuals' is* <u>*guaranteed to fail every expectation there is*</u>*!* Every group will find individuals within 'transsexuals' *who are diametrically opposite to what they themselves stand for.* Interpreted from this perspective it becomes easily understandable why no group wants to be associated with these 'transsexuals' - or with me personally *as long as I get assigned to this category!*

In addition there is always that other not insignificant problem that if I would like to associate with any intersex or lesbian group or one for physically handicapped people *I get identified as a person with a mental gender-identity problem,* not a physical one, **because this is the only accepted (and diagnosable) condition I am allowed to have!** **In fact I make this even worse by having accepted this, albeit only to obtain treatment, <u>*but that part is conveniently forgotten once that label has been stuck onto me*</u>! Having had the treatment I had - genital alignment - pretty much guarantees this!**

To give you an idea of *how fundamentally different* the two conditions actually are I would like to point-out a few major differences in the following very simplified table:

M/F Transsexuality	By Identification	By Intersex
- *Social:*		
Preferred gender-role	**female**	**any**[1]
Personal (sexual) identification	**any**[2]	**female**
Social identification	female, transsexual, other	male or female
Identifies LGBTTTQ2S…	any, *includes* gay male, trans or any combination	any, *except* gay male and trans
Sexuality and male genitals	may like male sex, genitals	dislikes/hates male genitals
- *Lived Gender Role:*		
Socially presented gender	**always** socially transitions	**may** socially transition[3]
Self-perceived gender	**may change**	**never changes**
Experiences "social transition"	big impact	small or no impact
Changes "role behaviour"	very likely	rather unlikely
Can live social role	female only	female, but likely both
- *Physical:*		
Phys. self-experience, pre-op	very likely **male**	**female**
Phys. self-experience, post-op	**male or female or other**	**female**
Other states (no-op)	many identifications[4]	does not exist[5]
- *Medical (surgical):*		
Requires genital alignment	**may need surgery**	**always requires surgery**[5]
Other surgery (feminization)	**very likely**, often extensive	**less likely**[6]
- *Hormonal (levels):*		
Typical pre-treatment testosterone	any normal male level	likely very low male level
Typical pre-treatment estrogen	any normal male level	likely very high male level
Testosterone suppression	maybe, dosage varies	to normal female level
Estrogen supplement	maybe, dosage varies	to normal female level
Testosterone (post-op)	suppression to supplement	suppression or none
Primary motivation for HRT	induce **physical** changes	induce **emotional** changes
- *Fundamental:*		
Emotional perception of sex-hormones	**reacts *male*,** "lives on testosterone"	**reacts *female*,** "lives on estrogen"
Reason for treatment: Adjustment of...	***...behavioural, social, possibly sexual* life**	***...biological and emotional* self-experience**
- *Trans is something…:*	**…to be *lived***	**…to *get rid of* a.s.a.p.**

---

[1] *While intersex-transsexuals typically feel female many may be quite ok with their "male social lives" or may find transitioning too much of an effort, too cumbersome, potentially dangerous, interfering, too much of an effort for the benefit, socially alienating, too costly or painful. They may also just have grown used to their lives and may not want change.*

[2] *Many trans-identified people may have some reservations to identifying female and rather say "I'm a girl, transwoman…"*

[3] *Intersex-transsexuals are currently forced to change publicly lived social gender-role even if they do not wish to do so!*

[4] *No-Op transsexual, transvestite, gender-queer, she-male, drag-queen,…*

[5] *With the exception of individuals who can't have surgery for some unrelated reason (i.e. medical counter-indication, philosophical, religious or other objection)*

[6] *In the current system many may opt for feminization surgery only to better qualify for genital surgery or may feel pressured into it for other reasons (peer pressure, therapist's or institutional expectation, fear of not obtaining other medical services…)*

Transsexual identification *is a <u>social</u> state[1]*. **It is defined as a person not agreeing with the social (or sexual) gender-role (the interaction with others and the personal expression of the individual) she was assigned.** Unfortunately at this time mental-health does not appear to differentiate between social, sexual and other motivations and *deems all cases to be of a sexual nature.* I believe this to be highly inappropriate and suspect that the social motivation may in fact be the one that gets seen by professionals a lot more frequently than the sexual one. The reason is obvious: If a *social* motivation exists, then social and socialization problems are expected to be paramount, *these are often highly visible and interfering in daily life.* If however a *sexual* motivation exists then intimate problems are expected to be paramount, *these are typically of a private nature and can be hidden more easily.* There are many other motivations and certainly *a combination of several factors* is also possible.

Transsexual identification is as much not a mental illness as asexuality, homo- or bisexuality aren't: If the individual is allowed to live her identification this expression can be very positive and enjoyable and no impairment of any kind, severe or otherwise, will result from it. If however the person is forced into the wrong social/sexual role then any and all behavioural, emotional or other <u>results from oppression or abuse</u> should be expected, ranging from depression to substance-abuse to neglect to anti-social behaviour to suicide. It is however important to understand that <u>all these are expected reactions to social oppression, *they are not a manifestation of some mental impairment the individual suffers from.*</u>

Transsexual intersex *is a <u>neurological</u> state[1]*. **It is defined as a persons brain reacting incompatible to her biological/biochemical combination (and level) of sex steroids, i.e. reacts positive to estrogen and negative to testosterone while the reproductive organs are male and (predominantly) produce testosterone(s) instead of estrogen(s).** People like myself don't tolerate the biological testosterone we produce ourselves and need estrogen for a fulfilling self-perception. Because there is likely a very close relationship between the brain's preference of either sex-hormone and the person's self-experience as female or male *I also experience myself physically fully and emotionally predominantly female, after all this is normal for an "estrogen-positive" individual[2].* Of course all this does not mean that we *have* to live socially visibly female, many women do not and enjoy this just fine. But it *usually* means that we will do just fine (even enjoy it) if this should be forced onto us, say by mental-health. It also means that I do not experience "intimate transition" (as mental-health defines it) *because I have always been female and simply remain female when I change!*

Transsexual intersex is by definition not a mental illness as it is biochemical in nature. Primarily it has nothing at all to do with either my behaviour or looks or the reproductive

---

[1] *I use the term 'state' here instead of the usual clinical term 'pathology' (or 'condition') because both a social female identification as well as a female physical self-experience <u>are entirely normal in every respect, medically as well as non-medically</u> and should therefore be seen separate from medical pathologies.*

[2] *It appears obvious that there is a much closer correlation between the brain's biochemical reaction to sex steroids and a person's (gender-) self-identification than between a person's self-identification and the looks of her genitals. After all self-identification is made-up in the brain and not in the genitals, isn't it?*

capacity of my genitals, other than their hormonal function. Therefore a castration and estrogen supplements could be a meaningful treatment for individuals who prefer not to socially transition. *Unfortunately dogma does not allow for such treatment as a permanent social transition is one of the preconditions for any genital surgery, including a simple castration.* If a person is denied treatment or finds herself unwilling or incapable to submit to the protocol then hormonally induced depression or suicidality may result. Some of the more likely reactions to this are an attempt at obtaining "illegal surgery" (castration or vaginoplasty) or at self-castration and self-medicated hormonal treatment. <u>That we have to do this under such de-humanizing (and dangerous) conditions isn't the result of us suffering from mental illness (as psychiatry claims),</u> *<u>it is the result of neglect and disregard by a society and a medical establishment in denial of our existence, our medical condition and our medical needs!</u>*

The people who stand behind today's established views and treatments of transsexuality will not welcome my view of it. ***There's the general issue of accepting a different view* <u>but likely much more important this would result in a significant loss of the dominance of mental-health in this field!</u>** However accepting this would result in *both* groups of transsexuals *getting vastly improved treatment* because many of the misconceptions the medical people have fallen for are a direct result of them observing people from both populations <u>who simply try to sneak through a system which is inappropriate for everybody</u>!

At first glance the main problem seems to be how to get a medical diagnosis as to which of the two groups any given individual belongs to. This isn't simplified by the fact that (virtually) every human-being has a gender-self-identification and that this isn't male or female at all but rather a result of many aspects of personality. People may be *predominantly male or predominantly female to various degrees, but there just isn't anybody on the planet who is "exclusively male" or "exclusively female"* in every stereotype there is, never mind these stereotypes may vary by culture and observer. ***As a result every person is to some degree trans (cross-gender) identified!*** *However this only ever seems to create problems in people who are identified extremely one-sided and are biologically of the other sex.* [This is one of Money mistakes: *Social gender-identification is at least in part learned, <u>biological identification however is not!</u>*]. Most people identify "somewhere near the middle" and would accept both social gender-roles, this is very obvious if one examines the population of people who currently are diagnosed medically intersexed: *Only a small minority will ever feel the need to change their social gender-role* while a much larger number does not agree or identify with the designation in their birth-certificates! *Medical practitioners finally had to accept that it is better for these individuals to decide this themselves.* This is the reason why today intersexed people are no longer subjected to mental treatment or protocols and don't have their lives (and how their genitals look) dictated to them by medical doctors (and rightly so!).

Because biological and social identification as well as physical appearance are (relatively) independent of each other *an individual can have either one or both transsexualities (and these can either be 'parallel' or 'opposite')*. If both are present the individual would be biologically male *while experiencing himself as (and seeking the life of) a female to male transsexual!* No problem? Ok, for individuals who desire genital alignment there's no problem because, honestly, it doesn't get any better for a transsexual than having been born with the desired genitals, does it? However the problem becomes just a little trickier if the person only identifies socially male, not sexually. So there we have *a biological male wanting to live the life of a no-op female to male transsexual!* And the person would seek *male to female* genital alignment *because he would like to live male, but from a sexually female perspective!* Now is *this* acceptable? Well, most certainly not by any stretch of today's psychiatric interpretation or according to dogma...[1]

Because we know that transsexual-intersex is biochemical in nature the following two assumptions are bound to be true *in a good number of these individuals:*

➤➤ If an individual who is intersex-trans gets her hormone levels adjusted she will feel a very positive change almost immediately (often within a few hours). In fact virtually all individuals will feel *some* change, however *for an intersex-trans person this will feel very positive, for everybody else this will be somewhat to extremely negative.*

➤➤ It is to be assumed that an intersex-trans person's natural hormone levels will be close to or even out-of-range of what is deemed "medically normal" for her biological sex. The reason for this is that there are several locations in the body where sex-steroids are produced (testicles and ovaries, but also the kidneys and the brain). *Some* of this production is (at least in parts) mentally controllable (at least the brain's own but possibly more), either on a conscious or a subconscious level. It is to be assumed that over time a person 'learns' to maintain her biological maximum estrogen production while suppressing testosterone to her biological minimum. This would not get her to female levels but it would get her outside normal male expectations.

However such presumptions should not be made into expectations and neither should these be interpreted or styled as a test because they don't in- or exclude anybody.

---

[1] *Today such an individual would need to live female, go through all the dogmatic treatments, obtain his surgery while claiming to be a woman and then revert everything, not implement his legal change-of-sex but instead change his legal name back! And yes, there are quite a few people who actually do this. There are in fact so many that psychiatrists have coined a term for doing this: They call socially reverting to birth-gender "de-transitioning" and (of course) take de-transitioning for yet another proof of instability in transsexuals, no matter how happy and functional and problem-free the individual may be afterwards . This, to me, is just another proof of how little the dogmatists understand, how limited their appreciation is of the spectrum human self-expressions comes in! It also is one more example of how absurd their seeing transsexuality as some form of identity-disorder is: Apparently these individuals know exactly, right from the start, what they feel, need and are! There's so little ambivalence there that they navigate and purposefully subvert the system, that they successfully pretend, submit to all the conditions and all the pain, in order to get what they've known all along they needed right from the start!*

In addition to these there is some circumstantial evidence: It is to be assumed that many in-tersex-trans individuals would have a social life to their expectation and fulfilment whereas quite a number of trans-identified individuals may argue that theirs is not satisfying before social transition. Furthermore if co-morbid conditions are present intersex-trans individuals and trans-identified individuals may typically have very different issues, the former predomi-nantly of a depressive kind, the latter more likely of a social, behavioural or possibly intimate kind, depending upon a persons particular motivation. Given the physical nature of intersex transsexuality I think that it is unlikely an individual would "find out about her condition" only late in life without having felt or suspected anything early. For transsexual identification on the other hand I do not know of any reason why awareness would have to be present at any specific time in life.

Social transition is a difficult, painful and long process for many trans-identified individu-als whereas for quite a number of intersex-transsexuals this is often not much of or even a complete non-issue. Or as they say: "This wasn't here yesterday, it must have changed over-night…". The very fact that we can do this as fast should show any mental-health-practitioner that this isn't actually a social transition as they define it because, honestly, *the transition they expect us to have simply is not possible overnight!* But as it isn't possible to "measure a dif-ference" from the outside they can't tell…

There is one more significant difference, but this one is only visible *after* treatment: After genital surgery transsexuals wake-up in the same world they left a few hours before - *and to some trans-identified individuals this ends-up being a very rude awakening.* **There's no "Cinderella-Effect" of waking-up and suddenly being a woman!** All social problems from integration to self-esteem and self-worth are still there, neither does uncertainty over transi-tioning suddenly vanish! True, the emotional relief of "actually be who one feels and says one is" can be of enormous help, a real boost to self-esteem. But surgery neither solves emotional nor social problems. Not this surgery anyway. *Genital alignment may solve sexual problems if the expectations are realistic and an appropriate surgical technique is chosen, **but no genital surgery will ever solve problems of self-identification!***

This is likely why dogmatic treatment puts such emphasis on us not to expect solutions from genital alignment. And this in turn is why intersex-transsexuals too are expected to reply to a therapist's question about our expectations *that we don't really expect anything from sur-gery!* Some therapists actually go as far as to define 'readiness' as *"a state of no longer hav-ing any expectations"* - then one's guaranteed not to be disappointed! For us this is just one more lie many have to dish out in these offices *because for intersex-transsexuals this really is different.* While we too wake-up in the same world we left a few hours before *our problem really can be solved by surgery because it is biological in nature.* **We never expect (or even want) our self-identification fixed, changed or reassigned in an operating theatre in the first place: We come out anatomically female, but we went in being women all along!**

To the question of medically diagnosing which group somebody belongs to? **Ideally no medical practitioner should ever have to determine this in the first place! If both types of transsexuality would be treated** *for what we need,* **all patients cared for with dignity and respect, openness and a problem-oriented approach then I am certain that virtually everybody would self-identify correctly - after all** *this would become the most efficient way for us to obtain the desired treatment while avoiding the undesired one!* The few who find themselves incapable to make this decision should be given support, but I expect these individuals to request this themselves or be rather easily identifiable by everybody involved!

A.27. BEING OF PERFECTLY SOUND MIND...

As expected my life, my emotional well-being deteriorated during treatment. Fast. Down from socially integrated and productive female to disconnected and, in the end, suicidal transsexual. And while this last bit, the suicidality, was medically induced by the effects of going off hormonal therapy in preparation to surgery (or more precisely due to the testosterone re-surge this created), I had managed to live for over 30 years on similar hormone levels without ever experiencing this kind of a depression. On the other hand my last pre-op testosterone report from the lab the day before I left for surgery was the highest I ever had in my life, including any tests prior to hormonal therapy and testosterone-suppression.

A couple of months into hormonal treatment I had figured out how to adjust the dosage so I would feel good (and consequently "look good") on any particular day, say when I had some kind of a medical/mental appointment coming my way. I figured out how to be a drug junkie really quickly because this is what made me look how I should and this in turn made me get somewhere. Of course "fabricating the good days" also meant getting the bad ones in between as every biological woman can attest to, I just had my own period 'engineered'. Well, I am an engineer, finding practical solutions to absurd problems is my job. (Whereas I often felt that finding absurd solutions to practical problems was what mental-health was all about). Under pressure people comply, under extreme pressure they comply irrationally, under ongoing excessive pressure they eventually break. It's normal, it's what's to be expected. No mental-health degree required to understand this, really.

I too complied. Like so many others before me. And I too came closer to being broken than most people ever will in their lifetime.

In the end, yes, I wanted to go to surgery, nothing but! I had a life with no other consideration in mind, no other social contacts except my immediate family (and that was at times difficult enough) and the handful of people I saw for healthcare reasons, no links to reality and no prospect to ever get any connection to reality back the way I was.

So, finally: Yes! I wanted that surgery! And I wanted it like never before! But not because I felt ill or somehow wrong or transsexual or even myself or not myself. Not because I needed it. Not anymore. These certainly were the initial motivators but over time these faded into oblivion, in the end I no longer cared at all. Not about myself and not about anybody or anything! *What remained was that I wanted it because to survive I needed the witch-hunt to end!* All the rest I didn't care anymore. Because I too couldn't live without a life forever. Because I too was and am incapable to live under such oppressive conditions endlessly. I was ready for the pyre. Not because I felt to be *but because nothing mattered anymore.* **Nothing.**

Is this what psychiatrists mean when they speak of readiness, mental health and sanity?

No, there was nothing crazy about me or my behaviour. If anything was crazy then it was the framework I was forced into. I find my reaction was the most normal I could possibly have had, my behaviour the most predictable anybody could possibly expect!

A few days later I had, somehow, made it to that faraway place where I had booked the start of my life. Fortunately I didn't have to travel alone, but I really don't remember much of getting there. I was just there and that was that.

First accommodation outside the hospital, then admission. A mountain of documents to sign: Declarations, releases, legal statements. I sign. Whatever they give me. I sign it. Who cares? They only want my signature and maybe my money and promise to help me for it, all these other people wanted my life and my soul and offered only ignorance, pain and suffering in return. I sign. Everything. Because this is now the only way to be alive in 24 hours.

Of all the documents I only remember the beginning of one. After I had spent so many months on how I could possibly get myself certified crazy I was asked to sign the following:

"I, the undersigned, being of perfectly sound mind, make the following declaration...".

Next morning, a few minutes before surgery, I was being prepped. Waiting. My surgeon came in. "Any last questions, concerns?". My first thought: *If for any reason this doesn't work as advertised there's no need to wake me up on the other side.* Of course I knew no surgeon would do this, so I just said "no, and thank you". I had bitten my tongue one last time... He: "Don't worry, you'll have another opportunity to thank me...". "I would not be here if I would worry". "Good! Then let's go inside!".

The anaesthetist started the drip. So this was finally happening! I was only some 14,000 days late, how inconsiderate of me!

Maybe another minute later, already on the operating table: "Is she gone?". "No, she's still smiling...".

A.28. Epilogue

Five Days post-op I felt physically healed. Of course I wasn't, I had a long way to go to complete recovery, but the problem was gone! I was also back on estrogen. A few months later I had much of my former social life back, I could function again. But I also had 16 months of abuse behind me no human being should ever be subjected to, 16 months of experiences nobody should ever have to make.

If I would be treated like this for punishment by any government or in any prison anywhere in the world I am certain Amnesty International would immediately call this torture. The Red Cross would certainly not tolerate such treatment on POW's.

Apparently if I get treated like this to obtain my healthcare then this is perfectly acceptable. My being seen as a transsexual and the kind of treatment I need makes this ok. Even warrants it. My way of being just a little different makes treating me like this right, doesn't it?

After I returned home one of the medical professionals involved said:

Thank you for playing along so nicely!

I replied: "You're welcome!". But what else could I possibly have said?

PART III - LIVING

A

HEALING

B

MADNESS NEVER AGAIN

The American Psychiatric Association, about the APA: "Its [...] member physicians work together to ensure humane care and effective treatment for all persons with mental disorder"[1]

The United Nations, General Assembly Resolution 46/119 of 17 December 1991,

Principles for the protection of persons with mental illness and the improvement of mental health care[2]

Principle 11, Section 12:

Sterilization shall never be carried out as a treatment for mental illness.

▸▸ Sex Reassignment is effective and medically indicated in severe GID [Gender Identity Disorder][HBIGDA-S]

▸▸ Genital Reassignment Surgery includes sterilization[3]

▸▸ Gender Identity Disorder is, as per its definition by the American Psychiatric Association, a mental illness[DSM]

---

[1] *Quoted from www.psych.org/FunctionalMenu/AboutAPA.aspx*
[2] *Office of the United Nations High Commissioner for Human Rights, Geneva, Switzerland*
[3] *Gonads (testicles in the case of a biological male) are, if present, removed during SRS*

A.29. BACK TO THE FUTURE!

People ask me from time to time about genital surgery. *That must have been quite a change* they generally suspect... Ok, it's major surgery. It's a month of pain, sometimes at unbelievable levels. After all the parts are some of the most sensitive our human anatomy has to offer. But of course one gets liberal amounts of pain-killers. Then there are a few months of recovery. It's surgery, that's normal. Recovery in the sense of physical healing, but also in the sense of hormonal re-adjustment. Hormone levels are fundamentally different afterwards, the biochemical process this sets off take a while to stabilize, a few months maybe. One has to find new levels of estrogen, testosterone suppression if indicated[1], possibly discontinue or adjust other medications if needed to feel comfortable. This all has to do with personal well-being, this all had a major impact on my level of physical and social activity.

Emotionally? That's simple enough to describe: **Surgical gender-alignment was the most overblown non-event of my life!** True, I'm not bothered by having the wrong genitals anymore, but that was the point, wasn't it? True, my natural testosterone-level is much lower now, but that was the point, wasn't it? Correction instead of suppression, that was the idea from the start, wasn't it? Physical as well as biochemical. True, I need a lot less medication now, but that isn't a bad thing either, is it? True, I don't feel 'wrong' anymore, I now feel, well, *actually I don't think about that anymore!* But that was the idea, wasn't it? This was the self-diagnosis I made some 40 years ago; this was, some 28 years ago, the treatment I thought would fit the problem when I learned that it existed; this was what I said when I came into the physicians office 18 months prior to waking-up in that hospital bed, wasn't it?

So what has changed? *Nothing?* Yes, nothing has changed, after all I'm still just the same woman I have always been. *Everything?* Yes, everything has changed, because I am now capable and allowed to be the woman I have always been! Because now who I am is right, understandable and acceptable. To me. It is even 'normal' to society - unless they rummage in their archives that is...

What I suppose is so difficult to understand for so many people is that <u>*genital gender-alignment does not change something from one to the other.*</u> <u>**I don't believe that making a woman from a man is actually possible.**</u> But neither does this surgery correct

[Medical professional] So they say you're done with transition? [Me] What transition?

---

[1] *Some trans-identified individuals find that they have too low a testosterone level to feel comfortable after surgery and s supplementing. Usually small amounts would be used but as so often this varies greatly by individual.*

"something that was wrong by making it right". This I presume would also not be possible. Though closer as an idea it still would never work *at the level this correction would have to be at.*

I don't feel *healed.* What I feel instead is *that there is not <u>and has never been</u> anything wrong!* **I don't experience myself 'gender-aligned', instead** <u>*I am now incapable to feel 'gender-mismatch'.*</u> **What surgical genital gender alignment does is** *<u>to remove something wrong in a way that afterwards it never was wrong!</u>*

But this is not the emotional context I live this in. This is, once again, the view "from the outside". My intellectual reflection and explanation of it when asked. <u>***What this treatment really gives to us is the ability "to*** *emotionally <u>open up to the world</u>"! And while this surgery may be the end of a long road for the physical aspect of this opening, it is merely another step on the road to emotional self-fulfilling!*</u>

The journey doesn't start here. It also doesn't end here. But it does make us capable to relate to the world in a meaningful and fulfilling way in many more ways than simply sexually!

This surgery was also the most absurdly absolute cut in life I have ever experienced. I am, as I am writing this, no longer emotionally capable to understand why I possibly ever wanted genital alignment. *How could anybody ever want this changed?* This would be absurd, even crazy, wouldn't it? Of course what I still understand is *that for me this was the only possible meaningful way out!*

I am a woman. *Why would I ever want to change this?* **These days life is that simple for me,** *just as it is for the great majority of people everywhere!*

B.41. LEGALIZE IT!

I have officially lived as a mental male who breaks the law every time she enters a public washroom for some 15 months of my life. I am now legally female, now it is unlawful for me to use the male washroom. Although I suspect punishment for a legal female who is found in a male washroom might be somewhat different from the one a legal male has to expect if found in a female washroom... Psychiatric dogma required me to do this, they force not few people to do this for decades or for their entire lifetime!

If ever anything would have happened during this time I might just have found myself in jail. *Male jail* of course as this would have been deemed "legally appropriate". It really doesn't take much: A bit of bad weather, a closed airport, a flight diverted. Maybe to a country where my gender-corrected documents aren't accepted but instead *are deemed fraudulent because they don't reflect 'reality'* - their reality. It could happen that easily!

I don't want to speculate what might have happened to me in a male holding-cell, but I suspect that this would not have been healthy, neither mentally nor physically. *Why they ask this of us,* **why any doctor would possibly force a patient to break the law before he is willing to dispense medical treatment** *and why this is deemed "good medical practice" is beyond me!* It doesn't help anybody, it doesn't make me "more female" and it most certainly does not make me non-transsexual, how could it? *It might however just get me killed!*

Because one is legally male while doing this one has to live with a set of official documents that don't match appearance, at least for some time. I have dual citizenship, one country blankly refused to change any and all of my documents including my legal change-of-name which they found to be "not gender-appropriate". For a legal male. The other country was a bit better, they at least issued me documents *in my new name.* Well, they'd better, after all it was *them* who had issued that change! They even eventually went as far as to grant me a gender-corrected driver's license and passport. Of course I was still deemed legally male, meaning that at times I had some absurd hurdles to overcome: Things like getting an insurance policy for a car. Males pay higher premiums than females do, but just explain to an insurance broker or company that I'd really like to pay the male-rate even though my driver's license as well as the vehicles registration (which is based on the data in the license) both say 'female'?

The whole absurdity fundamentally comes from a system which deems people to be male or female *not according to their self-identification, behaviour, appearance, or even*

[Male friend] And how does this... Hmmm... feel... now??? [Me] A lot better! [He] ...I still think I don't get the whole thing...

their genitals but *according to an entry in a dusty government database!* Sure, they could have changed that for me in about 10 seconds, the problem: *They didn't!*

From my perspective **having governmental files *reflect the current realities of life*** instead of data collected decades ago which may or may not be current and may even have been wrong back when it was collected would be one of the most fundamental, appropriate and meaningful improvements any government could introduce! Not just for transsexuals, after all it does seem very odd why anybody would *ever* want documents which do not reflect currently lived reality! Only this would create a problem for our dogmatists: Imagine I could have my legal gender-designation changed to female *by application?* What now? Suddenly the gender I say I am is the same that's on file! *Which means that I can no longer be gender-dysphoric!* And that can't possibly be right, can it?

So consequentially psychiatry says that it is mentally healthy for me to have a gender-corrected driver's license and possibly even a gender-corrected passport because it just makes sense for a woman to have female id. They recommend special legislation to cover this, hence my 'gender-corrected' documents. *But they stop short of recommending to the government to instead of dreaming-up a process to issue such "deliberately wrongful papers" to just make a correction and see me for who I am!* It would be far simpler if done this way, no special legislation for each and every governmental service would be needed! (Because I get *female* documents *while remaining legally male* directives now need to be drawn-up to cover any and all possible subsequent events: What to do with me if I'm found in a male or female washroom; what in case of a military draft; how to handle a potential arrest, body-search or incarceration; what to make of my potential request to adopt a child; in many courtiers rules and regulations need to be drawn-up in regard to the right to vote or for marriage: In spite of my *female* documents (and appearance) *I am to marry a woman,* not a man!).

Given how the legal system works and by what means our (mental) treatment is forced onto us *giving us legal rights just has to be the very last thing to happen in the whole process!* ***Because giving us this privilege would be the very last they'd ever see of many of us!*** So they let us live in legal limbo, drag this out as long as they possibly can (or a bit longer), never mind what this does to us, *because it keeps their control over us well established!*

After genital surgery they finally loose this power over us *because then not only will every doctor out there certify that "I am of female biological anatomy" (as lawyers describe it) but it will henceforth be risk-free for every doctor to prescribe me female hormones* (such as birth-control or post-menopausal treatment which is just what I get). *That all medications are, unlike surgery, easily available on the grey market without their consent is something they're acutely aware of, especially these days.*

In most jurisdictions midwives and doctors are *legally required* to ensure that a statement of live birth is filed *for every birth they have attended.* This document contains the newborn's gender which will become the basis of that person's legal gender. However *there are no rules in place which would in any way guarantee that a change in gender-designation would also have to be registered* (for whatever reason, be it the discovery of an intersex-condition, gender-alignment or a correction of a simple clerical mistake)! Transsexuals (as well as people who need such data changed for other reasons) do this *themselves* and some simply forget, de-transitioning being the prime suspect.

Only this double-standard of <u>mandatory registration at birth</u> and <u>voluntary notice of correction</u> very efficiently renders gender-designations in any and all legal documents and government databases useless! *<u>Because for every single entry we look at we now no longer know if it is a true representation of facts or not</u>! Of course Society would never admit that the whole legal gender-thing they've concocted is flawed and in reality reflects nothing else than government sponsored prejudice!*

B.42. No Future!

Treatment is over, normal life begins! Just as with every surgery there are a few medical concerns immediately post-op, there is post-surgical aftercare, but many of us have to fight another uphill battle just then. Most transsexuals get sent to surgery *by psychiatrists,* only psychiatrists are - while medical doctors - likely the most ill qualified when it comes to providing any kind of practical hands-on medicine other than pill-pushing.

It may indeed come as a bit as a shock to the psychiatric community to hear that genital surgery actually consists in cutting us apart pretty badly and then re-assembling us as good as it gets so when we come home we're managing everything from keeping infections at bay to a whole range of more or less typical post surgical concerns. And if ever something should go wrong and we do need an antibiotic or maybe a few stitches for a tear or whatever we find ourselves in a position where we first of all need to find a doctor who is actually qualified to do this, other than by psychotherapy that is. Only on top of being capable to help *that doctor also must be willing to accept a transsexual patient and not feel sick (or claim incompetence) when having to look at recent surgery in the genital area!* Neither dogma nor psychiatric practice in any way prepares us for this - *or in fact looses a single word over it!* So either dogma deems psychiatrists capable of dealing with all such medical issues without giving it any concern whatsoever - which I find at best *astounding* given the normal scope of a psychiatrist's practice - or it has escaped psychiatrists at large and dogmatists in particular that their medical colleagues aren't typically too keen on treating us? To put this mildly that is...

But even if we need medical care afterwards this is really a bit like the clean-up after Waterloo: The big battle is won and now the mess needs to be sorted out. Emotionally this is much rather like "if I die from this at least I am going to die free"!

There are a few lingering questions as to how this medical process called "elective surgery" works in general, questions outside the scope of the treatment of transsexuals. In my case one of these would be that I had a rather severe adverse reaction to one of the pain-killers I was given afterwards. Many surgeries and other "planned corrective measures" require medications either in preparation, during the procedure or afterwards. In some cases patients don't have a choice because there is only a single product for a given purpose available but often there is a large selection on hand. Pain-killers are one of the more obvious, there is a variety of substances available and one is pretty much guaranteed to need something for a few days after most surgical procedures. I was given morphine sulphate, only I don't tolerate this. Well, one always knows better, *afterwards...*

Being an engineer I would have deemed it prudent to test all the drugs I was bound to be given after surgery one by one *on myself before the event to find out if these would work as advertised.* I had to wait 9 months for the event, there would have been ample time for this. I'm not exactly the only person who has adverse reactions to certain drugs and I am not the only one for whom some drugs don't work as advertised. *Only I think it is a bad time to find this out exactly when one is in severe pain and needs all the strength to heal!* Particularly if this is avoidable, the problem could have easily been identified long before.

Identifying patients who react badly to drugs *before* any procedure may, in many cases, not even require a single dose of a substance, often a small fraction of it would identify a problematic drug immediately (with a potentially much less severe reaction *and at a time when this reaction would be the only medical concern at hand).* In an otherwise healthy individual this should not be a problem, *however having the same severe reaction after surgery instead just might make the difference between life and death* or at least between a speedy, pleasant recovery and a lengthy miserable one. In any case if it happens it isn't a nice experience. But eventually one recovers from this too, hopefully, it just takes a while longer.

And then this is done too. It may be two months after surgery, or four, and suddenly we realize that yes, *this now really is normal life!* We wake-up and find ourselves *deprived of the most important activities our lives were scheduled around for years, maybe decades:* There suddenly is no more need to behaviourally comply to obtain treatment, to find the means to survive oppression, to hope that this would ever happen and fear it never will! *Suddenly everything we ever needed in life is here! Suddenly everything we ever could achieve has been accomplished! And suddenly there's nothing left to do in life!*

For some this is the moment to start a completely new life. For others this at least includes some major changes to their current existence. However for yet others this leads to a more or less severe post-op depression. Nothing to do, no more artificial meaning, nothing out there for us to overcome or to achieve, nothing to fight or hope for! *No more irrational and artificial psychiatrically created meaning of life!*

The risk that this leads to a post-op suicide is very real. The psychiatric community says that 12 months post-op - and for the rest of our lives - statistics show that our probability of dying from suicide is the same as it is for biological women. They do not release figures for the first 12 months but I expect these to be *significantly* higher.

And yes, you know me by now, I am going to blame psychiatry and dogma for this! Of course I am! Because, honestly, none of us would fall into that kind of a hole *if they hadn't deliberately put it there for us to fall into!* If we hadn't had to wait for years, *if we hadn't had to focus any and all our attention, efforts, hopes and dreams into this one single issue and event for so long!* If we would not have had to rearrange our entire lives just for that one purpose! If we would have had an opportunity to get *a real life* in between *we would have that real life to return to and to carry on afterwards!*

But they deny us any form of normalcy before, so the normalcy afterwards becomes this never experienced absence of being told what to do, being told what to think, being told how to live. A sudden complete absence of being told who we have to be!

So there we are: Problem solved - and no reality to live in!

A.30. TRANSACTION WITHOUT A RECEIPT

I still hope to one day get this letter from a law-firm in a remote place somewhere on the planet: Please collect the billion-dollar estate a previously unknown aunt has awarded to me upon her death! Only these days there may just be a snag: *It is now impossible for me to provide proof that I ever was the person I used to be!* And if the estate just happened to have been awarded to my "old legal self", well, it may yet go down the drain because of a bureaucratic oversight - or should I say *a bureaucratic nightmare?*

Whenever somebody changes anything in her life's legal framework, say, somebody gets a mortgage or gets married or buys a car, even if this person just buys some groceries, it really hardly matters what it is, there's a legal paper-trail to follow and a descriptive document such as a receipt, a contract, even a government maintained registry *to show that this change or transaction has, legally, taken place.* Every single change leaves a paper-trail (or at least one's entitled to get one), there is no exception! Well, almost none... There is one exception I have found (but of course...): *Gender-alignment is not documented!* No, I'm not talking of the surgery, this left a sizeable hole in my bank-account and yes, of course I have a receipt *for the payment* I have made to the clinic and the surgeon. *I am rather talking of the legal change which takes place after surgery when I go and register the change that has taken place with the government!*

After surgery I apply to have all my personal documents updated[1]. By now some documents only need an updated gender while others, such as the birth-certificate, still need to reflect my current name as well. The officials accept this, change it, in some instances require the old original documents back, then new ones get issued. _What they don't do is to issue a proof of change, something that shows that, when and where the legal change has taken place!_ *Our government also has never issued any receipts for handing in old documents (or returned these marked 'cancelled') nor given me proof that these have ever existed and have been requested back (where these likely end-up in yet another dark basement-archive to collect dust instead of helping me to document my life).*

If you change your name, obtain a driver's license, buy a home, whatever, _you get some form of a document showing that this change has taken place, when it has taken place, how the state of affairs was before and how it is afterwards!_ For my legal gender-

---

[1] *Proceedings for this vary by the jurisdiction one lives in and or has relations to (i.e. is a citizen of, has a marital partner from, has a birth-certificate of,...). Some countries have legislation of varying degrees of what to do (if this is appropriate for a specific individual remains to be seen) while others have some procedural or administrative framework outside of legislation. What this covers and how this works varies greatly, the UK for example issues "proof of change of legal sex designation" which then entitles the holder to have any and all government-issued documents changed. This however is a rare exception*

reassignment I keep the old documents (if I'm allowed to hold on to these) and get the new ones issued (which is rather welcome), *showing for all intents and purposes a different person* (often the change-of-name and gender is reflected *at the same time* so a birth-certificate would change directly from "John Doe, male" to "Amanda Smith, female"). **And I get no confirmation whatsoever that there ever has been a change** *or that these two sets of documents belong together, that they in fact designate one and the same person!*

The problem really comes from the political as well as the legal community apparently being blissfully ignorant when it comes to dealing with us! Unfortunately it appears that the "trans community" or better "transsexual activists" are just as helpless - and so they end-up proposing solutions that don't prompt too many legal changes, cause no political wrinkles - *and solves hardly any of my problems while creating plenty of new ones!*

What that conglomerate of legal, political (and gender-political) 'experts' with some psychiatric insight have dreamt-up is that after surgery our birth-records get replaced. *Retroactively.* Now I don't know if that's the right thing to do or not, it may well be part of a meaningful package to solve the legal aspect. Only they have borrowed this solution from the neonatal ward where such corrections to documents are at times necessary. The legal gender of a newborn may need changing on paper because it appeared one way but on second inspection looked more like the other… It happens… Even to doctors...

More typically the reason for tearing-up an already filed birth-certificate and replacing it (though I am certain in truth these end-up collected in yet another government basement - "for historic purposes") would be *to cover-up for a childhood adoption.* Basically a fake is put in place of the original - it's the only way to prevent the child (or anybody else, say the birth-mother) to link the "former truth" to the "new truth" (or the simple fact that the child is an adoptee for that matter). If they'd keep the original on file or just put an amendment to it in the records (as would be the accepted legal practice), this would be easy enough. As it is every adoptee gets a form that looks exactly like everybody elses naming his/her biological parents (which are in fact *adoptive* parents and in all likelihood *not biologically related* to the child), they can see a doctor who was present at the birth and so on. *Only of course this birth never took place as advertised!* In both cases (early correction and adoption) nobody will ever ask for "proof of change", in fact everybody sighs relief if there isn't one! (Except possibly the adoptee who wants or needs to find his/her biological parents, but instead is told *that these problems are there by design* and he/she isn't entitled to know!).

So just applying the methods that work well (almost all of the time) for a newborn to an adult is best because??? *Because it is already there and nothing needs changing, no thinking is required?* **Or maybe *because nothing ever needs acknowledging and no acceptance is needed?***

Only, unlike a newborn, I have an entire life's trail of legal documents with binding obligations and privileges, all these carry my old name and gender and they all do not magically change *but they all become inconsistent, they suddenly no longer relate to myself!*

Having to obtain all these changes individually is a rather painful experience, it is expensive *and in many cases it isn't possible at all!* Some issuers simply refuse to re-issue documents (such as schools and universities), sometimes an equivalent document no longer exists or the replacement is in some way restricted (such as the duration of validity or by limitations the original did not carry[1]) and sometimes the issuing body or country no longer exist at all! As there is no legal mandate that anybody *must* issue an updated copy *everybody can get away with discriminating against us by not doing so!*

On top of this many documents that are re-issued leave a paper-trail of their own. If I have to change a land-title registration *this will appear as a change of title, not as an inconspicuous replacement or administrative correction of the original!* (Never mind I have to pay the full transfer-fee and may count myself lucky if there are no taxes levied on the 'sale' from me to myself!). Of course they haven't thought of transsexuals actually owning any property, I mean how could we, it's just preposterous! So now the entry in the registry suggests to anybody *that some kind of a transfer has taken place.* But even if I could have the original replaced this would not help because the government routinely sells their complete database to such interested third-parties as marketing companies, statisticians, journalists and historians. It would be very easy for anybody who owns an old copy to find any "corrected entries"! **Indeed their very method of how to sweep my legal change under the rug has by now caused my disability and medical record (and mental-health classification)** *to be put on public record, officially published and guaranteed to remain known forever!*

Public records now furthermore contain references to persons who officially never were born (as my old self has been removed from the birth register) and changes that have never taken place! For example there is now a change-of-name on public record from some old name to my current name *while I am also on record to have been born <u>under my current name</u>!* Such legal crap creates problems like me getting a letter from a foreign corporation (of which I own limited-transferable shares) saying that "to register your requested change please forward a notarized copy of an agreement of sale or a death-certificate of the previous owner & an affidavit that you are the entitled beneficiary of the estate". I have on at least one occasion a credit request refused on the grounds that the issuer thought the data they obtained from credit-bureaus suggested identity theft - and that's in the one instance I was advised of a reason, the ones who simply refuse without comment, who knows? Issues like these are difficult, not just legally, they are this emotionally also. The fact that after 50 years of the problem being known in legal circles *still no government anywhere is willing to put us into a position where we could deal with such matters unbureaucratically and efficiently* is a sad one and indeed doesn't show much willingness to do anything at all to facilitate our lives!

I don't want to start giving advice as to what could or should be done, this alone would easily fill an entire book. All I would like to do is point-out that these problems exist and for a

---

[1] *To give an example: My old foreign driver's license was valid for life and entitled me to drive cars and motorcycles whereas the replacement needs renewal every few years and no longer includes motorcycles as by now this requires a separate license*

good number of transsexuals they're not marginal at all. They in fact have the potential to screw-up our lives rather effectively!

One of the more questionable things in the current set-up is that the government issues me a corrected birth-certificate, but I still have to apply for a change-of-name before this! Could this not be done "all in one"? Well, it is not the legal community I will blame for that one but my favourite scapegoat, psychiatry! Because *dogma actually requires us to obtain a legal change-of-name,* apparently it's proof of our sincerity! *It's all part of what medical doctors feel they have a right to dictate to us!*[1]

The problem with this approach is threefold: First, as this is a change-of-name only I will get a legal identity and a set of papers *which about as clearly identifies me as being transsexual as it ever gets short of stamping a red letter 'T' on every document: These will all read* "Eva, male"!

Second, *this now requires me to change most documents twice!* Never mind that I have yet to hear of a government willing to give us a complete set of replacement-papers *free of charge, as a human right because replacing these is a necessary part in the course of treating our disability* (never mind paying twice over), the process of getting these isn't exactly as relaxing as going to the spa. It's not as if I could go to any counter and present a government issued certificate reading something like "The register of vital records has been updated to reflect the following correction(s)", followed by a list of changes, i.e. name, gender; "everybody is required to implement all listed change(s) upon presentation of this document...". But it is much rather like presenting a letter of my surgeon and saying something like: "Hi! Here's my old document. I know I don't look like the guy in the picture at all, but it's really me, and here is an affidavit from a doctor in a faraway place who gives evidence that he has cut off my male genitals in a way so it now looks female, please believe me I'm neither mental nor an impostor nor an identity-thief and could I humbly request that you replace this document even though there are no previsions in your guidelines to do so?" (Most rules and regulations as well as forms to change documents typically only allow to have a person's name, date of birth, place of residence and so forth changed, *but not her gender!*). If this works, fine! If not, stand back in line and try to get another clerk next time... Did I mention that this isn't exactly efficient or relaxing?

Jane says: When I left the hospital to go home I received a form to advise the police to issue me a handicapped parking-permit. I went there and received the permit to display in the dash. I can now use handicapped parking-spaces and if there aren't any I'm allowed to park my vehicle wherever it is safe to park for as long as I need to, free of charge, even if there's a parking-meter there. I'm thankful for this as without my car there are many

---

[1] *In some countries obtaining a simple change-of-name requires a court-order. Sometimes our new names are not accepted for a procedural change as they are not deemed "gender appropriate" (for our legal gender on file), this too will usually lead to a court-order. Typically the courts require a psychiatric expertise to grant such an "exceptionally inappropriate change". And do I have to mention that all this - in almost all cases - will have to be paid for by the individual?*

places I could not go to because I just could not get there! There are many things I could not do, simple things such as shopping for groceries, because I'm limited in what I can carry and how far. All this was free of charge and yes, I appreciate this, but honestly my disability is quite expensive enough and it would feel very wrong if the government would start charging me for having a severe disability, wouldn't it?

Third, *every such application and change leaves yet another paper-trail!* The more such traces I leave behind the less likely it is that afterwards I will ever be able to live a normal life. In my case the union of dogma and government-policy of treating my human rights with the utmost contempt has screwed-up that documented past so badly that I don't mind to publish this book anymore - *because everybody can find out about my sex-change as well as my previous name and identity by checking current and archived public government records or by just looking-up old government publications in a public library or on the internet.* It's not that I wouldn't care anymore, it's much rather **that I have been sabotaged at every step of the way** and this, once out in the public domain, just doesn't get put back again!

As a result it is today a lot easier *for everybody else* to find government certified proof that I had genital surgery than it is *for me* to provide proof that I was the person I used to be or to provide proof that the history of my life is in fact real and not fabricated. It's completely absurd, but it is a fact!

Just to give you an idea what I'm talking about: The public records now show that I was born Eva, female. Then I graduate from university as a guy. Next I immigrated to another country using a name for which there is no birth-record, claiming to be male. Even worse, upon immigration I state that I do not have a birth-certificate (I was never issued one) - which is nicely consistent to it not existing... Next I marry a female using that non-existing male pseudonym. Then I file several birth-records using that name claiming to be the father. Then I change that other name legally to one for which a birth-record already exists! Subsequently I claim to be that woman this birth-record identifies - and request that a certificate be is issued *to me!* Then I file to have our marriage re-designated a same-sex marriage while insisting that I, being born a woman, am father of our children and stand firm on retaining all parental rights. Just to make the confusion complete I on top of everything insist that I should retain all the rights and privileges *both* persons have ever obtained, including everything form academic qualifications to rights to inheritances to property to retirement benefits and much more! Honestly, if that were the scenario of a crime-story it would be considered a rather far-fetched set-up and wholly unbelievable. But, as it is: Welcome to my life!

Now can anybody understand why I might just have some problems to correctly fill out an application for, say, a police-background-check for some volunteer-work at our local school where it says *"state all previous names/identities used"?* Never mind that on top of everything else I am as stubborn as to have that absurd idea that I ought be treated without prejudice, just like everybody else!

A.31. MIRROR, MIRROR, WHO IS THE FAIREST...

How would I look today had I been allowed to start at age 17? Or at age 10? Well, in all likelihood better! Just to give you one example: I certainly would not have to loose half of my hair before I started, I could have had very nice natural hair without any intervention, pain, side-effects or cost!

It is rather obvious that the earlier one starts the better the result will be *in every respect.* Never mind there are body-features which can never be surgically corrected such as the overall height. If one just happens to be 198cm tall (6'6") - which luckily I'm not - one just is an exceptionally tall woman. If treatment starts early enough, before or early in puberty, *transsexuals could not only grow-up socially in line with their gender-identification, they could also in the end in appearance be like the average person of the identified gender, in every respect!* This would be ideal for most of us, it would facilitate integration, it would help to de-stigmatize transsexuality, it would for all intents and purpose be giving us the best possible life we could expect in a society which does not respect us for who we are, in a society where we have to comply, deny and hide!

It is true that not every transsexual says that she has known to be trans early in life. But many have. I have. It would just make sense to start with treatment *as soon as the condition has been recognized.* Or at least as soon as one can understand the differences - which would put early treatment at around 5 or 6, kindergarten age. After all the chances that transsexuality disappears spontaneously in an otherwise emotionally age appropriately developed individual are zero. After several hundred thousand psychiatrically documented cases we should finally accept this as fact!

Ideally the start of treatment would be before school-entry. If an individual would like to achieve fertility for procreation full treatment could start immediately after sperm has been collected but partial treatment could start much earlier, in particular social life could, if desired, start at any time. *Achieving biological fertility is necessary today if one would like to have biological children but it is to be expected that science will soon offer infertile individuals other means to procreate than collecting sperm- and egg-cells.* Doctors who treat transsexuals could borrow any reproductive treatment from there. During puberty every month counts, makes a difference - a difference in a potentially miserable life during this time as well as a lifetime of missed opportunities, a difference between a socially integrated, happy individual and suicide - or everything in between.

So far to the medical side. This part is important, it is in particular important as it may end in potentially insurmountable physical, financial and emotional problems. It is also

important because it leads many individuals who are intersex-trans via the biochemical hormonal connection more directly to depression and suicide. Or to put this differently: *We too*
would like to grow-up in line with our identification, in a matching social setting, with
peers we can relate to, with activities we like, expectations we understand. We too would
like to rise up to, maybe even excel at what we do, potentially be exceptionally good at
something!

Some transsexuals manage to "socially catch-up" later in life but we really shouldn't have
to. *And so many of us are later in life told that "they are not real women" <u>precisely because</u>*
<u>*they have been forced to miss out on growing-up female!*</u>

I could have been beautiful, I suppose. I still think I am, but if you know what to look for
you'll know that I have lived on a testosterone horror-trip for half a lifetime. It isn't completely reversible, not physically and definitely not emotionally. I'll now have to live with the
consequences of this for the rest of my life. *It doesn't take away any of my identification but <u>it</u>*
<u>*does potentially change how you see me.*</u> And it does make for half a lifetime of missing out
on life!

B.43. NEW: OBSESSIVE SELF-RIGHTEOUSNESS DISORDER

On a whole our treatment shows that many psychiatrists fall for a professional trap of trying to over-explain something they don't understand, thinking this gives them insight. In my case this would be *why I am a woman* or how they like to put it: "Why I *want to be* a woman". They float completely absurd explanations of a predominantly sexual nature, a desperate last-ditch-effort for not failing to provide *any* explanation at all! Is it ever tempting to propose sex as the motivational factor? Because sexual self-experience is by its very nature not measurable and if mine isn't what they say it has to be, well, *there's only my word contradicting their "expert opinion", is there?* So what I say can as well be ignored in favour of some made-up explanation by such "experts with superior knowledge" and once *they* have decided that *they* are right *I* can simply be "made to fit their explanation"?

Indeed this obsessive idea that psychiatrists are capable of "explaining everything" seems to be the very reason why they come-up with a completely oversexed, overgendered, oversimplified and overpathologized view of the entire world!

True, if one *absolutely* wants to see my transsexuality from a perspective of sexual self-arousal it would likely not be too difficult to find behaviours which could be misinterpreted this way and by sweeping all contradictory evidence under the rug one could then conclude that this is actually correct! After all I like my physical appearance a lot better now than I did before but why this would *have* to be interpreted *sexually* I don't know. Of course if I wouldn't like myself better now then *this* surely would be thrown at me by psychiatry for proof that I was wrong in the first place and should never have been allowed to go to that surgery? So really, I can't ever make it right for them, only they themselves can!

There are many views that can be put forward and I am certain one could find *some* supporting arguments for each and every one of these. Just pick the right arguments and ignore the rest, at over 45 years of age my life just happens to be complex enough to feature *some evidence* for every theory imaginable. I don't experience or see it like this, but then again, this isn't about me, is it? Because if it were, what I experience would have to be rated higher than what psychiatry implies. After all it is *my* treatment, not theirs. Or is it?

Taking a step back it is my impression that institutions and psychiatrists *tend to find cases along their view and expectations.* Scientifically of course it should not be possible that one population of patients suffers from a condition *which is impossible by the reasoning and experience of the treating physician next door,* after all the patients and their conditions clearly exist, even if they are professionally denied. However in spite of such truly basic reasoning (see Aristotle [ARIS-C]) many such scientific insights have been put forward in medicine in the past, have been "scientifically proven" only to be revised or deemed downright absurd a few years, decades or centuries later. I have mentioned phrenology and eugenics before, in the treatment of transsexuality notions such as "we're all undercover homosexuals" or the view that "transsexuality is an exclusively male phenomenon" would qualify. These should never have withstood scientific scrutiny at any time as clearly if they're found to be flawed now they can't have been right 50 years ago? The very fact that scientific research into such flawed assumptions, at the time, was crowned with success shows that, at least in part, *psychiatry designs and creates the illnesses they're looking for!*

Obviously there is the question if "making others fit to one's own beliefs or expectations" could be a mental condition. To qualify this would have to "impair emotional, behavioural or cognitive functioning", however it is obvious that there are a great number of possible reasons why a behaviour would be classified 'impairing' *but not seen as a mental illness.*

Jane, for example, uses a wheelchair to get around instead of her legs and feet. This isn't a typical behaviour for humans and it is 'impairing' in many ways. However because this "untypical behaviour" can be explained by a physical condition it is not seen as a *mental* illness. Or an illness at all for that matter. I suppose Jane would be rather upset if it were...

Usually - of course except in the case of transsexuals - a behaviour is seen as "being of a physical nature" if a physical cause can be determined, otherwise it is often, at least initially, believed to be "of a mental nature". Clearly there is no physical origin for thinking of oneself and one's own insights as being superior to others. But is this also 'impairing'? Just how inclusive should this definition be? Should this only include people who do this deliberately, out of malice, greed or narcissism? Or should it include any and all people who display such behaviour, even if they do not understand? Even if they "just follow orders"? Unfortunately there's a big problem here: The more inclusive one makes this the more of psychiatry itself (or medicine in general) would fit the profile...

I have always suspected that there must be a good reason *why some mental disorders are missing in the DSM.* On the other hand I agree that it is always more difficult to see one's own mental illnesses than these of others... But I have just the solution: May I suggest some therapy? *Any* therapy? Of course before we can get to that stage we would first have to find an appropriate diagnosis. A reason for 'any' therapy. So may I suggest the following:

[You may wish to add this page to your copy of the DSM]

Obsessive Self-Righteousness Disorder

This psychotic disorder is diagnosed when nonbizarre or bizarre delusions of one's own mental or moral superiority are present for at least three months and the symptom criteria for Schizophrenia have never been met. The behaviour may be destructive towards others and may involve breaking laws or rules, deceit or unethical behaviour. Other social functioning must not be impaired.

Diagnostic Criteria for Obsessive Self-Righteousness Disorder

A. Individual is convinced of his mental and/or moral superiority and of the truthfulness of his prejudices.
B. Such beliefs are maintained even in the face of clear contradictory evidence.
C. There is a pervasive pattern of disregard for and violation of the rights and integrity of others, their beliefs, behaviours, identifications or lifestyles.
D. Deliberate indifference towards others. (specify if this includes everybody or specific groups and if this includes malevolent indifference)
E. Considers criticism a personal insult or attack, rejects criticism on the grounds of status, claims that whoever doesn't accept his superiority is 'unqualified'.
F. Has a style of speech that is excessively impressionistic while lacking in detail, contents and often coherence. May use lingo to impress, claiming that it is not possible to express his superior insights in common language.
G. Exaggerates his own morality while rationalizing failure as fault of others, circumstances, social conditions or everybody else.
H. Expects preferred treatment and reverence of his superiority.
I. Mostly or exclusively socializes with people who recognize his superiority.

Specify if:

- delusions of infallibility are present (specify)
- the behaviour is part of a group or movement, if so specify if the group:
    - discourages or bans non-professional social contact towards outsiders
    - uses 'secret' language, codes and/or signs to communicate
    - deems indifference towards outsiders essential
    - deems presenting superiority towards outsiders essential
    - is highly organized and differentiated (specify structure and function)

If this scheme would, by any chance, remind you of a certain group of people that really does exist, maybe a certain profession whose members use lingo to describe common phenomenon of human life in a way so most people can't understand, distance themselves as a professional virtue so as to remain emotionally untouched by the consequences of their actions and generally keep to themselves to the extent that they make it illegal for each other to socialize with "the subjects of their work", maybe a group of people who think themselves uniquely qualified to provide certain services to the extent that they make it a crime for everybody else to provide the same, similar or better services, prohibit all the "unqualified people" from obtaining items that may be necessary for a person's well-being or survival (by declaring everybody 'incompetent' no matter what kind of insight, experience or education they might have, solely based on the fact that this person is not a members of their group) unless permission is granted by a member of this group at their sole and absolute discretion, even going so far as to force lifelong dependency on their repeated services onto outsiders **and if you think that this behaviour might just be far better explained by** *Obsessive Self-Righteousness Disorder* **than any other condition** I would certainly like to caution that *any and all resemblances to existing professions and any suggestion of current systematic abuse of the entire population of the planet by such professionals* **would be entirely unintentional, completely fictional and purely coincidental!**

I would also like to point out that *Obsessive Self-Righteousness Disorder* is most definitely an unfounded hypothetical condition, a literary invention, a fictitious imagination of a psychiatrically recognized sick brain as nobody in their right mind would ever think of something like this never mind doing it! [Please note the circular logic!]. **Because** *if there were even the most remote possibility* **of certain people** *ever* **behaving in this way,** *this surely would be recognized in the DSM and quickly dealt with by psychiatrists and professional regulatory organizations everywhere?*

A.32. I AM NOT MENTAL, IT'S EVERYBODY ELSE...

What I live is controversial. To quite a few people. To some it is unacceptable under any circumstance. There are individuals but also social organizations, governments and amazingly even churches who do not accept who I am or what I live. These days most governments have some level of acceptance, meaning they have makeshift solutions to getting our lives legally recognized. At least in most places we are issued legal documents that match our self-identification and the reality of our lives. Eventually.

But on a whole there is as of yet no country who takes our issues seriously enough to act and provide more than incidental support. There is an entire range of issues when it comes to dealing with governments, these all will have to be sorted-out but one of the more absurd would likely have to be our marital status. Quite a few transsexuals are married before they go to genital alignment. Only most countries - as of today - restrict marriage to heterosexual couples. Of course the designation 'heterosexual' is - you guessed it - not based on lived reality or even biological reproductive capacity but on archives in governmental basements. So countries have no problem if two anatomical females are married after the biological male has had her surgery - and thus the two are for all intents and purposes a married lesbian couple - *until such time as the partner who has had genital alignment asks for legal recognition and to have her documents changed!* **Because it is not the fact that two lesbians are married which apparently is offensive in some way, it is the fact that the government is forced to acknowledge that this exists already!** If this comes to the attention of a country where same-sex marriage does not exist the problem will be solved by a forced divorce or annulation, depending on circumstances and laws, in some places the two married woman may count themselves lucky if they don't get hauled into court for it! *In the end we get the choice of remaining faithful in marriage while not getting any legal recognition and protection or accepting a forced divorce in order to obtain a meaningful legal status!*

The problem gets incrementally absurd if the couple has biological children (either from before surgery or with the help of previously collected sperm and a fertility clinic afterwards). After gender-alignment the transsexual parent may not only have her marriage thrown out but on top of that *all her parental rights to her own biological children are likely affected or even cancelled outright!* Her children may retroactively be re-designated as having been born "out of wedlock" (although this may not have been true when they were born), some countries go as far as to re-issue birth-certificates with 'unknown' indicating the father because it can't possibly be a women, can it? (One only hopes science never invents something like egg-splicing which would enable any two fertile women to have their own biological children!).

My own case is, I suppose, a bit more absurd still. Being a citizen of a country where same-sex marriage is legal and of another where it is not I am now legally married in one country while at the same time I am legally "not married anymore" in the other. More absurd still: The country where our marriage remains legal (because they allow same-sex marriage and therefore don't question such changes anymore) *currently insists that it was and remains a heterosexual union* (which of course it officially was at the time of proclamation) while the other country insists *that we can't be married anymore because this would be an illegal homosexual marriage!* I can get my birth-certificate retroactively replaced but not our marriage-certificate. So I am now female at birth while I remain married as a male and this is unacceptable to the officials of another country because this constitutes "a same sex marriage"? Cynical me assumes this bureaucratic nightmare now exists *because same-sex marriage did not legally exist when we were married while female births did at the time I was born?* But we could solve this little problem by filing for divorce and then re-marrying each other: This *would* correct our marital state from unrecognized homosexual to recognized homosexual...

Of course if this were about a bank-account, a car or a house, a business or being in debt none of this would change in the slightest just because I change my legal sex-designation. I mean why would it? The one and only thing affected seems to be our family! Personally I don't understand why this should have to be the case, after all the marriage was consecrated legally so why should it not remain so "until death us parted"? This was after all the original idea when they invented marriage, wasn't it? But not so for transsexuals they now say: **I could *only* marry *a female* for the first part of my life, now I can *only* marry *a male!*

The two things I am not legally allowed - at least in that country where same-sex marriage is banned - is **to remain faithful in marital union to the same partner until death us parted** and **to raise our biological children within the legal framework and social protection of a family together with their other biological parent!** *And precisely because of what would I not be allowed this? Well, because, at least so I'm told, this would be 'immoral'!*

How wrong do social rules have to get in order to be recognized as being completely absurd? People who support such views pervert any and all meaning a religious context of marriage could possibly have! And as for psychiatry: I find they have a rather large field of activity they could get involved in! Only they don't. May I presume that society is not a well paying customer?

But in spite of all the problems, all the absurdity and all the social ramifications some of us do all this *while remaining faithful to their partner throughout a lifetime* *in a time where a 50% divorce-rate is considered normal among the general population!* **Surely this is unacceptable, even downright insane! Such things must be declared immoral, can't be tolerated, this demands prohibiting, punishment and persecution!** *Faithfully married transsexuals mind you, not that 50% divorce-rate. Of course!*

Yes, I understand full well that **if one accepts the reality of my life then one would in the end have to accept that the entire homosexual/heterosexual identification would have to be deemed meaningless** at least in my case. And if my lesbian marriage is ok, then why isn't every other lesbian marriage also? If my discrimination *in regard to marriage* is wrong it can hardly be right to discriminate against me when it comes to same-sex couples adopting children! Or tax benefits. Or annuities. Or discounts for couples. And so on…

So if people start accepting my life as real, *if they start accepting me as real,* **then… I suppose anybody can pretty much guess where this would inevitably have to go! Considering all the (few) options there are, isn't it so much easier to see me as a mental male?** *This way nobody needs to accept that a few major change in society are called for!* **Just to accommodate a handful of transsexuals whose marriages didn't fall apart during transition all by itself or therapists and surgeons didn't steer an ultra-hardline course and let something like this happen?** *After all this is something the mental-health community claims to occur in 1 out of 15,000,000 people?* **(Though I'm certain that this happens far, far more frequently).** *Should we possibly even consider to change our morals, beliefs and laws for a group of people psychiatry says count fewer than 500 individuals on the entire planet? Just because they prove with their lives that these morals are wrong?*

But then again, if I were "a fake", "a mental male" how come I have my marriage thrown-out on the grounds that this is now an illegal same-sex relationship? I mean they can't possibly take me for a woman for the purpose of marriage and at the same time for a mental male for the purpose of not having to overthrow their moral concepts? I can't be both a woman and a man at the same time - even if it would be very convenient for them, can I? *But if they nevertheless insist that this is how it is? Even in the face of clear contradictory evidence??? Well… Why does this now start to remind me of something and appears quite… insane???*

They could have let the whole thing rest in peace! Think of it as an administrative mistake, two married lesbians *of whom one had been taken for a male by mistake.* I'm certain this has happened before, somewhere! They could have avoided all these and so many other problems? But they didn't *because they just can't accept me as I am!* If they had just given me what I needed? Quietly, privately. Would have given me new documents to my new life? Quietly, privately. If they had just buried my old legal life and created a new one? Quietly, privately. They would never have to deal with all these problems! Their world would look unscathed while I would have my life! But that doesn't happen *because they just can never leave somebody who is different in peace?* Not quietly and not privately! *Honestly, somebody is definitely in dire need of some mental treatment here and I am rather certain it isn't me…*[1]

---

[1] *There are in fact two precedents of allowing some people to break many religious and social imperatives <u>because it isn't meaningful or possible to not allow this</u> - only most people aren't aware of this or don't understand it: (a)* <u>Adoptive children are socially and legally allowed to marry their biological sister, brother, father or mother.</u> *Of course this is incest and incest is neither approved of in a religious context nor allowed legally. But with adoption being secret it is not possible for the people involved (or the government or any church) to (officially) know! (b)* <u>People whose biological father is neither the husband of their mother nor the person mentioned as 'father' in their birth-certificates:</u> *<u>If such a child is a woman it is legal for her to marry her biological father,</u> knowingly or not. I am certain both cases exist - and the world hasn't come to an end because of it…*

B.44. NEW: THE REVERSE MUNCHAUSEN SYNDROME

While I am at suggesting additions to the DSM there's another one I find is dearly missing in there, I'd like to call it *the Reverse Munchausen Syndrome*.

For everybody who isn't on a first name basis with disorders of a mental kind, *Munchausen Syndrome* is a "factitious disorder". I have listed the definitions below:

Factitious Disorder[1]:

Patient's with this mental disorder are so eager to assume the role of a sick person that they intentionally feign or produce symptoms. Sub classification is according to whether the symptoms are predominately psychological, physical or combined.

Also: Ahasuerus's, artifactual, factitial, factitious disorder, hospital addiction, hospital hobo, hospital vagrant, malingering, Munchausen syndrome, pathomimia, peregrinating patient, Polle, polysurgical addiction, problem patient, professional patient, SHAFT

Munchausen Syndrome[1]:

Patients with this mental disorder want to assume the role of a sick person so they intentionally feign or produce symptoms and spend much of their life traveling from place to place and moving from hospital to hospital to be admitted as patients, often undergoing unneeded surgical procedures. (Named after Karl Friedrich Hieronymus, Freiherr von Münchhausen.)

Munchausen Syndrome by Proxi[1]:

Patient's with this mental disorder, rather than assuming the role of a sick person themselves, intentionally feign or produce symptoms in their child in order to maintain contact it [in] this role with medical providers. This can even result in serious injury or death of the child. (Named after Karl Friedrich Hieronymus, Freiherr von Münchhausen.)

[Government office, clerk] Hallo, how can I help you? [Me] I would like to have the sex on my document changed [She] Ok, I don't really know how to do that, I've never had a sex-change...

---

[1] *Text excerpt from www.behavenet.com/capsules/disorders/dsm4TRclassification.htm [DSM-IV-TR (online version)]*

[You may wish to add this page to your copy of the DSM]

Reverse Munchausen Syndrome

Therapists and/or medical practitioners with this mental disorder rather than assuming the role of the sick themselves needlessly pathologize their patients in order to establish and maintain a therapeutic relationship. This can result in serious emotional trauma or physical harm to the patient through either needless medication or medical procedures or self inflicted damage, including suicide.

Diagnostic Criteria for The Reverse Munchausen Syndrome

A. Inducing, feigning or inventing of physical or psychological symptoms in patient with subsequent pathologization and treatment.
B. The primary motivation is to assume the role of the therapist.
C. Additional motivations for the behaviour (such as economic gain, avoiding legal obligations, obtaining sexual services) may be present.

Specify if:

- the practitioner is aware of his behaviour (specify: intentional, subconscious)
- other motivating factors except maintaining a therapeutic relationship exist (specify: usually, often, always)
- the condition is an unnecessary extension or intensification of an existing real medical/therapeutic relationship or treatment/therapy was initiated for the sole purpose of obtaining such a relationship
- the therapist/medical practitioner inflicts emotional, physical, financial, legal, social or other harm on the patient, including harm such as self-harm by the patient due to any of the above and/or due to medication prescribed during the course of such therapy (specify all applicable)
- the behaviour is demonstrated independently or in collaboration with other therapists/medical practitioners (specify structure and type of collaboration)

The Reverse Munchausen Syndrome is similar to Munchausen Syndrome by proxy with the exception that (a) the relationship exploited is the one between a patient and a therapist and/or medical professional instead of the one between a child and a parent and (b) the patient with the mental disorder and the therapist/medical practitioner is one and the same person.

Assuming that such exploitative pseudo-therapeutic relationships in mental-health would actually exist, we could extrapolate the following *entirely hypothetical* conjectures:

➤➤ No patient would likely subject herself to such treatment *unless she doesn't have any choice or is hoodwinked or manipulated into believing that the therapy is actually necessary and helpful.* This could either be achieved individually or *by unnecessarily pathologizing whole groups of people* or entire segments of society

➤➤ The therapist would likely misuse *a long-term condition* which *is not diagnosable by testing* to avoid detection or contradiction by empirical data such as lab-tests

➤➤ It could be expected that the therapy applied *would never result in a treatment-success* (i.e. discharge of the patient)

➤➤ If any real medical conditions co-existed *treatment of such real conditions would be discouraged, subjected to conditions, delayed and interfered with* as the therapist would fear that his relationship might end if such treatment were successful

➤➤ Any potential positive effect *of other interventions* would be down-played by the therapist and *his therapy would be encouraged instead*

➤➤ The therapist might invent a completely new illness which he would in all likelihood define as: (a) *Not diagnosable by means of verifiable tests* (to avoid contradiction); (b) *To be incurable* (so if there is never any treatment-success this isn't seen as his failure); (c) *Of extreme severity* (to justify a lifelong relationship)

➤➤ *Subsequently a therapist might seek support from colleagues for his invented mental illness,* even general professional recognition as this would facilitate the recruiting of patients as well as increase social and professional acceptance

➤➤ Once professional recognition has been obtained the next logical step would be *to mandate this treatment on an exposed group of people whom the involved therapists define all to have this illness* in order to secure a lifelong supply of patients

If this scheme would, by any chance, remind you of a certain group of people who really do get treatment with no prospect of success, are deemed in need of such treatment without any evaluation or individual diagnosis for a condition which is abused to obtain therapeutic relationships **and if you think that this relationship might just be far better explained by** *The Reverse Munchausen Syndrome* **than any other condition** I would certainly like to caution that *any and all resemblances to existing psychiatric pathologies and any suggestion of current systematic abuse by psychopathologization of entire groups of people by anybody* **would be entirely unintentional, completely fictional and purely coincidental!**

I would also like to point out that *The Reverse Munchausen Syndrome* is most definitely an unfounded hypothetical condition, a literary invention, a fictitious imagination of a psychiatrically recognized sick brain as nobody in their right mind would ever think of something like this never mind doing it! [Please note the circular logic!]. *I'm certain that if there were even the most remote possibility of* doctors ever providing therapy or treatment **because providing such treatment and the perception to 'help' a patient gives instant gratification TO THE DOCTOR instead of because the patient really needs it,** *this surely would be recognized in the DSM and dealt with quickly by professional regulatory organizations everywhere?*

B.45. IT JUST NEVER GETS REAL ENOUGH

That comment about me "not being *a real woman*" just had to come-up? After all, it must be one of the most obvious remarks to make, in particular if one seeks a last ditch attempt to not accept who I am. Because apparently in some people's minds I can never be a woman and as they, particularly after genital alignment, run out of arguments awfully quickly they then invent the idea of *"the real woman"* which subsequently allows them to say that I am *something different*, i.e. *"not real"*, presumably *"a fake"*.

What is remarkable about this concept is that the 'fakes' are not the ones who *themselves* say that they are not women even though their birth-certificate says so (i.e. female to male transsexuals). The 'fakes' are always the male to female transsexuals when it comes to women or, to be more precise, *women who are perceived as transsexuals*, who "are known" because they have either self-identified or "have been found out". This is convenient as such a definition can't possibly be expected to be based on anything else but innuendo and an arbitrary combination of facts, speculations, discredit and distorted perception.

What this really comes down to is that some people would like to hide their prejudice against transsexuals behind a cloak of pseudo-science and pseudo-justification. The problem they have doing this is the very same I have also: *While I can't prove that I truly am a woman <u>they can't prove that I'm not</u>!*

If somebody wants to distinguish between 'real' women and 'fakes' what they have to do is to arbitrarily draw a line and *accept some, but reject others.* By doing this they define one - *and only one* - way to determine gender, usually this is the official entry in the birth-register. Or the first entry if they notice that we get these changed eventually. Only in real life things aren't as absolute, sometimes mistakes happen. So there are bound to be people who should be designated "real women" who are or have been mislabelled "real males" at some time, for however short or long. Does this bureaucratic mistake or that medical error make these people *less real?* On top of this there are people whose biological sex cannot be clearly identified! But because a designation needs to be made one will be chosen over the other. Is it the right one? *And if not, are these people "less real" than everybody else?*

Maybe we could get a hint of reality and fake if we ask John and Jane what they think about the issue:

Jane, would you like to have *a roll* with me? *A WHAT*? *A ROLL!* I mean your wheelchair *rolls*, so you're going to have *a roll* with me, while I *walk*? But if you'd rather like, I could push you, so that would then be *a push*?

This is nonsense? Yes, it is! I have yet to meet this paraplegic who doesn't refer to his getting around as "taking a walk" or 'walking' and not 'rolling'. Of course the walk is an obvious fake, but nobody would ever accuse Jane of faking walking with her wheelchair, nobody would give her a fine when she uses her wheelchair on a path marked *exclusively for pedestrians* because she uses wheels instead of feet...

If this isn't indication enough of how absurd this effort of trying to separate 'real' from 'fake' is or if somebody insists that being a woman (or a man) is not exclusively a self-identification but rather (or only) an external one, let's ask John what he thinks if we tell him that *he 'fakes' being healthy* as he clearly doesn't have a functioning kidney of his own and thus should be dead were it not *for the fake* he has in his body... True, his kidney is a fully functional human organ, but then again so are my genitals. They are in appearance, function and anatomy correct, the only difference between John's kidney and my genitals, apart from the generally different function, is that I did not need donor-tissue because I had every anatomically necessary part somewhere left to spare and plenty of my own tissue to accommodate the needs of the surgeon!

But this is not the point, is it? Organ transplants are quite ok and the people who get them aren't considered *freaks* afterwards! Crutches and wheelchairs, artificial joints, transplanted tissue, even from animals like pigs, are ok, right? Even artificial testicles or a surgically created or extended penis *for somebody who is already designated male* isn't a fake? Because, honestly, this could happen to anybody, *even to the people who hand out the 'freak' and 'fake' designations to us!*

But then again unlike being a paraplegic transsexuality doesn't just happen to people overnight and these to whom it does happen know it without being told! *So the others, the ones who hand-out the derogatory designation are, unlike Janes condition, 100% guaranteed that this will never happen to them! Because they too can feel who they are and they too know!* Isn't it easy to use one's own personal security to beat-up on somebody else? Particularly if this security doesn't come from some personal achievement or behaviour *but is rather handed-out by mother nature at random!*

So much for the superficial analysis. People have been beating-up on others ever since we climbed down the trees of Africa. Well, probably before that even only we didn't call ourselves 'people' back then. *But what really disturbs me, far more than the fact that this actually happens, is that we - transsexuals as we are called - quietly accept this!* We are told that we are *'transwomen'* instead of women by mental-health. And that's on good days because on the bad ones we're demoted to *"severely disturbed gender-dysphoric males"!* We comply. We play transsexual. We are kept as she-male pets for psychiatrists, our keepers tell us to accept this as a permanent identification *and we comply, quietly!*

By the time we finally get to be who we are *this false identification is so much part of us that many apparently just keep it!* **We have accepted that we are "transsexual women"** *instead of being women!* **And we have quietly accepted to remain just this - transsexuals - even after mental treatment ends!**

John no longer sees himself as a dialysis patient with a kidney disease because after a successful transplant he isn't anymore. Jane never defined herself as a paraplegic instead of seeing herself as a woman or as a human being, instead of seeing herself <u>as herself</u>, even though she is constantly paraplegic. <u>But then again, nobody has ever seen any need to require Jane or John to pretend otherwise to obtain medical treatment!</u>

John has never been able to overcome his infertility, he has had relationship and sexual problems throughout his adult life because of it. Nevertheless he was never deprived of medical treatment and while counselling was offered to him nothing was ever made conditional upon him having this issue addressed professionally. He never found himself accused of being a sexual pervert because of his inability to function sexually, psychiatric treatment was never forced onto him and neither was he ever diagnosed mentally ill because of it.

Nobody has ever seen fit to professionally degrade, de-humanize or de-value any of them for their disability or indeed John for his sexual problem! Nobody has ever suggested to Jane the fact of her using a wheelchair or to John the fact of him using a kidney donated by another human-being and inserted into his body surgically was due to an undiagnosable and incurable mental condition and that their need would disappear if they'd only pull themselves together and behave normally! Nobody ever told them - never mind for years and years and years - that what they wanted wasn't a medical necessity and therefore needed to be "talked out of them"!

We however are allowed on treatment no sooner than *when we've been broken enough to no longer seek our own true identification!* Because unlike John and Jane whose mental, psychiatric or psychological therapy, if they ask for any at all, *is geared towards making them self-confident and self-conscious, at making them <u>who they are</u>,* **our mental treatment is aimed at making us compliant, making us into what is expected, <u>making us into who we are not</u>: Transsexuals. For life!**

Obviously if psychiatry officially or at the very least by means of intent and treatment sees us this way *and we ourselves are compliant to a degree where we actually do see ourselves as told,* well, it is to be anticipated that everybody else does too! After all, <u>*if it's good enough for the patient and the therapist then it ought to be good enough for everybody else?*</u> So seeing us as "not real women" then isn't that much of a demeaning attitude with a good helping of discrimination at all, *it is much rather the verbal expression of what everybody agrees on anyway, including far too many of ourselves! It's obvious: In this framework of "gender-identification" one can't identify as a transsexual and as a woman at the same time! So as long as we say we are transsexuals we can't be woman! Not "real women" anyway.* Only as long as psychiatry forces some people into their gender-zoo who really do identify trans-sexual instead of female *because this truly is who they are* it becomes very easy to extend this onto everybody else!

Apart from psychiatry there is the social argument that we can't really be women *because we did not "grow-up as women"* or "have not been raised as women". Even judges seem to fall for this, given the fact that women (well, so called "post-op transwomen") have been barred from "women only" jobs and *such discrimination was upheld by courts precisely based on this very argument!*

If you ask me I would not be able to tell you what "growing-up a woman" actually means, but not because I presumably have not, but because this represents a personal framework of social prejudice and not an identifiable term. If a women grew-up among the amazons that "growing-up" would likely be *somewhat* different than if she grew-up to become Julia Roberts, right? Growing-up in the outback of Australia is totally different from growing-up in New-York on 5th Avenue & Central Park S., right? I would venture the thought that growing up designated male or female *in the same social setting* often makes less of a difference in social opportunities and expectations, social role-behaviour and -acceptance than, say, growing up designated White, Black, Indian, Asian and so on. Now please don't get me for these racist terms, *I'm just quoting what the US government[1] uses to officially classify and categorize human-beings!*

But if that's the case, then my ah so stereotypically male upbringing (which was in fact nothing but) contained any and all elements some biological females get exposed to somewhere in the world just as I did! So what's the great deal about that "growing-up" thing? Well, if it isn't social then it must probably be biological or - heaven forbid - sexual? Yes, I missed-out on a few experiences of a biological nature, some of these I missed dearly. And just if you were to wonder? The expectation I most often get from mostly male individuals is that these would be about breasts. But I'm sorry, I'm not talking about these here… On the other hand, I am not the only woman who failed to have these experiences which are by and large related to the primary female reproductive system. This is very simply true because not every woman is fertile, not every women has a functioning reproductive system. Quite a few actually don't have any at all, be it due to illness, accident, medical-intervention or a congenital 'disorder'. I just presume that the people who consider me "a fake", "not a real woman"

---

[1] *US Census-2000 had people classified in 14 groups: "White" (which of course they put first), "Black, African American, or Negro", "American Indian or Alaska Native", "Asian Indian", "Chinese",..., or "Some other race". (for a complete list see www.census.gov/dmd/www/pdf/d61a.pdf, page 1). Most notably* Homo Sapiens *is not a group a human can belong to!*

would not pin this same label on any of these individuals? Because that's different, right? Now just in what way this should be different I don't know...

Then there would be that "sexual bit". I am not quite a woman because the men did not whistle after me as often and they didn't drool at the sight of me? Well, let me point out here that I know quite a few women this has rarely happened to, and that's not because they weren't designated female at birth but because, well, they would not fall into the spectrum of people such men would identify as "an interesting subject"!

Last, but not least, there's that saying that growing-up male is so much easier than growing-up female? After all the males get all the perks and the females, well... But honestly, could we please ask somebody else about how happy it is to grow up male? Just in case somebody might not have noticed? I did grow-up *closeted transsexual,* not male. And growing-up transsexual sucks... (Sorry!). Now I don't know what's exactly meant by growing-up female or male, what I do know is that - measured by the rate of depression, suicide-attempts and successful suicides - there can't be too many things that are as difficult as growing-up transsexual in this society.

As from my personal experience: I am being treated a women these days. I now officially and effectively get "the second class treatment" in society. And obviously I am being asked why I would *choose* this - because it is just assumed that I used to get "the first class treatment" as a male before. Only I didn't. Because truth is that males by and large don't *get* "the first class male treatment", *they simply take it!* Whoever fails at taking it doesn't get it, male *looking* or not. And if then an individual is too emotional, too sensitive, one just finds oneself at the back of the queue - automatically. These days at least I'm being asked to get my turn every now and then *because I am a woman* and males are supposedly trained to let woman go first *in certain settings.* Well, if they have ever received such training and remember it, but then again, rudeness, selfishness and impoliteness aren't mental conditions because, after all, this only impairs *fellow human beings,* not themselves, it may even give the person who hands this out an advantage - temporary anyway!

It is true, I am still being mistreated. Many women are. Most in fact. Only now I know why! *And I know that I am no longer an exception!* I also often know ahead of time what to expect, which kind of abuse will be next, because for a woman it is to some degree predictable. To a woman forced to live male it is not.

I am a woman. But because I am a woman people - usually males - can just as well expect twice the effort and give me only half the credit for what I do. If *being a woman* is what I do then clearly I only deserve to be half a woman for putting in twice the effort...

Apparently my disability makes me quite woman enough *to deserve the treatment* that comes with being one. It's just never real enough *to actually deserve being one.* Right?

B.46. *SPIRITUAL SELF-EXPRESSION OR MENTAL ILLNESS?*

And just why does somebody feel male or female? I have to admit that I don't know either! However I can envision two possible explanations, only as a matter of principle none of these can ever be proven or disproven with absolute certainty. *This is, and in the end forever remains, a choice each and every human being will have to make for her/himself!*

I experience myself as a spiritual being with a body, a mind and a soul. This is how I define myself. I am alive, biologically, but I am more than just alive, I am also self-aware and I feel that I have the freedom to influence my self-perception, my behaviour, my perception of the world around me, my thinking and my emotional state to a certain degree by free choices I as a person can make.

I know that people can also define themselves in a materialistic way as having a body and a mind only, no soul. This Cartesian[1] view implies that my experience of "a soul" is really made-up in my brain and doesn't actually exist! Everything in life rolls-out according to physical laws of nature, I do not have any freedom to influence anything at all. All the choices I think I make are the ones I would have made anyway, because the outcome and my perception of it are all pre-determined in every respect and have been since the "big bang". In this view *the experience of self* or *the notion of a soul* are fictitious delusions.

I apparently have a choice here: I could see myself as a spiritual being or as a biological machine deluding herself into being spiritual. Nobody knows which one it is because nobody can prove any of these two views right or wrong! I for one *choose* the first, however I accept that *this is my personal preference* and <u>everybody is free to see this differently for themselves</u>. Nevertheless, I believe that my choice is the right one!

Quite a lot of people seem to delude themselves into thinking that they have a soul, there are in fact so many that they form some of the largest organizations on the planet to express this spirituality, to come together and share their experiences and beliefs in the context of religion. Their experience is in fact such a powerful force that even psychiatry finds itself forced to make a special exception for all these people! Presumably so they don't all get *accidentally pathologized delusional* and hauled away to the closed ward?

---

[1] *René Descartes 1596-1650, French philosopher*

[At the pharmacy, showing my insurance-card] But you are a woman, are you not? [Me] Yes, of course, legally and otherwise [She] They really shouldn't make these kinds of mistakes... [Me] I agree...

This then, psychiatrically, reads as follows:

Delusion: Commonly defined in behavioural health care as a fixed false belief (ex-cluding beliefs that are part of a religious movement). This psychotic symptom is present in a variety of serious mental disorders.[1]

As I am not a member of a "religious movement" but still experience myself as a spiritual being I am *highly offended* that psychiatry would deem *my* spirituality a mental illness *simply for the fact that I, as of this date, have not founded a club or 'movement' for it!* But if you have read my book this far you might just say "there she goes again, always offended by everything psychiatry says, they just can't make it right for her...". And no, they can't. Not unless they stop doing what they're doing!

Anyway, so I have yet another mental illness! This time I suffer from something like *"un-organized spiritual awareness disorder"?* This presumably comes under the umbrella-term *"religious identity disorders"?* Well, maybe I should just apply to have myself entered into the *Guinness Book of Records* for something like "Individual with more weak-minded psy-chiatric pathologies than anybody else"?

Now as a transsexual individual I experience myself female while being biologically deemed male. As I still experience myself female post-op I assume that it is quite usual for human-beings to experience gender, to somehow feel if one is male or female. After all, al-most everybody seems to know when asked!

People could derive this 'knowledge' from their physicality, their mind or their soul. Given the fact that people who are born with ambiguous genitals *still have an identification* and people who loose their reproductive organs or external genitals *retain their identification* **this apparently isn't physical.** Given the fact that people *seem to know even when they're not told,* i.e. they grow up solitary or without social interaction as has happened in rare cases or are raised "in the opposite gender role" for whatever reason, **this apparently isn't mental.** We also have the testimony of people who have suffered brain-damage and/or surgeries (in-cluding forced partial amputation of the brain[2] as a psychiatric treatment for homosexuality or transsexuality) to the end that *these individuals do not change their gender self-experience, no matter which part of the brain is damaged, destroyed or cut-out*[3].

But if none of these are the cause for our identification then *the one remaining possi-bility is that* <u>*the gender I experience is part of my soul*</u>, **if I happen to believe in one,** *or is of a delusional nature* **if I would not believe in the existence of a soul.** So there are "female

---

[1] *Excerpt from: www.behavenet.com/capsules/disorders/delusion.htm, highlighting added by the author*

[2] *Typically this would be what psychiatric practice refers to as a* <u>prefrontal</u> *lobotomy. In psychosurgery this is typically not performed as a physical amputation but rather a functional one, see footnote 1 on page 33.*

[3] *Of course if enough is damaged or cut then the individual looses her ability to communicate in a meaningful way - which I suppose solves the problem in some very questionable way. Well, it's psychiatric treatment and as I'm not a psychiatrist it is clear that I can't have the capacity to understand why such treatment would make sense, never mind be ethical.*

souls" and "male souls" if we want to put this very, very simplistic, just as there are "souls with different preferences of physical sexual attraction".

Again I apparently have a choice: I could see myself as *a spiritual being with a female self-experience* or as *a biological machine deluding herself into being spiritual and having fantasies of a female self-experience.* I for one choose the first, *but I understand that this is my personal preference and that everybody else is free to see this differently for themselves.* Nevertheless, I believe that my choice is the right one!

Now gender is the only spiritual attribute we know of which has a (normally strictly binary) physical and biological representation. Sexual orientation, religious identification, the experience of a higher presence (i.e. God or Gods, universal consciousness,…) and every other attribute we know of does not. **This is why only gender can be experienced along biological lines** *or in contradiction to these! If a person is born with a female soul in a biologically male body this inconsistent combination would then be called 'transsexuality'!*

Of course if this were true then transsexuality would be a spiritual experience, not a **mental illness and thus mental-health would be ill suited to explain, diagnose or treat it.** Now we all know that they can't explain transsexuality, need us to self-identify because they can't diagnose it and their treatment success is zero - just to mention some purely coinciden- tal and entirely immaterial observations…

If I may propose a typical reverse-deduction such as I have shown in this book psychiatry regularly pulls out of the hat *then I could reverse-conclude that the existence of transsexuality and the abysmal success mental-health has in treating it proves that human-beings in fact must have a soul!* But honestly, I find that's a bit far-fetched (and yes, I also know the deduc- tion is wrong *because the causality is in the other direction!*).

Nevertheless the one observation which seems well-founded is that psychiatry appears to see human-beings exclusively as bio-mechanical devices not allowing for the existence of either a soul or spirituality as otherwise they would have a very obvious explanation of trans- sexuality *albeit one that excludes their professional services!*

If I assume that psychiatrists see me as a biological machine then I must conclude that (a) psychiatrists themselves may not be members of religious movements, believe in God or experience any "meaning of life" (except Darwinistic procreation) or have a soul themselves? Or (b) that it would be *highly discriminatory* of them if they believed that *they themselves are at liberty to believe in a soul of their own* while at the same time founding their theoretical models and practical methods *on the premise that everybody else does not!*

As you might expect I see the world very, very differently from psychiatry. I have men- tioned that I experience myself as a spiritual being and that I believe in the concept of me having a soul. *I also believe that the root-cause of transsexuality is there - and nowhere else!*

Apparently as per current guidelines of mental-health psychiatrists are free to label me *delusional* **or certify me nuts for expressing this as clearly the concept of a soul has**

no meaning *in their reality* and is entirely a mental illness. But as we have seen neither they nor I will ever be able to prove one view correct!

The one thing that I - from my perspective - find more than a bit strange is that psychiatry would, based on evidence which is by it's very nature inconclusive, be allowed to behaviourally modify me, or better: To assault, torture, mutilate and abuse my spiritual identity, *to let loose a witch-hunt on people whose spirituality differs from what they dictate it to be,* to be allowed every method in the arsenal to force us into compliance, **even though we all perfectly well know that their views are nothing else but *their own improvable personal spiritual avowals!*** Are we really as medieval as to allow something like this? *In a time and a place where religious and spiritual freedom is considered to be a defining achievement?*

A.33. *IT IS ONLY A MATTER OF LIFE*

Except for a few decades of useless delay, a potentially unnecessary drug-addiction, a year's life on absurd levels of carcinogens, a body deformed by a puberty and life on testosterone, a medication-induced suicidality which luckily I survived without an attempt, having been denied emergency medical service, being stigmatized mentally ill and missing-out on half a lifetime I can't say that I have been treated badly by that system for having needed that gender-alignment...

But then I did keep away for 30 years, didn't I? I was in mental-health less than 11 months, some 20 sessions in all with two different psychologists, some sessions lasting less than 5 minutes. I was sent there because it is "the agreed upon way to do things", or at least the maximum they were willing to 'compromise' on that "agreed upon way". Because they thought they needed these signatures. Because they were told that they do absolutely need these. No matter how much they had to abuse me to get these. *And because they believed this and complied!*

Both psychologists as well as the medical people agreed that it was a painful and expensive waste of time and I suppose quite a few people sighed relief when I was gone. Though maybe not all for the same reasons...

Sometimes I got the distinct impression that abusing me was not all that easy for some of them because I was honest. I felt mistreated and I said so. I felt I was wasting my time and the time of other people and I made that clear as well. But they had their "professional standards" and these required them to put a certain minimum time and effort into abusing me before they thought to be in a position to declare themselves "compliant to doctrine" - and therefore entitled to sign the paperwork. Or ignore it. Like that half million or so cases before me. *Nobody ever admitted that what they were doing was wrong, but nobody ever dared to suggest that it was right either. But however friendly it was done, <u>in the end it was abuse nevertheless.</u>*

Of course publicly what matters is not what happened to me behind these closed doors. Not the pain I now have to deal with because I sought treatment and found institutionalized abuse instead, intermixed with a few people who didn't feel too good to hand it out. *What matters publicly is that this is seen as right!* That I have been branded a transsexual visibly, not just rhetorically but openly published in government records and of course this stays, even now when I'm no longer transsexual. What matters is that by some people, including sadly enough a good majority of medical doctors, I am seen as a person who is incapable to live independently or at best lives somewhere on the fringe of human society. A person who will be dependent on psychiatric support for life, somebody who's been medically declared mentally incapacitated, *a person whose mental processes are deranged to a degree which warrants government sanctioned forced intervention,* a person who can't be trusted to make sound decisions that match "common sense", not for herself never mind for others!

I am none of the above but people who duly appoint themselves to know better rather efficiently spread that idea. It doesn't help if they declare that what they do to us should not be seen as stigmatization and it should not be seen as if I were incapable to make decisions (this is stated explicitly in dogma) *when at the same time they go out and suspend my civil rights, severely limit my rights of making decisions about my healthcare and my own body, force their services onto me against my explicit wishes and get government-approval (and backing) for doing this!* It doesn't help if they say that I'm not crazy *when at the same time they officially state that my treatment, genital alignment, is solely accepted as a last resort treatment for the most severe otherwise incurable mental cases!* **What counts to me as well as to the public is not what they claim they *don't* intend, <u>what counts is what they actually do</u>!** Nobody is going to read (or believe) what they *presumably* didn't intend anyway!

Of course the solution would be very, very simple: **If it were true that they would not deem me mental then they should not just "officially state this", <u>but act on their own enlightened statement</u>! They don't - which proves more than any verbal declaration ever could that their statement is not to be taken seriously!** It doesn't take much to understand this, *in the real world everybody seems to get this just fine!* If expert psychiatrists still say that this isn't what they do then they are in complete denial of reality. Maybe not *theirs* but certainly everybody elses!

I suppose I could have gotten away with far less compliance to dogma. I was offered genital surgery to take place less than 8 months after my first visit with my treating family-physician, after less than half a year of mental-health and only 4 months on HRT. I declined because I could not provide proof of these dogmatic requirements, even though nobody ever asked for any. I had my surgery 367 days after commencement of medical treatment, the minimum requirement set by dogma being one year. (I suppose if it's a leap-year it takes people a day longer to "get ready", but then again, it's all mental anyway. Sorry. It's all mental-health, so I stopped trying to make sense of it and to understand what the reasoning behind things could possibly be because there isn't any. Just do as told!).

I have yet to see a psychiatrist and as I do not have any mental problems I couldn't easily solve myself why would I want to? I'm now just a woman, legally and otherwise, and I agree very well with it!

My "detailed psychiatric letter of recommendation bearing two signatures"? It is a one-page document, 14 lines of text, written by a psychologist from our local gay & lesbian community-counselling service. This is very much a personal treat as the dogmatic psychiatric institution in town who does trans, most cases in fact, one of these places where one takes many years just to be accepted as a transsexual, also puts-out one page letters these days - although they're mostly all the same, cut & paste using a word-processor. Theirs say that the person is mental and not otherwise treatable but "is stable", "has fulfilled 'their' criteria of the Real-Life Experience" (or in layman's terms: "complied to absurdly painful, excessive and abusive behavioural and physical modification and is damaged severely enough she's now deemed incapable to raise objection of any sort") and that the individual "presents as well prepared for surgery" (whatever they mean by this, but I am certain they think they know). They end their letters with the phrase "I trust this is helpful to you" and two signatures, M.D. psychiatrists, as required. Mine says that I'm an ordinary woman with an extraordinary life. It ends with "good luck and all the best wishes for your future!".

In the end nobody really cared about dogma, standards or mental treatment. But everybody still needed their behinds covered!

This is about dogma, about dogmatists, it is about homophobia and about having to submit to certain people's expectation as to what a human being or more specifically a woman is. How we have to think. How we have to feel. *But mostly how we have to look and behave!*

This is not about me, about my healthcare, about my life. It is not about us, it never was. This is all and exclusively *about them!* **It is not about my emotional life** *but about protecting their stereotypes!* **It is not about who I am,** *it is about who they say I must be!*

If there's a mental flaw in my personality then it must be that I'm "absurdly over-compliant". Or *pathologically* compliant? This, I think, might just be a rather common trait in transsexuals, after all we comply to society's pressure more than anybody else ever does, we can even be pressured into living a life that isn't ours! Of course you could see this differently and say that I'm simply far too stereotypical a woman! *Do as told!* I'll comply and do it! *Die as told!* I'll comply to that too.

If we - transsexuals - need coaching of any sort then I think it should be *coaching in non-compliance,* in not accepting what is been done to us! We do not need therapy to know who we are, this we know far better than most people ever will. *After all who we are is what doesn't work so we have a very good reason to think about this from a very early age on,* far more often and far deeper than most people ever will. *And when we've found the answer to this question, found who we are, we need to ask for it. Because what we find requires an afternoon in an operating room. And this, asking for gender-alignment, becomes for many of us the single act of social non-compliance we're capable of in a lifetime* and we can only do this because it hurts so badly. Because *this is asking for our lives!*

Society requires us to ask whoever they put forth as their representatives for consideration of our lives - because society isn't willing to give life to us freely without any conditions. *And we accept this and comply!*

Other people try suicide to show the world how desperately they need help. *We instead go to the doctor's office, wait in line and when we finally get in we say "In spite of how this looks I am a woman, I need gender-alignment, hormones and genital surgery. For me this is a matter of life, please give me what I need!".* This is such an unbelievable demonstration of strength every single transsexual shows to the world! I find this act of self-control, determination and strength should be honoured as such, it should be taken seriously, treatment should build on it, not systematically destroy it!

If we are among the lucky ones who get heard when we plead for our lives *we get religiously framed dogma instead, professional emotional detachment, we are told that our innermost self, our existence is deemed a sexual perversion and that we are not granted life as a human right or a medical matter of course but at the discretion of a self-appointed expert who makes it clear that he doesn't accept us from the get-go and that what we need may at best be given at grace, in a few years, maybe.* Or it may not, depending upon if he concedes that he is at the end of his wisdom before we're at the end of our lives. *Let us go because we can't be helped anyway, maybe even in spite of his better judgement...* They can't help us and they won't. *They know this yet they put their sole effort into preventing us form helping ourselves!*

The cost is some more pain, social humiliation, degradation and abuse, it is also the loss of a good part of our lifetime. That's the "best case scenario". We take it, accept whatever they hand-out! Because that's who we are. Because we're absurdly over-compliant! *Do as told! Because we're women!*

Should however the answer to our question be *no* many of us even comply to this and end their lives themselves. Many do so without ever entering treatment because they never expect a positive answer, never expect any decency there. *Or because they understand the set-up and are incapable of accepting the humiliation, degradation and abuse with open eyes. Or they know that for them this isn't survivable anyway. Or they're incapable to ever ask for anything, even their own lives! They die because they're incapable of that single act of social non-compliance!* They can never ask for anything in this male-dominated society. Because women don't ask for anything in male society. Never.

In the end they die for being women who aren't allowed to be women.

Is this mental? I don't know. But it is who we are. Many of us anyway. Treat us decently and we'll get decent lives. Give us our treatment expediently, with dignity, before this causes irresolvable or irreversible emotional or mental harm. Before 'issues' of any kind ever appear. *Accept us as we are!* But understand: ***The one thing many of us cannot do is to ever ask for it, <u>this will have to be given to us freely</u>. Because never asking is who so many of us are!***

Now if they continue to insist that this is "a sexual perversion" or "an identity disorder" then I don't think we'll ever get any closer to some form of understanding and the results will remain questionable forever. But whatever they say, we'll comply. Even if we die trying.

Psychiatry says that we are 'obsessed' by the thought of being women. We are 'obsessed' by the desire to get (surgical) treatment for our condition. Yes, for some of us this dominates their lives completely. For others it is one of the most important aspects. This then makes us mental *because we're obviously preoccupied with something completely absurd!*

John is looking obsessively at his kidney disease, his life turns around not much else than dialysis and obtaining a transplant, thoughts about the allocation of available organs, about how few there are, that there should be more donations, thoughts of hope and despair, sometimes thinking "this could be it" when the phone rings, disappointment when it's only a friend! *For him this is considered normal,* well within the bandwidth of expected human emotions in his situation. The desire to be cured and the importance he puts onto it, given the severity of his affliction is normal. *It is an expression of his humanity.* It is even *expected.* It is also accepted! *But if I do the same then I'm deemed mental for it!*

And there's something else: He has the advantage (if it is one) that he's in a position to understand why he can't be in the OR *right now.* After all he needs to wait until his "replacement organ" becomes available. Or to put this more directly: He has to wait until a matching donor dies somewhere in the world and he is chosen as the recipient!

With me this is very different. All that stands between me and a cure for my affliction is a signature from a self-appointed profiteer who has for all intents and purposes proven that he's incompetent to make the decision he has assigned himself to make!

For John this is despair. Maybe despair about people not offering donation, maybe despair about his medical profile not matching. For me this is despair also. Despair about people who put themselves between me and my healthcare *because they feel some kind of calling to do so!* For me there is no cause, no understanding, there can be no arguing, no reasoning!

They hide behind professional detachment when it comes to showing some compassion and empathy! They hide behind professional arrogance when it comes to explaining why they force their view of who we have to be upon us! And they hide behind professional ignorance when it comes to acknowledging their own personal shortcomings!

No, our behaviour isn't mental! I find it's the most appropriate, most normal, most fitting *and most human* reaction to this crazy set-up I can possibly think of! If society wants us to behave differently *all they need to do is change the framework we can live in.* We'll comply. It's what we do best. After all, it's all part of being a woman: Do as told! *This is what we are anyway!*

If they'd accept us for who we are, we would get what we need. Quietly and privately if they wanted it like this. They wouldn't have to know if they wouldn't want to. They wouldn't have to feel upset for any reason if they wouldn't want to. They wouldn't even have to look away![1]

Because they'd never notice us living among them even if they'd look right at us!

---

[1] *And they would never have to be upset by my book because I would never have written it!*

PART IV - REFLECTIONS

C

FAILING TO UNDERSTAND

The United Nations, General Assembly Resolution 217A(III) of 10 December 1948,

Universal Declaration Of Human Rights[1]

Article 2:

Everyone is entitled to all the rights and freedoms set forth in this Declaration, without distinction of any kind, such as race, colour, sex, language, religion, political or other opinion, national or social origin, property, birth or other status. [...]

Most countries have enacted laws on equal rights as well as against the discrimination of people with physical disabilities.

If transsexuality would be seen as a physical disability transsexuals would enjoy some measure of legal protection. But thanks to psychiatric insight transsexuality is not seen as a disability *but as "something else".*

Therefore:

As of today discriminating on the grounds that a person is living a different gender than she was assigned at birth is legal and such discrimination is government supported policy and practice *in every country on earth.*

---

[1] *Official wording quoted from www.unhchr.ch udhr lang eng.htm*

C.1.   AND JUST WHY ISN'T THIS THE END

Every normal book would have ended right at the end of the previous chapter. I've said my goodbyes, I've made my statement, so why isn't this over? Well, it isn't over because this is life, it isn't a Hollywood-script. Only in Hollywood the show ends with a well chosen statement followed by "The End". The good ones happily live ever after while the bad guys are dead for good! Then the lights go on, you find yourself in your seat. You leave the theatre, maybe considering if you've gotten your money's worth for the ticket you have bought two hours earlier, but maybe you're already in the middle of traffic and your thoughts are somewhere else.

And yes, at some time in my life I do too, I get these few hours only it isn't a movie-theatre, it is an operating-theatre and the curtain closes when I enter and (hopefully) opens when I leave. And then I too ask myself if these few hours or something I spent in that theatre were worth it! After all, I did spend something like a few hundred times more for every minute of entertainment than you did; but true, I did get the preferred seat and, for once, highly competent personal attendance. Though I wouldn't really know as I slept through the entire program!

"Would you do it again?", of course the question is asking if I'd have genital gender-alignment again, now knowing what it does and how it feels. And my answer would be a resounding yes, only that by now I really don't know anymore why I actually wanted to go there? After all, I'm quite all right, so why would I possibly ever have wanted a sex-change? And then it dawns on me, every time: This was in another life, another reality! I somehow didn't feel as good back then because there was something wrong with me... Yes, I wanted this fixed, that was the whole point back then. At some time it seemed this was all that ever mattered in my life!

And then I forgot about it.

So this isn't the end, because it really is the beginning! There is no "happily ever after" for me, but the beginning of a normal life instead. A life that feels and works and is just like everybody elses! Well, everybody elses who's not a transsexual that is...

[Medical professional, some time after surgery] The whole thing they made you go through to get here must have seemed like a bad joke to you [Me] The thought has crossed my mind...

C.2.   WITH MINIMAL COLLATERAL DAMAGE

That's it now I may have thought. But I don't think I ever was that naïve. Because there's really a trap here. One that psychiatry has set up very nicely for us! I was born a transsexual and the one thing I wanted all my life was not to be one. From my perspective this is just about the most normal wish I could possibly have: I was physically handicapped and all I ever wished for was that I were not! But from their perspective I was crazy and I suppose they will always insist in seeing me like this.

Today I have my life and it works better than I have ever dreamt it could. Emotionally, personally, socially, even sexually. True, there is that part about not having a past, about having to deny over 40 years of my life. This is wrong but that I can live with. Sort of. I am not secret about it, I have chosen to be quiet, I don't advertise myself, but I also do not hide! There is however one part of my life that does not work. One part that has been permanently damaged, one part I'll never get back: I have been pressured into compliance (or the anticipation thereof) to something I experienced as meaningless, unethical, immoral, destructive. *In order to survive, to navigate that system, what I had to do was to internalize the workings, the expectations, the theories and the methods of that system.* The problem: This system is life-denying, it is perverted, it is illogical, it is unethical, it is arbitrary and often completely absurd! It is in fact a conglomerate of at times contradictory systems of personal beliefs, a mixture of religious-, social- and personal agendas rather than what it claims to be: Science.

But this isn't just about studying the ideas of psychiatry. What I have been required to do is not the same as regurgitating the contents of a textbook or a lecture for an exam as students do, *I have been pressured into living that contents!*

In the final analysis living this is not unlike being convincingly male: I can't *learn* how to be male and then *perform* as if it were a spectacle. This never works, because I can't anticipate every possible scenario and then pre-emptively train appropriate behaviour! There is no such thing as an improv-show that is convincing *all the time*. This isn't acting, it isn't simply behavioural modification. What I do is to modify *not my behaviour* by doing things differently *but my perception!* I learn *how to experience the world 'male'.* Only if I can do *this* will I be convincingly male *all the time!*

We don't "do gender" or "gender-roles" because we get programmed to doing it like Skinner's[1] rats or pigeons. This isn't behaviourism, it isn't a behavioural scenario with

---

[1] *B.F.Skinner, psychologist, founder of "radical behaviourism" which explains all behaviour (animal and human) as a result of environmental 'stimuli'. It is, in essence, the Cartesian philosophy of a mechanistic universe applied to sentient beings.*

positive and negative re-enforcement. True, at times it is this too. And I agree, one *can* "do female" behaviouristically (as in acting), *Robin Williams* as *Ms. Doubtfire* or *Dustin Hoffman* as *Dorothy Michaels* (in *Tootsie*) are probably two of the best examples. There is "learned behaviour", everything from good manners to social expectations. But this isn't who I am, this is at best *how I present myself.* This doesn't "make my gender", it at best "presents my gender". But gender isn't presentation, *it is how we are born to experience ourselves and the world around us!*

The difference between *adapting how I react to the world* and *adapting how I perceive the world* (to react to it as expected, *always*) is that in the first *I behave in a certain way because I have learned to do so* whereas in the second *I behave in a certain way because I experience this as the right thing to do within the framework of my perception!* In the first my agreement is required: *I interpret what happens, experience the difference and I get a choice!* In the second I give this away: *When I change what I perceive as true and real[1] according to somebody elses specification I pre-emptively accept somebody elses choice!* But I still perceive what I do as 'strange', "somehow wrong" or "not quite myself".

What happens here isn't anything new and it isn't anything specific to what I find myself in. It is in fact the same mechanism that makes much of human discrimination, oppression and exploitation possible. It works by people modifying their perception and interpretation of the world in a way which makes them experience a particular behaviours as 'normal'. 200 years ago people didn't believe that slavery was wrong *because their perceptual framework showed them that this was a perfectly sound and justifiable thing to do!* 70 years ago the same was true when it came to eradicating Jews, homosexuals, 'gypsies', mentally and physically handicapped and many other groups. 300 years ago it was stealing the land from and killing first nations people. There are many other examples, many. Far too many!

In the specific psychiatric environment a transsexual finds herself in we are asked to accept that what psychiatry does is right, meaningful, appropriate and ethical. The frame of reference called 'psychiatry' (or mental-health) doesn't allow for criticism - not by a perceived or real mental-patient anyway - and it most definitely doesn't allow this by an individual who needs to get something out of that system (like a few prescriptions or a couple of signatures on a letter)... To achieve this and not get destroyed by that system on the way I change not how I behave *but who I am.* However there are problems with this: Psychiatric perception of the world isn't consistent, it isn't logical, it doesn't provide for a positive experience of life, it isn't even real or socializeable outside of psychiatry. It is, in large parts, nothing but a self-contradicting theoretical dreamland with no or little connection to the real world (psychiatry

---

[1] *HRT allows these transsexuals who take it* for emotional reasons *to perceive aspects of the environment differently (i.e. gender appropriate) as the sensitivity and range of sensory perception in males and females are different. This change can be very dramatic: Women, on average, can identify more colours and odours than men can, are more sensitive to touch and so on... We don't experience "a different reality" or "something delusional" but a significantly different view of the same reality!*

would pathologize this as *delusional disorder* or possibly *schizophrenia[1]*). And because this isn't meaningful, *what I get out of it, what I live, this life I'm getting from it isn't either!*

Now I haven't done everything as advertised. And I haven't completely changed as they wanted me to. Well, not all the way through anyway. For this the intensity and duration of my 'treatment' wasn't severe and long enough. For this my beliefs and my own frame of reference were too strong. I got by without really getting what I was set-up for, I was also lucky in many ways! Nevertheless a lot has been damaged and more has been lost. Today I experience the world highly oversexed, over gender-polarized and hyper-pathologized. But most importantly I now experience much of the world as a meaningless place of irrational activity instead of a meaningful place of positive emotion, it is now a place where exploitation and power reigns instead of caring and respect. Because that's what psychiatry does: **For psychiatry there's no emotional or spiritual existence (or values) nor meaning, there's only function and most of that they classify as pathological!**

Becoming this is not what I have been made, *it is what I have done to myself in order to comply with what was expected of me!*

I used to be an innocent little girl living in her intact world. Then I needed to learn to perceive the world how they think it has to be. Or maybe how they really experience it? Sick... Then I was expected to successfully self-pathologize *and to become their interpretation of this imaginary pathology.* Only then was I allowed to become a woman!

But still, I grew-up. My world wasn't intact anymore and I was no longer innocent, I felt stained and dirty, helpless and taken advantage of. But I was still reasonably intact and myself. *Because the one thing I was capable of was doing it all without actually believing in it!*

If I am being forced to comply to a system I don't believe in and therefore don't accept, even despise because of what it does to human-beings then I experience this pressure as highly abusive. I feel blackmailed by people who dream-up who we are to be and force their views onto us by means of their mental treatment *but don't stop there:* They also enforce their views and expectations of social behaviour, dress-code and intimate self-experience! They even try to enforce their expectations and views of sexual behaviour! *From my perspective doing only a small fraction of all this (never mind all at once) to another human-being is a sure sign that they lack in some important capacity and are in dire need of help! I personally see this as proof that it isn't me who is a sexual pervert, has a fetish problem or even one of identifying anybody's gender BUT THEM!* **Only thanks to the power they wield it isn't them getting help but me being forced into sickness instead!**

I'm not saying that this is a typical form of abuse - but it is abuse non the less! **Ultimately it is a form of brainwashing people into madness** and it perverts what transsexuality and in

---

[1] *Interestingly delusional disorder and schizophrenia are the two most common initial misdiagnosis for transsexuals. Cynical me would argue that this is to be expected: After all what many of us do is to reflect psychiatric expectations and with it a large part of psychiatric thinking back at the therapist. We present them a mirror-image of their own group-identity and if then their expert-opinion is 'delusional disorder' or 'schizophrenia' then this is in fact the very closest they could possibly get to an unbiased self-diagnosis of "the psychiatric thinking"!*

particular true self-finding and expression is all about (or 'transition' if interpreted from the outside): **Transsexuals do "gender-transition"** _so we can live who we truly are!_[1] But "coercive persuasion" is, be it self imposed or used as a form of torture, by it's very nature *a means _to make a person into somebody else than who she is,_* it is not suitable for self-finding! Or very simply put: _I cannot be brainwashed into being mentally healthy, only into being mentally ill._ And _I most definitely cannot be brainwashed into being myself!_

Why anybody possibly thinks that such a completely absurd approach could be in any way sane, meaningful and ethical and why the people doing this get governmental, professional and to a certain degree even social support truly escapes me!

On the other hand it is important to recognize that this isn't exactly "therapeutic abuse", I would rather call it _systemic abuse_. Professionally this ought to be called *"iatrogenic abuse"*. As you might expect the term doesn't actually exist *because abuse can never be caused by psychiatric theory, expectation or even therapy or therapists!* Ok, maybe it should be added to the DSM nevertheless, to complete *my* list of mental disorders? Then some bizarre psychiatric dogma could be dreamt-up as a "pretend-cure", we could call it's application 'therapy' and force it onto people we find to have it! Maybe we could even create a set-up in which people could be pressured into self-identifying [see B.44]...

And by now, in between all of this chaos I have grown up to be a woman! But thanks to mental-health I now live in an absurd world in which I don't believe, trying to overcome the abuse this system has inflicted onto me! But at least they now allow me to express myself freely. Well, the part of me that's left intact anyway[2].

---

[1] *This is by no means limited to "social transition", the highly visible public change for these individuals who desire or are forced into this but it is also true for "personal transition", the recognition and acceptance of who one truly is, just to oneself.*

[2] *Now I shouldn't have written this last sentence like I did! Because I know full well that some psychiatrists will interpret this sexually! The bit about "the part of me that's left intact"? After genital surgery? - But of course that's just it! I could really live without knowing how they will interpret this because from my perspective their interpretation is an expression of a seriously sick mind, a severe mental disorder which in all likelihood would substantially impair a person's cognitive, emotional or behavioural functioning - unless that person were to live his social life in the context of a mental institution!*

C.3. THE ULTIMATE CATCH

Sometimes people still call me 'transsexual', even now. From my perspective that's completely absurd. True, my appearance might certainly lead to suspect that I have lived on a testosterone horror-trip for a good part of my life if one knows what to look for, but even so, ever since shortly after genital surgery *I have lost the ability to feel "gender-mismatch"*. Of course I can still remember how I used to look *but I can no longer remember how this has ever felt!* **Because I was allowed to heal I am now incapable to experience transsexuality** - just like every other person on the planet who was not born transsexual or who has received appropriate treatment for it.

It was at first a bit disconcerting to me, particularly when talking to (pre-op) transsexuals, because they wanted to talk to me about the experiences I had during surgery, about the preparations and aftercare, about practical but also about personal and very emotional issues. I can hear, I can listen, I can empathize, but the one thing I no longer can is *understand*. In a way this puts transsexuals in a rather difficult catch: I can certainly be of help and assistance to a woman who is seeking treatment, after all I've been there, done that, know what to expect, know where to go and more importantly where not to go. But the one thing that's different to almost every other condition out there is *that by the very virtue of being healed I loose the capacity to emotionally identify with the people who are still seeking help!*

Everybody can sit in a wheelchair. For an hour, a day, a week. For the sake of the experience. True, this isn't the same as being paralysed but if this really were the issue modern medicine could simulate even this down to perfection. We can empathize, even experience paralysis and the life of Jane. *We can understand her.*

It is true, I can dress-up male should I ever want to, but I would not feel male as I used to. I would now feel that I were a female crossdresser or transvestite. The life I used to live is not replicable! If I would go off female hormones and on testosterone instead, to the same levels I used to live at for decades or even lower ones I would not tolerate this "induced male state" as I did for so many years, I would instead turn into a suicidal woman.

For a female identified "biological woman" this is the expected, normal reaction. It is this for me too, I was asked to test this when I needed to go off HRT prior to surgery. No testosterone treatment was needed as pre-op I still produced my very own in quite sufficient quantities. What I went through in these few days felt like a drug-induced horror-trip! If at any time in my life I had felt mental, had lost any and all control, experienced emotions and interpreted the world in a manner I could not account for, had thoughts as disconnected from reality as it ever gets, *these few days were it!*

The physiological changes and with it the changes in environmental perception and emotional self-experience that usually occur within days or a few weeks of going on HRT are far more permanent and go far deeper than psychiatric or even medical practice recognizes, accepts or even thinks possible! Because such changes normally don't happen and therefore can't be observed! *It is important to recognize that these changes were only possible because I was transsexual.* Applied to a male identified biological male the same medications may well induce depression, maybe even suicidality, within days or even hours. *My changes were possible because the result is normal for a woman and because this is who I am!*

We can make paraplegics from non-paraplegics, this works just fine as far too many victims of accidents prove. We can also do this on a temporary basis for medical purposes (it's called an epidural). The experience of loss of sensation and control is the same, the difference is in the setting and of course in the permanency of the effect. ***But we can't force males to become females. Neither on a temporary nor on a permanent basis. This will** never **work!* All we can do is to give a (predominantly) female identified individual a woman's life!**

We may not or possibly never will be able to understand why this is true. *But do we really have to understand this?* After all we have hundreds of thousands of cases to prove that surgery works just fine! We find that people know they need genital alignment and that they thrive after having received it! We also have hundreds of thousands of cases in a control-group to prove that this does not work and is not possible on non-transsexual individuals, that they too know *and would never accept such treatment were it not for ulterior motifs!*

Sometimes things are really simple! All we have to do is open our eyes! *And while we're at it maybe our minds as well. But most of all our hearts!*

C.4. Racism, Sexism And Featurism

In many countries it used to be legal to discriminate against people on the basis of their skin-pigmentation. Thankfully this isn't the case anymore! In most countries women didn't enjoy the same rights men did. Thankfully this isn't the case anymore, at least in a great majority of countries. In many countries it used to be legal to discriminate based on religious conviction. This too isn't legal anymore in most countries, though a fair number have signed declarations indicating that in their opinion religious discrimination is right and 'ethical'[1].

Discrimination is no longer seen as something that *just happens,* that *is inevitable* or that is *a necessary evil of life.* Discrimination can be fought, successfully! **Discrimination is wrong.** *Any* **discrimination! But the sad fact is that** *as of today* _discriminating_ _against people who live a different gender than assigned to them at birth is legal and_ _such discrimination is government supported policy and practice in every country on_ _earth!_

Should we stop discrimination on the grounds of what gender a person lives? Of course we should! *But there's something else we should do too:* _We should not draw_ _the line right behind us as so many other groups have done!_ Because it was the best they could get. Because they weren't aware of other people's discrimination or *because they didn't believe that the next form of discrimination was "their cause".*

Instead we should recognize that _discrimination happens because we group people_ _according to some features we assign to them and then draw conclusions on single_ _individuals or entire groups based on this assignment!_ The problem: *These features may or may not have anything to do with the conclusions we draw!* Even if we feel that we can prove a certain conclusion to *always* be true given a certain observation, *this still does not allow for the existence of future variations, errors, ambiguity and potential exceptions!*

Some psychologists have called this *'traitism',* an umbrella term to all the usual forms of discrimination, all the ones that are derived from 'traits'. The problem with this is *that the term 'trait'* _is a biological term used for a visible feature of an organism_ *(or empirically describable, in some way observable, independently verifiable feature).* So traitism would encompass sexism, racism, discrimination due to physical disability and so forth. However even if we were to interpret the term traitism very liberally and have it include

---

[1] *The Cairo Declaration of Human Rights in Islam (CDHRI), a declaration of the member states of the Organisation of the Islamic Conference. The CDHRI is their counterpart of the United Nations Universal Declaration Of Human Rights (UDHR) establishing Islam and Sharia as fundamental principles of government.*

discriminations based on behavioural observations (such as sexual practices) *this would still leave such discriminations as the ones based on sexual orientation, religion or nationality out as these are not (or not always) observable traits but rather self-identified or legal designations. It would also not include transsexuality as this too cannot be observed as a measurable feature of the person!*

I therefore think that *we should seek an even larger umbrella under which we define discrimination and laws against it!* For lack of a better idea I call this 'featurism' (from 'feature') *whereas any attribute of a human-being would qualify,* not just biological traits (this would include attributes of a social or legal nature, exclusively externally assigned or exclusively self-identified ones).

Transsexuality is not a trait, a physically quantifiable quality. Non the less it is an attribute or even at times an identifiable feature some people get labelled with. But whatever we look at it, discriminating against transsexuals because of who we are is still wrong!

C.5. THE MOST INVISIBLE MINORITY

"It"... yes, I've heard that one before. I suppose this would be how some people refer to me these days... And no, these same people would never use that designation on a post-hysterectomy female or a male who has had his testes removed for, say, testicular cancer. Obviously? Of course these and similar slurs are exclusively directed at us! And then, there's the one that we "besmear womankind" or are "a disgrace" or somehow "soil the image of women or femininity"? Obviously that one hits a little differently depending on if it's coming from a man or a woman... Ok, if it comes from a man it is more a laugh really because if he identifies as much a woman as to put himself into the position of determining what's a 'disgrace' for this group then maybe, just maybe he ought to see a shrink and have a decent talk about his own gender-identification?

But then again, why should I complain? We're such an obvious and easy target, are we not? Particularly if somebody is not yet easily 'passing' or it is just known about a person that "she is trans"? After all psychiatry not only nicely labels us, they present us on a platter to be exposed to this, have us declare our disability publicly, even print it in the government announcements to make absolutely certain everybody knows forever! (In some parts of the world these government announcements are put into every mailbox in town!). They have us live "she-male", something I find myself offended by doing it! If *somebody else* chooses this life I have no problem with it at all, each person should be allowed to find their own expression of 'self'. However I still feel abused *when I am being forced to do this myself!* So who better to understand than I myself that other people, be they male or female, may get similar feelings about myself *when even I get these?*

The way we're being set-up is bound to make it really simple to attack us *for not being real females* and it makes it just as easy to attack us *for not being real males*: Whatever demeaning viewpoint one prefers to choose, with us apparently everything goes!

If they make us into "fringe existences" and have us live that lifestyle for no other reason than testing the level of our submissiveness and we all seem to fall for it, comply and play along nicely then it is no surprise that a lot of people perceive us like this, perceive all this just as much as *'playing'.* After all we are all *"playing along nicely"!* This then rather obviously makes transsexuality look like "a choice" and "a lifestyle" or even "having fun on somebody elses cost" *rather than the only way of self-expression we are allowed to have!*

When it then happens that some people get offended our true motivation isn't important at all - *most likely the people who feel offended would not even know (or bother to inform themselves) that what we live isn't a free choice but forced onto us by psychiatric dogma and the power medical doctors wield!* It is then no surprise that many more people get offended than otherwise would, on top of the ones who always do, whatever happens, and the ones who do get offended because they don't or can't understand.

We are, as we are perceived, by and large *made into who we are!* The image we're being made into isn't flattering or positive, after all it is designed in large parts by egomaniac abusers with no consideration for others! People I would deem, from my uneducated and unprofessional perspective, as being seriously ill and in dire need of treatment! So what happens?

I can't be normal because their dogma requires me to behave and identify in a way I myself perceive as crazy! Then they put every effort into painting us mentally ill, lunatics, males with delusions of femininity... And just why should the public, even people who might know a transsexual, maybe have valued her highly before they found out about her identification, but in particular people who have no idea about the issue, the methods employed and the cause of my absurd or offending behaviour put any effort into changing *their* perception of me *when they get presented with so many fabricated and false depictions of who I am?* When they get presented this *by me, served-up by myself!*

Why would uninformed observers not believe *that what they see me doing was not really my idea, not really* **my own lunacy? Why should anybody doubt that I am crazy and the nice psychiatrist who is good enough to spend his time on a lost case like myself does his very best to cure me only I somehow manage to sabotage even the most competent doctors efforts? After all, not only does the nice doctor declare me nuts and not himself,** *I never even try to contradict his assessment!* **What reason would anybody possibly have to suspect that** *what I do and live is compliance to a mad psychiatric dogma, compliance to a degree nobody else would ever accept or could even imagine,* **that when I do this it is indeed not me who has lost her marbles?**

People, male and female, pick on these *who are different.* In our case this difference is in most cases not perceived as such, but even this is bad enough, maybe it is even worse! Because many of us can't be attacked openly for looks, behaviour, ethnicity or identification, after all we look as they look, behave as they behave and identify as they identify! *So they're doing it behind our backs,* likely even more so than this would happen with somebody who's part of a "visible minority". Because there is no physical feature to be picked on the target now becomes our mind - it is *an invisible attribute* to pick on! We are, after all, *the perfect prototype of an invisible minority!* Or we would be if psychiatry would not insist in dragging us out into their limelight!

C.6. ABSOLUTE POWER CORRUPTS ABSOLUTELY

No, I don't get a degree for having studied psychiatry and its inner workings for 30 years and nobody is giving me an Oscar for my performance as a male or a transsexual. And honestly, I don't want one. Well, maybe: That degree in psychiatry would have some appeal as then I could sign my own prescriptions! Because there is one more insult and degradation the system has in store: *Apparently the medical establishment sees a need to tightly control the substances I depend on for life!*

The motivation of this can't possibly be the protection of the public at large as estrogens are widely used in agriculture and it appears to be of no concern whatsoever that some of it ends-up in our food-supply! Some substances extensively used in the manufacture of plastics are 'mistaken' by our bodies for estrogens (these 'mimic' one of its forms) and as these can be found in things such as food-containers some of it will inevitably leech out and also end-up in our food. This too seems to be of no concern to the medical establishment, even if these chemicals are found in baby-bottles and -toys!

Maybe the classification of estrogens and testosterone-blockers as *medically controlled substances* is to prevent "the general public" from starting to self-medicate[1,2]? From my perspective it is difficult to see why there could be a significant problem along that line[3]. After all, the most likely effect any non-transsexual who uses these drugs would get is sexual dysfunction - and that's hardly anything that seems desirable to most people? So why do they think they need this kind of control? True, it could be nothing but a simple gender and power-issue: It is after all interesting that the substances used *to control the female sexual and reproductive function* (the pill) are tightly restricted and require the regular ascent of a doctor (and related costs and inconvenience) while equivalents *for the male sexual function* (Viagra, Cialis,...) are available freely by mail-order or at the grocer's, no potentially embarrassing and expensive visits to the family physician are required and no waiting-times or supervision are imposed or even expected?

---

[1] *Estrogens are listed for the following treatments: (a) To prevent pregnancy. The amounts that can be found in today's contraceptives are relatively small, except in certain "morning after" pills. Logically a prescription is needed for the low-dose contraceptive while the high-dose remedy is an off-the-shelf or over-the-counter product. (b) In HRT for women (biological and transsexual). Dosage typically follows the motto "listen to your body, you'll know how much to take!". Other applications include certain prostate-cancers (often in combination with other interventions such as surgery) but these are apparently so rarely used that they aren't even officially listed.*

[2] *Testosterone-blockers (anti-androgens) a transsexual would use are listed as diuretics, treatments of various prostate-conditions including cancer and precursors as well as to lower sex-drive, unlisted use include treatment of hair-loss.*

[3] *Estrogens can be purchased in virtually every pharmacy (in some countries in convenience-stores, from vending-machines or by mail-order) without a prescription if the stated purpose is the prevention of pregnancy (the "morning after pill"). Agricultural estrogens are available freely in many countries which have strict regulations on human medical equivalents, furthermore there are substances which 'mimic' estrogens (from both natural and synthetic sources) but the great majority of these are highly toxic, it would therefore be ill advised to use these as a substitute.*

But be this as it may, such control is necessary <u>when it comes to having some leverage to force continued behavioural modification onto transsexuals whenever it pleases the people in charge,</u> either in the medical or in the political system! Or maybe it is convenient to keep our mouths shut forever? But from the receiving end this indirect control then becomes nothing else but *a continuation of the oppression and general attitude I had to contend with all my life! <u>It extends the official view of who I have to be indefinitely, up to the end of my life!</u>* This system is apparently never, ever willing to let go of their prejudices against us!

In the end the only way for me to ever hope for a life free of such oppression is to ask for the otherwise unheard-of option of self-treatment! But I don't ask for this for convenience. What I ask for is not to forego checkups or lab-tests. I full well understand that these should be encouraged. Many people have long-term medical problems and need prescriptions for life and they too could ask for the option of self-care and the lifelong right to obtain what they need. I think this, while completely revolutionary[1], would make sense for many groups of patients. However my own case is very different: *What I ask for is not so much the right to write my own prescriptions (for the limited range of drugs used in transgender-care), what I ask for is an end to government sanctioned medical oppression <u>because I too should have the absolute right to express my personality freely, without limitations or control. What I ultimately really ask for are not prescriptions but the most basic human rights!</u>*

This is very different from such medical rituals as regular prescription-visits to treat everything from hypertension to diabetes or whatever it may be. Because what I have to ask for is not medical treatment, <u>what I have to ask for is a permit for my freedom of (self-) expression!</u> This is something no diabetic or hypertension patient is ever expected to ask for as neither of these treatments nor any other need for prescription drugs are self-expressions[2], these are given as "illness-management". And no, I don't want a life on probation with a hearing every 3-6 months to re-determine if I deserve my basic human rights for another few months! <u>Like everybody else I want the freedom to be myself for a lifetime!</u>*

In addition this is about the fact that - unlike every other long-term medical condition - I have been and still risk to be severely mistreated <u>by the medical system</u> for simply having the condition I was born with. <u>I have been forced into behavioural and physical modification to the dictate of this system. I had and still risk to again have my basic human rights denied, I have been treated with the utmost contempt for my personal integrity and my emotional well-being.</u> After all this I find it impossible to accept that I am asked to put my emotional, spiritual and physical well-being or even my existence into the hands of this very same abusive system once again. Indeed I find it absurd that this is even expected!

---

[1] *For example: Many diabetics use a blood glucose meter to self-adjust their insulin dosage. Diabetes is typically a life-long condition, treatment will be needed indefinitely. It is reasonable for a diabetic to see a doctor regularly but I do not understand why the individual should not be given the security of life-long continued treatment no matter if a doctor's visit is scheduled or not (or a doctor is in fact available). Or to put this differently: <u>A patient should be allowed to attend follow-ups for insight of usefulness,</u> he should not be forced there by means of violence (the threat of the death penalty due to unavailability of medication). Such behaviour is disrespectful and unethical, it may in fact severely disrupt the doctor/patient relationship.*

[2] *Except for substances used to control reproductive functions (contraceptives) and for spiritual and religious practices. This is in fact one of the most often quoted reasons why medications such as Viagra and Cialis no longer require prescriptions!*

Many psychiatrists seem to wonder why a good number of transsexuals don't come back to 'therapy' after their surgery and instead prefer to self medicate[1] ('illegally', as doctors call it). Honestly, how much ignorance can they get themselves into? After all the grey-market only wants our money while the medical system demands full control of our lives! How much detachment from reality does it take to not recognize *that we too, just like everybody else (including they themselves), value our freedom of self-expression and that we too will escape oppression, abuse and blackmail in any way we can?*

I would have liked to respect the medical system, not fear it. I don't think this will ever be possible but I still would like to see my doctor because I honour his dedication and intentions, appreciate his knowledge, welcome his advice. Not because the system uses violence, coercion, oppression and abuse to have me hauled into his office four times a year!

Reality is that my condition as well as my treatment is *to this day* not generally accepted by medicine! Many of us have, either temporary or over long periods of time, *great difficulties to find a physician who is actually willing to treat them* (to write the prescriptions and the occasional lab-requests because under normal circumstances there's nothing else to it). *This is about the fact that, even now, my treatment is still given to me conditionally upon approval of my behaviour,* as defined by the medical system, enforced to whatever degree a treating physician chooses. There is no entitlement to *medical* treatment, only to the mental kind; there is not even a general agreement that I need it! *Or that I merit it if it comes to that!*

This is not about personal mistrust, I trust my doctor, I would be looking for somebody else if I wouldn't. *But I don't trust the system he works for, the people who decree what he can and cannot do, how he has to see me and my condition. I don't trust the decisions they make!* After all, they have proven time and again that they can't be trusted, that they act unethically and that my best interest is none of their concerns. This is about the fact

➤ *that I too should have the unequivocal right to life, to long-term care and to a predictable supply of the drugs I need just as every other patient with a lifelong medical condition does - even if more than a few doctors would refuse to treat me.*

➤ *that I too am deemed mentally sane and competent to make any and all decisions in regard to my own life unless there is clear and tangible evidence to the contrary.*

➤ *that I will never again be subjected to another witch-hunt at mental-health as a condition to obtain medical treatment - or anything else for that matter.*

➤ *that the system never again uses its power of threatening me with an implicit death penalty to enforce some kind of behavioural conditioning!*

---

[1] *Skipping medical treatment most often occurs when an individual has to pay for her drugs herself. The added weight a prescription carries via full or partial drug-coverage has the effect to pressure more people into a physician's offices as some may simply not have the option or do not want to pay for everything themselves. Doctors thus exploit financial circumstances, poverty and the behaviour of insurance-companies to increase their power!*

This is not about a prescription, all the drugs are easily available without one by mail-order anyway. *This is about basic dignity. And it is about drawing a line:*

The medical establishment declares me *insane*, then concludes that *they now have the duty* to intervene in my life to an unheard of degree. But this isn't medicine, it is a sick form of abusing power: I am not declared insane for evidence of mental illness *but because doing this is convenient (and necessary) to enforce any and all behavioural modification of their choice!* But when medical treatment is not given *unconditionally of sociobehavioural change* IT IS NOT MEDICINE, IT IS SOCIAL ENGINEERING!

Ultimately this is about what medicine should never be used or abused for. This is about recognizing, acknowledging, preventing and, insofar as it is possible, correcting such mistakes. This is about how we define our human society in general and medicine in particular: Nurturing, supporting and healing or judging, enforcing and abusing?

This is about an absolute guarantee *for everybody* that medicine is there - whenever we may need it, for whatever reason we may need it and for however long we may need it - to care for our lives, well-being *and personal dignity* in whatever way is possible in any given circumstance, without any conditions!
This is about the principles of medicine, as laid out in *The Declaration of Geneva[1]:*

➤➤ *The health of my patient will be my first consideration*

➤➤ *I will not permit considerations of age, disease or disability, creed, ethnic origin, gender, nationality, political affiliation, race, sexual orientation, social standing or any other factor to intervene between my duty and my patient*

➤➤ *I will maintain the utmost respect for human life*

➤➤ *I will not use my medical knowledge to violate human rights and civil liberties, even under threat*

Yes, doctors are routinely asked to deliver what some people describe as 'miracles'. *But as long as medical associations and their members collectively, as a "professional standard" (referred to as "good medical practice") interpret the above in a way that permits premeditated murder as a 'treatment' (as in abortions, in particular the ones on request, doctor assisted suicide, participation in administering the death-penalty or in the research for weapons of mass destruction[2]) the miracle called 'ethics' may be one we will have to wait for a very*

---

[1] *Principle 4,8-10 of* The Declaration of Geneva. *The text has been adopted as a "modern version" of the* Oath of Hippocrates *by the World Medical Association in 1948. It has been updated numerous times since then. Quote from the 2006-edition*

[2] *It isn't my intention to judge any of these. I personally value all life and it's dignity above everything else but I also accept that this is my choice, everybody else is free to see this differently. However if our society allows any or all of the above (and many other practices from a very long list) then such services can never be provided by medical doctors! An alternative system for "physical treatment" should provide these hence clearly separating medical professionals whose only objective is to*

long time. Subtleties such as medical doctors recognizing their personal limitations or even admitting these and restricting their actions to within such limitations or acknowledging that other people may have contributions to make or are capable to acquire the capacity to make their own educated decisions even if they are not med-school graduates may remain a dream forever.

For transsexuals one more important question needs to be answered: As apparently so many individual physicians as well as their professional organizations *prove incapable to uphold or enforce their own ethical standards while at the same time denying us any option to obtain medical treatment elsewhere, **just where should transsexuals**[1] **turn to if we ever need medical help?** **After all THEIR OWN SYSTEM MAKES TREATING OURSELVES A CRIMINAL OFFENCE!***

---

guarantee the best possible health of an individual **from these other interventions.** *Such other physical treatments could range from piercing and tattooing to surgical body-modifications (religiously motivated procedures, vanity surgery,...), providing legal recreational drugs to any legitimated form of murder (assisted suicide, abortions, death-penalty) - whatever society (not medical doctors!) may choose to allow.*

[1] *In this context 'transsexual' means "anybody who is perceived by the medical system or an individual medical doctor as such"*

C.7.   LOOK, IT'S ALL A GAME!

Throughout my ventures into the healthcare and mental-health-system I have actually been told this twice, by people involved in the official process: *"Look, it's all a game!"*. I know who's being played all right, what remains to be figured out is *by whom* and *why*. None of the people I met on this journey seemed to have taken much pleasure from what they were doing to me, in fact some seemed honestly and personally depressed about sending me to suicide instead of treatment. Depending on the personality of whoever was on that other side people noticed that they could increase the entertainment value (ok, psychiatry would probably see it negatively and refer to it as "lowering the depressive potential") for everybody involved dramatically by doing something completely different than what was expected, others just chose to show me the door after 3 minutes instead of waiting until they risked getting seriously depressed over what they thought they were obliged to do. Still others just pretended and probably booked an hour with their pre-ferred therapist each time right after they saw me leave their offices. Honestly, I didn't mind to be shown the door as early as possible just as long as this came with a piece of paper to show that I was there!

I don't understand why these people do what they do, why they don't simply refuse to do this. After all, *they're in the business of improving lives, not destroying these!* That's at least what I thought and all the people I have met along this journey apparently thought so also. They let me feel this and showed me this by their compassion and their humanity. But they still did what they were told to do! I honestly do not understand how they could.

I suppose I know a thing or two about social pressure and compliance, after all I was compliant enough to live the wrong gender for half a lifetime before I openly started asking to have this changed. But *I did this to myself, not to another person* and I had some reason for doing it, but I quite understand that this eventually leads to an unful-filled, lonely life of depression and suicide. So are they too just compliant? Is this nothing but a hierarchy of a few people who exploit us, exploit *everybody?* Because they are (or have accepted to be) in a position to give directions, write dogma? *And everybody else plays along nicely, no criticism and no protest?*

It does seem absurd! But could it just be true? After all I complied by living the wrong life! Is this the final solution? A few sick people in control: Sadists, perverts, exploiters, people who don't care - except maybe for themselves? Them giving the orders? And we, the rest of humanity nicely in compliance? You and I, many of the medical people, *eve-rybody compliant?* Just differently? I comply by living the wrong gender while the medi-

[At the Driver's Licensing Office, she] I am sorry this is taking so long... [Me] Don't worry, I have gotten used to the experience that in my life things only work on second try...

319

cal people comply by mistreating patients instead of treating them? It's both absurd, isn't it? Or *mental* if one prefers that term? Just differently!

They did comply well, I *almost* believed it. I complied well *and they really did believe it!* But then again, I had an advantage, didn't I*? I could actually prove to everybody that my compliance was anatomically justified...*

So, in the end, is *this* the difference? Is *this* who we all are? Is *this* how society gets us to live a life that isn't ours to near perfection? It does appear to be strong enough at least that the medical people cross every moral and ethical line, disband with every human right there is in order to comply to their *"professional expectations"!* It does appear to be strong enough to make me cross every line of my own ethics if social rules call for it: I can be non-compliant, break rules, even mistreat people - to prove that I am *who I am not,* to make everybody believe that I am indeed male. *But I would never do this to be or become myself?* Because it is not who I am. Who I *really* am! Nevertheless I comply - *just as everybody else does!*

But ultimately there *is* a difference: Their artificial compliance is socially induced, *it is social and behavioural only.* My artificial compliance is all this also *but it is biological, physical as well.* This appears to be why my compliance will get me killed eventually while they can get away with theirs, live it for a lifetime, happily or not. Because of this difference I face a choice: My body or my mind! I could choose death: This would supposedly be the acceptable solution. *For them!* Or I could... Actually do this? *Do what in all likelihood will be the worst incident of social non-compliance of a lifetime?* **Go and ask society for my life <u>because I have grown arrogant enough to think that my life is more important than their social comfort?</u>** To actually <u>break all their rules so I can keep my life?</u> A life which, if they allow me to have it, will be so dramatically different that nobody will even notice that I am there? *But on the way there, while getting this most ordinary life, I show society and particularly the people I meet during my treatment that they too are living a life of absurd compliance - only they don't do anything about it!*

Is *this* why transsexuals are so unacceptable? Is it just easier to declare us mental for wanting to live *than society for how it treats us - <u>and how they treat each other?</u>* Is this the game society wants me to play? **Be mental and they let me live that unacceptably non-compliant life in a hidden corner <u>because then they don't have to look AT THEMSELVES?</u>**

If so, I am sorry! I am not playing along nicely anymore! But then again this doesn't matter now because I am already certified nuts! If not on paper then I have at least proven it by having that sex-change, haven't I?

C.8.   FOREVER GUILTY FOR WHO I AM

If I had received the typical treatment, never gotten anywhere and being abused at every turn, I would have it easier now: I could just *hate* the people I went to for healing. Many transsexuals do, given the treatment we get this seems rather normal. However because of all the emotional abuse and because of who we are this, for so many, *ends in simple acceptance of what is* - which is good in a way as it alleviates many negative feelings. It is unfortunately also the base on which a lot of this system can be built on and maintained!

Only I didn't get that typical treatment because I was selective in where I went and because I was simply lucky. I did get some of that "never get anywhere treatment", but very much cut to the bone: Do minimal compliance and in return nobody ever cared about anything!

The problem for me now is *that I end-up being in the absurd position of feeling thankful towards the people who didn't enforce routine-abuse onto me to a level which would most certainly have killed me.* It's just another catch of that system: *Ultimately it makes us feel grateful, somehow, towards the people who finally "sign us off"* because no matter the harm they inflicted onto us, no matter how badly they abused us, *they in the end approve our lives!*

Of course the way this has been concocted the people who so far haven't gotten that nod will never write a book and never become a problem to that system! <u>*Because they're either still hoping and waiting and complying and keep very, very quiet or they're dead silent after suicide!*</u> On the other hand a great majority of the people who have received their treatment will not want to look back and are quiet also. *And thankful...*

Yes, in the end I hate and despise the system that treats people like this, that has treated me and so many others I personally know (or have known) in this way or even worse. But I can't hate the people I have met personally, indeed I feel very, very thankful towards *them!* This is rather absurd as it makes the abuse I have taken from this system, abuse which was inflicted onto me *by people,* into one *I can't assign an abuser to!* There's no "evil person" to blame, I have nobody to call to account! Well, there is... But I have never seen *these* people and I have no intention to ever change this...

Ultimately this is a hierarchical structure of systematic abuse like so many before. I have only ever met the lowest ranking people, the ones who play along nicely, just as I do, the ones who may struggle to give me what I need within the confines of a system they may find inappropriate, wrong, even abusive themselves, but which they don't want

[Consulate, secretary] You understand that having your sex changed will result in annulment of your marriage? [Me] Thank you for telling me this but honestly, it's a little late for such considerations now...

321

to, don't dare to or don't feel are capable to ever change. But this still isn't quite a typical hierarchy of abuse, *this psychiatric-therapeutic system of abuse is more refined and better camouflaged than any I have ever come across:* True, this dogma is just as much a set-up where people treat each other unethically, where they are hurt needlessly *but it looks so inconspicuous that most people don't recognize it for what it is: Evil, hurtful and wrong!* **Because in it's deviousness it makes precisely these people whose intentions are the very best behave unethical** *as this becomes their only way out to help people like myself!* **And it makes me blackmail all of them into doing it!**

This is much more subtle and it is much more perverted than a simple top-down power-scheme such as the Nazi-State. **This set-up works by exploiting the nature of my condition** *and the humanity and compassion of these few people who really care* and the only way out for everyone within this framework is to behave unethical or immoral and get hurt! Because in the end it makes me seek-out the help of the most decent and caring human-beings by telling them **"this is who I am and what I need. But I'm not going to survive dogmatic treatment and waiting, I'm going to die if you behave as you are told and expected to!".**

I give them a choice between my life and their professional duty, accountability and integrity. **Maybe even the insight that ultimately there can only be *one* ethics.** But however that may be, *there is a choice to be made.* **And I make this *their* choice.**

And yes, I admit it: *I am quite devious enough to put that choice before the very people I suspect will have the most of a personal problem with it - because these will be the people who are most likely to give me life instead of dogma! Because I understand this system and I understand that in this set-up this is my only chance!* I understand that this is abusive and I understand just how abusive it is. I understand that what I do is wrong, that I go after the very best people in this system instead of the very worst ones. I also know that acting like this is the only way for me to get life instead of death.

And then I'm done, everything has been taken care of, my life should be working just fine now, in every respect. Only it doesn't! Because this set-up is so completely hair-raisingly absurd *that I now feel guilty for having asked for just this - my life!* I feel guilty for being the one who survived while so many others did not! I feel guilty for having picked the people I put that question to, for having understood the system and for having taken full and complete advantage of this knowledge. I feel guilty for the pain I inflicted on some of the people I met on my way, pain I inflicted *for the simply reason of having been there, for having asked for my life!* And I feel guilty for having been the one who has been let go "too easily" and thus lived, *for having been "the lucky one"!*

Yes, I quite understand that this is irrational and it isn't called for. Nevertheless I now have to live with these 'side-effects' of all these so very enlightened psychiatric theories. They used to call it *"survivor syndrome"* but in the DSM-IV merged it into *posttraumatic stress disor-*

der[DSM] (PTSD). ***So now I have to live with posttraumatic stress disorder thanks to psychiatric insight, theory and therapy!***

And just in case this would ever cause "clinically significant distress or impairment in social, occupational, or other important areas of functioning"[DSM], or just any kind of distress for that matter, I would have to be truly nuts before I'd ever look for any professional help for anything like this ever again! Or they'd have to force their 'help' onto me. *Again.*

C.9.   *IN AN IDEAL WORLD WHERE WE ARE FREE TO CHOOSE[1]*

Have you asked yourself the question yet??? I have... For the past 30 years, ever since I have found out about the conditions medicine puts on our lives... The question: If I would live socially as a woman or as a man *if I had a free choice? Would I have done social gender transition or just continued to live who I was if I would have been given treatment (genital and hormonal alignment)* as a free choice, *without behavioural modification in the form of social transition (and life as a woman) as a condition?*

Yes, I have asked myself this question over and over again. Apart from the question 'why' - no, not *why am I transsexual?*, but *why do they do this to us?* - this is most likely *the one question I have asked myself more often in my life than any other.* And the most honest answer I can give is that I really do not know!

However what I do know is that I would have done many things very differently. First and foremost I would have, decades ago, started with genital surgery and *only after that* would I have started estrogen only treatment. If that would have worked, if the testosterone reduction from surgery would have been enough, I might have had a life on far less medication and consequentially far fewer side-effects, less cost and fewer potential complications. Now I can't tolerate my own residual physiological testosterone anymore, now I will very likely have to continue suppression for the rest of my life. *Because now I am an addict. Not to some drug but to not having my own testosterone that's left!*

Socially? I was living integrated in society as an active member of our community. A normal life. True, as a stay-home-parent I was living a rather stereotypically female role, my activities included children, school, playgroups, running a household and so on. But nobody minded and I didn't either. I suppose for all intents and purposes I would have done what every other intersexed person does: I would have tried to find out if this would have continued to be a workable solution after surgery! Nobody would have had to know about my "intimate correction", I neither see a point in publicly advertising how my genitals look nor in alienating myself unnecessarily!

They all knew me being male, father of my children. Many, particularly women, treated me as a woman (or "just one of us") anyway. Not because I told them, not because they *knew,* but simply *because they felt this to be the right way to relate to me!* I looked male, sort of, and they just overruled what they saw because what they felt was so much stronger.

Now they know me as a woman. They don't have to 'overlook' anything anymore *and they still treat me as "just one of us".* Not because I tell them, only now it is obvious

---

[1] *Lyrics from the song "Ideal World" by* The Christians

even from afar. It doesn't take somebody new five minutes anymore to make the adjustment. Only now I can't be the father of my children any longer without a lot of explaining. Now I have to hide something and I have to do a "coming-out" every now and then to explain the situation to somebody while before I wouldn't have to. *If that's an improvement to my mental health then tank you very much, but honestly, that kind of improvement I could nicely do without!*

I have never had any behavioural or social problems living my (legally male) life. I have never felt that I 'needed' to transition socially. True, I have lived in my small social space where male-ness was just about as unheard of as it gets, but there are quite a few people - biological females as well as males - who do just that, so it wasn't a problem to find people I could relate to. Yes, this limited my social activities to some degree but never going to Hooters or picking up a prostitute didn't truly appear as a 'limitation' to my life, never mind while my social (and intimate) transition would potentially allow me to do this now, "from the other side", I still don't feel in any way limited by not doing it...

On the other hand I am predominantly female identified. I like living my identification to the best of my abilities, I enjoy doing this greatly. I like being identified and taken for who I am instantly and yes, this does make my life easier, even socializing has become in many ways easier. But I also know what kind of potential problems this change could cause. Not only to myself because this affects a lot more people than just myself. So far it has worked well, *however I still think that this should have been a decision we as a family should have taken ourselves! A lifestyle, never mind one that is deemed by still quite a few people as "completely unacceptable" or at best "borderline acceptable", should never have been forced onto me as a condition for my life!*

If I would have been allowed to get surgery without public transition and if I would not have felt good and complete in any way afterwards or if we, as a family, would have deemed the effort, alienation, cost and potential side-effects of public transition to be the smaller of two disadvantages, I could have done that lifestyle-change at any time in the future! It would actually have been *a lot easier* not having to deal with all aspects at the same time: Obtaining medical treatment, the public lifestyle-change, the coming-out and all the legal issues. But maybe just continuing would have been quite ok! There are many legally female individuals living visibly male or androgynous lives and this is by far not limited to intersexed and transsexual individuals. I would just have been one more! I would not even have been living an exotic gender-role, it would have looked like before, somewhat unusual but quite acceptable, *because I would have continued to be deemed a male in a female role.* This I had been for many years and it worked just fine. I could simply have continued to do what had always worked! But then again, that's an engineer offering a practical, workable (and honestly, very obvious) solution, not a psychiatrist's delusional dreamland...

C.10. JUST TRUST ME!

Quite a few authors write *"they let us jump through so many hoops before we get what we need"*, but then they usually stop short of saying *"therefore we should be trusted and allowed to be women, because we have proven the deepness of our conviction by the level of pain, exploitation, abuse and alienation we were willing to accept"*.

This dogmatic process is not about having to do self-finding for a year or two or seven before we're allowed to go to surgery, *to make sure only the ones who need this actually get it*. This isn't even about us. It is about enforcing compliance, about having to submit to arbitrary control, about enduring physical pain to a level which otherwise would be called torture, about enduring emotional pain which would break the great majority of people, about repeatedly and freely having to choose to go to de-humanizing 'treatment', about the ultimate form of behavioural conditioning - and if we tolerate all this, accept it willingly, without any protest, pay for it ourselves and don't either kill ourselves over it or go mad, then who could argue that we aren't women beyond any doubt? I mean who else would take something like this and call it a life but a woman?

Few authors and none of the people who write dogma admit this. But at the end of the day it gets that simple and that unbelievably absurd: *Because whatever they do there will never be any verification for our self-identification either way. Because ultimately there can't be any.* There can never be! ***Because any division of humanity into nicely labelled groups - any number of groups short of one group per person - is always to some degree arbitrary unless it is exclusively self-identified!*** *So finally they make the absolute limit of pain we are willing and capable to endure the ultimate substitute-proof before they "let us go"!*

But proof *of what?* Proof *of who we are?* No, I don't think so. Because even though I am now considered a woman by the legal system, by the state and its bureaucracy, even by the military and the revenue-service, *I still do not get a re-designation in the medical system! To them I forever remain a transsexual male or, depending upon a doctor's personal point of view, a severely mentally challenged guy who has had his genitals cut-off. Some of them address me friendly and call me 'she', nevertheless I won't get re-designated a woman with a birth-defect to and by the system, <u>instead the medical system continues to argue that such a birth-defect does not exist and therefore a re-designation is never possible, re-interpretation or re-evaluation is never needed and rethinking is never indicated!</u> I must truly be mental to think otherwise! Period. <u>Be-</u>*

cause to them the idea that gender - "medical gender" - never needs to be rethought, reassessed or reconsidered remains a fact in spite of all the evidence!

The words "to hold an absurd fixed false belief despite clear evidence to the contrary" come to mind here. But as this is the definition of *delusions*, a mental illness, I think it might just be safer not to develop this thought any further!

So no, I don't think they take the pain we endure as a substitute-proof of who we are. At best they mistake it for proof of our 'incurability' and this in turn lets them agree to our surgery. Sadly enough ultimately it is not their understanding or (as this isn't really possible) their acceptance *but THEIR CAPITULATION* that makes them give us our lives!

There are these sick rules, that perverted dogma. With it our lives are stolen from us *because the one thing they can't do, the one thing they can never accept is that all it would take is a little trust!* Trust in us, trusting that we in fact do know who we are! Trusting that we understand what we need and that we understand what we ask the medical people to do. Trust in us that we understand our lives far better than they think we do. Than they think we can. Even admit that many of us probably understand ourselves a lot better than they ever will understand *either us or themselves! Have enough faith to accept that our emotional lives and self-experiences are more real than their personal moral values. Accept that their beliefs too are emotions, philosophical viewpoints and personal values, not proofs!*

In the end they still don't have "hard evidence". All the abuse, the compliance, all the behavioural modifications, the financial exploitation, the control, the de-humanization, even the pain, the forced medication and physical modifications they often insist upon still give them no definite proof of who we are! *In the end they are where they started: They still have to trust us, they still have to accept that we are woman on faith alone - faith, nothing else! Nothing! BECAUSE PROOF IS IMPOSSIBLE - EITHER WAY!*

In the end all the abuse hasn't changed a thing! *Except for the fact that because of it there are a lot fewer of us left alive to receive treatment and these who are left have been severely damaged!*

I am a woman - because this is how I experience myself. I can't prove this. But just as the many hundreds of thousands before me *the one thing no abuse, no torture, no brainwashing is capable of changing is that for me this is and remains an absolute truth!*

C.11. HOPE

If you have taken one thing from this book I hope it is the understanding that mental-health doesn't help us while medical help does. *Because transsexuality is a medical condition, not a mental illness. Because transsexuals need medical treatment, not psychiatric therapy to live with or overcome their condition.*

If there's something else you take from it I hope it is that you understand our need for treatment, in particular hormonal and genital surgical alignment. That we depend on getting it, *that many of us die because they're not getting this treatment in time or at all!* Our surgical treatment is not optional, it gives us life! This is just like any other severe medical condition or disability. It is true that our surgery makes a few things a little more complicated because the looks of our genitals have, at this point in time, legal, social and maybe other ramifications. *But these aren't medical considerations and should best be left out of medical treatment.*

I have given you some insight into my life in this book. It is not what I wanted, *it is not what I in all likelihood would have chosen to do under any other circumstance.* I have given you insight and a glimpse into what I consider are some of my most personal and private experiences. I have done this because I was mistreated by a system which continues to mistreat human-beings and does so right now!

I may have given you some ideas about why this happens, how this happens and maybe even what might be done about it. Above all I may have given you a glimpse into the suffering this causes. Suffering which is caused by one of the more exotic conditions out there *but mostly by one of the most absurd treatments people get subjected to!*

I may have given you some insight into something simple, gender, which may turn out not to be that simple after all. And I have given you some insight into who I am, because while I am probably not who you expected to find *I am most certainly not who I am made out to be!*

You may think that I am unusual. Maybe a little different. But whatever I am or whatever you think I am, *I am human!* For that - *and nothing else* - I believe I merit to be treated humanely, respectfully, with dignity and decency, without prejudice and with equal rights. *Just like everybody else!* For this to happen mental-health needs to declare itself incompetent to treat people like myself. They need to stop telling us who and what we have to be and they need to stop enforcing their view onto us *just because we are different from what they want us to be!* Our treatment needs to be a personal decision in a medical context, not a one-for-all wash-up in a mental one. The care of mental-health or psychological support *may* be called for *in some cases,* but like every other medical condition this should rest with the patient and the directly involved medical professionals, *it has to be a case-by-case determination.*

But more importantly I ask all mental-health and medical professionals to stop deciding if human beings are to be male or female by taking the decision of who gets surgery and who does not away from us! I ask the medical community to start respecting our humanity, our self-identification, our right to self-determination. I ask them to respect our freedom to be who we are, I ask them to respect our freedom of self-expression.

I ask all medical professionals to understand and accept that there are limits to what they are capable of! I ask all medical professionals to understand and accept that there are limits to what they can decide "in the best interest of somebody else". And I ask them to accept that stepping over this line, taking something that isn't theirs to take, making a decision they can't make, declaring themselves competent in matters where it is impossible for them to be competent is wrong!

Only *I* know who and what I am, because only I have been given the emotional context I live my life in. *I am the only person who can ask my soul what I feel and who I am - and I am the only person who will ever get an answer!* Whatever they do to us, *this will never change!* **If medical doctors say they know better then they're playing God. This is unethical, it is unprofessional and it is very, very arrogant!**

I hope that one day life will be granted to us as a human right. Not as an arbitrary decision of somebody who is by definition incompetent to make this decision. *I HOPE THAT ONE DAY WE TOO WILL HAVE THE UNEQUIVOCAL RIGHT TO LIFE!*

I hope that one day abuse and oppression will end. *Every* abuse and *all* oppression. I know that this very wish has been the one so many people and groups have had before me. **The right to equal treatment. The right to life.** *The right to be who we are!* **The right to express ourselves.** *The right to choose.* **Freely.**

But for us there's something else: Our right to express ourselves as we are and the means to doing it *will have to be given to us freely, without any conditions.* Because so many choose no life over asking for it. *Because never asking for anything is who they are!*

Some of us learn to express this later in life. After treatment. After healing. Finally, after not just finding and accepting *who* we are and *what* we are but also *how* we are. Some of us start to express this. Some of us even get strong enough to speak out later in life. But this isn't who we are, it is at best an acquired capability. *Because who we are never changes, who we are can only be freed and lived or damaged and killed!*

I am a woman. I have always been a woman. I always will be a woman. This is who I am and if you don't let me be myself I can't be somebody else for you. I have tried to comply but this is one compliance that is not possible. If you insist that I try again I will die trying.

C.12. FINAL NOTE

There's one last bit to address: Why do I write this book and why do I write it now? I suppose the average psychiatrist might say that this is an expression of a therapeutic workup of some of my problems. Well, *some!* Because surely, there must be more? There always are, aren't there? *It's really only a matter of creating them...*

The not so average psychiatrist who actually takes the time to read it before passing judgement might conclude that this is my reckoning with psychiatry, putting myself into the role of the victim and lashing out. Or one could say that I wanted to drop a few hints to some people who, hopefully, would listen if the hints were direct and open enough so as not to be misunderstood. Or it could be my concern for people just like myself who are still waiting, hoping. Or for people who potentially are just about to give up that hope.

But of course being myself I could see things a little more differentiated and a lot more complex and say that it's a bit of all of the above and a whole lot more. As for the part about dropping hints and seeking change? Well, I don't believe this book will be of any use for that one. There have been many changes in psychiatric thinking before *but whenever this happened there was only ever movement into the wrong direction.* More psychiatry, dreaming-up more and more absurd theories about transsexuality. Making more things mandatory, allowing fewer. If there ever will be change it will have to come from somewhere else. But there is hope. There always is, isn't there?

To the question why I have published this now? Well, that one is easy: I have been denied anonymity by psychiatrically and politically enforced medical and government procedure, by psychiatric practices and requirements. Thanks to this most people who know me also know that I am what they call "a post-op transsexual" - and a lot of people who don't know me know at least this about me! So I suppose I have nothing more to loose, haven't I? Honestly, I don't think somebody's going to force a phalloplasty onto me any time soon, after all, apart from the public record and psychiatric insight I am now no longer a transsexual, am I?

And that last bit? "Having a go at psychiatry"? Well, I find that's a bit over-generalized as I have only ever had contact with a very small segment of psychiatry and I have no idea how representative this experience might be for the rest of it. However the part I have been in contact with doesn't need to be exposed as implausible or ridiculed, I think they're doing a rather good job at that themselves - just holding-up a mirror does it nicely... If this shows us anything at all about a more general state of mental-health or the medical system as a whole then it would be that medical professionals by and large fail at "self regulating their system in our best interest", that while they may be good at presenting a perfect image of medicine they are by far not as good at practicing it and they fail dismally when it comes to defining what medicine should be or where limits need to be set. But this isn't really the point, is it? What I have a go at is the violation of every human right there is if it comes to how transsexuals get treated by society and its various organizations. Medical doctors and in particular psychiatrists just happens to be, for whatever reason, the people who assign themselves the task to enforce most of these violations.

As with every such task some people step away from becoming accomplices, some go along grudgingly, some pretend and find a way around the violations they're asked to inflict onto others (a few may even take personal risks to help), some justify their action by the reasoning that this is the only way to help us. Sadly enough as always there are a few individuals who use this as an excuse for profiteering and some actually cherish the opportunity of getting away with doing things to their fellow human-beings they would not possibly be allowed anywhere else in society. This is very, very human, it isn't new and it isn't particular to psychiatry at all.

At the end I would like to invite each and every reader to look at the quote on the next page. To maybe understand why in the beginning I said: *"The simple fact of interpreting a life's experiences differently by different people can lead to misunderstanding, pain, impossible expectations, absurd treatments and death".*

Because the reason for all the pain, the impossible expectations, the absurd treatments and all the deaths isn't their interpretation. *It isn't even their* divergent *interpretation.* **The reason for all this pain and all these deaths is that a group of people is given free reign and absurd absolute powers to act-out on THEIR interpretation of OUR lives:**

Explanatory Memorandum of the Rome Statute of the International Criminal Court

> *Crimes against humanity are particularly odious offences in that they constitute a serious attack on human dignity or grave humiliation or a degradation of one or more human beings. They are not isolated or sporadic events, but are part either of a government policy (although the perpetrators need not identify themselves with this policy) or of a wide practice of atrocities tolerated or condoned by a government or a de facto authority. However, murder, extermination, torture, rape, political, racial, or religious persecution and other inhumane acts reach the threshold of crimes against humanity only if they are part of a widespread or systematic practice...[1,2]*

---

[1] *Explanatory Memorandum of the* Rome Statute of the International Criminal Court. *Quote as given by* Guy Horton *in* Dying Alive *(in turn referenced as RSICC/C, Vol. 1 p. 360)*

[2] *As of January 1, 2008 a total of 105 nations had ratified (or acceded) the Rome Statute, a further 41 had signed but not ratified it. The USA, the nation where WPATH (the de facto authority on treatment of transsexuals) is incorporated, had initially signed the Rome Statute but later withdrawn its signature.*

I have dedicated this book to all the woman who have paid the ultimate price for being denied life-saving treatment.

I could easily have been one of them, instead I have met a few understanding and accepting people.

I would like to thank all of them for my life!

I love and value life.

ALL LIFE!

APPENDIX.I. THE YIN/YANG TEARDROP (COVER)

In Chinese philosophy Yin and Yang are generic symbols of opposites in nature. The Tai-jitu (the traditional symbol for Yin and Yang, also known as "Yin/Yang") symbolizes a unity of these opposites by combining both: Two halves, a combination of contradictory aspects which nevertheless are similar in many ways and are both necessary parts to form a complete Circle of Life.

Taijitu (Taoist and Neo-Confucian philosophy)

The black part (Yin) represents passivity, darkness or night, it is consuming and symbol-izes femininity, the white part (Yang) stands for activity, brightness or light, it is producing and symbolizes masculinity. There are many other interpretations, traditional opposites such as fire vs. water, air vs. earth or sun vs. moon, just to name a few.

Each of the two parts of the Taijitu is a perfect half of that whole called 'unity'. While each half is an ideal of an absolute, they're both exactly equal in area and shape. Each also con-tains an element of the other (called 'seed'): While each half symbolizes *an absolute extreme* that absoluteness never truly exists in nature because every expression of any extreme *always contains a part of its opposite* and cannot exist without it. In nature Yin and Yang are in con-stant movement, change and interaction.

I have chosen this symbol because it exemplifies an understanding of nature and human-beings I find much more appealing than simplistic designations such as male and female. We all see ourselves and each other as male or female, however we all have and recognize aspects of the other in each and every one of us. But while how much of each and which specific attributes we have is different and individual to every human being, the one thing we all have in common is that we all need to express who we are within that framework of opposites we are born with in order to feel good about ourselves.

If a human-being has many or most of these opposing attributes of life on one side and this side just happens to be the one that cannot be expressed (for whatever reason) then the result will be pain. In the Yin-Yang-Teardrop it is the female side that weeps, becomes a tear. Because it is there but can't be expressed.

Yin-Yang-Teardrop

Over a lifetime some of the attributes that make-up who we are change. Some are relatively easy to change, some change all by themselves (i.e. age, puberty, stage in life, personal development, illness,...) and some are very difficult to change. There are also some we can never change.

Just as the Taijitu has two sides, Yin and Yang, such attributes usually come in pairs: Pairs of attributes of which one is changeable while the other one is not. Sexual orientation and sexual activity for example. We can change our sexual activities, we cannot change our sexual orientation. The better somebody is capable of bringing these pairs in line during a lifetime, the better that person will feel about herself, be capable to express herself, interact with others and have a fulfilling life!

There is one case, *and only one* I know of, where a human-being can be born with a pair of contradicting attributes *that are both unchangeable*. This pair is "biological reproductive capacity" and "self-perception of gender". For such a person to live one of the two will, sooner or later, have to give.

APPENDIX.II. CHAPTERS THAT DIDN'T MAKE THE CUT

EQUAL - NOT ANYMORE!

Transsexuality is *the only disability for which some form of official government registration is required* and, upon such registration, one looses equal rights, equal access to government programs and later finds oneself subjected to bureaucratically sanctioned discrimination, extortion and harassment, not the least by government officials.

A WINDOW INTO ANOTHER WORLD?

Many transsexuals find a very specific understanding of life and society. *This could be of great value to society at large* if we were accepted for who we are.

THE ICING ON THE CAKE?

Genital surgery as "the icing on the cake" must be the most often quoted sayings in trans-care. Truth is that we live a divergence *because for a biological woman this all starts with her genitals being right. For us however genitals while are appropriate will be the very last thing that we ever deserve!*

MALE SEX, FEMALE SEX AND PSYCHIATRIC SEX

How the two sexes usually see and live sexuality and how psychiatry interprets this. How psychiatry describes, uses, understands *and misunderstands* sexuality.

SELF-MUTILATION

The pressure insane testosterone-levels put onto us, the despair this creates at times and how this pressures some individuals to use the "do it yourself" approach to castration.

DAMAGING OUR CHILDREN - ONLY A LITTLE

The attitude mental-health has towards transsexual parents - from forced child-removal to mandated family separation to today's slightly more enlightened view that *"we only damage our children a little"*, but not quite enough to warrant having them removed from us.

UNTIL GENDER-ALIGNMENT US PARTED

Thanks to psychiatric insight a divorce between a woman and a transsexual woman is often seen as *a separation between "a normal female"* and *"a mental male"* resulting in the transsexual partner (and her transition) almost always being blamed for the separation, and hence her being guaranteed to loose her children, even visiting rights, often in the end finding herself with nothing at all.

HUMAN MEDICAL EXPERIMENTS HIGHLY WELCOME!

There have been reports of transsexuals being abused for sick medical experiments, particularly in the area of "human sexual research". About such experiments and what this does to the people who get subjected to these.

SELF SUPPORT: LEARNING THE LINES

Self-support often ends-up being nothing else than *government organized learning centres for compliance to mental-health* and a test-arena for approved behavioural self-modification.

WHEN HUMANS ARE INFALLIBLE

Transsexuals have the right to correct their legal existence *but not their mental records.* Government administrations may make mistakes that need correcting, *but doctors never make mistakes!* Therefore, as a matter of principle, *no correction or removal of mental-health records is ever permitted,* no matter how prejudice or wrongful the reason for obtaining these was!

PUT A MOUNTAIN THERE, THEY WILL CLIMB IT!

The more absurd the restrictions on gender alignment surgery are the higher the chances that people seek it for the wrong reasons, for the sake of getting there, to prove themselves or even as a "replacement treatment" or mistaken solution for a different physical or a real mental problem or illness.

MEDICAL SELF-UNDERSTANDING

How western medicine *deliberately defines its scope in a way as to discretionarily exclude social, environmental and educational issues* which cause illness or may prevent these, such as malnutrition due to poverty, burn-out due to stress, illness due to lack of public hygiene or sex-ed including education on sexual orientations, gender issues and transsexuality.

NOT BELONGING ANYWHERE - EVER

We never find belonging anywhere! Because we can never "grow into a social setting" we can't find either emotional nor social belonging to a place like a neighbourhood or to any group of people: *This is because we so often end-up being accepted for who we are not or we are not accepted for who we are!*

ALL IN ONE: LAWMAKER, JUDGE, JURY, ENFORCER, VOYEUR AND BYSTANDER

Doctors assigning themselves all the roles that are by the "separation of powers" for good reason supposed to be held by different people in our society: They are lawmaker, judge, jury, enforcer, voyeur and bystander all in one - the roles left to us are death row inmate and executioner - of ourselves!

BORN TO BE MYSELF!

Many transsexuals feel the need "to learn how to be a woman". Initially I was sceptical why I would possibly need "to be taught how to be myself" but eventually I understood that for many this is appropriate, even needed *because there is often so much social and psychiatric damage that true self-expression without this "external help" is no longer possible or would take an unreasonable length of time.*

WHY ME?

About me having survived this absurd treatment while so many others do not and about the subsequent discovery that survival sometimes comes at a very high price...

FIRST ORDER OF BUSINESS: ASSIGN BLAME

In medicine it is usual that the patient and her immediate healthcare *comes first,* reasons and causes are investigated later, if at all. But this isn't true in transgender-care! Here finding "somebody who's guilty", *assigning blame to parents, social conditions, education, sexual behaviour, even sibling-order seems to be the most important thing to do for many therapists!* Only when "somebody or something to blame" has been located will there be treatment but because they only look for absurd reasons they are very likely to find only explanations of the most mental kind!

A BROTHERHOOD IN...?

About the statement *"My Colleagues will be my sisters and brothers"* in the medical oath [The Declaration Of Geneva, WMA, principle #8[WMA]] and if this means "to watch your brother and help him to avoid mistakes, support him correcting these if he does make any and treat him if that mistake is the result of a medical or mental condition he suffers from" or if it means "to let one's brother roam freely and if he screws-up, creates mayhem, starts to hurt and kill people that then calls for rolling-out the best cover-up money can buy for him"?

A LITTLE RESPECT AND SOME HONESTY

The most important qualities a human-being who makes any decisions in the best interest of somebody else are: (a) To know, understand, accept and respect one's own limitations, (b) an unassuming nature and (c) honesty. The fact that neither of these is a prerequisite or a subject at med-school (in fact the opposite is true: Doctors learn how to cover-up for not knowing instead of learning to openly admit their personal and professional limitations) nor is it a continually upheld standard for anybody who is licensed to practice medicine, even insofar as it can be defined objectively.

RE-INVENTING THE WHEEL - ONE PATIENT AT A TIME!

In many cases transsexuals know a lot more about their treatment than the treating doctors do. There is no open organized professional exchange of information either for treatment or for resources in spite of this condition affecting millions of people. Therefore doctors who are confronted with their first case may find themselves without guidelines and end-up (re-) inventing a treatment of their own - as it is of course impossible to trust "some non-medical advice"!

DON'T CARE 101

What does mental-treatment really teaches us: The "Don't Care Lesson!". Just how hurtful it is to be subjected to a weekly (or whatever) ritual during which the most predictable mantra is that what I am is not taken seriously, what I need is not acknowledged, what I say is irrelevant and who I am is deemed to be impossible! We learn not to care about any therapist, not to care about any views or labels. We learn how best to be abused and how to submit to absurdity. In the end we learn how to not care about ourselves!

THE MORALIST PANEL HAS SPOKEN!

The difference between 'ethics' and 'morals' and why so few people understand this difference. About why the term 'ethics' is so often abused to cloak moralistic preachings, the fact that there can't ever be an "Ethics Commission" who hands out ethics by decree as a majority consensus and that such organizations are and correctly ought to be named *Moralist Panels*. About the absoluteness of ethics *and why "true ethics" isn't thought at med-school.*

THE MIRACLE EFFECT

About the media showing-off "the miracle-cure" or "the effect of transition" and setting this in perspective to other "medical miracles". The public loves to gape at such 'wonders' as Siamese twin separation, weight-loss by gastric bypasses and plastic surgery for aesthetic purposes. Only that "miracle transsexual" would be completely invisible and uninteresting, thus they portray something different as being transsexuality *because they get better ratings and more money doing this instead!*

NO PAST - AND NO FUTURE EITHER!

About transsexuals being cheated out of their past because society doesn't allow us to have the past we have had and about society denying us the future also *because they never allow us to truly leave that past behind* they say we aren't allowed to have had!

BETTER FLUSH TWICE

Some transsexuals resort to simulating mental illnesses because simulated mental conditions are an easy way to show "progress in mental treatment"... They gladly take the respective prescriptions or dispensed medications and report that these have a very positive effect, show the anticipated changes *while in reality it all ends in the toilet, flushed down the drain!*

SEX, LIES AND GOVERNMENT TAPE

Most governments prefer "government sanctioned lies" over an orderly process to have our legal status recognized and corrected. Maybe they mean well but in the end implementing such half-lies which ultimately make *us* look dishonest *end-up being the basis for continued life-long discrimination!*

JUST ANOTHER ROTTEN APPLE FROM A ROTTEN TREE

Medicine forces any and all medical services under their control which makes them end-up having to provide such treatments as "abortion for convenience", "murder on demand" (such as providing or assisting in administering the death-penalty), "assisted suicide" and more. This completely perverts all medical ethics. *In the end the greed of wanting to control every medical intervention guarantees ethical bankruptcy!* Therefore how transsexuals get treated isn't an absurd excess but rather the normalcy one has to expect from such a system, *transsexuals are in fact but the tip of an iceberg - with a lot more under the surface we just can't see. Yet!*

APPENDIX.III. QUOTES THAT DIDN'T MAKE THE CUT

[Me] You know, gender isn't just "plug and play"... [He] ... Well yes, there's watching and the picking-up and so on? [Me] You're confusing sex and gender again! [He] You're really making that whole thing so darn confusing and un-enjoyable...

[She] You know that the medical treatment of transsexuals goes by the three-'s'-rule? [Me] Three 's'? [She] Steroids, stereotypes and sex!

[He] Why do you cry? [Me] It's what women do when things get emotional... [He] You really don't need to do this *that* convincingly...

[Medical professional] That morning-sickness is rather normal at your hormone levels... [Me] Ok, but how long is this going to last? [He] Well, normally for the first trimester, but in your case...

[The morning after surgery, I wake-up in a pool of blood... The morning nurse] Welcome to your first period! It's going to be a heavy one...

[At mental-health, me] Have you noticed: Every major organ has a society these days! There's the lung association, there's heart and stroke foundation, the kidney foundation, the pancreas has the diabetes foundation, even bone-marrow has it's own society - only the brain does not!! [She] ...To promote mental-health? [Me] ...To promote *thinking*...

[Mental-health professional, about me] ...Just an ordinary woman with an extraordinary past!

[Medical professional] You must have noticed that you are quite exceptional for a transsexual. [Me] That may be so, but isn't the idea of medicine to treat each patient according to her needs? [He] I'm not talking about medicine here...

[To a friend] There's something about me I'd like to tell you: You know, I am trans... [Friend] Finally! You know I thought you'd never get it!

[Me, at mental-health] The fact that you can't make sense of me doesn't mean that I have a mental disorder!

APPENDIX.IV. NOTES AND REFERENCES[1]

Mentioned in support

[ARIS-C]   *Categories* by Aristotle, approx. 350BC, translations available in good book-stores everywhere

Critically mentioned

[DSM]   *DSM-IV-TR, Diagnostic And Statistical Manual Of Mental Disorders, fourth edition*, The American Psychiatric Association. An online-version of the DSM may be found at www.behavenet.com/capsules/disorders/dsm4tr.htm [Somewhat abbreviated and slightly simplified version]

[HBIGDA-S]   *The Harry Benjamin International Gender Dysphoria Association's Standards Of Care For Gender Identity Disorders*, Sixth Version, available for download at www.wpath.org[WPATH]

Further references

[KINSEY]   The self-definition of *the Kinsey Institute* and references to the works may be found on www.kinseyinstitute.org

[WMA]   *The World Medical Association.* A self-description, short introduction and some key-documents may be found on www.wma.net/e/

[WPATH]   The self-definition of *WPATH* and references to the works may be found on www.wpath.org

No psychiatrists have been harmed in the production of this book.

---

[1] *(a) In my opinion appendices in which authors list every book they have ever read are utterly useless. (b) I think it would be useful for the scientific community <u>to adopt a system in which references are denoted as supported, criticised or simply mentioned for convenience</u>. This would greatly facilitate research as it would then not only be possible to see if a publication is quoted often or the work referenced frequently, <u>it would instantly become possible to see if this work is referred to positively or negatively</u>, deemed credible or incredible - <u>and by whom or which group of researchers</u>! It would furthermore become obvious if a researcher who lists references actually has knowledge of the contents and refers to these appropriately. Additionally it would help a reader to specifically look for materials with similar or dissimilar ideas and it would enable the scientific community at large to 'evaluate' authors (and the typical quality of their work) according to who they reference positively and negatively and by whom and how often they themselves get quoted or referred positively or negatively. What a scary thought!*

Diversity makes our world beautiful.

Our world exists because of it, through it, and for it.

We all are this diversity.

My best estimates:

There are at least **5,000,000** m/f transsexuals alive today

By the year 2008 at minimum of **300,000** women have received
psychiatrically approved m/f genital gender-reassignment,
most of these women live among us today, a great majority of them in
Europe and the Americas, mostly unseen and completely unnoticed

Patients who have been approved for m/f genital surgery have received in
excess of **50,000,000** sessions of compulsory psychiatric therapy[1]
The number of individuals cured from transsexuality by this therapy is **zero**

The number of patients currently receiving psychiatric therapy while
waiting to be approved for medical treatment **remains undisclosed**

The total number of therapy-sessions billed as a direct result
of the "Standards Of Care" **is at least 300,000,000**[1]
The cost of these therapy sessions **exceeds $35,000,000,000**[1,2,3]
All approved m/f genital surgeries ever
performed **have cost less than 10% of the above**[2]

The number of "in treatment suicides" of transsexuals waiting to get
psychiatric approval for their medical treatment or as a result of
psychiatric denial of such treatment **remains undisclosed**

The average cost to treat one m/f transsexual for life is **$65,000.-**[4]
The average cost of refusing one treatment is one life

---

[1] *Worldwide (where reliable numbers of therapeutic practitioners are available), number of patient-sessions, any form of therapy including single and group, by any dogmatically approved therapist, since its first inception*
[2] *Inflation-adjusted to 2008, US$*
[3] *Estimate of US$160 session for individual M.D. psychiatric therapy, US$80 session for other therapy (as of 2008)*
[4] *Average lifetime payments by health insurance in US$ when treatment is fully covered. Insured expenses typically include medical lab & prescription-visits, partial drug-coverage, genital gender-alignment surgery and psychiatric therapy (to get there). In some countries facial hair-removal as well as some other medical and non-medical expenses are also covered*

LaVergne, TN USA
05 December 2010

207496LV00001B/6/P